16.50

D0876268

The
Limits
of
Change

HARVARD EAST ASIAN SERIES 84

The East Asian Research Center at Harvard University administers research projects designed to further scholarly understanding of China, Japan, Korea, Vietnam, Inner Asia, and adjacent areas.

This book was sponsored by
the Joint Committee on Contemporary China
of the Social Science Research Council and
the American Council of Learned Societies

Contributions by

Guy Alitto	Lin Yü-sheng
Martin Bernal	David E. Pollard
Hao Chang	Laurence A. Schneider
Arif Dirlik	Benjamin I. Schwartz
Lloyd E. Eastman	Tu Wei-ming
Charlotte Furth	Ernest P. Young

THE
LIMITS
OF
CHANGE

**Essays on Conservative Alternatives
in Republican China**

EDITED BY

Charlotte Furth

HARVARD UNIVERSITY PRESS

Cambridge, Massachusetts, and London, England   1976

Copyright © 1976 by the President and Fellows of Harvard College
All rights reserved
Printed in the United States of America

Preparation of this volume has been aided by a grant from
the Ford Foundation.

Library of Congress Cataloging in Publication Data

Main entry under title:

The Limits of change.

    (Harvard East Asian series; 84)
    "Essays . . . presented in their original versions as
papers at a conference on intellectuals and the problem
of conservatism in Republican China . . . in 1972."
    Includes index.
    1. China — Intellectual life — Congresses. 2. Con-
servatism — China — Congresses. I. Furth, Charlotte.
II. Alitto, Guy. III. Joint Committee on Contemporary
China. IV. Series.
DS721.L565   951.04   75-23490
ISBN 0-674-53423-9

Preface

The essays which make up this book originated as papers presented at a conference on "Intellectuals and the Problem of Conservatism in Republican China" which was held in 1972 under the auspices of the Joint Committee on Contemporary China of the Social Science Research Council and the American Council of Learned Societies. Like many conference volumes, this one grew out of a sense among a small group of us that collective effort was needed in opening up a new perspective on a subject. In choosing to examine conservative styles of thought in Republican China, our aim is better to understand alternatives as the Chinese themselves saw them, and to illuminate the framework of common concepts of the age — a framework which cannot be understood by analyzing radical movements alone. Our aim is not to confirm exaggerated theories of the power of historical continuity in modern China, nor to offer a judgment, pro or con, on the historical inevitability of Mao's revolution. Rather, the essays here indicate how rapidly wide strata of the postimperial elite adapted to change within the framework of continued preoccupation with native history and culture. They help us subsume the impact of the "West" upon China under the broader rubric of the impact of "modernity." They show us more distinctly than radical movements alone can do what issues of political and intellectual controversy were essential in defining the revolution which finally occurred, and what ones only seemingly so. They suggest problems of value Chinese considered important which survived the dramatic transformations of 1949, and which have continued to play their part in the ideological struggles of recent years.

In most non-Western societies emerging from preindustrial isolation to fight for modern power and national independence, resistance to change per se has been understandably weak, by comparison with the forces of traditionalism in Asian empires or those of gradualism in European democracies. Far from being an exception to this generalization, twentieth-century China is a place where revolutionary impulses have appeared especially totalistic and far-reaching. Some readers undoubtedly will feel that the analytic framework of conservatism applies to certain of the individuals and movements described here only in a quite attenuated sense. Disagreement on the issue is amply represented in the essays themselves, among whose authors the question of the exact scope and meaning of the idea of conservatism as applied to their subjects has been a topic of vigorous debate. However, even given a variety of interpretations, the concept has maintained its usefulness as a common denominator, because — as over and against "traditionalism" — it has suggested we are dealing with a group of *modern* Chinese alternatives; and because it has facilitated comparison within the framework of the worldwide triad, conservatism/liberalism/radicalism, inherited essentially from the Enlightenment.

Our essays discuss intellectual currents, and to a lesser extent political and ideological compromises of revolutionary programs. We have not been able to deal with the obviously massive social obstacles to change in Republican China; while the vast subterranean area of unanalyzed traditionalism in custom and psychological attitude is also, for the most part, tantalizingly beyond our reach.

Many people have contributed time, money, and thought to making the conference and this volume possible. The Joint Committee on Contemporary China was generous in its financial support of the 1972 conference; and its staff members, William R. Bryant and John Creighton Campbell, deftly facilitated its organization. For their stimulating contributions, we owe special thanks to the other conference participants: Albert Feuerwerker, Barry Keenan, Herman Mast III, Mary Rankin, Richard Rosen, Roger Swenson, and C. Martin Wilbur. John King Fairbank offered invaluable guidance and support. During various stages of the total project Ralph Croizier, Jerome Greider, Thomas Metzger, and Ross Terrill also provided suggestions and help for which I am grateful. My own work as editor and in the preparation of my individual contributions was supported by grants from the Harvard East Asian Research Center and the John Simon Guggenheim Memorial Foundation.

In the stylistic preparation of these essays for publication, I have followed guidelines for the elimination of male-oriented language drawn up by the Los Angeles Westside Women's Committee. I wish to thank the contributors for their cooperation in this effort, and also to thank my friends Norma Farquhar and Marina Preussner for their inventive editing and meticulous work in the preparation of the typescript.

C.F.

Contents

I Introductory Perspectives: The Conservative Idea and Chinese Realities

   1 Notes on Conservatism in General and in China in
      Particular   3
      Benjamin I. Schwartz

   2 Culture and Politics in Modern Chinese Conservatism   22
      Charlotte Furth

II National Essence

   3 National Essence and the New Intelligentsia   57
      Laurence A. Schneider

   4 Liu Shih-p'ei and National Essence   90
      Martin Bernal

   5 The Sage as Rebel: The Inner World of Chang
      Ping-lin   113
      Charlotte Furth

   6 The Suicide of Liang Chi: An Ambiguous Case of
      Moral Conservatism   151
      Lin Yü-sheng

III Political Modernization Against Revolutionary Politics

   7 The Hung-hsien Emperor as a Modernizing
      Conservative   171
      Ernest P. Young

   8 The Kuomintang in the 1930s   191
      Lloyd E. Eastman

IV   The New Confucianism of the Post May Fourth Era

   9   The Conservative as Sage: Liang Shu-ming   213
       Guy Alitto

  10   Hsiung Shih-li's Quest for Authentic Existence   242
       Tu Wei-ming

  11   New Confucianism and the Intellectual Crisis of
       Contemporary China   276
       Hao Chang

V   Modern Historicism and the Limits of Change

  12   T'ao Hsi-sheng: The Social Limits of Change   305
       Arif Dirlik

  13   Chou Tso-jen: A Scholar Who Withdrew   332
       David E. Pollard

       Contributors   359

       Notes   361

       Glossary   413

       Index   419

I INTRODUCTORY PERSPECTIVES: THE CONSERVATIVE IDEA AND CHINESE REALITIES

1 Notes on Conservatism in General and in China in Particular

BENJAMIN I. SCHWARTZ

The study of "conservatism" is a swamp which one approaches with reluctance. Not only is one skeptical of discovering the "essence" of conservatism but one is also constantly tortured by doubts whether the whole enterprise is worthwhile. Yet we all find ourselves using the terms "conservative" and "conservatism." In China the term has come to be used as a conventionally accepted description of personalities and movements which have been neglected because the study of Chinese conservatism has not been popular. It is one of those terms which will neither submit to the dogmatic criteria of meaning imposed by certain rigorous linguistic philosophers nor allow itself to be dismissed as meaningless.

At first approach, it seems not at all difficult to identify what might be called a conservative disposition. The inertial disposition to persist unreflectively in established ways of acting, feeling, and thinking may be called conservative. J. G. A. Pocock, in defining tradition, says that "a tradition in its simplest form may be thought of as an indefinite series of repetitions of an action which on each occasion is performed on the assumption that it has been performed before; its performance is authorized by the knowledge or assumption of previous performance." The trouble with this statement as a description of a mere conservative disposition is the fact that the words used suggest a reflective conscious justification of action rather than an unreflective persistence in habit and custom. While one will find everywhere people who say that they do things because "they have always been done that way," the fact is that this mode of justification of behavior is much more rare (Weber to the contrary) in the history of human thought than one might suppose. Most of the thinkers, prophets, and sages, even when they have justified the "way things are," have done so on the grounds of revelation, intuition, or reason which reveal universal and eternal normative truths. They will justify established traditions in terms of universal norms and rarely say that the traditions are true merely because they have persisted or grown. In Chinese Taoism, to be sure, we find the notion that the unreflective, unconscious persistence of the routines and uniformities of nature is itself a proof of their perfection—of their embodiment of *tao*—and it is interesting to note that the contemporary conservative British philosopher Michael Oakeshott is fond of quoting Lao-tzu and Chuang-tzu. Yet the paradox is, of course, that neither Lao-tzu nor Oakeshott are themselves unreflective or unconscious. Moreover, Lao-tzu and Chuang-tzu tended to regard the sociopolitical order not as an example of *wu-wei* but of deliberate conscious meddling with the order of *tao*.

Thus, while conservative dispositions may be found in all times and places, Karl Mannheim and others have been quite correct in maintaining that conservatism as an "ism" only emerges in the West in the late eighteenth and early nineteenth centuries; and it is only since the early nineteenth century that individuals have tended to be described by others or by themselves mainly as conservatives. Conservatism as a conscious doctrine thus emerges as an inseparable component of the triad conservatism/liberalism/radicalism. The fact that all three categories emerge roughly simultaneously is, it seems to me, good evidence that all operate within a framework of common concepts which emerge at a given period in European history. One way of dealing with conservatism is to say that with the French Revolution and the rise of the idea of progress, certain people (whatever their motives) who were bent on maintaining things the way they were created a conscious doctrine of conservatism. This formula seems to me very inadequate because it overlooks the fact that the definition of the way things are was itself very much conditioned by common concepts of the age. Thus while radicals will often say that they wish to smash the whole "system," and conservatives will often defend the "system," the concept of "the system" is shared by both.

It is often asserted that conservatism was a reaction to the French Revolution, but it is probably more correct to say that the doctrine of conservatism rose in dialectic reaction to certain major trends of the Enlightenment. Edmund Burke had certainly developed many of his ideas before the French Revolution and, as Klaus Epstein demonstrates in his book on German conservatism, certain German conservatives such as Moser had also developed their ideas before the revolution. The revolution, to be sure, very much clarified and intensified the polarities.

One of the dominant tendencies of the Enlightenment was the overwhelming concentration of attention on the sociopolitical realm — on the social, political, and cultural environment within which individuals live. There was a growing conviction that the solution to the major problems of the human condition was to be sought within this realm. It has often been said that the optimism of the Enlightenment was based on a faith in the ability of "man" to master the sociopolitical environment in the same way in which Newtonian science had made it possible to master the physical environment. There is, however, a paradox here. The fact is that if most individuals are determined and conditioned by their sociopolitical environment, as individuals they have little actual power to shape either their own individual lives or the environment. All of this implies that those systems of behavior which are embodied in institutions or legal and political systems are conceived of as being "independent of the wills of men," to use the phrase of Marx.

This view was further strengthened by the sensationalist epistemology which implied that people are passively molded by their sense experiences, which are in turn molded by the sociopolitical environment. In Montesquieu we also find the germ of the idea of cultural as well as social determinism. Each political system has its own correlative set of mental attitudes which are again independent of the wills of individual persons. The characteristic attitude of the Enlightenment toward the sociopolitical and cultural systems bequeathed by the past was on the whole negative. (We are, of course, simplifying. Thus the believers in Enlightenment despotism were convinced that they could use the monarchy as a lever of reform. On the other hand, people like Turgot and Condorcet, while sharing the general view of the bad past, believed that in the realm of the arts and sciences there had been general incremental progress.)

The dominant Enlightenment view tended to seek in the sociopolitical order the cause of much, if not most, human suffering and wickedness and its optimism was based on the assumption that a new sociopolitical order based on reason and corresponding to nature can be constructed. The problem, however, is: who will construct this new order? There were, to be sure, eighteenth-century thinkers—particularly some Americans such as Jefferson—who seemed to believe that the average individual possessed an actual (not merely potential) rational power to control his or her environment. Hence, they could believe in the immediate implementation of democracy. Those who believed that the overwhelming mass of human beings are totally conditioned by their bad environment could not believe this. Hence, the enormous stress on legislators and educators, the *homines ex machina* as it were, who are somehow able to transcend the environment and change it. Hence, it is not "man" but some select individuals who change the environment. It is to the problem involved in this notion that Marx refers in his third thesis on Feuerbach when he states that "the materialist doctrine concerning the change of circumstances and education forgets that circumstances are changed by men and that the educator must himself be educated. Hence this doctrine must divide society into two parts—one of which towers above the other."

This solution to the problem of how one changes a bad society also highlights another dominant aspect of Enlightenment thought, namely its political emphasis. We have referred to the sociopolitical realm, yet the fact emerges that the notion of the social system as a kind of superior organism transcending politics with its own inbuilt dynamism and power of growth does not yet seem to have been established. It is, of course, possible to treat the political realm itself sociologically as a kind of realm where suprapersonal institutions have an inner power of persistence and growth "independent of the wills of men" and it was precisely this view of the British constitution which was developed by the conservative Burke. To the leaders of the Enlightenment to whom I refer, the political realm was a realm where a vanguard could change the environment through their deliberate, conscious decisions. Indeed, the genesis of the bad social order of the past is often ascribed by some to the malevolent decisions of tyrants and priests just as the good social order of the future would be fashioned by noble legislators and educators.

Now the dichotomy we here note between ordinary individuals shaped by their environment and the sociopolitical order as an independent realm which shapes them is actually taken over—and even carried further—by those we call conservatives. What they reverse drastically is the evaluation of the sociopolitical order inherited from the past. The institutions, social structure, and traditions of thought which have endured and grown over time embody a wisdom and reason higher than anything the feeble individual can devise. They doubt both the capacity and the wisdom of any individual to change the entire inherited social order. In his famous defense of prejudice in "Reflections on the Revolution in France," Burke stated: "We are afraid to put men to live and trade each on his own private stock of reason because, we suspect that this stock in each man is small and that the individuals would do better to avail themselves of the general bank and capital of nations and ages. Many of our men of speculation, instead of exploding general prejudices, employ their sagacity to discover the latent wisdom which prevails in them."[1]

Mannheim stresses the conservative contribution to the idea of the historic growth of societies. This seems correct even though the idea of growth appears to involve the notion of change and even progress. Men such as Burke or Möser or Adam Müller were not nostalgic for archaic utopias and were well aware that the prevailing system which they were prepared to defend had grown and even progressed over time. It was simply their conviction that the organism had substantially reached adulthood—a healthy maturity. Thus Burke, who was after all a moderate conservative, believed in piecemeal change in the present to improve society, but he regarded those changes as modest embellishments of a magnificent structure already in being. There have been conservatives who have not been as happy about the actual existing state of affairs as Burke and have preferred the social order of the day before yesterday which had in some unaccountable way been upset by the meddling intervention of ideologues and politicians. Yet even those German conservatives who stressed the German medieval feudal heritage (which still survived in part) were convinced that this earlier order had grown organically over time. This leaves us, of course, with the difficult problem of whether those who hanker after utopias in the distant past, like the "feudal utopians" in traditional China, ought to be called conservatives. They share with the present-minded conservative the conviction that the good has already been achieved in human experience. However, I would suggest that this conviction is perhaps a not very significant aspect of what they represent, for the fact is that they see enormous tension between the way things are and the ideal state of affairs.

Conservatism of the Burkean variety not only approves of the general manner in which the history of society has moved but also asserts the power of social-historic forces. De Tocqueville, Hegel, and many nineteenth-century historicists were able to explain the French Revolution itself in terms of the historic growth of cultural and social forces. Thus, as Mannheim and others have asserted, late eighteenth- and nineteenth-century thought gave an enormous impulse to both sociologism and historicism.

Another aspect of this conservatism again stressed by Mannheim is its "holism." What Burke asserts is that the British sociopolitical order is good as a "whole" even though there may be defects in the parts. It is good not only because of most of the sum of the parts but because the parts fit together as an organic whole. The system is basically good and it has grown as an organic whole.

Finally, another characteristic of this conservatism is its involvement with the growth of nationalism. I use the expression "involvement with nationalism" because it can hardly be asserted that nationalism as such first emerged only within the environment of conservative thinking. It has often been pointed out that radical nationalism in the writings of Rousseau and in the practice of the French Revolution emerged as early as, if not earlier than, conservative nationalism. The British constitution which Burke so ardently loved was, of course, produced by its social bearer —namely the British nation. One might say that the sociopolitical and cultural order has its organic quality because it was produced by a social organism—the nation. One can conceive of forms of conservatism in nineteenth-century Europe which take as their societal base something other than the nation—such as ultramontane catholicism—but by and large when speaking of a society, since the end of the eighteenth century one has meant the national society. It may be urged that in the case of Burke, his real commitment was to the social-political order as such and that he deeply believed in its intrinsic superiority in terms of universalistic criteria. Yet the logic of his thought forced him to concede that there were other societal organisms which followed their own patterns of organic growth. Even if he felt that British history had taken a happier course than French history, he constantly attacked the French revolutionists for not acting within the framework established by their own history. Thus the relativism inherent in this kind of nationalistic historicism is even discernible in Burke himself.

Now if one can speak of modern conservatism in terms of historicism, holism, sociologism, the idea of organic growth, and nationalism, Mannheim's essay on conservatism, which develops all these points, has the further merit of pointing out that while some of these notions and orientations may have been given their first impetus in a conservative milieu, the concepts themselves are highly ambivalent common concepts which could be appropriated to radical ends. Hegel was the bridge to Marx as well as to other forms of nineteenth-century radicalism. Marx was able to weld together the seemingly incompatible elements of revolutionism and the doctrine of sociohistoric growth simply by assuming that growth proceeds not in a smooth continuity but in a continuity interrupted by a series of crises in the "life cycle" of society. The idea of growth itself was indifferent to any judgment of whether the full maturity of the race had already been achieved or was yet to be achieved. To be sure, Marx seems to return to the Enlightenment's negative evaluation of the whole historic past, but his dialectic approach actually allows him to characterize the modes of production of the past as both exploitative and objectively progressive. A common element here between mature Marxism and the kind of conservatism we have been discussing is the common disbelief in the power of the individual to affect the longer course of events. (In Leninism, to be sure, there is a kind of retreat from the faith in larger impersonal forces and a kind of recrudescence of the Enlightenment view that unless legislators in the form of a revolutionary vanguard consciously take action, the forces of history will bog down.)

Nationalism has also proven to be a common concept. It may be urged that many forms of nineteenth-century radicalism — including Marxism — were antinationalist, regarding nationalism as a conservative device. However, the general overall tendency from the nineteenth century to the present has been in the direction of reappropriating Rousseau's radical nationalism. The common subjective element in nationalism is the supreme commitment to the societal entity known as the nation as the focus of ultimate loyalty. A radical nationalist would, of course, tend to identify the nation with the people and the people would be seen not only in terms of transnational functional categories like the industrial proletariat but also as bearers of national characteristics. If the conservative nationalist would stress that one can have no sense of national self-esteem unless one can believe that the national biography has produced great things, the radical nationalist (like Li Ta-chao in China) would stress the power of the nation-people to renew itself completely on the analogy of the individual soul which can by an act of conversion and self-renewal slough off the whole incubus of the evil past. To the conservative nationalist, it seems impossible to separate the transcendent national soul from the national life history. To say that all the past accomplishments of the organism have been unworthy is to devalue the organism.

If modern conservatism and radicalism draw on common concepts, what can be said of that other entity, liberalism? Presumably, liberalism, with its emphasis on individual autonomy and capacity to shape the human environment, would resist the stress on the primacy of impersonal sociohistoric forces as well as the collectivist bias inherent in nationalism. Yet the fact is that throughout the nineteenth and twentieth centuries liberalism also became deeply involved in the overwhelming powerful notions discussed above. It seems that a good deal of what is called liberalism came to stress not so much the capacity of individuals to shape themselves and the environment as the notion that the individual should be the beneficiary of all sociohistoric change. Nineteenth-century liberal philosophers such as Spencer and Mill and twentieth-century American philosophers of development have been just as insistent as Marx that the realization of their good society is the culmination of a long impersonal sociohistoric process. A good deal of American liberal sociology credits the individual with as little responsibility for social change as do nonliberal sociologies. Freedom is, no doubt, one of the cherished goals of all liberals. Yet the question of what freedom means to the sociologistic liberal is a most difficult question indeed.

As for the relationship of nationalism and liberalism, one may ultimately love one's nation precisely because it is the "sweet land of liberty" or argue, as do Yen Fu, Liang Ch'i-ch'ao, and even Hu Shih up to a point, that liberalism is valuable precisely because it strengthens the nation.

Another characteristic which is often ascribed to liberals is a tendency to believe in piecemeal change, while conservatives and radicals tend to believe in a total integrated social order which must be maintained as a whole or smashed as a whole. Liberals like John Dewey and Hu Shih, his Chinese disciple, believe that societies must contend with all sorts of problems which can be dealt with quite separately. Now the relationship between the piecemeal social engineering approach and individualism in the sense discussed before is by no means an easy one to unravel. Most eighteenth-century Enlightenment thinkers in France were committed to piecemeal change, and many of them even believed that piecemeal change could be brought about by enlightened despotism even though their ultimate aim was an entirely new order. Most of them did not anticipate the revolutionary concept of instant total transformation. On the other hand, it has been pointed out that moderate conservatives like Burke, while they regarded the whole as eminently sound, also believed in piecemeal change around the periphery. This has led many who regard themselves as radicals to identify piecemeal liberalism with conservatism. In their view, the liberal favors piecemeal change in order to forestall "deep structural" change in the whole.

The latter view claims, of course, to unmask the deep real motives of liberals. However, if one is dealing not with supposed conservative motives but with conscious intentions, I would tend to say that within the Chinese context, Hu Shih was a sincere liberal in this sense. Like some eighteenth-century philosophes, he believed that piecemeal changes would gradually dismantle the evil structure of an old society and build an entirely new society. He was, by no means, merely interested in making improvements on an existing structure which he regarded as basically sound. Above all, however feckless he may have been as a political actor, he believed in principle in the power of human beings to shape historic forces. In the case of the United States, where a majority of the people operate within the framework of a polity whose general structure they still tend to affirm, it may perhaps be argued more plausibly that piecemeal social change is conservative. A great deal would depend here on whether one regards a commitment to the basic rules of the game of the polity as being equivalent to an acceptance of the whole system or the whole social order. A democratic socialist who is in some sense a liberal would deny the allegation of conservatism.

All of this leads to a much larger problem. Is the general definition of modern conservatism as an ideology put forth here—a definition which roughly corresponds to the Burke-Mannheim formula—sufficiently elastic to cover many of the ways in which the word "conservative" has come to be used in the twentieth century both in China and the West? May we consider Barry Goldwater a conservative? Can people who are wholeheartedly committed to modernization ever be considered conservative? Is it appropriate to call Stalinists in the Soviet Union and Eastern Europe conservative?

Now in attempting to answer this question, it must be stressed that while we have tried to relate modern conservatism to a certain syndrome of ideas, these ideas are still of a rather high order of abstraction. The notion that the social-political and cultural heritage of the past and present must be affirmed as a whole tells us very little about the content of any specific heritage. There is nothing here as specific, for instance, as the idea that all conservatives must believe that human beings are sinful — an assertion which can readily be undermined by the known fact that many Chinese conservatives believe that human nature is basically good. Many would argue that Goldwater is not a conservative because America is a land which has never known *true* conservatism in the British Burkean sense. Michael Oakeshott, who uses the term "rationalism" rather than "radicalism" as the antonym of "conservatism," sees in America the land of rationalism par excellence.[2] Born in a revolution, its leaders attempted the ultimate rationalist act of creating a whole constitution on the basis of their own rationalistic deliberations.

The fact remains that during the last two hundred years both the revolution and the Constitution have become particularly hallowed parts of an ongoing American tradition. Since it is my view, as against Burke and Oakeshott, that human deliberation and conscious purpose have always played a considerable role in the formation of all institutions and culture down through the ages, I found no difficulty in accepting the possibility that a product of conscious deliberation, like the Constitution, can become a tradition. In the case of Goldwater, we find that he accepts not only the revolution and the Constitution as he interprets them but also the American way of life as it grew throughout the nineteenth century. The American sociopolitical heritage grew smoothly and harmoniously until it was upset by the meddlings of the New Dealers. Individualism, corporate organization, and the cult of technology thus emerge as part of one unproblematic whole. Above all, Goldwater is an extreme nationalist who believes that the American heritage, as he understands it, and America's strength as a nation state are inextricably interdependent.

Revolutions, which in Burke's view represent the deliberate meddling of doctrinaire ideologues in the majestic flow of history, give birth to social and political orders which convert the revolutions themselves into glorious traditions, thus providing new status quos with a sanction even stronger than the sanction of mere continuity. I see no problem in calling the Daughters of the American Revolution conservative.

If it may be possible to accommodate Goldwater and sociopolitical developments which arise out of revolutions within our definition of conservatism, what can we say of the relationship of conservatism to modernization?

The fact is that during the last few years it has become common for people in the American left and in the "counterculture" to refer to preeminent protagonists of modernization as conservatives. Nathan Glazer has even been willing to accept the term for himself. Yet as Guy Alitto suggests in his study of Liang Shu-ming in this volume, modernization would seem to be the very antithesis of conservatism. Modernization seems to involve the systematic universal application of technological rationalism both to nature and society. It thus seems to be the very paradigm of the deliberate effort to shape the social order according to conscious ideas in people's heads. Yet the fact is that as modernization has proceeded, it too has come to be viewed more and more as a sociohistoric process independent of human wills. It has thus also come to be viewed as a kind of organic societal growth which has already achieved a mature state of development. While there no doubt have been forms of aristocratic agrarian conservatism in Europe which resisted industrialization, the fact is that conservatism of the Bismarkian variety wholeheartedly based itself on bureaucratic and industrial rationalization and clearly perceived the link between industrialization and national power.

Many American social scientists had become convinced during the forties and fifties that the system based on the achievement of modernization had proved itself in solving many of the problems of the human condition and would go on to solve more. They thus came to view the attacks on this particular form of historic growth, whether from the new left or the "counterculture," as again a kind of meddling with an essentially benign and inexorable social process. To be sure, the meddlers with the course of history are now viewed not as irresponsible rationalists in Oakeshott's sense but as irresponsible irrationalists. In this kind of context, it may not be implausible to call such modernizers conservatives.

All the variants of conservatism we have discussed thus far may be called happy modes of conservatism. They positively affirm the prevailing sociopolitical order and the prevailing drift of history and thus affirm the historic processes which have brought it into being. One may, of course, feel that it was better in the recent past than it is now, but the dominant attitude is affirmative. There are also some modes of conservatism which might be called unhappy or skeptical. They accept the overwhelming power of the social, political, and cultural heritage of the past but not its benignity. They may even accept the Enlightenment view of the past as a record of error, folly, and ignorance but believe that it cannot be changed, that change is not worth the effort, or that any order no matter how bad is preferable to disorder.

What we have here suggested is that this limited definition of conservatism, whether happy or unhappy, is sufficiently elastic to apply to many varied contexts, and that it is quite possible for wide varieties of people to fall within this category in many times and places. This may limit the scope of the concept as an explanatory concept, but I will here confess that it does indeed seem to me to be a concept of limited explanatory power.

Before turning to China, something should be said of the linkage of conservatism to social interests. Mannheim, as a sociologist of knowledge who had come out of a Marxist tradition, simply and mechanically links conservatism to the social interests of the aristocracy, liberalism to the social interests of the bourgeoisie, and radicalism to the social interests of the proletariat. One need not doubt that in the modern world a majority of those who enjoy power and privilege, however one defines them, will tend to favor conservative movements which rationalize the prevailing system. They implicitly accept the modern notion of the system as a total Gestalt. There have, however, been times and places where flexible ruling classes or sections of ruling classes have realized that the preservation of their power and privileges involved sharp and radical breaks with important parts of the prevailing system. As for intellectuals, as Mannheim himself points out, they are an indeterminate group who might embrace conservatism out of sheer conviction or because they have no predetermined view of where their interests lie. The masses, including the urban proletariat, may often support conservatism because they are unreflectively but deeply attached to many established ways of life as true and valid and are thus willing to accept the conservative position that these ways of life are inextricably bound up with a total prevailing sociopolitical system. Nationalism has in many parts of the world become a deeply held mass religion, and the conservative interpretation of nationalism may also come to be widely accepted.

Turning to China a case can be made that the syndrome of ideas which we have here defined as conservatism as an intellectual orientation did come to China from the West as part of the conservatism/liberalism/radicalism triad. (A case can perhaps be made that something like the idea of conservatism as here described may have developed within the Chinese culture sphere. We shall not pursue this topic here.) In the Chinese situation, however, it was to assume its own modalities. One is first of all struck by the dominance of the nationalist component. To the extent that people as diverse as Chang Ping-lin and T'ao Hsi-sheng can be described as conservatives, nationalist pride and frustration (which is not of course inherently conservative) was the dominant passion to which the other elements of their conservatism were subordinate. What makes their nationalism conservative is a conviction that China can survive and flourish as a national entity only if it can somehow draw on its own sociocultural heritage. It must either be able to draw sustenance from its own "national essence" or — as T'ao Hsi-sheng believed — it must have a deep sense of a Chinese society growing organically and inexorably out of the Chinese past however much its future may depart from this past. If the Chinese spirit were to divorce itself from its own past it would not achieve national greatness. The idea of society as an organic entity on a biological model was the crucial element of this conservatism.

Another particular aspect of modern Chinese conservatism is that it is largely cultural conservatism and not basically a sociopolitical conservatism committed to the prevailing sociopolitical status quo. Many Chinese cultural conservatives are, of course, much more definite about the elements of the culture which are to be preserved. Here they often become vague or highly selective. Above all, they do not often see the culture of the past fully realized in the current sociopolitical order (the period of the National government provides some exceptions.) Edmund Burke did not approve of everything in the sociopolitical structure and culture of late eighteenth-century England but he did approve of a vast number of things in general and of the political order in particular. His commitment to the whole involved a deep commitment to the myriad parts. In China, however, by the beginning of the twentieth century we find few members of the articulate intelligentsia who are prepared to defend the current sociopolitical order as a whole. What Chang Ping-lin's conservatism amounts to is a vehement insistence that Chinese derive their categories of thought from their own racial heritage, and it is this insistence which defines him as a cultural conservative.

Yet when we look more closely at Chang's specific commitments within the Chinese cultural realm we are forcefully made aware of the limits of the notion of conservatism as an explanatory concept. As a man who still lived quite naturally within the traditional culture, he in fact regarded that culture not as a harmonious, integrated whole but as a reservoir of conflicting tendencies. He was, first of all, committed to a kind of philosophy of scholarship (Ch'ing scholarship) which turned out to be nihilistically neutral toward all the dominant alternatives of Chinese thought. He was also committed to a kind of Taoist-Buddhist philosophy which blended easily with an anti-Confucian Legalist political philosophy. His experience led him on one level to a violent revulsion against the Confucian fusion of the ethical and political orders. On another level it led him to seek solace in a brand of Taoist-Buddhist philosophy which made it possible for him to raise questions about the degree to which human life can ever be moralized or freed from suffering.

Chang Ping-lin reminds us that conservatism can by no means be simply equated with commitment to ideas drawn from the Chinese cultural past. Indeed, his sociopolitical ideas were to lead him into the radical revolutionary camp. The issues with which he became involved far transcended the conservatism/radicalism dichotomy. One can indeed discern a contradiction between his conservative racialist organicism which seems to posit a unitary Chinese spirit and his own very particular predilections and aversions within the realm of Chinese thought. Other Chinese cultural conservatives less deeply immersed than he in the particularities of the Chinese past were to have less trouble expounding the doctrine of a vague unitary Chinese spirit. Chiang's thought in particular highlights the difference between the conservative commitment to the idea of "Chinese culture" as a construct and the actual contents of that culture which may have either conservative or radical implications.

One might, of course, use the term "traditionalist" rather than conservative to describe all those in modern China such as Chang Ping-lin, Hsiung Shih-li, Liang Shu-ming, and others who have claimed that ideas and values of the past had present validity for them. The late Joseph Levenson drew a distinction between "traditionalist" and "traditionalistic" thinking. Traditionalistic thinking in his view refers precisely to the kind of cultural conservatism which professes to cherish values and ideas of the past not because of any deep sense of their inherent validity but because of their usefulness in enforcing national pride (as in the case of the traditionalism of the Nationalist government). It was, of course, Levenson's view that in a society inexorably committed to modernization (hence a society in which traditional values were no longer relevant) all invocation of past values and ideas was inevitably traditionalistic and hence conservative. Levenson's approach seems to suggest that a simple way to define conservatism in modern China would be to identify it with all attitudes which seem antithetical to the project of modernization. All forms of commitment to tradition could thus be called conservative.

To those who are by now troubled by the semantics of the word "modernization" and who are not necessarily convinced that modernity on a Western model is an inseparable whole, the possibility of a genuine commitment by modern Chinese to ideas and values of the past cannot be precluded. A case may thus be made that Liang Shu-ming, who claims to derive truth from the traditions of the past and who is only partially committed to the project of modernization in the full Weberian sense, is not fundamentally a conservative. He certainly never committed himself to support of the current sociopolitical structure. On many issues he seems to have had a greater affinity with the type of radicalism represented by Mao Tse-tung than with the conservatism of T'ao Hsi-sheng.

Conversely, it is possible to speak of conservative modernizers in twentieth-century China. The goals of modernization, it is argued, particularly the goal of national power, require an environment of stability. They require the consolidation and development of moral and physical energies in being. Thus Yen Fu at the beginning of the twentieth century and Yuan Shih-k'ai after 1911 could both argue that given the retarded evolution of the Chinese masses, the symbolism of traditional monarchy could alone provide a focus of meaningful political authority around which a program of modernization might be developed. Such a conservatism may be more or less happy about the extent to which the evolution of Chinese history provided factors favorable to modernization. When Chiang Kai-shek launched his New Life movement, which was based on the assumption that traditional values could be revitalized and harnessed to the purposes of modernization, he presumably expressed a high faith in the "modern" utility of Confucian tradition. On the other hand, T'ao Hsi-sheng was far less happy about the consequences of China's social history. Operating in the intellectual environment of the thirties, he actually uses Marxist categories to analyze the past and even shares the Marxist sense of the "badness of the past." Yet given the determinative weight of social history, China had no alternative but to use whatever sources of strength and stability it had available to it. Above all, what China required if it was to move forward to national power and socialism was not class strife but class unity and political order. This national unity also required a certain positive sense on the part of Chinese of their unique cultural history. The Nationalist government after 1927 seemed to be the only force in being which held the promise of the kind of national unity which might facilitate the process of modernization. Thus, while Tao Hsi-sheng's conservatism may have been relatively unhappy about China's historic past, it was nevertheless clearly used to support a political order in being by appealing to a kind of attenuated cultural conservatism.

One can also find in modern China a kind of conservatism of despair exemplified by Chou Tso-jen, treated in this volume by Mr. Pollard. Chou Tso-jen — at least on the conscious level — does *not* affirm the social, political, and cultural heritage of the past. Indeed, as an "Enlightenment" thinker he finds the past, taken as a whole, evil and repressive, and in his later development he is not even driven by any nationalist impulse to affirm that past. What impresses him is not the benignity of the past but its overwhelming power. It is, to be sure, true that he clings to certain minor strains in the cultural heritage—the solace of scholarship and a kind of aesthetics of daily living which he finds in the tradition of Su Tung-po and others. In the end, however, he is overwhelmed by his sense of the culture of the past as a vast inert power independent of the wills of individuals and beyond their power to change in any fundamental way. Indeed efforts to change it are only likely to make matters worse.

Thus, in surveying some of the modalities of conservatism contained in this volume, we find that we rarely encounter in twentieth-century China the kind of robust Burkean conservatism which rests on the ringing affirmation of prevailing sociopolitical order as a whole. What one finds is rather a kind of cultural conservatism in the service of nationalist passions which are rarely linked to any deep commitment to the prevailing political order although such commitment can be found after the establishment of the Nationalist government. One also finds that while there are Chinese forces of conservatism which insist that elements out of the Chinese past can be harnessed or used for modern purposes, there are other unhappy modes of conservatism which are skeptical about the usability of China's past, but which are nevertheless based on a profound sense of the determinative weight of that past.

It must thus be asserted that the problem of the relationship of modern articulate Chinese to the total cultural heritage cannot simply be equated with the conservatism/radicalism problem. The cultural crisis of twentieth-century China becomes involved with problems which transcend this dichotomy. One cannot predict whether traditional or antitraditional views will necessarily have radical or conservative consequences within a given historic context.

Finally, a word should be said about the limited scope of this study. We are considering the explicit views of a small intellectual and political elite. We are not dealing with the vast mass of sect leaders, Buddhist monks, secret society members, and others who still lived, in the twentieth century, unreflectively within the older culture; nor are we considering the ways in which habits of thought and action out of the Chinese past continue to influence people on an unreflective level.

2 Culture and Politics in Modern Chinese Conservatism

CHARLOTTE FURTH

In their various ways, the essays in this book represent an effort to reevaluate the relation of recent Chinese intellectual movements to Chinese tradition, and to trace the changing face of conservatism in an avowedly revolutionary modern society. Although the fate of Chinese tradition in the twentieth century is a well-worn theme, our images of the issues involved have come mostly from two sources. The first is from those radical young Chinese who actually led the May Fourth movement, and who then passed on to history their totalistic interpretation of the evil dragon, "tradition," slain once and for all in the streets of Peking in May 1919. By portraying the preceding reform generation as one still steeped in feudal culture, in spite of its leadership of an abortive political revolution in 1911, New Culture inconoclasts glossed over the profound cultural changes since the 1890s which in fact had made their own total revolt possible. By describing the battles of the 1920s and 1930s as those of progressive movements—identified with liberalism or socialism—pitted against the stubbornly traditional masses and/or those who fattened on mass ignorance, they tarred their political opposition with the brush of cultural reaction, and so tried to appropriate for themselves the precious symbolism of modernity. Prevailing images of Chinese culture under the Nationalists, by students from left or right, have been powerfully affected by this view.[1]

For those of us in America especially, the second formative source of our image of "Confucian China and Its Modern Fate" has come from Joseph Levenson.[2] His books have been guided by a theoretically historicist belief that old forms of thought and behavior must in some sense inevitably change their meaning in new historical contexts. Accordingly, he has stressed that the twentieth-century Chinese conservatives' failure to be authentically traditional came not so much from their aspiration as from the new situation they could not help. On the empirical level, therefore, he has seen cultural conservatives as motivated by the tension between their nostalgia for the past and their nationalist consciousness. It is true that cultural nationalism has certainly been a very real modern phenomenon, nowhere more than in colonial and semicolonial Asia. Nonetheless the habit of explaining modern Chinese intellectual movements in terms of the presumed nationalist motivations behind them can lead to psychological reductionism—to unprovable assumptions about people's actual motivations, and to a genetic fallacy of giving priority to the historical process of "thinking" over the formal content of "thought." The habit of suggesting a special relationship between conservative thought and nationalism in China can lead to a mistaken analysis of nationalism as an ideological quantity. To a certain extent everywhere, and especially in anticolonial countries, modern nationalism has taken the form of a popular sentiment so universal as to transcend the categories of sociopolitical debate. To take as a primary category of analysis the nationalism of any Chinese may distract our attention from the cultural and sociopolitical issues that actually were of central concern to them. We can now see that Mao's nationalism did not alter the fundamentals of his social vision; it seems reasonable to grant that the same may be true of Chiang Kai-shek. The new form of political community—the nation—was with equal plausibility identified with almost the entire range of sociopolitical issues in dispute, suggesting these must be considered on their own merits independent of the national factor.

The various authors in this book present a number of different interpretations of the idea of conservatism as a political concept, but there is much agreement concerning our approach to the study of modern Chinese conservatism in particular. First, it is important to see the pre- and post-May Fourth generations in a dialectical rather than an antithetical relationship, and to reject totalistic conceptions either of Chinese tradition or of the character of modern criticism of it. Second, rather than focus on their psychological relation to tradition, it is more useful to try and focus on the content of what Chinese have said and done in the context of their immediate situation, and in light of the serious ongoing conflicts inside China which could not be papered over by appeals to a common spirit of national solidarity.

Such an approach suggests placing the beginning of China's modern intellectual crisis in the 1890s, and seeing it as involving challenges not only to the preexisting sociopolitical order but also to what might be called the moral-spiritual order as well. Recognition of what was happening was widespread enough so that it seems possible from a very early date to isolate a conservative response which less resembled attitudes common to imperial China than those characteristic of other worldwide conservative movements of our last two revolutionary centuries. The label "conservative" here denotes conscious points of view, rather than unanalyzed traditional assumptions, and has been adopted to indicate one constellation of essentially postimperial attitudes.[3] In China, as elsewhere, modern conservatism has been a response to new issues, a response in which reevaluations of tradition have gone hand in hand with competing models for change.

In his essay here, Benjamin Schwartz points out that in the West as in China conservatism as a self-conscious ideological phenomenon has been a historical reaction to real or threatened challenges, and that it has tended to share a framework of common concepts with the alternative innovative movements it opposed. Though historicism, sociologism, and nationalism have been thought of as characteristic of nineteenth-century European conservative thought in reaction against the Enlightenment, they can also be shown to have shaped liberal and Marxist categories of analysis as well. Similarly, in China modern conservatism like its rivals was a reaction to imperialism and the introduction of Western ideas. It emerged when the breakup of the monarchical ideal, widely recognized as inevitable, forced people to see the national political order as having an existence independent of the web of social custom and moral-spiritual belief which the imperial system had also symbolized. Questions of culture had to be divorced from questions about politics. As a consequence of this, attachment to the political status quo or immediate past became increasingly difficult to maintain. At the same time hitherto novel questions about culture — its essential definition, historical origins, and relation to other aspects of human experience — became a subject of special importance for intellectuals of every stripe. To characterize the particular conservative response to these issues shows not how modern Chinese conservatives have been behind the times, but how they have been a reflection of them.

The mystique of the imperial monarchy began to crumble in the 1890s, with the dynasty's foreign disasters and the reform movement stimulated by them. The new Darwinian view that adaptation to the times was a necessity of historical evolution soon made the demand for institutional reform almost universal among the literati. Of course the theory of imperial monarchy had always allowed that dynasties should fall when they failed to meet practical tests of leadership, but the mandate of heaven had been a sacred, not a utilitarian, conception of political legitimacy. After 1898, however, even loyalty to the throne began to be interpreted in ways that not only demanded pragmatic accountability but also questioned the sacred character of the imperial institution itself. With this the decisive separation of the political realm from the cultural and moral orders had begun.

The sexagenarian Chang Chih-tung was probably the last important Chinese leader to maintain that preservation of the Confucian doctrine (*chiao*) depended upon the continued existence of an imperial Person to serve as the concrete symbol of its manifest presence in the political order. In spite of the well-known pragmatism of his educational and other reforms after 1902, Chang believed himself to be within the framework of the forty-year-old *t'i-yung* formula for change. That is, he believed that reform would not prevent social and political practice from continuing to reflect the cultural and religious norms of recent Confucian orthodoxy. Yet even he emphasized pure literary culture in his educational schemes for preserving the Confucian heritage. K'ang Yu-wei's equally famous loyalism to the dynasty was based on more novel premises. It went hand in hand with his plan for the institutionalization of

Confucianism as a state religion — a move inspired by what he considered to have been the role of Christianity in the West, and designed to protect the *chiao* from becoming demythologized as a result of political innovations.[4] K'ang's Protect the Emperor Society (*Pao huang hu*) and provincial constitutionalists alike argued for monarchism on the basis of the new criteria of the needs of the times, unwittingly implying that those unready for the throne's abolition were other people, not themselves.

For most constitutionalists, formal loyalty to the old order must be seen as a device to usher in the new. Once imperial rulers ceased to be perceived as in some sense sacred, they were soon seen to have no reason to exist at all. In spite of the heritage of centuries, monarchism has played almost no role in modern Chinese conservatism. Even such a superficially traditionalistic experiment as Yuan Shih-kai's attempt to establish a new dynasty in 1915 was, as Ernest Young shows here, conservative in terms of postimperial political alternatives. It was a strategy pragmatically conceived in the interests of nation-building and, like that of the constitutionalists whose legacy it tried to co-opt, was aimed at outsiders — the presumably more old-fashioned common people.

Cultural commitments to tradition, then, were uncertain guides to postimperial political allegiances. On all sides the search for new political forms was perceived as necessary. All the diverse kinds of cultural conservatives discussed in this book claimed to be looking for modern, even radical, political alternatives. The pattern appeared even before the 1911 revolution, among the anti-Manchu "national essence" (*kuo ts'ui*) classicists associated with the National Essence Protection Association and the Southern Society. Individuals like Chang Ping-lin and Liu Shih-p'ei exploited native alternative traditions as a source of political criticism of imperial orthodoxy. Their efforts amounted to a scarcely conservative manipulation of history to undermine the present — a "restoration strategy" reminiscent of the seventeenth-century British use of the idea of a pre-Norman "ancient constitution" or the French revolutionary evocation of the Roman Republic.[5] Alternative traditions especially important to these Chinese were Ming loyalism, now given a sharpened racialist interpretation, the tradition of critical scholarship identified with the school of Han learning, and the non-Confucian theories of the philosophers (*chu tzu*) of the ancient Chou.

However, their restoration strategy appealed largely to a presumed lost spirit of ancient institutions — that of public-mindedness (*kung*) — and therefore contributed little to the issue of the institutional forms of postrevolutionary political construction. Their attack — devastating against the selfishness (*ssu*) of imperial despotism — continued to appeal to the same spirit against republican performance after 1912 and ended up being merely anti-Western. Nonetheless, their combination of nativism in culture and innovation in politics, so novel in the reform generation, became quite commonplace later on. By refusing to be politically anti-Western, Sun Yat-sen was far more able than they to seize the political initiative, in both his republican and his Leninist phases. But his small learning in Chinese culture and history, much of it acquired from National Essence scholars, supported their negative opinion of the New Culture movement.[6] In modified form the national essence style of revolution was carried on by the Kuomintang, and Sun's combination of political radicalism and cultural nativism, far from being an anomaly, fit an established pattern.

Neotraditionalists of the 1920s and 1930s often followed a style of thinking about politics first given wide currency by K'ang Yu-wei, purporting to find precedents for the spirit of democratic institutions in Confucius and Mencius. Also somewhat like K'ang, many endorsed the forms of liberal politics, though without much inner conviction, since the genius of the spirit of Confucianism was, they said, after all in "men" and not in "laws." Nonetheless, whether they supported democratic oppositionist groups, as Chang Chün-mai and Liang Shu-ming did,[7] or pledged allegiance to the "Three Principles of the People" like most KMT supporters, they acknowledged that modern politics gives formal sovereignty to the whole people, and showed how much cachet attached to being politically up-to-date.

To make the idea of political conservatism in twentieth-century China meaningful, then, a contemporary worldwide perspective must be adopted. Rather than simply comparing movements inside

China, we must take global historical patterns as the basis for establishing a periodization and defining issues, which means to accept the framework of industrial and political modernization.

Ernest Young's essay here on Yuan Shih-k'ai defines modernization in terms of two important historical movements. The first is the one toward national independence and integration, which has been part of the twentieth-century anti-imperialist stage of a global evolution toward the organization of peoples into nation-states. The second is the movement for mass participation in politics, which has been occurring on an increasing scale as the pattern of mass society spreads within individual countries and to more and more peoples throughout the world. In this setting, both Yuan Shih-k'ai's regime and Chiang Kai-shek's were committed to the modernizing goal of nationhood, and their conservatism lay in their opposition to its achievement through increased public participation in politics. Yuan defeated the liberal gentry and their constitutional program. Chiang suppressed the mass movement of the 1920s. Moreover, both leaders wanted control of the political process by a small coterie at the top and the concomitant political centralization. Yet the attitudes toward both the traditional political order and its symbols were instrumental and manipulative, and both turned to the West for models of government organization in areas like law, finance, and military affairs.[8]

In his discussion of the Kuomintang in the "Nanking decade," Lloyd Eastman sees a slightly different global movement to which the politics of modernization in China may be related—the worldwide wave of militarism in the 1930s led by fascist Germany and Japan and Stalinist Russia. To some extent, Nationalist China could be seen as a would-be totalitarian dictatorship. It is true that among the complex kaleidoscope of KMT factions, only the Blue Shirts consciously came close to adopting a fascist ideological model, and that KMT performance, developmentally sluggish and militarily beleaguered, was somewhat lacking in totalitarian dynamism. But Eastman's point is precisely this contrast between aspiration and achievement. From the point of view of goals, a national dictatorship like Chiang's, committed to rapid economic development and military mobilization, wished to be like Western totalitarian governments rather than like liberal regimes content with an evolutionary pace. From this perspective the most important conservative force in Nationalist China was not so much the explicit governmental policy as it was the natural drag of a still traditional political culture inhibiting the mobilization of resources to carry out rapid change; it was not so much conscious political conservatism as it was unanalyzed traditionalism. Rather than reflecting an explicit preference for old ways, it reflected old habits that were not thought about at all.

The Chinese Republic had a government national in scope only in those years when it was under the leadership of Yuan Shih-k'ai or the pre-1949 Chiang Kai-shek. Their common style of nation-building therefore marks an important continuity in postimperial politics which the period's dramatic military history has often obscured. Nonetheless, while agreeing substantially about the behavior of these political leaders and the administrations they headed, Young freely characterizes Yuan Shih-k'ai as a conservative modernizer; while Eastman, on the other hand, observes that China in the 1930s fits Clinton Rossiter's typology of a truly revolutionary society in which fundamental changes are so universally regarded as necessary that people of conservative temperament have no viable movement to attach themselves to. This contrast points to a basic analytical disagreement over whether it is possible to understand any among a group of competing models for political change under the category of "conservatism."

Eastman assumes that conservatism must be analyzed in terms of the rate of change occurring in a total political system. In a revolutionary situation this will be rapid under a wide variety of policies. An industrialization program such as the Nationalists envisaged, based on rapidly developing a mixed public-private industrial sector and encouraging urbanization, would change the lives of the masses of people just as fast and just as much as Mao's agrarian-oriented socialism. The first might bankrupt the countryside while leaving rural social organization prey only to market forces; the second would actively reorganize rural work and property relations but in so doing inhibit urbanization. Such an analysis, which comes close to seeing all forms of modernization outside the West as inherently radical, gains clarity in analyzing conservatism as a function of time and change, conceived as the abstract totality of a historical process. But in so doing, it loses sight of the competing goals of change and explicit sociopolitical conflicts over these. The discussion of politics becomes depoliticized, as a regime's abstract relation with history takes precedence over its political relationship with the contemporary people at whose expense it rules. In discussing Yuan Shih-k'ai, Young is less concerned with whose beliefs are more old-fashioned than with the battle over property and power between haves and have-nots, in the context of a presumably populist tide of modern history. His implied analysis of the forces of change includes a projection of future trends. Regardless of the fact that as a professional military politician Yuan's outlook was just as historically novel as that of his enemies the constitutionalist gentry, his refusal to share power with them is meaningfully characterized as conservative in this political sense.

If republican politicians, however variously their programs are interpreted, all aspired to be modernizers, then the cultural conservatives discussed here, from Chang Ping-lin to Hsiung Shih-li, all accepted the necessity of political change and had to consider cultural-moral questions apart from the political process. The cultural conservatism of these years was the work of individuals who found it necessary to separate their ideals and values from political necessity, to move with the times in part, while denying the power of those same times to corrupt what was most precious to them. Two main currents of conservative thought emerge from the essays gathered here, both predicated upon the discovery of a deep cleavage between the cultural-moral and the sociopolitical realms. The first is the nativist National Essence school, and the second is the movement for the modernization of Confucianism, embracing thinkers as diverse as K'ang Yu-wei and Mou Tsung-san.

One of the first signs of people's perception of the separation of culture from politics was the emergence shortly after 1900 of a new body of conservative analysis concerning the question of culture itself. If the May Fourth movement represented the logical culmination of a generation of thinking that cultural westernization was the spiritual foundation necessary for progressive change, the National

Essence (*kuo ts'ui*) movement was the almost equally long-lived countercurrent. The Meiji neologism *kuo ts'ui* (*kokusui*) apparently entered the Chinese vocabulary around 1903—shortly after Liang Ch'i-ch'ao's call for a "new people"—as a slogan to refer to the presumed essence of China's classical heritage in philosophy, history, and art. The association of the term with literary culture was clear from its first use to designate the academy proposed by Chang Chih-tung in 1904 and founded in 1907, which was to be responsible for the preservation of national learning in the face of the necessary westernization of general education. As Martin Bernal and Laurence Schneider point out, people from a fairly wide spectrum within the reform and revolutionary movements began to promote the national essence around the time the examination system was phased out and the constitutional movement gathered momentum. Thus the idea stood for the classical heritage disassociated from the institutions which for centuries had integrated learning with political practice.

But culture, however detached from existing institutions, has to come from somewhere and be transmitted by someone. The contribution of the revolutionary wing of the National Essence movement was to mix classicism and social Darwinism—fueling the anti-Manchu revolution by suggesting that the national essence had been the creation of the Han people, an organic product of their ethnic genius and historical experience. Briefly in the years before 1911 national essence suggested populism of a sort—it invoked a national community based on race, soil, and history; and briefly this call to community went hand in hand with efforts to organize the people to rise up as a nation against the Manchus. However, for the national essence classicists the myth of ethnicity proved less durable than the myth of culture, which quickly regained predominance again after 1912. In spite of the widespread acceptance of the idea that cultures are the creation of peoples, culture was far more commonly discussed by scholars like Chang Ping-lin and Liu Shih-p'ei as if it had a life of its own, capable in turn of transforming those people with whom it came in contact. Moreover, rather than being directly identified with the existing customs of the people themselves, particularly those which might be presumed to reveal the people's moral and spiritual values, the national essence was located in the historical and literary record.[9] By the time of the May Fourth movement, the advocates of the national essence were once more identifying the creators and transmitters of culture with men of genius—if not the sage-kings themselves, then the historical poets, philosophers, and scholars who acted as their surrogates. Culture, which provided the evaluative standard against which the actual social life of the people might be measured, was to be known in the form of "objective geiste"—the record of the high civilization.[10]

In this way national essence came to stand for more than the preservation of the particular Chinese heritage against the corrosive effects of Western civilization. It was a new way for Chinese to conceptualize the idea of culture itself. National Essence scholars and poets symbolized the conservative opposition to the New Culture movement because they offered a nontraditional, yet conservative, alternative to the radical demand for cultural revolution. Rather than calling for broad educational and social change to bring culture and polity back into harmony with one another, the national essence solution was to accept the finality of the disjunction.

In the May Fourth period, this new conservative perception of the autonomy of culture drew interestingly close to a type of new cultural liberal attitude. The literary revolution itself was energized by the demands of poets, scholars, and artists that culture stand apart from social utility and serve as the theater for inner personal self-expression. The plea of a Chang Ping-lin or a Wang Kuo-wei that people should be allowed to devote themselves to disinterested private scholarship as a matter of right bears a family resemblance to Chou Tso-jen's call for a literature of personal "interestingness," or even the demands of romantics like Kuo Mo-jo and Hsu Chih-mo that the function of poetry should be to express the poet's untrammeled inner voice. The difference between the liberal and conservative perceptions of the autonomous cultural realm seems to lie in their contrasting conceptions of what, on the deepest level of meaning, the inner sphere of personal experience signifies—whether it reflects ontology, or only expresses the self; whether it is guided by personal choice or a sense of moral necessity.

For conservatives at least, the historical Chinese culture came to be seen as a spirit embodying suprapersonal values. The social Darwinist outlook of the National Essence movement encouraged formulations which conceived of the spirit as dynamically evolving. Organic models were available to explain how changing historical forms went hand in hand with unchanging essences. May Fourth iconoclasts scoffed at this as *t'i-yung* thinking — a convenient smear which glossed over the basic shift in emphasis which had taken place since 1900. As conceived by the late Ch'ing self-strengtheners — technology (*yung*) had been the category set apart, while the foundations of society (*t'i*) continued to be conceived as socially, politically, and culturally unitary. Advocates of national essence had not only rejected the late Ch'ing political system, they had also participated in the reform critique of the orthodox Confucian social norms as particularistic props of despotism. Whatever their private behavior, they had offered a revisionist theory of Confucianism: as rational morality, skeptical historical tradition, or universal value system, based on benevolence (*jen*) and righteousness (*i*), not ritual (*li*). Thus their theories were to some degree detached from traditional social as well as political forms. In idealizing culture, they were adapting to their contemporary situation as much as resisting it.

Nonetheless, as was logical for the last generation of classicists China ever produced, the early National Essence group had linked cultural essences with classical forms of literary expression and, as Laurence Schneider points out, such a movement could hardly survive the universal triumph of the vernacular language. In the 1920s the Harvard-trained *Critical Review* clique tried to bring the heritage of Greece and Rome to the rescue, defending classicism as a formal principle divorced from native content — a solution that pleased hardly anyone and marked the end of the trail. After the early twenties, the slogan *kuo ts'ui* was largely abandoned by cultural conservatives themselves, as regrettably old-fashioned, evocative of a dead scholasticism.

What did survive, however, was the idealization of native Chinese culture, based on the Darwinist premises of the earlier movement that it had grown from natural organic roots in the people, history, and land. Nationalist intellectuals and propagandists of the late twenties and thirties disdained *kuo ts'ui* but talked freely of *kuo hsing* or *"min-tsu hsing"* (national character).[11] The term evoked unitary ethnic consciousness more and classicism less, but still in the final analysis served to identify the people with the cultural ideal of traditional morality. What the "national character" claimed to establish, as both ideal and fact, was the unitary nature of the Chinese people's historical experience and its fruit in their unique devotion to moral principle. These ideas had political uses, exploited fully by KMT anti-Communist polemicists like Tai Chi-t'ao. But beyond politics the denial of the existence of deep social cleavages in Chinese history and the claim that the Chinese people and their way of life were simply morally superior symbolized something important about the presumed values of the Chinese cultural spirit itself.

A sophisticated example of such thinking is found in Ch'ien Mu's widely admired history of China, which was a basic text in many colleges in the 1940s.[12] Ch'ien Mu identified the spirit of Chinese culture with the moral principle of public-mindedness (*kung*), interpreted as the synthesis of the best in Legalist and Confucian tradition, both unitary and altruistic. The actualization of the spirit of public-mindedness was traced from dynasty to dynasty—from the philosophical unification of the Ch'in and Han, to the assimilation of alien peoples and foreign cultural ideals (Buddhism) in the Six-Dynasties-T'ang period, to the perfection of the centralized state in Sung-Ming times. For Ch'ien Mu, the literati were not a self-interested class, but the developers and transmitters of those legitimate institutions (*chih tu*)—chiefly the examination system and the central government bureaucracy—which established a society organized around principles of unity and public benefit.[13] Like Chang Ping-lin earlier, Ch'ien Mu was concerned about the problem of origins and about the relation of historical forms to abiding spirit. Although with more sophisticated detail, drawn from archaeological sources, he followed the earlier scholar in emphasizing that the national character had been the creation of the natural environment itself, mediated by time. Rather than statically originating at a point in history, this cultural spirit emerged as a historical metaphysic; that is, as the unending consequences (*yeh*) of the collective spiritual accumulation of a people. By analogy with the Buddhist notion of karma (*yeh*), the spirit was perceived as both detached from all its many historical manifestations, yet continuous with them.

KMT nativism emphasized the populist Darwinian themes of the national essence but continued to give culture a special, preeminent place in defining the nation. In modern nativist thought elsewhere, as in Japan or the Muslim world, it has been common to find the more backward country population praised as a last reservoir of uncorrupted traditionalism, and the centers of cultural conserva-tism have often been located in the provinces, and have articulated regional, rural interests.[14] But natives in this sense were not the focus of Nationalist nativism. They rarely praised the moral superiority of rural life as such; they brought severely rationalistic and orthodox standards to bear on those untidy and often superstitious popular customs which were under their power to control; they might extol the moral spirit of the old family system, but they did not by law or example encourage the perpetuation of the clan model of family organization, nor did they honor familistic values as primary over those of the larger national community. The New Life movement was as much a drive for the modernization of people's social behavior according to contemporary urban standards of orderliness, hygiene, and decorum, as it was an effort to restore the endangered traditional moral fiber of the populace. All in all, the Nationalists celebrated abstract unity, not intimate community. Culture was correspondingly an abstract ideal, objectified in historical tradition and ethical precept, which could be presented instead of living popular custom as the theoretical basis of the people's presumed true national character.

Nonetheless, however we may criticize the social and philosophical limitations of much nationalist ideology, it cannot be seen solely as an instrument serving state power without denying that the symbols appealed to had any authentic power to stir feeling—if not among the masses, certainly among the educated. The original National Essence group had been passionately nationalistic, but because they saw national survival as the only way to keep alive their cultural heritage. In Ch'ien Mu the modern nationalist ideal pioneered in *kuo ts'ui* historiography was carried on, and the Chinese nation was portrayed as the historical bearer of universal moral values capable of being realized in progressively more perfected historical forms. The idealization of Chinese culture could serve either as a tool for the manipulation of social reality, or as an evasion of it or an alternative to it. It could be instrument, opiate, or dream.

Although National Essence thinkers tended to moralize culture, they and the Nationalists after them also tended to rationalize Confucius. The scholarly roots of the original national essence clique lay in the Ch'ing Old Text tradition of Han learning, which had pioneered the critical approach to classical texts which in turn evolved into the revisionist scientific historiography of the 1920s.[15] Following the lead of Chang Ping-lin, the national essence approach to the modernization of Confucianism was to encourage a view of the sage as a social moralist and rational scholar, in contrast to New Text-style apotheosis of the sage. Moreover they emphasized pre-Ch'in non-Confucian philosophical schools as independent sources of tradition, equal to or even preeminent over Confucianism itself. In promoting a Chinese Renaissance, they both suggested a new world-historical framework within which to conceptualize the origins of Chinese culture and also offered a cultural program which stood as an alternative to New Text Confucian utopianism.

In other words, during the pre-May Fourth period the partisans of the national essence either wanted to deemphasize Confucius or to make Confucius relevant to modern conditions by emphasizing the secular nature of his teaching. Their debate with K'ang Yu-wei and his followers over whether Confucianism is a religion[16] was itself a sign of the emergence in China of the modern problem of religion. Morality in its relation to social custom was for the first time perceived by Confucians themselves as analytically separable from morality in relation to cosmic truth, leading to searching questions about what Confucian tradition might in fact have to say about the ontological foundations of normative belief, or what contributors to this book call "the problem of meaning." Beginning with K'ang Yu-wei, an increasing number of Confucian reformers felt it necessary to characterize Confucianism as a functionally religious system of thought.[17] If National Essence partisans located value in an abstract cultural ideal, advocates of Confucianism as a religion located it in an even more rarefied region of metaphysics.

Even among cultural conservatives, K'ang Yu-wei was not a popular figure after the May Fourth movement. His New Text Confucianism was seen as motivated either by Christian example, which was a concession to Western superstition, or monarchical loyalty, which was a concession to Chinese reaction. Nonetheless, though he and other advocates of a Confucian state cult lost decisively in the debates of the May Fourth era, the problem of religious meaning they had raised did not go away, but instead acquired new urgency with the spread of scientism. Liang Shu-ming stated it in classic form when he argued in 1921 that human beings all need religion as such, for their psychological comfort and for dealing with the side of existence which the intellect is helpless to explain.[18] In the science and metaphysics debate of 1923, Chang Chün-mai, Chang Tung-sun, and others, faced with the claims of the new scientific rationalists among the intelligentsia, defended the autonomy of value — and by implication Confucianism — with arguments drawn from the European *Kulturkampf* between science and Christianity.

So, although Confucian rationalism might superficially seem a more up-to-date strategy for a cultural conservative, in fact the most seriously acclaimed neotraditional thinkers of the 1920s and 1930s followed Liang Shu-ming in interpreting Confucianism within the broad modern framework of the problem of religious meaning in an increasingly secularized world. These included Hsiung Shih-li and the Taiwan-Hong Kong neotraditionalists discussed here by Tu Wei-ming and Hao Chang, and also the philosopher Fung Yu-lan. For these individuals, issues of Chinese tradition were subsumed under the more universal ones of the ultimate cosmic-moral forms of truth.

The complexities of the "new Confucianism"[19] as a religiophilosophical movement are given some preliminary exploration in essays presented here. Recognizing an inevitable oversimplification, I would generalize about the following religious dimensions to new Confucianists' thinking. They thought within the framework of a cosmology which attempted to characterize the total universe in both its spaciotemporal and supraphenomenal aspects; they described an intimate relationship between moral values and these ontological foundations; and they explored areas of psychological experience which they felt enabled human beings to know the sublime and the character of their unity with it. Their ontological formulations all developed the classic formula of the Doctrine of the Mean (*Chung yung*) which affirmed the unity of humanity and heaven. Their ethics was based on benevolence (*jen*) as both a cosmic and moral principle. Psychologically Liang Shu-ming's "intuitive knowledge of the good" (*li-hsing*), Fung Yu-lan's "seriousness" (*ching*), Hsiung Shih-li's "experiential recognition" (*t'i-jen*), Mou Tsung-san's "awakening" (*chueh-wu*) were all terms designed to call attention to the fact that understanding and living by these truths was no simple intellectual matter, but the result of consciously directed spiritual and moral energies. New Confucianists generally felt special affinity with the idealistic forms of Buddhism and also with the Lu-Wang wing of neo-Confucian philosophy, which supplied much of the technical vocabulary in their writings.[20]

As a difficult and highly philosophical route to truth, the new Confucianism obviously had little to do with the types of popular worship, including ancestor rites, which historically had functioned as forms of religious expression for most ordinary Chinese, and actually most leaders of the movement were academic philosophers. However, their claims for the academy were not modest, since schools, unlike monasteries or mountain retreats, function *in* the world and so presumably could carry out some part of the historical Confucian social mission of ordering society. They expected that the learned activity of reconstruction of Confucian metaphysics would not only illuminate the heritage but also, in the words of Tu Wei-ming here, shape the meaning structure of society as a whole. Teachers were not simply to be moral guides, but, it was hoped, *chün-tzu* and sages — indispensable active agents in the symbolic ordering of the world. While recognizing and even participating in the rapid professionalization of academic life about them, the new Confucianists nonetheless saw themselves as guardians of the "religion of the intellectuals."[21]

What I have outlined here are two styles of cultural conservatism found under the Republic. The followers of the nativist or national essence variety were generally secular-minded, concerned with the preservation of cultural ideals which they saw as the creations of the historical genius of the Chinese people. They were likely to emphasize non-Confucian contributions to the historical tradition or to see Confucianism itself as rationally humanistic. Concerning the relationship of science and value, they followed what might be called the strategy of amalgamation — claiming to find in the prescientific cultural tradition itself elements compatible with modern science and upon which it could be expected to build. Their emphasis upon national culture and the integration of traditional philosophical systems and science made their approach adaptable to the political outlook of supporters of the Kuomintang. Neotraditional Confucianists, on the other hand, insisted that the central core of the tradition lay in Confucianism, for precisely the reason that through Confucianism Chinese historically had dealt with human problems of an essentially religious nature. They tended to emphasize that the personal search for spiritual truth could not be thought of as having national or cultural boundaries, though it might take national or culture-bound forms. Concerning science, they followed what might be called a separatist strategy — insisting that Confucian truth exists on a plane of insight separable from that governing science, and superior to it.[22]

The emergence of these two styles was of course a response to the forces of nationalism and the secularization of society — things Chinese were experiencing along with most other people in the modern world. At the same time much in the Chinese situation kept the two styles from being sharply antithetical. In the first place, the external crisis made Chinese nationalism a universally shared sentiment which flavored every point of view, so that a nativist like Ch'ien Mu could make world-historical claims for the Chinese cultural mission, while a cosmopolitan like Liang Shu-ming saw China, not some other place, as the homeland of universal religiomoral value. Perhaps more important, older forms of rationalism and mysticism had been closely intertwined in the Confucian tradition itself, so that even as modern Chinese newly perceived a gulf between sacred and secular realms, they looked for ways, drawn from their inherited store of syncretic symbols, to overcome it.

Nativists, who placed value in the ideal of culture rather than in accessible forms of social custom or political practice, often went on to make explicit or implicit claims for the religious nature of culture itself. In the 1920s Wu Mi and Ts'ai Yuan-p'ei spoke for such an approach, treating cultural products like art and literature as an up-to-date substitute for religion. They did not just say that art performs the religious functions of providing inspiration for right conduct and imaginative release; Ts'ai Yuan-p'ei argued further that "art shows ontology in phenomena," and Wu Mi that it "draws on the mysterious to manifest the true."[23] The most extreme development of such a point of view may be found in the philosophy of culture of Ma I-fou, who spoke of the "six arts" or classic departments of knowledge as objective manifestations of the human spirit, and therefore one with all things in the universe.[24] Alongside *kultur* religion may be found scientific religion, as expounded by Ch'en Li-fu, for example. His claims for the scientific spirit of Confucianism took the form of a speculative materialist cosmological system which identified the metaphysical ideas of the *Book of Changes* and the Doctrine of the Mean with the constructs of physics and biology as he understood them.[25]

If the nativist approach to culture and Confucius seems often to become highly spiritualistic, the new Confucianists often insisted upon the rationality of the Confucian faith. In such contexts rational came close to signifying humane, in the Mencian sense that humane values are assumed to be the natural possession of the human mind and thus principles of reason. As a humane faith, unlike theistic Christianity or life-denying Buddhism, Confucianism affirmed the ontological unity of what Fung Yu-lan called "the sublime (*kao ming*) and the commonplace (*chung yung*)," or in the beautiful traditional symbol, of the "sage within and the king without" (*nei-sheng wai-wang*).[26] Moreover, this symbol, which evoked the humanistic claims of Confucianism in the many complex meanings it acquired over a long historical tradition, continued to suggest in metaphorical form that Confucianism, like other great world religious systems, had a social mission integrated into its ontological vision.

Such metaphors are ambiguous; but the nuances given this one by new Confucianists consistently skirted the sphere of political action historically associated with the sages' task of pacifying the world in favor of other more inward forms of kingliness. Was the sage within linked to the world by the ontological fact that the mind and the world are interdependent constructs, each contributing to the creation of the other in an ongoing process of dependent causation? In thinking so, Hsiung Shih-li made the relationship a vital part of his idealistic conception of the structure of reality itself, above and beyond any particular historical or social forms reality might take. Was it the case, as Fung Yu-lan suggested, that the sage within is simply a man whose outer kingliness lies in the fact that he does what everyone does but understands it differently?[27] Such a one who knows how to wander in the transcendent Beyond while living as an actor in the ongoing human world of history necessarily will adapt to all of the changing social forms imposed by the historical process. Or was it in the teacher-student relationship, literal or implicit, that Confucian social action was possible? Some believed this, but in so doing they restricted the sphere of social or political action to the theater of personal relationships.

The special place which Liang Shu-ming holds in the history of republican cultural conservatism may come from the fact that he alone seems to have insisted that the sage's action in the world must be explicitly political — at least to the degree that its aim is the creation of a larger social community recognizably Confucian in style — and to have so acted in his unique rural reconstruction program. Although it existed side by side with other model counties like Ting Hsien, which were organized along guidelines of Western social science and philanthropy, Liang's districts, as described briefly by Guy Alitto here, were more Mencian in inspiration. In his external aspect, the sage was to be a teacher; the central institutional agent of government was to be the school; and the cadre were to be the spiritual hierarchy of dedicated students. Rather than assuming scientistically that a pilot project is an experiment, Liang asked that it be a morally inspiring and socially transforming example, and so created the rural reform which was China's closest approximation to Gandhi's village movement.

If Liang Shu-ming's example was a talisman, it was also an ex-

ample of how quixotic the effort to undertake an explicitly Confucian program of political action could appear in the atmosphere of
the 1930s. By and large, new Confucian efforts to give social meaning to their faith's professed humanistic core were less successful
than their effort to demonstrate the metaphysical implication of
that humanism; namely, that moral action has ontological significance.

Where the nativist religion of culture and the new Confucian
humanistic faith overlapped most closely was on the common
ground of ethical concern. It was ethics that best bridged the sa-
cred-secular gap, and also, it was hoped, the politics-culture gap as
well. If the new Confucianists moralized ontology, and the nativists
the imaginations of almost all Chinese had been haunted by images
of the struggle for survival which the needs of the times seemed to
require. In place of the familiar old Confucian social relationships
(*li*), they had focused on universal moral ideals of Confucianism:
benevolence (*jen*) in the sphere of human relations and public-
mindedness (*kung*) in the sphere of public action. Where the old
morality had valued a style of poise, equilibrium, and centrality,
now people demanded of themselves a dynamic engagement with
history, and aspired to lose the self not through detachment from
things but through struggle with the circumstances of the times.
The collapse of customary standards of morality visible to the revolutionary generation left those who continued to respond to Confucian symbols no alternative but the far more difficult and demanding Confucian tradition of moral heroism, in which what is expected
of a person is not bound by what he or she may reciprocally expect
from others in a net of personalized loyalties but extends to the most
total disregard of self for public goals.[28] To live by such exacting
standards in a world which no longer supplied established forms for
the expression of Confucian belief, either in ritual, canon, or commonly accepted political or social norms, placed an enormous burden on the inner commitment of the individual, while leaving fluid
the exact mode of action commitment might require.

These were among the circumstances which gave the school of
Wang Yang-ming its special appeal to cultural conservatives as
diverse as Liang Shu-ming and Chiang Kai-shek, and made com-

mentators by the war years see the Lu-Wang tradition as a main-stream of Chinese Confucian thought in the twentieth century.[29] Historically this school had affirmed the capacity of the subjective human consciousness to shape cosmic reality as well as reflect it. In the notoriously difficult doctrine of the "unity of knowledge and action," it had insisted upon the unity of such perfect forms of consciousness with action, probably intending less to suggest a method of arriving at spiritual truth than to call attention to the psychological experience of it. As such, Lu-Wang teachings not only provided the most satisfactory basis for new Confucian religiomoral ontology, but also lent themselves to individualist and activist ethical interpretations.

In Wang Yang-ming's example, modern cultural conservatives found a characterization of the moral life which seemed to suit their need to commit themselves to the publicly directed struggle and self-sacrifice the revolutionary age demanded. When they praised the school for its individualistic spirit of emancipation,[30] they did not mean to condone the pluralistic tendencies which were in fact inherent in this as in any other dominantly inner light approach to truth. That was the job of critics of the Lu-Wang philosophy in the twentieth century, as it had been in the seventeenth. Rather they thought Lu-Wang taught that the moral life was universally accessible ("Every man can be a Yao or Shun"), and that it stressed the individual, personal commitment which must, they thought, characterize the essence of the moral experience. Nonetheless, as seen in these pages, in the socially chaotic world of republican China, Lu-Wang inspiration was claimed for actions as diverse as the poetical heroics of a Liu Ya-tzu, the lonely introspections of a Hisung Shih-li, the struggles in the countryside of a Liang Shu-ming, or even the revolutionary organizing of a Sun Yat-sen. If the modern Confucian ethic called for moral heroism, the ambiguities of this code in practice draw attention back to our original problem of the relationship between cultural conservatism and political and social action in republican China.

Moral heroes may serve any cause, so long as they serve it without thought of return. The new Confucian ethic left undecided the question of what sort of sociopolitical consequences of acts could be allowed to stand as an authentic expression of the moral ideal. The question of authenticity could be decided only by the inner standard of the relevant individual's experience of commitment. The new morality which was designed to bridge the culture-politics gap in fact only illustrated its magnitude. In spite of the incessant moralism of Kuomintang propaganda, the people who benefited most in the long run from the very genuine moral energies aroused were not conservatives at all, but the communists. The difference between communist and new Confucian morality, ironically, was not that the latter did not emphasize struggle and self-sacrifice for public goals, but that the communists believed people ought not to be exploited, something which established limits to self-sacrifice and introduced in a materialist form the ethical concept of rights.

The one kind of moral behavior that was naturally questionable in new Confucian eyes was just what was most practically necessary — work for the creation of material wealth. The *Great Learning*, believed by many Nationalists to be the foundation of Chinese political theory,[31] indeed affirmed that sincere thoughts and a rectified mind would lead to tranquility in the state; but making one's heart sincere was never something which an individual could undertake in a spirit of utilitarian calculation. These attitudes made moral commitment to the utilitarian goal of modernization very difficult. Guy Alitto here points out that Liang Shu-ming could not urge the peasants in his model district to work at improving living standards simply for their own benefit. Success might accompany their efforts, or even after the fact validate them in the eyes of others, but it could not be the *inner* wellspring of their motivation. Similarly, Chiang Kai-shek admired the Chou statesman Kuan-tzu for his nationalist spirit, but balked at the ancient sage's observation that the people must be well fed before they will have a sense of shame.[32]

Just as Confucian philosophy historically had a rationalist potential which in the twentieth century was eclipsed by the more thoroughgoing rationalism of scientific thought, so also the utilitarian thread in the Confucian social ethic was deemphasized by modern Confucianists. In both cases, the pressure to define Confucianism as a system of belief in dialectical opposition to the secular forces of science and materialism led modern interpreters away from the practical in doctrine, and toward the ethereal. This meant that the more cultural conservatives relied upon the idea that social and political change would come about through the agency of the sage acting in the world as moral hero, the harder it was for the gap between their religiocultural ideals and contemporary sociopolitical goals to be bridged. Where historically the sage within found a sphere of political action for himself in the world, now the sage symbolized the reification of ontology. Where historically statecraft and moral action had seemed compatible, now moral action was stressed the unique moral nature of the Chinese people as a national community, both did so with reference to ideals of behavior which they understood to be central to the Confucian persuasion. Moreover, their conceptions of the moral life had undergone a common transformation in the revolutionary century. Ever since the 1890s, premised upon the perfection of one's inner mind, while statecraft — in the 1930s more than ever — meant devotion to the pragmatic task of economic modernization. The logic of the historical situation that made people define politics solely as a function of morality also made them think of morality apolitically.

However, we cannot conclude that the gap between politics and culture which opened up in the reform generation had by the 1930s simply become a permanent feature of conservative attitudes, crystallized in the various idealistic forms of new Confucianism and echoed in the *kultur* religion of many nativists. By the 1930s, in fact, it is possible to observe a resurgence of social thought among many Chinese conservatives — thought which was not just a reply to Marxism in the narrow sense, but a consequence of broader intellectual changes which had occurred since the May Fourth movement. Once again, categories of analysis in conservative thinking can be seen to reflect orientations shared across the ideological spectrum. People of widely different viewpoints were coming to believe that autonomous social forces are responsible for historical change, and therefore to see politics and culture as in some sense dependent upon them.

A view of the May Fourth period as the decisive watershed in twentieth-century Chinese intellectual history has been questioned by some scholars recently. This book as a whole shows both that cultural conservatism certainly survived the heavy guns of *New Youth* and the iconoclasts, and that a modern theoretical approach to questions about the nature of Chinese culture, religion, and ethics had taken shape during the earlier reform period. Nonetheless, before the 1920s, most people thought about structures we would call socioeconomic (technology, livelihood, education, family) as concrete manifestations of a particular moral-cosmic spirit working itself out in history. (This was true whether the spirit was imagined to be that of Western liberal society or Chinese Confucian society.) They might see human evolution like Yen Fu, more as a process of Darwinian natural history, or like K'ang Yu-wei, more as the working out of a cosmic-moral destiny; and be, like both these men, deeply troubled at the dissonant element introduced into their organic view of change by the harsh facts of political revolution. But if they had been asked what institutions were the primary agents of human contributions to the pattern of history, they still would have wanted to think first of the political realm, not the social one. They discussed science as a vaguely rational spirit or as an extension of practical technology, but not, like the later generation, as a material force capable of generating total social systems including the views on culture and human life of the people living under them. They imagined the people as ethnic and national wholes, but they did not see groups of people as classes fundamentally tied to the material economic base which determined their power, privilege, and social attitudes. If the pre-May Fourth divorce of the idea of politics from that of culture made this earlier organic conception of history impossible to maintain, many in the post-May Fourth generation found in the sociological view of historical evolution an acceptable new method for their reintegration.

In our book the conservative mode of the new sociology is represented by the KMT ideologue, T'ao Hsi-sheng, described here by Arif Dirlik. T'ao was not like Ch'ien Mu, or Tai Chi-t'ao, both of whom recognized the categories of the new sociologism (like social "class") only to deny their implication, insisting still that the spirit of the Chinese people transcended class divisions and historically had been an autonomous generator of values and custom. T'ao acknowledged the materialist view of history and its social consequences. Although he insisted in the manner of these other nativists that China's pattern of historical development had been unique and special, and that national unity was a deeply moral as well as practically imperative goal, he remained a historian of development, concerned primarily with the social and economic preconditions of revolutionary construction. T'ao together with a considerable number of other conservative intellectuals—some like Ch'en Li-fu closely identified with the Nationalist government, and some like Fung Yu-lan critical of it—were all explicit theorists of modernization (*hsien-tai hua*) as a process of linking sociopolitical change with changing cultural norms. They looked to a future reintegration of politics and culture as a consequence of the social process of modernization.

The conservative context of these theories of modernization lies politically in their advocacy of Nationalist goals (if not always methods), but more important in their critical analysis of both the New Culture movement and programs for violent social revolution. They spoke on behalf of the spreading backlash against the new culture not by denying that social and economic development was necessary, but by disassociating the process from the imitation of the West. The idea that historical change follows worldwide socially determined patterns did not have to be interpreted only to condemn China's past, but also could excuse it. Alternatively, the idea that culture is a superstructure whose changing forms are largely determined by the pattern of other more basic economic institutions meant that the post-Confucian customs of "present-day China" must, as a matter of historical necessity, be accepted as legitimate. Asians discovered before most Americans that modernization is not westernization.

Such was the temper of Fung Yu-lan's materialist defense of the historical Chinese cultural spirit, and his rationale for industrial and social change.[33] Since all social change derives from changes in the material productive forces in society, he argued, the New Culture radicals' emphasis upon *cultural* revolution had been fundamentally misguided. It had led them to a foolish moral condemnation of traditional culture, which had in fact simply been the culture appropriate to an agrarian community in which production was organized around family units. Further, it had led them to praise the spiritual culture of the West, without recognizing the latter's necessary association with an urban industrialized social productive system. He recommended that Chinese concentrate upon the immediate practical tasks of economic development, recognizing that the social and cultural changes which would accompany these are both inevitable and necessarily gradual. In a remarkable evocation of K'ang Yu-wei's *Ta-t'ung shu,* he presented world evolution as a benign, impersonal process leading naturally to higher and more universal forms of moral community. But in Fung's case the agents of historical change were conceptualized as the material forces of production, not as the cosmic-moral forces of change itself; moreover, in keeping with this view Fung envisaged the future Great Commonwealth (*ta-t'ung*) not as based on a utopian political order, but rather on an economic one: "the social control of social [that is, industrial] production."[34]

As a new Confucian metaphysician, Fung accepted the social implications of rapid industrialization for China, believing that Confucian ontological truth exists on the metahistorical level of the formless "empty" as opposed to the phenomenal "actual."[35] He also distinguished between absolute moral values—the ideal of duty as such—and historically conditioned social values. Ch'en Li-fu and the "ten professors" (including T'ao Hsi-sheng) spoke for the officially sponsored campaign for "cultural construction on a Chinese base," which received wide publicity in 1934 and 1935 primarily in *Cultural Construction* magazine.[36] They shared Fung's critical attitude toward the new culture and also his historical materialism.[37] However, the *Cultural Construction* group located value in the secular realm of the national culture itself, and in keeping with this their modernization theory was based on a scientistic syncretism. They emphasized technology as the agent of historical development, scientific thought as the natural correlate of a modern social order, and the strategy of harmonizing the best in East and West according to scientific standards. Claiming that the May Fourth liberals in their idealization of all things Western had departed from the scientific objectivity they claimed to value, the *Cultural Construction* group turned the earlier westernizers' own syncretic method against them. The new group saw no reason why a scientific culture could not harmonize with China's "special characteristics" including the rational spirit in Confucianism. Supporters of the "ten professors'" manifesto, then, combined criticism of the New Culture movement with the co-option of many scientistic outlooks, and to the extent that new cultural pragmatism had indeed inculcated scientistic values more than liberal ones, Chinese liberals found their positions undercut.[38]

Although Fung Yu-lan and the *Cultural Construction* group represent our two contrasting orientations toward the essential meaning of Chinese tradition — the nativist and the new Confucian — their views on the social and political issues of the 1930s show broad areas of agreement. On the assumption that national culture and customs reflect the stages of social evolution, they believed that the solution to the social problems of peasant poverty and backwardness, and the development of a humanistic, urbane modern culture, would come about more or less naturally as the consequence of successful national and productive revolutions. Like K'ang Yu-wei they combined an optimistic view of the long-term course of historical evolution — in their minds toward an urbanized, industrial society with some sort of collectivist social system — with a tendency to accept rather than to strain against what they perceived to be the limits of the present stage. This meant allowing for some present accommodation with a capitalist phase of development, or with more enthusiasm, looking to a Chinese form of national socialism.

Nonetheless their sociological determinism was no more ironclad than K'ang Yu-wei's cosmological determinism had been. They did not feel it necessary to choose between it and a belief in the conscious human factor as an agent in evolution. In Ch'en Li-fu this might take the form of rhetorical calls for a militant spirit or the statement that politics (read the Nationalist government) should be the mediator, arbiter, and organizer of other social changes. Fung Yu-lan, more subtly, implied that sages assent to the historical process and in so doing lend their moral energies to its advancement. *Ta-t'ung,* the universal moral community of the future, hovered before both their imaginations, something naturally destined and to be created by human effort, a vision that lay between prophecy and those vulgarized secular forms of it found among political speech-makers. In sum, their modernization theories combined a style of Chinese utopian thought recognizable in outline since K'ang Yu-wei with elements of a politically conservative sociological theory of modernization of a kind familiar in the West. The common denominator is a sense that moral teleology works naturally and benignly through material means, making violent sociopolitical conflict along the way appear at best unnecessary and at worst a betrayal of the grand historical design. When Chinese moral utopianism married the technological utopianism of the West, it can be said that some Chinese conservatives had indeed found their own version of the "culture of modernity."

It must be clear by now that the category "cultural conservative" is being used here in ways which again raise interpretative questions about the concept itself. Some will argue that the sociologists of modernization described here were both tolerant of the prospect of modernizing changes and only minimally attached to the substance of Confucianism or any other important Chinese cultural tradition. Others, like Tu Wei-ming in his contribution to this volume, suggest that the new Confucianists in their search for religious meaning emphasized needs which are timelessly human and transcend the sociopolitical circumstances of any time or place. The first group appears to have lost both love of this particular cultural tradition and intimate knowledge of it; while the second makes their love and knowledge the basis for ahistorical claims. Nonetheless, there have been in the thinking of both groups presumptions of continuity of a kind which makes it reasonable to interpret them within the context of conservatism.

When the new Confucianists ask whether some principle validated their moral intuitions, justified their pain, and explained what the universe is fundamentally all about, they asked it as people sharing a universal human condition, transcending the social circumstances of any time or place. To call conservative those who have continued to use Confucian symbols to allude to their meaning is to say that the historical specificity of the religious form is inseparable from the timeless truth being expressed, and that this embodiment of the eternal in the historically conditioned human is seen by the believer as both necessary and right. New Confucianists certainly accepted this view. Furthermore their assertion of Confucian value has taken place within the historical context of a worldwide post-Enlightenment trend toward the secularization of society and thought, to which contemporary restatements of the believer's message, by Chinese and others, have been a conscious response.

On the other hand, T'ao Hsi-sheng and other Nationalist-oriented sociologists of modernization, for all their vaunted scientism, believed that the organic processes of change itself set limits upon what can be expected of the present — a view which suggests a final analytical approach to the nature of conservatism in general and in China in particular. If there is a true conservative ideology, distinguished from the widely variant forms of conservatism determined by the issues of specific historical situations, it lies in a kind of historical consciousness: the belief that society is so profoundly conditioned by circumstances beyond individual control that change through willed human action is scarcely possible, least of all in the directions of our utopian desires. Such a sense of history may be either mystical or skeptical: it may rest upon an optimistic faith that the suprapersonal historical process itself is responsible for patterns of life we most wisely assent to; or it may come from a somber sense of the existential imperfection of things.

One mainstream of Chinese metahistorical thinking — about the nature of time and change as such — transcended the radical-conservative dichotomy. This line of thinking was observable in Li Ta-chao as much as in K'ang Yu-wei and Chang Ping-lin, in Mao Tse-tung as in T'ao Hsi-sheng, Ch'en Li-fu, or Fung Yu-lan. It involved a combination of progressive Darwinism and a more traditional outlook on the times derived ultimately from the cosmological theories of the *I ching*. Time, in this view, is not just a matrix of human action, but a palpable cosmic force, and adapting to the demands of the historical situation is not just pragmatism, but rather the necessary and right means by which people both fit their destinies to the unalterably given structure of the world and also make that structure reflect human purposes. In traditional metahistorical thinking, such as we see in Wang Fu-chih, the human being strikes the balance between history and his or her own will. In the midst of the overarching pattern of change itself, understanding the times is an inspired human act, and appropriate human action makes its independent contribution to the ongoing teleology of history.[39]

However, after the 1890s, as people adapted this style of historical consciousness to the idea of Darwinist evolution, and felt themselves drawn into the hectic flow of revolutionary events, it was harder to maintain the old sense of balance between voluntarism and determinism. More and more the predicament of revolutionary times suggested either the possibilities of change, or its limits; the opportunities for decisive human action, or the constraints upon it. Though the choice between these was still subject to such elusive yet sweeping shifts as are made by the direction of wind on water, our conservatives emerge as those for whom on balance the message of the times came to be that in China and the world, changes follow rhythms they could only submit to. Even this was not always unambiguous, for in the setting of an almost universal dislike of the present, the heritage of metahistorical mysticism encouraged some like K'ang Yu-wei or Fung Yu-lan to be at moments as much utopian as conservative, so that although K'ang in 1912 could feel that the pace of actual institutional change was too fast, Fung in 1949 could feel that the revolutionary process itself must be assented to.

Nonetheless, what was suggested more than stated by a variety of the subjects of this book was a belief that too much human meddling in the historical process is foolish or immoral or both. Whether the meddling was presumed to come from New Culture rationalists in the May Fourth period or from advocates of social revolutionary action in the thirties, the conservative sociologists of modernization contrasted what they saw as an arbitrary, dogmatic *will* to change on the part of radicals, with the natural, benign modernization process which would provide both continuity with the past and an alternative to violent social revolution. In this their modernization theory and those of the past generation in America have served similar ideological functions.

What separated a T'ao Hsi-sheng from a Chou Tso-jen, our other ambiguous modernist analyzed here by David Pollard, was not so much an acceptance of the limits of change, which both shared, as different existential psychological attitudes toward those limits. In spite of a belief in the autonomy of the cultural realm which suggests liberal individualism more than conservative idealization of culture, Chou Tso-jen was at heart a cultural anthropologist, who drew from nineteenth-century Darwinian science pessimistic conclusions about the capacity of human beings to overcome the limitations imposed by history and their own biological natures. Both T'ao Hsi-sheng and Chou Tso-jen felt obliged to make their peace with China's backwardness, but the deterministic flux of history which the first, in the final analysis, could optimistically assent to became for the second a prison. Understanding his own commitment to personal emancipation less as a political ideal than as a quixotic private hope, Chou displayed the skeptical conservative's classic pessimism over the possibilities for human progress. Here he was unlike most other frustrated modernists in China, and instead closer to the classicist Chang Ping-lin, another intermittent hermit touched by the spirit of Taoist withdrawal. It is interesting and I think significant that, in the face of twentieth-century problems the rest of the world has persisted in regarding as just about overwhelming, our survey of recent China has turned up so few instances of this kind of conservatism of despair.

II NATIONAL ESSENCE

3 National Essence and the New Intelligentsia

LAURENCE A. SCHNEIDER

We will perish;
but poetry persists!
(*The Southern Society Anthology,* 1923)

While it is possible to speak of an integrated imperial Confucian order prevailing in China during much of the nineteenth century, it must be recognized that that order was disintegrating from about 1895 to the destruction of the monarchy in 1911, and beyond. Before this disintegrative process was set in full motion, it seems reasonable to understand China as a system in which the state, society, and the arts were viewed as inseparable parts of a whole — which in turn was believed to be integrated with the cosmos. If the terms "politics" or "the political" are used in regard to this system, they must be used generically, for the state and its attendant bureaucracy were expected to be not only sources of ultimate temporal authority but also the perpetuator of ethical and aesthetic norms, if not their originator.

From the late nineteenth century this integrated system and holistic world outlook began to fall apart. One of the earliest symptoms of this disintegration was the "discovery of culture," by scholars who, in their approach to dealing with China's contemporary crises, saw a special body of native literature and art as a thing-in-itself, independent of and even more fundamental than the political and even social institutions which until then had been intimately associated with it. Even before 1911, leaders of the intellectual community were speaking as if politics and culture were two distinct and increasingly incompatible realms. This tendency was developed in a number of different directions after 1911, and no matter to what purpose the argument was applied, it was persistently felt that the whole of human experience in China contained (or should contain) distinct cultural and political spheres.

Inseparable from the discovery of culture in the early twentieth century was the incipient emergence of a modern Chinese intelligentsia, itself initially the product of the process of fragmentation that made possible the perception of distinct political and cultural realms. And from the outset, this intelligentsia assumed the task, outside of and usually in conflict with conventional institutions, of defining, protecting, and perpetuating culture.

The idea of "national essence" (*kuo ts'ui*) and the activities of the social groups associated with it are among the earliest manifestations of the emergence of this intelligentsia preoccupied with culture. National essence was seen as culture detached from the traditional organic order; and its purveyors became the intelligentsia, severed from state and society by new forms of association, as well as by the abolition of the traditional examination system and the fall of the monarchy.

The preservation of national essence and of an elite group capable of acting as its bearers was a fundamental goal of the three overlapping circles of poets, scholars, and educators which are the focus of the present study: the Society for the Protection of National Studies (*Kuo hsueh pao-ts'un hui*) whose *National Essence Journal* (*Kuo-ts'ui hsueh-pao*) was founded in 1905; the Southern Society (Nan she) founded in 1909; and the Southeastern University (Tung-nan ta-hsueh) faculty who published the *Critical Review* (*Hsueh heng*) founded in 1922. By juxtaposing these three, it is possible to see a continuous development of conservative attitudes and values formulated in response to the fear that Chinese civilization was threatened with extinction. It is also possible to see consistent variations on these attitudes and values developing in the series of new contexts following the 1911 revolution.

In spite of the fact that the initial formulators of the idea were often leaders of pre-1911 anti-Manchuism and antimonarchism,

advocacy of the national essence was already acquiring a conservative aura when the first rumblings of the New Culture movement
were felt in 1915. By 1919, within the circles of the Southern Society
and the *National Essence Journal* there was an explicit tension
between what was perceived as their radical political functions and
as their conservative cultural ones.

Radical politics was initially perceived in these circles as a means
of serving an ultimate goal: the preservation of traditional Chinese
civilization — or at least that part of it treasured by the activists. The
crucial need to perpetuate the national soul (*kuo hun*) or national
learning (*kuo hsueh*) was repeatedly expressed, and from as early as
1904 there was much talk of a national essence which was separate
from the physical national itself and which comprised the true
source of the people's identity. While the physical nation might
perish, it was argued, its essence was indestructible and eternal. But
essence, especially under pressure from a foreign nation, could be
lost, obscured, or forgotton, perhaps forever. True to traditional
Chinese immanentist proclivities, the basic national essence
argument suggested that (like the Confucian *tao*) essence required a
medium through which to manifest itself. This medium was the
stream of traditional scholarship, poetry, and to a lesser degree,
painting of which National Essence scholars approved and made the
core of their own studies and teachings. These patriots did not
believe that the national essence could save them; it was required
that they do the saving by way of the publications, libraries, and
educational efforts that overlapped their subversive activities.[1]

Moreover, during the decades preceding the May Fourth
movement the National Essence intellectuals were not the only ones
preoccupied with the new problematic status of culture. After the
1911 Revolution, National Essence advocates continued to find
themselves part of a larger preoccupation with cultural change, but
now advocates of cultural revolution jarred them into defensive and,
apparently, untenable positions. The New Culturalists reflect the
discovery of culture even more dramatically perhaps than their
antagonists of the National Essence group; and it was to be expected
that after May Fourth national essence approaches to culture would
find new modes of expression. From its vantage in the 1920s, the

Critical Review (hereafter *CR*) coterie was the only National Essence group in a position to attempt a reintegration of culture and politics. It made its bid to achieve this end, in effect, by changing Chinese culture through infusions of the spirit of Western culture.

However, though patent changes occur in National Essence thought from its beginnings down to the *CR* period, there persisted a number of fundamental ideas. The basic national essence argument rested on two premises which represent a fundamentally conservative outlook: first, the assumption that there is indeed a transhistorical essence; and second, that there are historical men and women — scholars, poets, and artists — who both recognize this fact and are able and willing to act in the ways required to protect and preserve the essence. Because this essence is embodied and conveyed in the Great Tradition, the result is a new social-intellectual nexus: poet (or scholar), high culture, and nation. In this discussion, the new set of relations is seen as a function of the alienation of the educated elite from its traditional sociopolitical base. The poets' compulsion to preserve and transmit essences and traditions was in part a drive to save for themselves some essential role in the envisioned new society.[2]

The idea of national essence was first nurtured to prominence by a group of young scholars and poets primarily from the wealthy southeastern coastal provinces. These scions of comfortable bourgeois, rentier, or literati-official families initially came together as an association to make war, in their own peculiar fashion, on the Manchus and on the institution of monarchy. In 1905 they founded the Society for the Protection of National Studies in Shanghai, and soon after, a number of similar groups sprang up. From the outset, the membership of these National Essence associations clearly overlapped with that of the Revolutionary Alliance (T'ung meng hui), also founded in 1905.[3]

Initial tendencies notwithstanding, the National Essence societies' membership soon manifested ambivalence and even reversals of feeling about the proper form and goals of their political activities. Liu Shih-p'ei, as Martin Bernal describes in detail in this volume, was a founder, editor, and the major contributor to the *National Essence Journal*. He was a member of the Revolutionary Alliance but within a few years caused a serious disruption in the National Essence circle when he changed his sympathies and threw his support to the monarchy.[4] He nevertheless continued to publish in the *National Essence Journal* and to carry on the deeply rooted scholarly traditions of his family, one of the most prominent literary families in China at that time. Co-founder of the *National Essence Journal* was Huang Chieh (1874-1935), an intense poet from Kwang-tung province who was completely devoted to anti-Manchuism. He was a major coordinator of all of the National Essence society's activities, and he brought to this circle an unusual mistrust and dislike of party politics which is evident in his refusal to join the Revolutionary Alliance. His active role in the journal came to an abrupt end with Liu Shih-p'ei's conversion to monarchism.[5]

Still another kind of participant in the National Essence circle was Ch'en Ch'u-p'ing (b. 1883), a native of Kiangsu and son of a wealthy Soochow (Wu-chiang) merchant. Ch'en's career involved him in most of the major subversive organizations and actions that make up the history of anti-Manchuism in the southeast coastal region. Even before becoming a regular contributor to the *National Essence Journal* he was initiated into avant-garde politics in 1904 as a member of the Shanghai-based Chinese Educational Association (Chung-kuo chiao-yü hui), under the guidance of Chang Ping-lin and Ts'ai Yuan-p'ei (1868-1940). After a *Wanderjahr* in Japan in 1903, Ch'en responded with typical revolutionary spirit to the *Su pao* case, a cause célèbre that fed the fervor of the National Essence circle in its early years. Liu Shih-p'ei was probably responsible for bringing Ch'en into the Revolutionary Alliance in 1906.[6] In the following year, the National Essence circle and the radical movement of the southeast were both shaken and stirred to higher levels of dedication by the martyrdom of Ch'iu Chin (1875-1907) and Hsiu Shih-lin.[7] In 1907, in the wake of the deaths of these two friends of Ch'en Ch'u-p'ing as well as the death of the *Su pao* martyr Tsou Jung (1885-1905), Ch'en and some close associates laid the foundation for the Southern Society (Nan she), a poetry club which soon became a prominent sister organization of both the Revolutionary Alliance and the Society for the Protection of National Studies.[8]

Reveling in the spiral of radical activities in the southeast, the founders of the Southern Society stormed the Shanghai politico-literary world in 1909 in the spirit of the traditional knights-errant with whom they regularly identified. The charge was led by Ch'en Ch'u-p'ing and his young Kiangsu friends Liu Ya-tzu (1887-1958) and Kao Hsu (1887-1925), and they were joined by fourteen other charter members, mostly from Kiangsu as well. Fourteen of the seventeen charter members were also members of the Revolutionary Alliance; and three had been charter members of the Society for the Protection of National Studies.[9] This political heritage and regional focus characterized the Southern Society throughout its life. Almost immediately the Shanghai-based society acted as a center for many subchapters south of the Yangtze.

Like their friend Ch'en Ch'u-p'ing, Liu Ya-tzu and Kao Hsu had been intimate with the piecemeal radicalism radiating from Shanghai before they gave themselves over to the leadership of the Southern Society. Guided by Ch'en and by Ts'ai Yuan-p'ei, the two young nationalist poets expended their robust adolescent energies on the organizational duties required of Revolutionary Alliance operatives. They established or participated in revolutionary front organizations (usually schools), and were prominent in local subversive activities until their nemesis, the Manchu viceroy Tuan-fang, closed in and forced them in 1907 to leave Shanghai and seek more legitimate looking work.[10]

The Southern Society met formally as a whole only twice a year, and in all it published twenty-two weighty anthologies of its members' poetry and prose. With a large and fluctuating membership and no structure to speak of, the society could not be said to have had a formal philosophy or platform, though individual members ventured their opinions, and readers of its collections could easily make inferences for themselves. Ning T'ai-i (1885-1913), the society's martyr in the Second Revolution, suggested that the society's purpose was "to use our southern accent to keep alive the memory of our ancestors."[11] Another member wrote that the society was "using literature to promote innovation" in China.[12] And a reader soon becomes aware that the Southern Society used its poetry and prose "to separate the Han from the barbarian," that is, to foster the anti-Manchu republican revolution. A short 1909 manifesto subtly identified the Southern Society with the political-literary Fu she (Revival Society) which had flourished at the end of the Ming dynasty.[13] In 1908 Ch'en Ch'u-p'ing had explicitly identified the idea of the Southern Society with the Fu she and the Tung-lin Academy of the late Ming dynasty.[14] But the Society's fundamentally subversive intent was most clearly evident in its elegies and obituaries written for fallen radicals (like Ch'iu Chin) and in its constant allusion to Ming loyalists.

Southern Society members were associated with a number of anti-Manchu republican periodicals, both as editors and staff.[15] Most important for this discussion was their involvement with the *National Essence Journal* and its affiliates. In effect, the two societies and the Revolutionary Alliance shared in a functional division of labor as they all worked toward more or less the same ends. (According to Liu Ya-tzu, the Southern Society was sometimes thought of as the "cultural arm" of the Revolutionary Alliance.)[16] Both literary societies offered anti-Manchu propaganda, sometimes of a very similar nature, and both, by extension, aimed at destroying the monarchy and instituting a republic.

Nevertheless, much of the work of the National Essence circle was devoted to scholarly and educational ends directed not at subversion of the Manchus but at keeping alive "Han" culture. Indeed, despite a fundamental political antimony, there was some overlapping of purpose between this circle and that of the late Ch'ing reformer Chang Chih-tung, who was a monarchist. The National Essence circle in some instances seemed to be implementing the proposals of Chang's turn-of-the-century "Exhortation to learn" (*Ch'üan hsueh p'ien*). Certainly the circle could have been in sympathy with Chang's idea of national essence as he discussed it in a statement made on the opening of his Academy for the Preservation of the Heritage (Ts'un ku hsueh-t'ang) in 1907:

The finest of a country's teachings, skills, rites, doctrines, and customs which are especially treasured and protected are called "national essence." [Other] countries attach special importance to [its] preservation. They do so to nourish feelings of patriotism and an awareness of one's own kind. Actually, the sources [of strength] of the powerful nations in the East and West may be found herein.[17]

In contrast to Chang, however, the National Essence circle focused its vision of essence rather sharply on some specific traditions of literature and scholarship. The *National Essence Journal*, for example, began to depart from Chang's concept where it emphasized Ming loyalism, the scholarship of Ming loyalists, and following from this, a revision of the distortions of Ch'ing official historical writing. Repeatedly, the journal placed its own contributors in a line of succession of critical scholarship carried on by scholars in a state of tension with politics (because of their disillusion with the government and/or the government's displeasure with them). According to the journal, it was precisely these kinds of scholars who transmitted the national essence each time it was threatened with obscurity.[18]

The National Essence circle further veered from Chang Chih-tung where it adhered to the school of Han Learning (Han hsueh) which Chang had criticized as excessively scholastic. From this followed still further departures. In the *National Essence Journal* one clearly sees efforts in philological and philosophical criticism, best exemplified by Chang Ping-lin and his students. And later issues of the journal contained the literary criticism of Wang Kuo-wei. Collectively, this scholarship pioneered attitudes and methods which were later developed by the National Studies school (Kuo hsueh) of the 1920s where its consequences were by intention culturally iconoclastic and subversive.

By contrast, in his "Exhortation to Learn," Chang Chih-tung had expressed impatience with the philological tradition of Ch'ing classical studies; his self-taught courses on classical traditions advocated short-cut textbooks so as to waste as little time as possible on such burdensome chores. Chang also regarded the study of pre-Ch'in noncanonical philosophers (*chu tzu*), who were standard fare in the *National Essence Journal*, as potentially subversive as well as wasteful.[19] Thus Chang Chih-tung seemed to emphasize the variety of imperial Confucianism which was informed by Chu Hsi's sense of orthodoxy and by the ethical teachings of the sages as they were conveyed in the Four Books. The National Essence circle preferred a variety of traditions reflective of tensions between orthodoxy and the circle's understanding of the true spirit of classical learning. Yet in practical procedures, there were similarities between Chang and the circle. Both were devoted to preserving the literary heritage, and to that end, established academies and published bibliographies, textbooks, and detailed study guides. And both paid lip service to some kind of East-West syncretism, a goal to which neither devoted much serious effort.

For the purpose of teaching and perpetuating its favored traditions, the National Learning Protection Society established an academy in Shanghai where superb classical scholars like Liu Shih-p'ei could lecture to young scholars from the area. The society also undertook the writing and publication of middle-school textbooks, and Huang Chieh and his colleague Teng Shih reputedly spent all of their respective and considerable family inheritances on a fine library which they established in Shanghai in 1905.[20] The library and the academy (before Liu Shih-p'ei bolted) might be considered fronts for Revolutionary Alliance activities; for everyone from Chang Ping-lin to Sung Chiao-jen frequented them. But they are solely described as places of legitimate scholarly activity which served as refuges where anti-Manchu activists could take a moment's respite and quietly marvel at the cultural glory of Han literary traditions.[21] Scores of books from the library's holdings were reprinted and circulated on the Shanghai market.[22] Here, then, were concrete statements that Chinese national essence was somehow crystallized and conveyed in classical scholarship and in traditional aesthetic forms, and that it could be perpetuated by broadcasting its various expressions throughout literate society.[23]

The *National Essence Journal* also sought to promote the kind of syncretism originally formulated by Chang Chih-tung:[24] Western learning was to be employed to illuminate Chinese learning, and the journal was to become a liaison between Chinese learning and Western science.[25] But these elegant formulations were just that, and those in the National Essence circle who were even casually familiar with things Western were rare and notable exceptions in a largely ethnocentric milieu. The National Essence group would have to wait for the *CR* circle in the early twenties for an effort to implement the kind of syncretism it theoretically advocated before 1911.

The *National Essence Journal* devoted more serious attention to the problem of Chinese racial and cultural identity. Huang Chieh's "Yellow History" (Huang shih), serialized over a period of four years in the journal, represented the most extreme expression of National Essence reliance on race and ethnicity in coming to terms with Chinese identity.[26] Where it does not sketch biographies of scholarly leaders of resistance to barbarian invasions, the "Yellow History" is primarily a kind of philosophical ethnography. Each of its many installments deals with the peculiar historical Chinese forms of government, marriage, burial, alimentation, clothing, housing, and the like. The "Yellow History" sought to trace the sources or origins of each of these in order to see guiding Chinese essences in all their purity.

The most dramatic aspect of the "Yellow History" is its introductory essay—a theory of the origins and primal identity of the Chinese race, as formulated by the French scholar Terrian de LaCouperie and adapted by Liu Shih-p'ei and Chang Ping-lin.[27] The Yellow Emperor figures prominently here as the father of the Chinese race, ultimately an offshoot of stocks from farther west.

Within a year after it began to appear, the "Yellow History" started to devote more space to scholar patriots, southerners for the most part, who resisted northern barbarians. Such subjects became the dominant mode of showing China's ethnic distinctness as well as the cultural legacies of national essence. Huang Chieh's ethnography gave way to a less subtle anti-Manchu propaganda campaign which fed on endless examples of Chinese martial skills exercised not for the sake of Chinese habits of government, marriage, or burial, but rather for Chinese scholarship and literature. In this way, Huang's theme of ethnic origins of cultural identity was gradually overshadowed by the theme of Ming loyalism.

Pointed allusion to seventeenth-century Ming loyalism was nothing new in 1905, but with the *National Essence Journal* it became an art. The first issues of their journal are filled with biographies of loyalists (most of them scholars of repute) and by 1907 a whole series of books, including the works of these loyalists, was reprinted under the auspices of the society. The National Essence Series (Kuo ts'ui tsung-k'an) comprised twenty-seven titles, some having more seditious implications than others: we find Lu Liu-liang's writings (proscribed under the Ch'ien-lung Emperor) as well as Wang Yang-ming's *Ch'uan-hsi lu*; a piece by Huang Tsung-hsi and a detailed bibliography of literature previously forbidden by the Ch'ing.

In 1910, under Teng Shih's editorship, another eleven titles from the holdings of the Shanghai library were reprinted. More varied this time, they included writings of Ku Yen-wu (1613-1682) and Chin Sheng-t'an (1627-1662).[28]

The founders of the Southern Society engaged in similar kinds of activities, but the publications sponsored by the *National Essence Journal* were more erudite and scholastic, and their efforts in the realm of propaganda were seldom separated from their efforts to keep alive China's great literary traditions, as they understood them. Southern Society poets were able to use less roundabout means to express their anti-imperialist patriotism and contempt for the Manchus—sentiments often difficult to separate in their poetry. Before his twentieth birthday, Kao Hsu had written a "Patriotic National Anthem"—

> How can you be anything but proud
> of your invaluable gifts to the world!
> Opening fresh flowers of civilization . . .[29]

and effervescent verse such as this from 1903:

> To preserve our country, I think of the Violent Men
> ascending the tower and loudly chanting
> "The Song of the Typhoon."
> So few will give up the Five Corruptions
> and sacrifice themselves;
> but there are blood-sucking jackals and tigers
> in the Central Plain.
> Ten thousand families are divided
> and without a national history.[30]

Liu Ya-tzu, in the same year, the year of the *Su pao* affair, was equally strident:

> People's rights are subjected to oppressive exactions;
> evolution has brought things to ruin.
> All life slumbers and the people's spirit and suffering
> are obscure.
> Wolves and jackals block the roads . . .
> The people are being colonized —
> Oh where is the Old Home?[31]

Patriotic anguish was repeatedly expressed by contributors to the *National Essence Journal*. But how recondite their most passionate classical prose all seems when compared, for example, to the poetry of young Ma Chun-wu (b. ca. 1879) even before he became a stalwart of the Southern Society. "For a century our sacred land has been engulfed by aliens," he wrote in 1903, "the sun and moon themselves mourn China."[32]

The Southern Society fought national despair and shame by evoking, nurturing, and even merging with the rebel traditions of the past — especially those which recalled southerners who resisted northern barbarians. Greatest emphasis was placed on the seventeenth-century resistance to the Manchus. The Southern Society itself did not publish compilations of politically suggestive historical documents like those of its sister organization. However, such compilations were privately undertaken by active members; and the prefaces and apologias to these documents were regularly reprinted in the "Prose" sections of Southern Society anthologies.

Ch'en Ch'u-p'ing was a prolific compiler and reprinter of such materials. His native district of Kiangsu was a particularly rich source for traditions of poetry that reached back uninterrupted for many centuries, and Ch'en devoted almost three decades to gathering and publishing fragments of them. A 1911 Southern Society publication explained that Ch'en's *Sung-ling Literary Anthology* was explicitly conceived as a dramatic continuation of a seventeenth-century anthology, compiled by a Ming loyalist martyr from Ch'en's home district.[33]

Southern Society publications also regularly contained short biographies of southern loyalists like Kiangsu's Yang Shih-fu, whose resistance to the Manchus in the mid-seventeenth century cost him his life. And of course biographies of recent anti-Manchu martyrs and short historical sketches of their uprisings and campaigns were a mainstay. But even in these essays on contemporary rebellion, the past was never far away: Southern Society writers depended heavily on the seventeenth century and much earlier periods as well for the archetypes and metaphors that give depth and meaning to their descriptions. Thus, in his 1907 "Epitaph for Ch'iu Chin," Liu Ya-tzu compared Ch'iu Chin to Yueh Fei, the southern Sung warrior who fought in vain against the northern barbarians, and in this same poem Liu alluded to the Manchu massacre of Chinese during the "Ten Days at Yangchow," comparing the plight of contemporary anti-Manchus to that of their counterparts of the seventeenth century.[34]

In the lives and thoughts of the poets and scholars of the Southern Society circle, one may thus find ample evidence for arguments about the tenacity of tradition, and, equally, for arguments about the elasticity of tradition and its potential utility for radical change. The Southern Society, especially where it overlapped with the *National Essence Journal*, was devoted to political radicalism largely as a means to protect China's high culture and to guarantee the continuity of its literary and scholarly traditions. Their radicalism was complicated by the need of this culture to respond over time to two related, but analytically separable, problems. On one hand, these scholars and poets were reacting to a purported Manchu corruption of traditional values and failure to properly perform traditional functions. Here such images as the Ming Tung-lin Academy and the Fu she were called in, and, in traditional parlance, the job at hand was a rectification of names; that is, a restoration of values last seen, it was argued, under the Ming. From this derived the call to separate the barbarian from the *Hua*. On the other hand, there was the challenge of the West. Here the issue was more than the alleged corruption of true Chinese values; it was loss of identity, and perhaps extinction. In the face of this challenge, the very possibility of resurrection or renaissance became a question. Neither knights-errant nor Tung-lin scholars were relevant here. This called for living individuals to devote their own lives and energies to the efforts to ward off China's death or prepare for China's rebirth.

In these efforts, publicists of the National Essence circle gave priority with increasing frequency and eloquence to what was "inner" — culture and morality — over what was "outer" — the nation and its law and government. The latter were now important only because they were needed to save the former. And revolution was in turn necessary to save the nation.[35]

The basic concern for continuity was coupled with an awareness of irresistible external pressure for change and a passion for substantial though circumscribed internally instigated changes. Nevertheless, the early National Essence circle showed little concern for the problem of how to preserve culture in times of calamitous change without diluting it — as the syncretist might express the problem. Journal contributors in effect placed themselves at the end of a long line of successful transmitters of the Chinese essence from the time of Confucius through the Ming loyalist scholars of the seventeenth century. The National Essence circle believed that even with the evolution of the times (*pien*), the true culture could be transmitted intact and without damage. From this point of view history was not in itself a threat to the continuity of Chinese civilization; history merely provided new settings in which the fixed essentials of China could display and realize themselves. The danger lay in believing that "ancestral customs are exhausted" and therefore permitting the national essence to become eclipsed through inanition, ignorance, or false goals.[36] Westernization was never seriously discussed as a potential false goal that would lead to cultural discontinuity. But as 1911 passed, the goal of political action became increasingly questionable as part of the program of protecting the essence.

Politically, the National Essence movement fragmented after 1911. The initial division occurred between those who withdrew from party politics entirely and those who were active in the new Republican government. A more serious challenge to the integrity of the movement arose from Yuan Shih-k'ai's ascension to power.[37] Most of the National Essence circle seems to have remained loyal to the Kuomintang throughout the Second Revolution. The Southern Society found in the poet Ning T'ai-i a useful martyr to the republican, anti-Yuan cause in 1913.[38] But, according to Liu Ya-tzu, when it came to Yuan's monarchical plans, many of the National Essence group broke with the prevailing anti-Yuan sentiment and joined Liu Shih-p'ei in supporting the restoration.[39] In this situation the cultural mission of the group was now its sole source of solidarity; and that mission had become even more sharply divorced from politics. The group's solidarity was maintained in large part until controversy over culture itself arose in response to the challenge of cultural revolution. The waves set up by the *New Youth* and the new culture appear to have brought about the final disintegration of the original National Essence circle.

The original Southern Society fell apart not over the advent of Yuan Shih-k'ai but rather under the early blows of the New Culture movement. The questions that divided its membership irreversibly concerned not constitutional forms, but rather literary forms (such as the use of the vernacular), and the value of fundamentalist devotion to the preservation of China's heritage in the fashion of the now defunct *National Essence Journal*. By the end of 1917, the Southern Society had stopped publishing its literary collections and thereby lost the only source of its always tenuous cohesion.[40]

Even as the Southern Society disbanded, prominent members of the National Essence circle were coming together for a last outburst against the new culture in the electric atmosphere of Peking University under the chancellorship of Ts'ai Yuan-p'ei. In 1917, Ts'ai Yuan-p'ei had gathered to the university a very mixed crew of scholars under the banner of scholarship-exclusive-of-politics. He was personally responsible for bringing to Peking the so-called Kiangsu-Chekiang faction — a group of literary men schooled under Chang Ping-lin and now under Liu Shih-p'ei's leadership; it featured a number of former leaders of the early National Essence-Southern Society circle.[41]

Ts'ai Yuan-p'ei's idea of what the university should be can be regarded as the first post-1911 institutional manifestation of the culture-politics split which we are pursuing here. His "aesthetic" world outlook can well be considered the expression of his personal "discovery of culture." From this point of view, it is understandable why Ts'ai, who had once been the close colleague of Ch'en Ch'u-p'ing and Kao Hsu and a contributor to the Southern Society forum, should expect his Peking University to be able to contain simultaneously a Liu Shih-p'ei and a Ch'en Tu-hsiu.

However, the university did not contain them for long without friction and outright hostility. Taking up the cultural burden of the National Essence circle, Liu Shih-p'ei's *National Heritage* (*Kuo ku*) launched an outright attack against new culturalism in March of 1919. Much of the short run of four issues of this journal was devoted to high scholarship in the vein of the *National Essence Journal*; but there were now bitter and panic-stricken essays addressed to the new youth instead of the Manchus. Where the earlier National Essence publications reserved the simile "book burners like the Ch'in" for barbarians, now it was applied to advocates of the vernacular and other literary reforms.[42] The dominant fear which the *National Heritage* expressed so eloquently was that an abrupt engorgement of Western culture would destroy the integrity of Chinese culture and the continuous filiation with the past would be lost.

The bifurcation between old and new which the *National Heritage* group thought they detected at the foundation of the New Culture movement (especially in its prototypical journal, *Renaissance* [*Hsin ch'ao*]) troubled them more than any other problem. But their only response was to invoke the old syncretic formula which National Essence advocates had largely managed to do without until then.[43] This they leavened with an explicit reliance on an organic historical viewpoint emphasizing the gradual, cumulative nature of institutional growth. They feared the destructiveness of nonevolutionary change, and they feared absorption into an alien culture as well.[44] "If you call contemporary science *alive* because of its widespread use now," the journal pleaded uneasily to the younger generation,

then so is our national heritage, the evolved product of our past learning, which has directed the spirits of our nation's multitudes and has been preserved in the minds of our people. Moreover, what is "alive" and "dead" cannot be fixed once and for all; what is "dead" today is not without the ability to begin resurrection tomorrow.[45]

The confidence and aggressiveness of the old National Essence arguments were gone; the metaphysical props were down, and all that remained for the moment was participation in those cultural phenomena which signified national essence. When Liu Shih-p'ei died in 1919, the *National Heritage* stopped publication.

Nevertheless, within a few years after the short-lived efforts of the *National Heritage*, Huang Chieh and other seasoned advocates of national essence found a new, broader base of opposition to the New Culture movement developing in the *CR* circle at Southeastern University in Nanking. The *CR* and a significant element of Southeastern University were rather self-consciously setting themselves up as an intellectual counterforce to the New Culture movement centered in Peking University. By this means national essence thought came to be understood as the antithesis of the New Culture (that is, the Vernacular Literature movement, the iconoclastic new history, philosophic pragmatism, and the like).

By the time of the founding of the *CR* in 1922, the idea of national essence had acquired a rather mixed set of associations in the minds of New Culturalists. It was sometimes applied to the thought of men like Chang Ping-lin, whose scholarship and politics after 1911 were rejected by many young scholars who nevertheless respected his role in the 1911 revolution as well as his earlier scholarship. It was equally used as a derisive catch-all for the likes of Liu Shih-p'ei, K'ang Yu-wei, or Yen Fu, who to many young people were symbols of political reaction and perhaps even of betrayal of revolutionary principles.[46] In spite of the fact that from at least 1919 the term "national essence" had acquired unpleasant connotations of anachronism and reaction, the contributors to the *CR* used the concept unapologetically to describe their own goals.

The *CR* circle, the most prominent publicists at Southeastern University, was most famous for its aggressive, outspoken, young, American-educated leaders, many of whom had studied with Irving Babbitt at Harvard. But it was also a haven for many more conventional scholarly types, like the classicist Liu I-cheng (b. 1889), whose roots were solidly planted in native Chinese literary tradition. Wu

Mi (b. 1894), a co-founder of the *CR*, was one of Babbitt's students who later also became a professed disciple of Huang Chieh.[47] Wu had known and respected Huang's poetry since the days of the *National Essence Journal*. Other personal links between the *CR* group and the early National Essence crowd were Mei Kuang-ti (1890-1945) and Hu Hsien-su (b. 1894), both also co-founders of the review. They had contributed poetry to Southern Society publications as early as 1915.[48] More significant was the association of Ch'en Ch'u-p'ing with the literature department of Southeastern University from about 1922. The following year he was already considered to be one of the "bishops" of the school.[49]

The *CR*'s definition and defense of national essence or culture took place in a context markedly different from that of Ch'en Ch'u-p'ing's youth. With the emergence of the Vernacular Literature movement and then Marxism during the 1920s, intellectuals were newly conscious of the workings of "society" — as seen in folk culture, popular literature and language, and in such collective social phenomena as social classes. The *CR*'s advocacy of culture as the key factor in Chinese survival was aimed not merely against corrupting politics, but also against what it perceived as corrupting and diluting mass and democratic values, and against the evolutionist and historical materialist arguments which appeared to support them.[50]

If the context of the *CR*'s pursuit of national essence was considerably changed from the pre-1911 context of its forebears' efforts, so were there jarring changes in its modes of expression. While traditional Chinese scholars and poets continued to be cited as its authorities and models, classical and recent Western authorities had gained a prominent if not preeminent place. Matthew Arnold and Irving Babbitt, and numerous Western writers of all fields, were thrust before its Chinese audience. This literature was invoked not only to bolster arguments against contemporary Chinese social and intellectual currents; the *CR* further saw itself as a medium for accomplishing that grand goal heralded by Chang Chih-tung and weakly echoed in the *National Essence Journal,* that is, using Western learning to foster the appreciation and survival of Chinese learning. Moreover, now, after the First World War, Chinese learning was thought to be in a position to guide global culture toward an ecumenical renaissance.

In keeping with these views, the *CR* balanced Liu I-cheng's essays on National Learning and his guides to the Chinese classics with Mei Kuang-ti's translations from Plato and his history of classical Greece, an essay on the classical scholarship of Chang Hsueh-ch'eng with one on recent German historiography, or one on Chinese poetics with translations from Arnold and Babbitt. Equivalence between China and the West cannot be the sole explanation for this bicultural approach. Wu Mi, Mei Kuang-ti, and their colleagues themselves explained that their primary goal was to better understand *true* Chinese traditions and to evaluate China's contemporary cultural plight by using the insights of the West. Regarding Western influence, they argued that unless the West's truest and most valuable traditions were introduced to China, naive Chinese intellectuals would be seduced and led astray by false Western gods. Thus, the *CR* rejected Communism, Marxism, and "mass democracy" and looked favorably on aristocratic values and the leadership of a cultured elite or "saving remnant." It said *no* to Dewey, Marx, Tolstoy, and Ibsen, and *yes* to Nietzsche, Babbitt, Aristotle, and Dante.

A collage of *CR* values would include traditional aesthetic forms, continuity, precedent, discipline, standards, morality, absolute value, and individualism. *CR* was obsessed by fears that relativism would become the predominant mode in art and ethics and that positive values and norms (where there were any) would become a function merely of what was new and what was derived from or related to the masses.

The *CR* circle, like the earlier National Essence circle and the Southern Society, funneled their many ideas about national essence through the dramatic image of the heroic scholar-poet who bore the burden of rescuing China's past, and hence China's future, at the risk of self-sacrifice. For all of these groups, consideration of the essence to be preserved went hand in hand with admiration of the special group of persons whose destiny it was to transmit that essence —that is, scholars, poets, and artists.

Early National Essence anti-Manchu patriots admired scores of such semilegendary heroes as Cheng Ch'eng-kung or Yueh Fei. However, these figures were not merely propaganda vehicles. The pattern of their integration into National Essence literature strongly suggests that reference to them was related to the National Essence advocates' problem of their individual and collective identity as modern intellectuals. This problem began to emerge in China at the turn of the nineteenth century, and it was formalized by the abolition of the examination system in 1905. When the Southern Society began a few years later, the newly ambiguous situation of the scholar was the institutional fact that underlay its members' peculiar search for identity.

"Take the Fu she as our example; continue the tradition of the Fu she and arise!"[51] This was one of Liu Ya-tzu's war cries early in 1911. As we have seen, reference to the seventeenth-century literati protest coterie was a common and quite casual mode of self-identification for the Southern Society.[52] Sometimes the reference was broadened: "Men of the Southern Society are contemporary prodigal warriors (*ch'i-shih*). Its eminent members compare most favorably with the men of the Tung-lin and Fu she."[53] Whatever the form of the allusions to these groups, they are highly suggestive in that they beg the question of how far beyond traditional literati protest groups the Southern Society generation had come.

Mary Rankin has begun the exploration of this question in her fine study of the larger political milieu of the Southern Society. She has found that in spite of the trend at that time of constructing modern Western-style institutions, such as radical schools, these associations paralleled in their style of operation late Ming academies like the Tung-lin.[54] Rankin suggests that loose nonparty groups like the Southern Society are more typical of then current styles than groups like the Revolutionary Alliance. This is so because of their impermanence, their scant structure based on personal connections, and their contentiousness.[55] Partly because of these factors, "the intellectuals in Shanghai as a group remained divorced from political power and separate from conventional society."[56]

It is this divorce and separateness that compels us to inquire if more had changed than the parallels with conventional elitist styles of association and protest would lead us to believe. If Frederick

Wakeman's recent study is our guide, then the answer must be that in spite of vestigial conventions, there had come about a fundamental social change at this time which had begun to yield "intellectuals in the modern sense."[57] From the Ming dynasty, when the Tung-lin flourished, down to the end of the nineteenth century, "Scholars alone, acting as individuals, were respectably impotent. Scholars together constituting a faction, were dubiously partisan."[58] Individual scholars neither had nor claimed a right to express any idea they wished. But they did have an often mortally costly "self-defined right of evaluative dissent"; there was no conception, individually or group generated, of "group rights for intellectuals."[59] Sacrifice of autonomy was worth the compensation that the literatus gained from his position as broker between state and gentry.

It is Wakeman's argument that at the end of the nineteenth century, new kinds of literati societies were being formed which were at least partially devoted to creating intellectuals of a new kind — "scholars of resolve" — who were to be drawn from all strata of society and made equal within the structure of the group: "Membership replaced status; the *hsueh-hui* [study society] created its own 'scholars of resolve,' instead of the contrary."[60] When these people then began to define their own corporate legitimacy they could also begin to be called intellectuals in the modern sense. The abolition of the traditional examination system took place in the context of the erosion of the "amateur ideal" by imported pragmatic and utilitarian values and in the "differentiation of the intellectual from both the state and the traditional gentry." In the hopes of complete autonomy, intellectuals had surrendered their role as broker; but ultimately, Wakeman concludes, the price of autonomy was political estrangement.

The cult of suicidal heroics which characterizes the political milieu of the Southern Society may well be more a function of this new estrangement than of the "tenacity of tradition." The cult was central to the self-perceptions of Southern Society members. In Rankin's words, "Radicals posed as embattled defenders of virtue and appealed to public opinion through dramatic denunciations. At times they virtually invited government suppression. Immediate defeat became moral victory in the long run."[61] This is certainly reminiscent of one of the Tung-lin's major orientations, that is, heroic action when "critical situations" arose to test the depth of one's moral commitment.[62] However, there is no evidence that Southern Society intellectuals were following the Tung-lin's philosophy of critical situations. On the contrary, there is much reason to speculate that the de facto and de jure extinction of the literati-official *Stand* was coming at a time when only inadequate conventional symbols existed to make that fact intelligible, and even less adequate means were available to give direction and meaning to the new role of the new intellectuals. In such a condition, action per se, especially violent action, can become a mode of achieving meaning and identity—the more so if a band of poets waits, pen in hand, to immortalize the deed.

Ambivalence toward oneself is to be expected under such trying conditions, and the Southern Society's reverence for the poet Kung Tzu-chen (1792-1841) was an important expression of such feelings. Kung, a native of Hangchow, was well known through his poetry as a frustrated activist who had failed the examinations many times before becoming an official and who died with many unfulfilled plans for reform. He had expressed his unhappy ambivalence toward life by means of two symbols: "the flute" (poetry, withdrawal into art) and "the sword" (politics, heroic action).[63] These symbols were directly borrowed by Liu Ya-tzu and other writers of the Southern Society.[64] Kung's poetry idiosyncratically blended bits of Buddhism and knight-errantry, Ch'ü Yuan's legend and the lore of Taoist abandonment. Piecemeal, these all appear in the most characteristic expressions of the Southern Society.

Kung's poetical influence was especially important to the eccentric Southern Society poet Su Man-shu (1884-1918), who managed to become a legend in his own time by taking the Buddhist tonsure and writing patriotic verse and fantastic "autobiographical" fiction. To Su, Kung was matched as a model by Lord Byron, an appropriate Western hero for Chinese patriots half in love with poetry and martyrdom. Su was among the first to translate Byron into Chinese.

In 1923 Liu Ya-tzu, reflecting on the halcyon days of the original Southern Society, wrote, "In the mountain fastness we grasped our swords and aroused many a chivalrous warrior!"[65] Self-consciously mimetic, Liu and the Southern Society circle identified not only with Tung-lin and Fu she models, but also with a colorful array of heroes from China's past, including the outlaws of the popular romance, *Water Margin* (*Shui-hu-chuan*), from which the above quotation may well have derived its imagery. Believing that without great sacrifice and much bloodletting China could not be bettered, the members of the Southern Society constantly referred to themselves by designations like "knight-errant" (*yu-hsia*), "valorous warrior" (*ying-shih*), or "chivalrous knight" (*i-hsia*).[66]

Sung Chiang the *Water Margin* bandit, the *Tung-lin* scholars, Byron, mad monks, and revolutionary martyrs—all these filled the lively Southern Society pantheon. Divergent and incompatible though they might have been, they all share a self-righteous place on the fringes of conventional society if not in direct conflict with it. Not merely exemplars for selfless action or models for nationalistic sacrifice, these heroes past and present seemed also to help explain —even glorify—the estrangement of the poets who wrote about them. In time, to the Southern Society the act of creating poetry itself came to approximate the heroic act; it differed in form but not in value from the heroic deed.[67]

By the time the *CR* was established, the Manchus were gone and the monarchy as well, so that the tasks at hand for poets were more diffuse and less consonant with singular and strikingly dramatic acts. Now the images of the Tung-lin Academy, the Fu she, and the knight-errant were set aside for a more recent and Western-derived model—Matthew Arnold's poet-*critic*. Here was contemporary society's hope, *in* but not *of* the world, aloof but compassionate, dispensing "disinterested" judgments by drawing on a special fund of sweetness and light, the perennial wisdom, the absolutes which by Arnold's day had come to be signified by culture.[68] Arnold's poetry-criticism, as understood by Wu Mi for example, was to take over the role of religion, to order society, and custom, and human spirit. In the *CR*, Wu Mi and others explained the relevance to China of Arnold's generation's experience by suggesting that China's central problem was the loss of the old beliefs and the painful difficulty of achieving new ones. Arnold's time was also "an age of disillusion"; Arnold's poetry was left "standing between two worlds, one dead, the other powerless to be born."[69]

The *CR* reached back to the Southern Society for its Chinese equivalent to the Arnoldian poet and found such a person in Huang Chieh. By the mid-1920s, Wu Mi had all but apotheosized the gentle, retiring poet who had been instrumental in narrowing the idea of national essence down to a body of literary culture. In the quality of his poetry and in his unification of teaching, study, and method, Huang Chieh was claimed to have had no equal in China but the great Tu Fu himself. And he was further appreciated for his early defense of national essence against the New Culture movement as well as his self-imposed isolation from political factions and from the government. Though invited on a number of occasions after 1912 to take on various administrative posts,[70] Huang Chieh preferred to devote himself to poetry, which he saw in a fundamentally meliorative role. Before all else in post-1911 China, Huang argued (with echoes of the scriptural Great Learning), the human spirit had to be ordered by poetry "to help people know what makes them human; after which the nation can be strong, and the chaos of the world arrested."[71]

Besides venerating poets, the *CR* looked to the intelligentsia (*chih-shih chieh-chi*). Repeatedly the fear was expressed that Chinese civilization was caught between the end of the old beliefs and the birth of the new; and equally dangerous was the fact that the "old intelligentsia had been obliterated while the new intelligentsia still had not been established."[72] This "excellent minority,"[73] this priestly cultural elite, was central to China's future.[74] Liu I-cheng, the *CR*'s chief classicist, put it this way: Those basically responsible for contemporary China's calamity, he wrote in 1922, were not the anti-intellectual provincial military leaders, the national assemblymen, or the cabinet ministers, but rather the intellectuals themselves, who needed "to reform their minds (*hsin*)."[75]

This emerging intelligentsia was seen to be threatened, and therefore China's fundamental culture or national essence was threatened. If the poets of Southern Society days saw the enemy as the Manchus or Yuan Shih-k'ai, the *CR* saw its nemesis in the emergence in China of the masses and middle class liberalism. Where moral and patriotic poets once fought against the corruption engendered by the state, they now turned their attention to the onslaught of commercialism and misdirected appeals to the masses.[76] Mei Kuang-ti explicitly lamented the destruction of the scholar-gentleman ideal under these pressures, and by the mid-1920s he was calling for a "reaffirmation of the old Chinese view of the social structure, with the scholars at the top and the tradespeople at the bottom."[77] While Mei was perhaps the most extreme of his circle in his view on these matters, he was not alone in fearing an increasingly populist trend amongst the purveyors of the new culture and vernacular literature.

The *CR*'s answer to the encroachment of mob values on culture was to reassert the inseparableness of the national essence and its elite interpreters. The intelligentsia, they repeatedly argued, are an intellectual aristocracy, and scholarship, art, and truth are totally dependent on them; no advances in civilization come from the common people. Civilization, properly understood, is strictly a function of the leisured minority "who sacrifice themselves for humanity."[78] And in place of the prevailing dangerous trends of crassness, vulgarity, commercialism, and callowness in literary circles, the *CR* advocated values more than faintly reminiscent of the warrior ideal of the Southern Society: strict discipline, standards, a high, clean spirit, sacrifice, reverence for the master-disciple relationship, and the inherited traditions of schools (*chia fa*).[79]

The touch of sternness in the *CR* image of the poet, which separates it from Southern Society models, was in keeping with the *CR* group's admiration of classical as opposed to romantic values. This opposition, so foreign to all earlier generations of Chinese classicists, had been taught them abroad, by Irving Babbitt. In a sense they recognized its ambiguity as an aesthetic ideal among people whose favorite poets included Huang Chieh and Liu Ya-tzu of the Southern Society, Byron, and even the younger Matthew Arnold; so they explained that form and content must be differentiated: Byron and Arnold were "romantic in sentiment but classical in form."[80] In fact for the *CR* group classicism in aesthetics represented an attempt to moralize pure form in art, a manner of thinking that went to the heart of national essence concerns.

In keeping with this manner of thinking, a number of basic questions ranging from the issue of conservatism to the way in which poetry would serve national essence in modern China all were couched in discussions on form and content. Wu Mi, who was most concerned with these discussions, had a simple formula which he repeated in a score of contexts: "old forms with new materials" (*chiu ke-lu hsin ts'ai-liao*).[81] His way and the way of *CR*, he said, was a middle way between the alternatives offered in the nineteenth and early twentieth century by the so-called Old School and New School of poetry.[82] Though Wu Mi's predecessors in the Southern Society characteristically favored the aesthetic of the New School and deplored the Old School, the *CR*, no longer involved in the pre-1911 political milieu, typically selected guidance from both sides.

The New School featured the poetry and poetics of leaders of the 1898 Reform movement, especially Huang Tsun-hsien[83] (1848-1905), and Liang Ch'i-ch'ao. It received what little definition it had at the time from Liang's 1903 "Poetics" (Shih hua), the Chinese locus classicus for Wu Mi's form/content formula. Liang's characterization of the school emphasizes its topicality or involvement with contemporary history, its infusion of a new spirit into old forms, and its serious attempt to use a syntax closer to the vernacular.[84] Nonetheless, with the exception of Huang, who was uniquely innovative, and Liang, who was occasionally experimental, the New School adherence to most traditional poetic conventions persisted.

While I have not yet discovered any dialogue between the New School and the Southern Society, the latter to some extent carried forward the tendencies of the former. The Southern Society generally was close to the intent of the New School in its use of poetry directly to define and arouse nationalistic sentiment and to record and reflect on contemporary events. (Kao Hsu once called his work "now poetry.") Both coteries of poets experimented with national anthems and popular songs about China; both apostrophized Korea and its plight or wrote laments on the deterioration of their home provinces, which they identified with all of China.

In poets like Kao Hsu and Ma Chün-wu, the Southern Society produced poetic innovators. Kao seems to have experimented with the vernacular, though he later refused to join the Vernacular Literature movement. And he regularly admonished his colleagues to eschew hackneyed classical models and clichés, to strive for a more simple and lucid style and syntax, and even to break with the conventional *lu-shih* form which usually dominated Southern Society poetry.[85] But even Kao Hsu did not go as far as his colleagues Ma Chün-wu and Su Man-shu. The former advocated the avoidance of all earlier models in favor of "casting poetry in a mold of your own making."[86] Yet neither Ma nor any of his colleagues was really able to make that strenuous leap to the kind of novelty that only came with the vernacular movement.

The strongest expression of Ma Chün-wu's position was his promotion and personal translation of foreign poetry — Byron and Shelley being the favored subjects. Within the Southern Society, Ma's only rival in this was Su Man-shu, who not only translated the same poets, but went so far as to compare Byron favorably with Li Po and to suggest that in Chinese poetry only Tu Fu could compare with Shakespeare and Tennyson. Su wanted more translation done, especially of poetry, to give the Chinese new sources of inspiration.[87]

In spite of these strivings for modernity, both the Southern Society and the New School found it difficult to come to terms with the relationship of new subjects and old poetic forms. The fundamental and unresolved problem here was not a question of the adequacy of forms (as it would be after the vernacular movement began in earnest) but the reality of change. A question of adequacy is being asked when something like the cliché "old skin/new wine" is invoked. The wine ferments but the skin, already stretched, cannot give, and therefore bursts. But when an equivalent to the "old wine/new bottle" cliché is used, then we are dealing with a problem of illusory change, or disguised continuity. In Liang Ch'i-ch'ao's oft-cited formulation of the latter issue (in his 1903 "Poetics") one can see, among other things, how casually the shift is made from questions of poetic to political forms:

A transitional period must have a revolution. But revolutionaries must change spirit (*ching-shen*) not form (*hsing-chih*). My group currently favors a revolution in the world of poetry. Now in the instance of filling paper up with new terminology and calling this revolution — here is the kind of thing we see with the Manchu's political reforms and modernization. Real revolution can be facilitated by using old modes (*feng-ke*) to embody new states of meaning (*i-ching*). Contemporary poets [must be] able to cast new ideas (*li-hsiang*) in old modes.[88]

The Southern Society's Ma Chün-wu rejected such a formulation, suggesting that not enough was changing if merely the content of poetry was changing. Yet this is really all he saw — even in the realm of translation, where prolific translators like Lin Shu turned volumes of European literature into classical prose. Even Liu Ya-tzu in the early 1920s still had not broken away from "classical acrobatics," in spite of his new post-May Fourth political and social commitments.[89]

Here was the start of a dilemma for the *CR*. On their part (and this was not merely their own problem) considerable concessions had to be made to modernity and the West; but if new and imported ideas could be contained and controlled within indigenous structures, perhaps at least a semblance of Chinese particularity could be retained, and palpable continuity with a premodern China supported. To this end, the *CR*, in addition to retaining traditional poetic forms, rejected the use of the new vernacular language and its published writings on all subjects developed a modified (some would say bastardized) classical literary syntax.

This preoccupation with form might be a simple indicator of conservatism, but it is complicated by the contemporary social role which the *CR*, envisioned for poetry and the poet. The preeminent ethical role which it wanted for both could be undermined by the potential of form to be at once moral and amoral, and even antimoral. In Erich Heller's words:

[Form is] moral because it is the expression and result of the artist's immense inner discipline, but amoral or even antimoral since by its very nature it is indifferent to morality, indeed intent upon subjecting the moral to the rule of the aesthetic.[90]

In order to have ethical relevance, the *CR* poet had to infuse his inherited forms with contemporaneous materials. If contemporary poetry is sick, Wu Mi argued, it is not because of its continued use of long-evolved and tested forms, but rather because it has not come to terms with modern materials (such as modern topics or modern feelings).[91] In strong contrast, Wu Mi's enemies in the Vernacular Literature movement argued that form itself must be a function of ethical realities; that the failure to come to terms with modern materials was inseparable from the failure to establish modern forms.[92] Here is the place to understand radical-romantic Kuo Mo-jo's "deep loathing of form," and his declaration in 1919 that "when substance and form are one, then we shall see the appearance [in China] of good poetry, true poetry."[93]

The *CR* fascination with the problem of form completes the discussion of the conservative direction of national essence thought down to the mid-1920s. This thought, as it evolved in and responded to a changing context, is summarized below.

Before the New Culture movement radically transformed the context of the National Essence circle, contributors to the *National Essence Journal* labored to counteract the seemingly inescapable evolutionist and historical relativist tendencies of contemporary thought in China. Their product was a transhistorical and even antihistorical essentialist argument about the fundamentals of national identity. But where a historical framework seemed to be useful, they adapted it to their needs. Hence the desultory references to a simple parallelism between the development of Western and Chinese history, culminating in a renaissance stage that, in the nature of things, guaranteed a resurrection and even a new preeminence for China. The poets of the Southern Society, however, were more simple and lyrical. They lamented the passing of time, and the failure of the past to transmit eternal verities to the future.

By the late teens, defenders of national essence began to couch their resistence to history in an argument which said in effect that the current bifurcation of the old and the new was false and misleading. Liu Shih-p'ei's *National Heritage* eloquently laid down the line which was soon elaborated at length by the *CR*. Here it was argued that the mere passage of time is not socially meliorative, nor can judgments of value be a function of proximity in time, or even suitability to a particular time. The world, alas, was going to change, it was acknowledged, but change did not necessarily require discontinuity or loss of identity. If there was going to be a new culture, the *National Heritage* argued, then it had to be remembered that both Chinese and European culture evolved gradually to their present conditions: all streams have a source; all flowers a stem. And from this Burkean caveat, the old syncretic mood was revived with new images: if making the so-called new culture were thought of as the making of new paper, then European civilization was like old paper and Chinese civilization was like old cloth — both were needed in an artfully blended mixture to produce the new product.[94]

Another element of National Essence resistance to encroaching ideas of flux and change was its emphasis on locale and site. The Southern Society in particular was obsessed with the *tao* of the South, and individual poets were encouraged to cling to the immediate and concrete details of their own villages, counties, and provinces in the South. Building on a tradition that was begun perhaps in the southern Sung period, or even as early as the Six Dynasties era, National Essence poets and essayists saw their region below the Yangtze not in historical terms of political economy or geopolitics, but rather in timeless aesthetic or moral terms: the Yangtze was a moat,[95] an outer perimeter between barbarism and the pure traditions of Chinese civilization; the north was corrupt, destructive, and subject to deterioration by time and barbarians. The south was a preserve of morality and heroism, and the fertile accumulations of great scholarship, poetry, and painting.

This focus on place does not seem to have inhibited thinking about China as a national unit. There is some evidence that concerns for the south, or for a special part of it, were meant to be poetic devices — concrete and personal expressions of concern for the Chinese nation as a whole.

Inseparable from these considerations of space were the timeless archetypes that crowd the National Essence circle's thought about its mission. Down to 1911, and perhaps even through the end of Yuan Shih-k'ai's regime in 1916, the circle fostered a Chinese variety of the European cult of blood and earth. But the preoccupation with ethnicity in the revolutionary period was rapidly superceded by cultural definitions of the nation's essence as 1919 approached. In 1905 Huang Chieh had felt it necessary to introduce his "Yellow History" with a summary of current racial theories. This emphasis was consistent with the racial theme found in most of the anti-

Manchu propaganda that the National Essence circle manufactured down to 1911. However, soon after the revolution, talk of the Yellow Emperor and the barbarians was lost to discussions of language, scholarship, and literary forms.

For all its emphasis on energy and action, the early National Essence circle engendered little if any sense of historical movement or change, with the one exception of its involvement in the 1911 Revolution. Yet even this was thought of in close retrospect as a false millennium, superseded by—again in a conventional paradigm—a usurper. For all their noise and frenetic motion, the National Essence scholars and poets very often sought and evoked stillness.

The *CR* eschewed most of the histrionics and virtually all of the dramatic forms of identification with past exemplars to achieve their more self-conscious, more studied conservative effect. They did explicitly defend the mode of historical thinking which relied on Confucian archetypes. This can be seen in Liu I-cheng's battles with the iconoclasm of the new history, an important corollary to *CR's* efforts in the realm of literary theory. They directly addressed themselves to the "sophistry" of evolutionist thought and condemned "running with the times." The *CR* group complemented their nonevolutionist literary criticism of Chinese traditions (a rarity in the twenties)[96] with serialized introductions (in the manner of Chang Chih-tung) to classical scholarship (*kuo hsueh*). And this in turn was matched in bulk with introductions to studies of classical Greek culture and Renaissance humanism—clearly with the aim of illustrating extra-Confucian expressions of ordered system, and of hierarchy, composition, quality, limits, perfection, and so on. When Confucius and Chu Hsi were inadequate to explain the idea of an eternal national essence, Plato was close at hand.

Where the *CR* and other advocates of national essence were concerned with the *continuity* of Chinese civilization they were in the company of many of their New Culture antagonists who stand outside of our "conservative" classification. But where the *CR* sought *persistence*—with the help of Confucius or Plato—there they began to part company. Important leaders of the new literature and new history schools explicitly sought out Chinese traditional foundations for their versions of modern China; at the same time they eschewed any ideas which implied that there was either a historically transcendent Chinese identity, or that a historically meaningful identity for China, old *or* new, could ignore folk, popular, or mass considerations. And these same leaders, from Ts'ai Yuan-p'ei to Hu Shih and beyond, also shared a conception of culture which overlapped with that of the National Essence advocates. All shared an experience within which a body of values and literary or artistic forms, necessarily under their stewardship, was seen to be independent of the realm of the state and of political action, yet fundamental to the construction of a Chinese nation.

The course of National Essence thought, from the turn of the century to the early twenties, was influenced by the parallel growth of the New Culture movement, as well as by the disappearance of the monarchy and attendant institutions. The conservatism of the early National Essence circle, for example, would seem to qualify as Mannheim's "unconscious" variety; whereas that of the *CR*, certainly amongst its younger leading members, was "reflective."[97] The Southern Society spoke to a kind of conservatism "which still lives in the heritage of the past, for which the past is not yet a memory and an object of reflection."[98] When its membership wrote in classical idioms it was because that was what they knew; alternatives were then just beginning to be considered. But when the *CR* used the classical idiom, it was a conscious choice, expressing a systematic rejection of the series of recently constructed alternatives to traditions transmitted, frayed or intact, down to very recent times.

National Essence thought also evolved toward increasing attention to questions of politics and society. Latter-day exponents were much more explicit and formulaic in their conception of a separate cultural and political realm; and they were quite different from their predecessors in their effusive yearning to reintegrate the two into a new organic unit in which their priestly functions might be appropriately effective. At the same time, the concept of national essence (or culture) was in fact accruing social connotations in response to the emergence of quasi-populist tendencies and Marxism in the New Culture movement. Early National Essence rhetoric and creative writing was notably lacking in concern for either institutions (with the exception of the monarchy), or social groups other than the people (*min*), by whom they meant the population of the Chinese nation, or the "Han," which meant the same but from a racial or ethnic point of view. National essence began as a concept differentiating Chinese from non-Chinese, but by the time of the *CR*, the term *kuo-ts'ui* had come to be identified with what the *CR* called "aristocratic" values and aesthetic forms; national essence was now something that could not be expressed by the folk, mass, people, or proletariat. In spite of their flirtations with the idea of a syncretism between China and the West, the early National Essence advocates feared the undermining effects of Western and Japanese high culture. In contrast, the *CR* circle feared that the Chinese national essence was in greater danger of being obscured by internal democratic tendencies in the definition of culture than by the elements of Western civilization, upon which it drew so freely.

The idea of national essence which grew out of prerepublican nationalism failed to survive the 1920s. In spite of profuse and energetic efforts to breathe new life into the idea, the *CR* circle succeeded only in fossilizing it. They tied national essence to specific traditional literary forms just at the moment when new forms were being widely accepted and employed. They welded the idea to aristocratic values in an era when respectful attention to the masses was increasingly the order of the day. In a context of change and upheaval, they clung to an idea of national essence which connoted fixity and order for China's fundamental identity and stressed coexistence rather than succession for the essential qualities of its history. From Kao Hsu to Wu Mi, all those who contributed to shaping the idea of national essence were defending what the French conservative Barres called "not the past, but what is eternal."[99]

4   Liu Shih-p'ei and National Essence

MARTIN BERNAL

The development of the concept of "national essence" in China is
intrinsically interesting, but it has a broader significance as a key
element in the cultural backlash against the small degree of
westernization that had begun to appear after the 1890s. After
1907, although the dissemination of foreign culture continued in
China, there is no doubt that many of the individuals who had
originally propagated it, as well as important sections of the intellectual elite, turned their backs on the West. Inevitably they became
conservatives, not traditionalists. No longer accepting their culture
automatically without question in a truly traditional way and
unable to avoid an awareness of other alternatives, their acceptance
of Chinese culture became a matter of deliberate choice. However,
the very consciousness of this decision transformed the culture they
wanted to preserve into something artificial and their own position
from traditionalism into conservatism. The main concern of these
conservatives became the analysis, articulation, and preservation of
"traditional" Chinese culture.[1] Thus one finds the paradox that the
political revolution of 1911 took place during a period of cultural
reaction among the elite.

This essay is concerned with the life and thought of Liu Shih-p'ei
up to the beginning of 1907 and, in particular, with his association
with the National Essence group. Liu's life illustrates in a dramatic
way the acutely uneasy relationship between political revolution and
cultural conservatism among the elite of his generation. His entire
family history prepared him to be a transmitter of traditional cul-

ture. For eighty years before his birth in 1884, his family had been one of the most renowned scholarly clans in Yangchow, a city famous as a center of commerce and culture. Too central to have a distinctive school of its own, Yangchow was a microcosm of Chinese literati culture as a whole. In the nineteenth century almost every school of Ch'ing scholarship was represented in the city and indeed within the Liu family itself. The latter were professional scholars, who lived largely from the patronage of high officials, notably Juan Yuan and Tseng Kuo-fan. The strain of being heir to such a tradi-tion of scholarly accomplishment was clearly enormous. Two of Liu's immediate family, an aunt and a cousin, committed suicide during his youth, and Liu himself felt extraordinary pressures both to rebel and to conform. Even more than most of his contemporaries of the same social class he found it difficult to extricate his individ-uality from the corporate family identity, and to some extent he felt he *was* his ancestors.

Liu's education and home environment were orthodox and Confucian, but within the orthodoxy there were influences that predisposed him to revolutionary and anti-Manchu ideas. The two figures to whom he acknowledged the greatest debt for such ideas were Wang Fu-chih and Huang Tsung-hsi.[2] In this respect Liu was like T'an Ssu-t'ung, Liang Ch'i-ch'ao, and many others of his own generation.[3] However the Liu family had a special connection with Wang Fu-chih. Liu Shih-p'ei's grandfather had supervised the prep-aration of the definitive edition of Wang's collected works in the 1860s when he was chief editor of Tseng Kuo-fan's publishing house in Nanking. The suggestion that anti-Manchuism may have been included among the family traditions is strengthened by the fact that Liu's great-grandfather, Liu Wen-ch'i, gathered materials in the 1840s on the barbarian invasions of the fifth and sixth centuries A.D., producing work that Liu Shih-p'ei was able to use to devasta-ting effect sixty years later.[4]

Although Liu's background was in many respects similar to that of his contemporaries, his proximity to the centers of the political and intellectual worlds gave him a quality of being larger than life. This effect may also be related in some ways to Liu's idiosyncratic behavior, the many shifts in his political and professional careers, his flair for the extreme, and his apparent disregard for consistency. In 1903 at the age of nineteen he became famous as an anti-Manchu journalist and pamphleteer in Shanghai and later endured persecution and exile as a revolutionary. For the two years 1907 to 1908 he was regarded as one of the leading Chinese anarchocommunists. Yet during these years he also organized literary societies, promoted publications to preserve national essence, and even maintained contact with a number of high Ch'ing officials. In 1909 he made public a switch which had almost certainly taken place two years earlier by openly declaring his loyalty to the Manchu dynasty. He remained a monarchist for the rest of his life, even supporting Yuan Shih-k'ai's attempt to found a new dynasty in 1915. His disciples and friends have tried to draw a sharp distinction between what they see as his powerful intellect and his weak personality and — falsely in my opinion — put the blame for his betrayals on the evil influence of his strong-minded wife, Ho Chen.[5]

Actually Liu Shih-p'ei only exhibited in an exaggerated form an ambivalence shared by many other would-be preservers of the national essence. Chang Ping-lin, for instance, supported the revolution wholeheartedly when he could do so in the name of restoring the Han but his eventual political conservatism can be seen as the inevitable consequence of the priority he gave to his mission as a classical scholar.

The effort to preserve the national essence was one of the most consistent threads in Liu Shih-p'ei's disjointed life. It was an integral part of his work as an anti-Manchu journalist and pamphleteer before 1907; it continued in tandem with his anarchism; and significantly, the last six months before his death from tuberculosis in December 1919 were spent in an attempt to defend national culture against the onslaughts of the May Fourth movement.

Liu saw his two major pamphlets before 1907 as continuations respectively of Huang Tsung-hsi's *Plan for a Prince*, with its attack on the authoritariansim of the Chinese imperial system, and Wang Fu-chih's *Yellow Book*, with its appeal for Chinese "racial" solidarity against the Manchus.[6] He completed the first, *The Theme of Social Contract in China*, during the winter of 1903-1904 in collaboration with the revolutionary educationalist Lin Hsieh, but the work as a whole appears to have been largely Liu's.[7] It is a tour de force. The authors took Rousseau's *Le Contrat Social*, which had been translated through the Japanese by Yang Ting-tung in 1901, and applied it to sixty-two Chinese classics and other written works, and though they never lost sight of the social contract, they broadened their scope to include virtually all classical Chinese references to popular control and democracy. The theme of the whole work was stated to be based on Huang Tsung-hsi's view that the people are hosts (primary) and the princes guests (secondary) and that the weakness of the Han people can be attributed to excessive authoritarianism.[8]

Like *Le Contrat Social* itself, the pamphlet's historical framework was vague. It simply assumed the existence of a Chinese social contract before the earliest classic. Natural freedom and chaos was followed by social control: "In high antiquity the government of the whole country was held by the people."[9] According to the pamphlet, during the Spring and Autumn period power was usurped by lords and aristocrats, but traces of the old democracy persisted in institutions and in the writings of philosophers.[10] The pamphlet assessed those writings for their positive and negative features, but because it was an exercise designed to show the "equivalence"—in the Levensonian sense—and equality of East and West, most of the writings were praised. Even Hsun-tzu received credit for his emphasis on the right to kill rulers who had become "enemies of the people." However, Hsun-tzu's version of the social contract is compared unfavorably to that of the *Lü shih ch'un-ch'iu*. Hsun-tzu, who believed that order had to be maintained to prevent people from harming one another, was compared to Hobbes, while the *Lü shih ch'un-ch'iu*, which maintained that a sovereign was established to benefit the people, was compared to the more "perfect" Rousseau.[11]

Implicitly, there were two villains in the *Theme of Social Contract in China*. The first was imperial Confucianism, with its stress on the power of the ruler and unconditional obedience to authority. Even Wang Fu-chih, the hero of nationalism, was attacked on this score. However, the authors did not swing to the other extreme and accept Taoism or any kind of anarchism. Indeed their other major targets were the utopianism of *Ta-t'ung* as expounded by K'ang

Yu-wei and Hsu Hsing's radical egalitarianism, both of which were seen as equivalents to Western anarchism. K'ang Yu-wei was attacked for demanding an impossible selflessness similar to the Mohist "general love," while Liu and Lin maintained the more limited Confucian position which they saw as the Chinese equivalent of the Western "enlightened self-interest."[12]

When dealing with the dialogue between Mencius and the followers of Hsu Hsing, Liu and Lin accepted the former's victory over the egalitarians, and maintained his argument that as long as there was a division of labor there would be a distinction between rulers and ruled: "Some work with their minds, some with their strength. Those who work with their minds rule others; those who work with their strength are ruled by others."[13]

They even buttressed Mencius' argument by quoting Adam Smith on the necessity of the division of labor.[14] Thus rejecting authoritarianism and anarchism, they argued that China had a tradition of democracy which would make it natural for her to adopt constitutional government.

Liu's *Book of Expulsion* (*Jang shu*) dealt with the problem of nationalism. For Liu and all men and women of his class and generation the word *jang* (expel) was invariably attached to the word *i* (barbarian). The expression *jang-i* was associated with a remark by Confucius about Kuan Chung. When asked why he praised Kuan Chung, who, in serving Duke Huan of Ch'i, the first hegemon, was serving the murderer of his former master, Confucius replied that Kuan Chung's failings were overridden by his defeat of barbarian invaders.[15]

The *Kung-yang Commentary*, referring to Duke Huan, described the hegemon's duties as supporting the emperor (*tsun-wang*) and expelling the barbarians (*jang-i*).[16] By the Sung dynasty there was an esoteric tradition that *tsun-wang* and *jang-i* were the hidden messages of the *Spring and Autumn Annals*. In the seventeenth century these terms and Confucius' implication that expelling the barbarians was a primary virtue were being used by Ming loyalists against the Manchus.[17] In the nineteenth century they became widely known in their Japanese forms, *sonnō jōi*, which were used as the slogan against the Tokugawa and the foreigners by the promoters of the Meiji Restoration.[18]

As followers of the *Kung-yang* tradition, supporters of the emperor, and passionate admirers of the Meiji Restoration, K'ang Yu-wei and the other reformers might have been expected to use the phrase. However, *jang-i* was quickly taken over by conservatives opposed to any kind of westernization; and of course the reformers' championship of the Manchu emperor also made the term unacceptable to them.[19]

Liu as a revolutionary did not mention the words *tsun-wang* but concentrated on *jang-i*. This he claimed was different from *kuang-fu* (glorious restoration), the term used by Chang Ping-lin and other revolutionaries. According to Liu, *kuang-fu* referred to the expulsion of the forces of another civilized state; for example, Polish attempts to gain independence from the Russians were aimed at *kuang-fu*. *Jang-i* meant to "expel barbarians" and was therefore the appropriate term to apply to the Chinese struggle against the Manchus.[20]

The *Book of Expulsion* began with a line reminiscent of Wang Fu-chih and Herbert Spencer on the differentiation of nature and the separateness of human races. Liu's attitudes toward race and culture were complicated but were similar in many ways to those of his contemporaries, particularly Chang Ping-lin.[21] In a traditional Chinese way Liu and Chang saw a close connection between culture and physique: they believed that human beings without culture develop the physical characteristics of animals. Liu was able to invoke Spencer for a Western equivalent: "Roughly speaking, the more barbarous human beings are, the closer they are to animals, and the more civilized the further away."[22]

Liu discussed the evolution of the human race from animals—to which he added the half-animal figures of Chinese mythology—and the survival of animal traits among contemporary primitive peoples.[23] He believed that the backwardness of these peoples would disappear eventually, and like K'ang Yu-wei and the latter's Western mentors, he equated the world of *t'ai-p'ing* or *ta-t'ung* with the concept of the spread of civilization and the elimination or absorption of "inferior" races.[24] In China's case this apparently meant sinicizing the barbarians. However Liu could not support an argument that would justify the acceptance of culturally assimilated Manchus. To avoid such a position he drew on two traditional lines of attack against barbarians. First—going against his main argument—he said they were physically incapable of becoming civilized.[25] Second, he followed the view put forward by the Ming loyalist Ku Yen-wu and others that if Chinese and barbarians were allowed to mix, one could not be sure which would prevail.[26] To illustrate the danger, Liu gave examples of Chinese states that had lost their culture. Thus there were two dangers: "Abandoning barbarism and approaching Chinese culture is usurpation. Abandoning Chinese culture and approaching barbarism is rebellion."[27]

These dangers led Liu to add a gloss to Wang Fu-chih's repeated theme that the spirit of China had moved south, a view which was later to become the rationale for the Southern Society.[28] Liu attributed the shift to cultural and racial mixture. According to him the North, which had been the original seat of Chinese culture, had been weakened by barbarian conquest and settlement. Spirit and culture had moved to the South. Of course there were barbarians there too, but these had submitted and become sinicized.

This dichotomy between North and South pointed up the whole issue. To Liu and most of his contemporaries—seeing the Manchus clinging to their caste privileges—it was clear that barbarians in a position of power refused to accept Chinese culture or only pretended to do so in order to trick and weaken Chinese. Those Chinese who helped them in this pretense were the ultimate traitors.[29] And since barbarian rulers only pretended to have Chinese culture, they were to some extent nonhuman. Weak barbarians on the other hand tended to retreat in the face of civilization and die out. However, in certain circumstances they could gradually be raised to Chinese culture and physical humanity by a process of adaptation.

With the possible exception of Herbert Spencer, the dominant Western influence on the essays making up the *Book of Expulsion* was Terrien de Lacouperie, who also had a fundamental but unacknowledged influence on Chang Ping-lin.[30] Terrien de Lacouperie (1844-1894) was a Frenchman brought up in Hong Kong where he appears to have been educated in the Chinese classics. In the 1970s he went to Britain where he established a position on the fringe of academic life, editing his journal *The Babylonian and Oriental Record* and propagating his theories.[31] These were based on the contradiction — common among Westerners of the time — between his admiration for Chinese culture and his contempt for the Chinese people. His solution was to postulate that Chinese culture had been brought in from outside and preserved by the Chinese, who were "renowned for their character ultra-conservative and non-progressive."[32]

He proposed that the "Baks," a "semi-civilised, ruddy, blue eyed people" left Mesopotamia for Central Asia, and in the third millennium B.C., after years of wandering entered China (*Hua-kuo*, the Flowery Kingdom), under their leader Huang-ti, whose name was supposed to be a version of Nakhunti, the generic title of the kings of Susiana. The model for this migration clearly came from the wanderings of the children of Israel.[33] The next part of Lacouperie's scheme was analogous to Gobineau's racial theory that the superior and virile Germanic Franks had conquered the indigenous Latin population to create France. In China Huang-ti, the Yellow Emperor, was supposed to have defeated the aborigines under their leader Ch'ih Yu. Some of these had fled south to become the Miao while others remained as serfs of the conquerors. Lacouperie saw a crucial difference between two of the terms used for "people" in classical Chinese. According to him the *pai-hsing* (literally "hundred surnames") were the "Bak" conquerors, and the *li-min* (black-haired people) were the black-haired, or black natives.[34] Lacouperie's work was largely written in the 1880s, and by 1900 most of its themes had been incorporated into a Japanese *History of Chinese Culture* to which Liu frequently referred.[35]

It is strange that nationalists like Liu and Chang should have accepted a theory that stressed the derivative nature of Chinese culture and divided the Chinese people, whose homogeneity was so important to most patriots. Indeed these drawbacks did later lead them to modify and abandon that explanation.[36] For the time being, however, the scheme had several attractions. It helped them rationalize their ambivalent feelings about China by attributing her good and vigorous aspects to the *pai-hsing* and her weakness and servility to the *li-min*. It also described Chinese class divisions as originating from racial castes in the same way that they were supposed to have arisen in the West.[37]

Lacouperie's scheme had appeal also because several of its components were firmly rooted in Chinese tradition. Thus Liu and Chang were attracted to it because it gave Western "scientific" validity to the classics, which were under attack from new text scholars. Lacouperie and his friends who were aware of these attacks agreed with old text scholars on the authenticity of pre-Confucian classics and on Confucius' position as a transmitter of tradition, not as its creator. Lacouperie and his colleagues also disliked the *Kung-yang* emphasis on Confucius, preferring Taoism and Lao-tzu with his references to Huang-ti.[38]

In China as in most societies the differences between reformers and conservatives can often be seen in their attitudes toward the past. Both use the past to justify their actions, but conservatives want to defend or restore the near past — life as they knew it — while reformers, particularly radical ones, prefer the distant past, which is easier to reconstruct according to their desires.[39]

K'ang Yu-wei and Liang-Ch'i-ch'ao wanted to go beyond Sung or even Han Confucianism to their model of Confucius himself. Lacouperie encouraged Chang and Liu to outbid the reformers by returning to a still more distant past. His theories enabled them to say that the equivalences between the West and ancient China were not mere coincidences but common features that arose from the same stock.[40] Chang and Liu's monistic cosmology, or belief in a single origin for diverse phenomena, was as strong as that of Lacouperie. They were able to claim that the foundations of Western and Chinese civilization were not merely similar but were the same: "The Chinese race came from Chaldea . . . Early Greeks were from Chaldea as were the Romans, Saxons and Slavs."[41]

While apparently accepting Lacouperie's belief that Chinese culture originated in West Asia, Chang and Liu usually played down this aspect, seeking instead to fit the theory into a more satisfying and traditionally Chinese scheme in which the Chinese culture heroes Fu Hsi and Shen Nung were universal rulers who introduced all civilization. Liu quoted Huang-fu Mi (A.D. 215-284), one of Lacouperie's favorite writers: "Before Shen Nung there were nine *chou* (continents) . . . After Huang-ti virtue could only spread to Shen Chou (China) so the nine were divided."[42]

Thus apart from establishing a scholarly justification for anti-Manchu agitation, the diverse essays in the *Book of Expulsion* set China in a world context while giving it an identity of its own. In their writings of this period Liu and Chang were most concerned with Huang-ti, the Chinese ancestor whom they saw as linked by direct lines of descent to every Chinese. Huang-ti had been seen as the ancestor of the Five Emperors since at least the fourth century B.C.[43] The Ming loyalists had stressed his importance, and Wang Fu-chih appears to have named the *Yellow Book* after him. However he was mentioned less frequently in the eighteenth and nineteenth centuries, and the reformers tended to subordinate him to their hero, Confucius.

The revival of interest in Huang-ti was relatively sudden and was almost certainly connected with the appearance of Lacouperie's theories in Japanese. It was reinforced by the discovery on the part of Chinese intellectuals that Westerners spoke of their people as "yellow" and by the effective use the Japanese had made Jimmu, the imperial ancestor.[44] Huang-ti provided an excellent symbol for the new national revolutionary movement. In May and June 1903 — the months of the *Su pao* affair — Chinese student magazines in Tokyo started using dates based on the alleged year of Huang-ti's birth. In August in his first published article, Liu urged the establishment of a calendar based upon Huang-ti. He specifically linked Huang-ti to the revolutionaries' stress on the survival of the race as opposed to the reformists' emphasis on Confucianism.[45] This article popularized Huang-ti still further while making Liu's reputation. At the beginning of 1904 the article was incorporated as the first chapter of *The Soul of the Yellow Emperor* (*Huang-ti hun*), a collection of articles that became one of the key revolutionary tracts.

The use of the word "soul" or "spirit" in the title was significant.[46] The search for spirit preoccupied Liu, and like many of his contemporaries as well as many thinkers of other cultures, he was caught between determinism and voluntarism. Despite his interest in the inevitable historical stages in the "sociology" of Herbert Spencer and other nineteenth-century Europeans, Liu, like nearly all those around him, had great faith in the power of will. He believed that the most intense form of will was that of men of violence who were willing to sacrifice their lives for their cause, and he maintained that all the great achievements of history came from violence and creative chaos.

In antiquity the men who concentrated this fearless will were the assassins, or *tz'u k'o*. These were the knights-errant described very sympathetically in the *Records of the Grand Historian*. However they had been suppressed during the former Han dynasty. Since then, though folk culture had maintained an intense interest in the subject and in violence as a way of righting wrongs, there had been no recognized cases of political assassination for the purpose of correcting injustice.[47] In the eyes of the revolutionaries this decline had matched the decline of Chinese "spirit" since the Ch'in dynasty. Therefore Liu and his friends promoted assassination both for immediate political ends and to revive national spirit.[48]

Early in 1911 Kao Hsu, founder of the Southern Society and disciple of Liu Shih-p'ei, wrote:

A nation with spirit (*hun*) will survive; a nation without it will perish. But where does the "national spirit" lie? In national studies (*kuo hsueh*). If one wants to preserve "national spirit" one must start by preserving national studies.[49]

The term that linked the incorporated *kuo hun* "national spirit" or "national soul" with *kuo hsueh* "national studies" was *kuo ts'ui* "national essence."

The idea that a country has a fixed national spirit grew up with the nation state itself. It became particularly important for culturally peripheral countries which were forced to admit their borrowings from outside, satisfying their self-esteem by describing these as "informed" with national spirit. The country in which this concept reached its peak was Germany. By the end of the eighteenth century national spirit had become a fundamental principle of the German romantics. But the supposedly fixed and distinctive nature of national character—with its links to the organic community—became a major theme of conservative writers everywhere. As the leading French conservative de Maistre wrote: "I have seen in my lifetime Frenchmen, Italians, Russians, etc. . . . But I declare that never in my life have I seen a man."[50]

The term *kokusui* (national essence) first came into common use in Japan in 1887. It arose as a reaction against Meiji efforts to convince the Western powers that Japan was "civilized," that is, westernized enough to deserve a treaty revision which would abolish foreign concessions and extraterritoriality. The wave of westernization which had been gathering momentum since the 1850s came to a head as the government promoted European customs at every level.

The winter months of 1886-7 were for Tokyo a season never to be forgotten. Among the lower orders the wearing of foreign articles of dress was advocated, and in every direction it was evident that "foreign" ways were to be adopted with all possible speed.[51]

In this atmosphere groups formed for the purpose of protecting the national essence. Their intellectual champions were Miyake Setsurei and Shiga Shigetaka. In 1888 the latter wrote in the declaration of principles of their new paper, *The Japanese (Nihonjin)*:

Through tens of thousands of years the Yamato *minzoku* (race) was seen to grow. In this mystery a special *kokusui* (nationality) [English in the original] emerged and developed. This *kokusui* fits and follows the existence of Japan's national territory by responding to the environment and reacting chemically. With this gestation, birth, growth, and development it is an heirloom of the Yamato people handed down and purified through the millennia.[52]

Although Shiga translated *kokusui* as "nationality," it clearly meant something closer to "national spirit" or "national essence." With its emphasis on mystery, land, and organic growth, it was a profoundly romantic and conservative concept. Its phrasing and scientific terminology showed the influence of Herbert Spencer, whose "sociology" dominated Japan during the 1880s and 1890s.[53] Spencer's belief in gradual evolution and adaptation to specific conditions—a view shared by many other nineteenth-century thinkers—carried with it the implication that the existing pattern of historical development was logically necessary and therefore morally right.

Shiga went on to discuss the problem of preservation of national essence (*kokusui hōzon*). Since Japan had borrowed so much from abroad, it was impossible to take a stand against all cultural borrowings. But Shiga was opposed to sweeping changes, maintaining that foreign innovations should be made carefully and selectively so as not to damage the national essence, which he saw as the key to the nation's survival.

This line of discussion left open the crucial question of what national essence actually was. Their inability to answer this problem satisfactorily caused Shiga and his colleagues considerable difficulty. They refused to link it up to Shinto Buddhism, Confucianism, or any specific religion or philosophy; all Shiga could do was to point to Japan's "artistic sense," which he contrasted with the mathematical and scientific West. This aesthetic definition, which was probably influenced by Western Japanologists, later became important for the Chinese movement. However, it was not widely accepted by the Japanese National Essence group, who preferred more general definitions. According to another statement *kokusui* was (1) an intangible spirit, (2) the special property of one country, (3) a characteristic that could not be copied by another country.[54]

Both Shiga and Miyake had had several years of Western education and had formed many of their cultural and political ideas during the 1880s, a period of drastic westernization. Nevertheless in 1888 when Miyake and Shiga set up *The Japanese*, it quickly became the opposition to the leading journal advocating westernization, *The People's Friend*. Whatever their actual position both men were anxious not to be considered conservative. In fact they shared many of the new assumptions common to all Japanese schools of thought in the 1880s. They believed in youth, in spirit, and in a biological evolutionary process, and their concern not to appear reactionary led them to replace "preservation of the national essence" with the more progressive "development of national essence" (*kokusui kanshō*). Later, they were genuinely shocked by the virulent nationalism that emerged in the 1890s; nevertheless they always maintained clear links with conservative or at least anti-Western forces. The phrase "preserve the national essence" continued to be widely used by all kinds of cultural and political conservatives, for whom it remained a rallying cry throughout the 1890s.[55]

The idea that the preservation of national essence strengthened the nation was extremely attractive to many Chinese intellectuals. Not only was the term borrowed from the Japanese, but the Japanese movement was a direct inspiration to them, especially after the first wave of westernization in China from 1895 to 1906. Although the scale of this wave was far smaller than that in Japan in the 1880s, the two situations were comparable in many ways. As with the Japanese the concept that the preservation of the national essence could save the nation appeared to provide a resolution to the contradiction between the attachment of many Chinese to the traditional culture in which they had been brought up and their country's need to become strong. It suggested that instead of sweeping traditional culture aside one should sharpen and improve it—two very congenial tasks for scholars. For Chinese too the new scheme was clearly conservative, not traditional. It represented two major breaks with the mainstream of earlier Chinese thought. First, it admitted the need to justify the tradition in terms of other values; and second, it recognized China as a nation, not "all under heaven." Historically China, unlike Japan and Germany, was not culturally peripheral. Rather, like Italy and France, she had created enough of her own culture to maintain the illusion of being civilization itself. Thus accepting the concept of national essence meant accepting that there were other different but equal national essences.

In 1902 Liang Ch'i-ch'ao, even at the peak of his radicalism, was sufficiently attracted to the idea to propose the establishment of a journal called *National Studies* (*Kuo hsueh pao*) to promote it. As he wrote to the old reformist official Huang Tsung-hsien, who had backed his previous publications: "To nourish the *kuo-min* (nation) one should have preserving the national essence as a principle. One should take old studies, polish them, and increase their brightness."[56]

Huang, a diplomat who had served in Japan and Europe, had written a history of Japan in 1887. In his reply he showed the inadequacy of the analogy between China and Japan. According to him the latter was a country with a long history of cultural borrowing, and in recent years it had "worshipped" the West. Therefore, it was healthy for Japanese to develop a theory of national essence. In China the problem was persistence of bad old customs; therefore, "new" studies should be encouraged, and it would be a long time before any movement for national essence would be necessary.[57]

After that, although Liang continued his practice of "preserving national essence" by using new scholarly methods to analyze traditional culture, he did not use the phrase, presumably accepting Huang's arguments against it. If reformers like Liang Ch'i-ch'ao, who promoted the introduction of Western thought and tolerated the "barbarian" Manchu rulers, were attracted by the concept of national essence, one would have expected culturally conservative anti-Manchu revolutionaries to have been even more interested. The only surprise is that they did not take it up sooner. However it is clear that by early 1904 ideas of "preserving national essence" were current among Liu and his group.[58]

In January 1905, while still editor of the revolutionary *Alarm Bell* in Shanghai, Liu joined with Teng Shih and Huang Chieh, two wealthy Cantonese scholars, to establish the Society for the Protection of National Studies (Kuo-hsueh pao-ts'un hui). Its aim was to preserve Chinese culture, which the founders claimed was essential for the survival of the nation. Its activities included a project to establish a national archive to save rare writings and other treasures of Chinese culture. The *National Essence Journal* (*Kuo-ts'ui hsueh-pao*), which was conceived as a magazine to present these treasures to a wider audience, began publication in February. Its issues were made up of scholarly articles and "family heirlooms" — previously unpublished letters and manuscripts. Politically the journal had a radical if not a revolutionary tone, stressing the ideas of Wang Fu-chih and other Ming loyalists and strongly implying that the Manchus and their collaborators were polluters of the Chinese essence.[59] Teng and Huang financed the paper and took responsibility for its publication, but Liu dominated its contents. Throughout the six years of its existence he wrote well over half the articles, and a high proportion of the "heirlooms" came from Yangchow, many being directly associated with the Liu family.

In 1904 and 1905 Liu argued that China had lost her national essence at the end of the Chou period, and the National Essence group as a whole claimed to be critical of all but the most ancient historical epochs and traditions. Unlike Shiga and Miyake, who believed that the Japanese essence had been refined as it passed through the generations, Liu, Teng, and Huang often implied that Chinese national studies and essence had for centuries been polluted and buried by tyrants and barbarians. In theory they regarded later manifestations of national essence as feeble flickers from the original pre-Ch'in sources. In practice, however, their interest in Sung, Ming, and Ch'ing studies made them more catholic. At the same time, the admission of these late imperial objects and writings into their definition of national studies increased their attachment to the recent past and provided a powerful pull toward political conservatism.

Like their Japanese predecessors the Chinese group laid great stress on the visual arts as repositories of national essence, and the number of illustrations of paintings and calligraphy increased steadily throughout the journal's life. Despite the group's indebtedness to the Japanese movement, however, at least one of its members, Huang Chieh, was concerned with Japan, which, because of its geographical and cultural proximity, he saw as even more dangerous to Chinese culture than the West.[60]

Nevertheless the Chinese group followed the promoters of *kokusui* in their primary idea that the survival of the nation depended on the survival of national culture. They were probably borrowing directly from Miyake and Shiga when they attributed the fall of Sung to the adoption of Mongol customs and the restoration of Alsace to Germany to the survival of German culture there.[61]

In 1903 Liu had been one of the first to point out the distinction between the reformers and the revolutionaries; namely, that while the former wanted to preserve the *chiao* (teaching), the latter wanted to preserve the race. It was ironical though not surprising that eighteen months later Liu should be in a group that advocated the view that protection of the nation's classical culture was essential to its survival. This position did represent a shift from Liu's earlier pure racialism but it was still profoundly different from that of K'ang Yu-wei and the reformers. In theory at least K'ang and his followers were opposed to the decadent society around them, and they turned to the New Text school and the figure of Confucius as a redeemer. However their "teaching" and their image of Confucius were not seen as ends but as the means by which to create a strong country.

Influenced by the less exclusive preoccupations of the Old Text school, the National Essence group saw Confucius as just one among many classical philosophers. They rejected the *Kung-yang* tradition's view of him as a redeemer. Like K'ang they saw Confucianism as an equivalent to Western Christianity, but for them it did not correspond to the invigorating Protestantism of the nineteenth century, but rather to the stifling medieval Catholic church. Most members of the group clearly associated Confucianism with the uniformity and sterility of imperial China. By contrast, the other pre-Ch'in philosophers were seen as representatives of a period of Chinese vitality and spirit and as the equivalents of their contemporaries, the classical Greek philosophers. The National Essence group wanted a revival of classical philosophy, a Chinese renaissance equivalent to that in the West, which they saw as having started with a refinement of classical culture that led to the creation of strong national states.[62]

The concept of a twentienth-century renaissance justified in patriotic terms the intensive study of China's classical period. Liu's first major work in the *National Essence Journal* was an "Introduction to the Schools of Thought at the End of the Chou Dynasty." This was followed over the next six years by detailed exegeses of the writings of Kuan-tzu, Yen-tzu, and Hsun-tzu.[63] Given their Carlylean view of history, the National Essence group believed that to carry out a true renaissance it was necessary to have great men and superb scholars. Liu, an obvious candidate for such a role, was promoted as the "literary hero" to pursue the task.[64]

Although there was no noticeable change in his scholarship, Liu's arrival in Japan in February 1907 marked a crucial watershed in his life and political thought. It is likely that he had just betrayed the revolutionary movement, and it is certain that he soon declared himself to be an anarchist and began his hectic career as a promoter of anarchocommunism among the Chinese students in Tokyo.

However, 1907 was not merely a turning point for Liu Shih-p'ei; it also marked a major change in the intellectual ambience of the Chinese elite. As in tsarist Russia and many other societies, most members of the Chinese revolutionary and reformist intelligentsia belonged to the relatively small ruling class. The number and intimacy of Liu Shih-p'ei's family connections and personal ties with high officials were unusual, but close personal contacts between revolutionaries and the Manchu establishment were by no means exceptional. Furthermore at this stage revolutionary students, reformists, and officials were linked by their common and exclusive classical culture. Thus it was possible for intellectual movements to take place across bitter political divisions.

In the year 1907 Ch'ing officials, notably Chang Chih-tung, first began to make public use of the slogan "preserve the national essence." Chang first mentioned the term "national essence" in 1904.[65] In 1905 he sent a telegram to an assistant proposing the establishment of a "special School for the Preservation of Antiquity (Ts'un-ku hsueh-t'ang) to protect the national essence."[66] This proposal was probably influenced by the establishment of the *National Essence Journal* four months earlier, and Chang referred to "talented and spirited men" — a term that by this time was almost exclusively reserved for revolutionaries — "who know the principle of preserving the national essence."[67] In the short run nothing appears to have come of the scheme. However two years later Chang formally memorialized a request for the establishment of a School for the Preservation of Antiquity which would "have the transmission of national essence as a principle [in order] to cherish ideas of patriotism."[68] The school's name and general purpose had clearly been in Chang's mind since 1905, but the final proposals came out only in July 1907, shortly after Chang had had prolonged talks with one of Liu Shih-p'ei's closest official contacts, K'uai Kuang-tien, who had also previously advised Chang in his educational reforms.[69]

At the end of 1906, on court instructions, Chang had been involved in the establishment of a school at Confucius' birthplace in Shantung.[70] If this school was a concession to the reformers' cult of Confucius, the School for the Preservation of Antiquity was a move toward the National Essence group. Apart from frequent use of the term itself, Chang's whole proposal had a flavor of national essence. There were, for instance, constant references to the importance that other nations placed on the preservation of national culture to encourage patriotism and the growth of national strength.[71]

The school opened in Wuchang at the end of August and bore all the signs of being a rushed job. It had only one professor and very few students. By this time Chang had gone to Peking to organize education nationally. He maintained some interest in the school, sending a telegram to his successor in Wuhan instructing him not to let it collapse, but despite this concern there is no evidence of the school's existence after 1908.[72]

Many people saw Chang's promotion of this school as a repudiation of his earlier career as China's leading westernizer.[73] This view is misleading if only because it neglects Chang's consistent emphasis on the primacy of the Chinese *t'i* (substance or essence) over the Western *yung* (utility). Paradoxically his founding of the school can also be seen in some respects as a move away from tradition. Previously he had hesitated between culturalism and nationalism: did one protect the country to save the culture, or the culture to save the country? Now in theory at least Chang had chosen the latter: "If there is no national culture, how can we hope for strong national power?"[74] The Chinese past had become a *yung* for the new patriotic *t'i*. Chang felt that he could use national essence to win over or find common ground with young "men of spirit." In this way he believed China could avoid the situation he described in January 1907 wherein "many patriots, having the principle of destruction, aim at confusion."[75]

The National Essence group apparently resolved for him the contradiction that had plagued him most of his life, that between preservation of traditional culture and national survival. The group appeared to provide a way in which by following his natural scholarly inclinations he could harness the spirit of patriotic youth to maintain the status quo. The extreme desirability of the scheme blinded Chang and the others to its obvious weaknesses. However Chang retained his natural caution, planning only one School for the Preservation of Antiquity among hundreds of other schools. Nevertheless, it was an important symbolic step which helped to swell the new wave of cultural conservatism.

Before 1907 revolutionaries, reformers, and "enlightened" officials were united in their efforts to introduce European institutions and ideas into China. After that year, the reaction against the West set in, giving rise to two mutually opposed groups: on the one hand there were the new cultural conservatives, who were concerned with safeguarding Eastern values against Western materialism; on the other there were cultural radicals like Wu Chih-hui and the Paris anarchists who, while accepting Western science and the future it promised, were bitterly opposed to existing Western society. From 1907 Liu was consistent in his opposition to existing Western culture and political forms, but for two years he tried to champion both of the mutually incompatible forms of opposition to it, anarchism and cultural conservatism. However his position as the young personification of the Chinese literary tradition made his eventual choice of the latter inevitable.

During 1907 Liu and Chang Ping-lin changed the key revolutionary magazine the *People's Journal* from a popular radical organ into something almost as scholarly and esoteric as the *National Essence Journal*. During the same period the revolutionary students Ch'ien Hsuan-t'ung, Lu Hsun, Chou Tso-jen, and others set up the Society for the Promotion of National Studies (Kuo-hsueh chen-ch'i she) in Tokyo. Early that year Liang Ch'i-ch'ao, previously the greatest popularizer of Western thought in China, wrote a long essay on Chinese philology and expressed his concern about the "withered" state of national studies.[76] Later in the year he gave up his journal, the *Renovation of the People*, for political work on behalf of the constitutional movement. He resumed journalism in 1910 with a new magazine called *National Customs*, in which he stated his opposition to the discarding of indigenous culture. For the rest of his life he devoted his intellectual efforts to the use of Western techniques of scholarship in the study and preservation of traditional Chinese culture.[77] Yen Fu, the other great transmitter of Western culture, appears to have changed about the same time. In late 1906, he made a public attack on "youths who had contempt for ancestral thought" and declared himself to be a conservative.[78]

As the intellectual shift took place across the political spectrum — though within the same social class — the pattern of causal factors pushing the different groups in the same general direction was extremely complicated. For all groups, but primarily for the revolutionaries, the Japanese victory in the Russo-Japanese war was very important. The years between 1900 and 1904 were a time of despair. Intellectuals saw China as a country and even the Chinese as a race threatened with annihilation by the "white peril." They tended to accept the European claim that "oriental" characteristics were synonymous with inefficiency and weakness. Thus they were prepared to jettison these in the interests of national survival. The destruction of the myth of European invincibility led them to reconsider these pessimistic conclusions and gave them hope that it might be possible to save both the nation and the culture.

By the end of 1906 it became clear that the momentum for the establishment of a Western-style constitution was irreversible, and a significant portion of the gentry began to take part in political activities associated with it. Thus essentially cautious members of the ruling class like Chang Chih-tung, Liang Ch'i-ch'ao, and Yen Fu began to see excessive change, rather than stagnation, as the major source of danger.

However there is little doubt that the most important single factor behind the shift to cultural conservatism was the abolition in 1905 of the traditional examination system. The lives of all members of the Chinese educated classes had been focused upon it, and its removal was traumatic. Even many of those who had struggled against the examination system appear to have been terrified that its abolition would destroy classical studies, making their own huge investment of time and effort in these studies worthless. However, Liu Shih-p'ei and others at the pinnacle of the elite could disguise this fear with enthusiasm for the opportunities for a new genuine classical scholarship untrammeled by the examination system.

At least among the revolutionaries, immediate contingent causes were very important in the timing of the shift to cultural conservatism. Chang Ping-lin's release from prison in the summer of 1906 and his arrival in Japan, followed six months later by that of Liu, obviously helped to stimulate increased interest in the classics among Chinese students and exiles in Japan. However their presence would not have had any effect without a favorable predisposition toward the change among the intellectuals.

Although some Western institutions were beginning to be

introduced into China and Western ideas had been discussed in limited circles during the first six years of the twentieth century, this wave of westernization was much less overwhelming than the one that had provoked the Japanese *kokusui* movement. However, the Chinese literati, whose status was bound to classical culture partly through the examination system, felt threatened and turned readily to cultural conservatism.

In China even during the "westernizing" period 1902-1906 the hold of tradition had not been broken even among the intelligentsia The awe in which scholars like Chang Ping-lin and Liu Shih-p'ei were held was almost religious. Their academic prestige gave them an extraordinary power even over the most radical. This power of scholarship appears to have been an important factor behind the lack of challenge to their cultural conservatism between 1907 and 1915, the year when Ch'en Tu-hsiu, a close friend of Liu and a prestigious scholar in his own right, founded the iconoclastic *New Youth*, a step that can be said to mark the beginning of the New Culture movement.

When describing the "conservative wave" it must be remembered that it only affected a minute elite even within the literati. The *Kung-yang* tradition used by the reformers was esoteric, but the concept of Confucius as a redeemer was relatively easy to convey. By insisting on a detailed knowledge of the extremely complicated philosophical schools of the late Chou period, the National Essence group excluded most of the literati, let alone the people as a whole. Furthermore, their style of writing was almost impossible to understand, and its general effect seems to have been to impress and intimidate rather than enlighten. Twenty years later the historian Ku Chieh-kang remembered that in the *National Essence Journal*:

The learned articles by men like Liu Shen-shu [Shih-p'ei] and Chang T'ai-yen [Ping-lin] rather overwhelmed me for they contained many abstruse passages I could not understand. The chief thing I learned from these, aside from certain new ideas about racial revolution, was the fact that Chinese scholarship of the past had been carried out by many conflicting schools of thought.[79]

While the academic elite were swept up in the "conservative wave," the vast majority of the population remained deep in tradition. However, among the more aware members of the general populace, the new ideas introduced before 1907 continued to spread. There were many students who, like Mao Tse-tung, between 1907 and 1915 were excited by Western ideas that had been published in China five or ten years earlier. It was this progressive "middlebrow" culture that swept China in the period of political freedom between November 1911 and the defeat of the Second Revolution in August 1913. Among academics and the intellectual elite, however, the atmosphere was much more conservative. The New Culture movement from 1915 to 1922 was not only directed against the traditional life and values of the population as a whole but also against the cultural conservatism of the academic elite, which, as the career of Liu Shih-p'ei demonstrated very clearly, could easily turn into political conservatism.

The weakness and superficiality of the conservative position was revealed by the speed and ease with which it was overthrown. However, with some modification, elements of its ideology survived the iconoclasm of 1919. Hu Shih, Ku Chieh-kang, Fung Yu-lan, Kuo Mo-jo, and many other academics who dominated the 1930s and 1940s and even later are almost as much heirs of the National Essence group as they are of the May Fourth movement.

5 The Sage as Rebel: The Inner World of Chang Ping-lin

CHARLOTTE FURTH

In the history of the Revolution of 1911, the role of Chang Ping-lin at first appears a puzzle. One of his generation's most famous classical scholars in the philological tradition of *Han hsueh,* he joined in reform and revolutionary movements from the 1890s on. After supporting K'ang Yu-wei and his followers and sharing their disgrace and exile after 1898, he was one of the first to break with the idea of modernizing the existing monarchy, declaring openly in 1901 that no political solution was possible without over-throwing the Manchus and restoring Han Chinese rule. He offered a scholarly and recondite analysis of the foundations of his anti-Man-chu views in the *Ch'iu shu,* a short book first completed in 1902;[1] and in 1903 he collaborated with other anti-Manchu militants in Shanghai on a provocative journal, the *Su pao,* for which he wrote biting and passionate indictments of the Manchus and of the reformism of K'ang's constitutionalists.

When the dynasty pressured the British to withdraw the protec-tion of Shanghai's international settlements and imprison the paper's editors, Chang was jailed for three years — but he had made his cause famous throughout China and had won for himself the halo of a revolutionary martyr. This reputation, plus his prestige as an intellectual and his genius as a polemicist, made him welcome in the Tokyo Revolutionary Alliance (T'ung meng hui) after his release from prison. He was entrusted with the editorship of the Tokyo group's journal, *Min pao,* but eventually it was banned, and Chang fell out with most of his revolutionary associates one by one, including Sun Yat-sen, Wu Chih-hui, and Liu Shih-p'ei. In the last years of his exile before the Revolution of 1911 he pursued an interest in Buddhism and religious thought which had been stimulated by his prison experience and made a precarious living as a teacher of classical philology to Chinese students abroad. At the same time he continued to be politically active, supporting the anti-Sun Restoration Society (Kuang-fu hui) of Chekiangese militants in their rising of 1907 and in their efforts to create an independent organization. After 1912, Chang at first appeared more inclined to support Yuan Shih-k'ai than oppositionist party politics, but Yuan's inability to protect the northern frontiers against Russia as well as his vendetta against the Revolutionary Alliance drove Chang into opposition again. He paid for this intransigence by spending two years under house arrest in Peking, being released only by Yuan's death. After a short-lived reconciliation with Sun Yat-sen, in 1918 Chang severed political ties and devoted the rest of his life to pure scholarship.[2]

The career sketched above was that of a determined enemy of the monarchy in the years which saw the final, decisive erosion of Chinese imperial power and prestige. In a revolutionary movement already noted for its eclecticism, Chang Ping-lin has been especially resistant to clasification. Communist historians had trouble deciding whether he represented feudal or capitalist social forces; the Kuomintang suspected him in its youth but embraced him in its old age; Western students argue over whether he was a radical or really a conservative at heart. Some have concluded that in the last analysis he was a maverick — the kind of natural eccentric whose reigning spirit is one of individualist opposition to all established social norms — who would have been an outsider in any age, and therefore was a revolutionist in this one.

To most of his contemporaries, Chang's important theoretical contribution to the revolutionary movement was his doctrine of *min-tsu chu-i*, the first formal expression of a nationalist ideology in China. For Chang, nationalism meant opposition to the Manchu dynasty and by extension to all foreign influence in China, both political and cultural. He believed that the Chinese should find their revolutionary inspiration in native Han history and culture, and that the most important mission of the revolution was to preserve China's unique "national essence" (*kuo ts'ui*). Chang's ideas on these matters became so much a part of revolutionary thinking that it is hard to credit him as their sole source, even though their widest early dissemination came from tracts written by his younger admirers, Tsou Jung and Liu Shih-p'ei. Side by side with anti-Manchu action and polemic went the National Essence movement, a more erudite effort to foster national cultural revival through a reexamination of history and antiquity. Chang, the senior and most renowned classical scholar in the revolutionary camp, led its intellectual debate against the sage of the reformers, K'ang Yu-wei. On the mainland, his writings appeared regularly in *National Essence Journal*; as a teacher, author, and editor in Tokyo, his ideas and personality touched a wide circle of contemporaries and younger people.

Linguistically, both *min-tsu* and *kuo ts'ui* (*kokusui*) were Meiji Japanese neologisms which entered the Chinese vocabulary shortly after the reform movement of 1898. Their meaning, and Chang's thought as a whole, must be understood in the context of the larger fact that the reform movement laid the intellectual foundations for the breakup of the imperial system, and with it the Chinese conception of China as an integrated social, political, and cultural order. Imperialism had finally breached the famous mandarin cultural isolation. For the 1898 generation, Western power threatened China's extinction; and Western thought, in the form of social Darwinism, was the basis for a dangerous new set of assumptions about the world. All sorts of people were becoming reformers, believing that change, dynamic and irreversible, must be considered a law of all natural and social existence, and that the people of the world are grouped into cultures and nations which of necessity must compete for survival and dominance. Adaptation to changing conditions was regarded as a law of survival. In China, these ideas meant institutional reform.

Within that framework there took place a reevaluation of Chinese history and thought, carried out most boldly by Chang Ping-lin and K'ang Yu-wei, who began to explore possible historical foundations for change in ways which dissolved for good the possibility of an integrated Confucian world view. Chang and K'ang, each in his own fashion, exploited and developed long-neglected sets of ideas now recognized as offering alternatives to prevailing Confucian orthodoxy. The fact that their heresies were rival ones, presenting interpretations of the classics and of history as much at variance with each other as they were subversive to conventional viewpoints, only increased the corrosive impact of their views.

K'ang was basically a religious reformer. He answered a modern, Western-inspired question—is Confucianism a religion?—in the affirmative, based on his understanding of the prophetic New Text Confucian tradition which had flourished in the Han dynasty. Chang was a rationalist who wanted to demystify Confucius, claiming that Ch'ing textual scholarship showed Confucius to be no more than a historian, a transmitter of the known record concerning antiquity, and a figure whose life and work contained no privileged message concerning either politics or ethics. Where K'ang worked from an esoteric and mystical, not to say mystifying, interpretation of the Confucian canon, Chang denied any canonical status to the Confucian literary corpus. Both men accepted the Darwinian view that change was necessary and inevitable, but where K'ang thought New Text Confucianism justified an optimistic theory of the inevitable progress of humankind to a utopian future age of universal harmony, Chang drew upon Buddhist and Taoist thought to offer a more skeptical view, which questioned progress as a value, and on the level of spiritual truth, even denied its reality. While both saw their society as engaged in a struggle for survival, K'ang hesitated to throw out the *t'ien-hsia* ideal totally, and so imagined that in the utopian world of the future, Chinese moral and spiritual truth would at last be truly universalized. Chang was more ethnocentric, insisting that the future survival of Chinese values required the people to become aware of their organic nationhood rooted in time and place. While both believed that institutional reform required a new development of the rule of law, K'ang wanted the spirit of the laws to reflect the ideals of Mencius, which he identified with Western constitutionalism; while Chang advocated a development of law based on the precedents of Legalist statecraft under the early empire. The historic Confucian *li*, or social norms, seemed to both too particularistic and "private" to provide a satisfactory basis for the moral life of a modern national community. But K'ang believed that modern institutions, including a secular state, might someday come to be radiant with the universal Confucian spirit of *jen*, while Chang accepted painfully the Legalist view that ethics and politics occupy separate spheres, and, with less despair, the Taoist view that the universe is finally indifferent to good or evil as human beings define them.[3]

In this way ideas drawn from the Chinese past were made to function for the reform generation as a form of contemporary social criticism. As such they demonstrate that the intellectual foundations of the breakup of the traditional Chinese order began not just with the introduction of Western ideas, but also with the alteration of native belief systems from within. Yet while both Chang and K'ang presented native alternatives, only Chang's was "nativist," carrying the message that China's national identity, which depended upon the maintenance of her particular historically defined culture and ethnically defined people, was the supreme value. If K'ang was a religious seer who disguised in nationalist dress a prophet's universal claims, Chang was an ethnocentric nationalist whose thinking logically led to a more tribalized image of the future, in which the values Chinese treasured could only comfort and strengthen a special, parochial community.

Nonetheless, both of them were seeing history in the same way, appealing to the remote past against the recent present in an obviously "radical" use of tradition. Their rival "nativist" and "religious" solutions had other important novelties in common: both men largely disliked Western cultural models, and in the process of that rejection began to believe that a supremely valuable abstract Chinese spiritual heritage was capable of maintaining its integrity through changing sociopolitical circumstances. These attitudes became basic assumptions guiding modern forms of Chinese conservative thinking down through the republican period. In the following sections on Chang's thought, my aim is to present his ideas in a way that will help us understand how they played the two-sided role of providing a revisionist interpretation of tradition that set patterns for a modern republican cultural conservatism. I am therefore passing over his prodigious writings on political strategy against the Manchus and concentrating on those which show his views on questions about history and language, race and evolution, and politics and religion.

Language and Scholarship

Han hsueh, or the study of antiquity through analysis of the earliest surviving Han dynasty texts of the classics, had been the great scholarly movement of the Ch'ing period, and Chang Ping-lin was one of its last generation of masters. Specialists in Han learning, while accepting the orthodoxy and authenticity of the "old text" versions of the Five Classics as originally established, saw their mission as purging these texts of accumulated centuries of distorted interpretation. The causes of these distortions, they believed, lay partly in the philosophical biases of neo-Confucian metaphysics, and partly in the difficulty and obscurity of the archaic Chinese language itself, a problem which had been recognized in the Han dynasty, but increasingly neglected by commentators since then. In the seventeenth century Ku Yen-wu had pioneered techniques of linguistic analysis, particularly phonology, which gave the new scholarship its most powerful analytic tool. This linguistic tradition, or *hsiao hsueh,* formed the basis of Chang's earliest scholarly training and remained a subject of lifelong devotion.

In Hangchow, at an academy on West Lake, Chang associated intermittently between 1890 and 1897 with the famous master, Yü Yueh, who was in the tradition of the Anhui school considered to have been founded by Tai Chen in the eighteenth century. In his own writing, Chang identified himself with this school, accordingly praising Tai Chen and his successors Wang Nien-sun and Wang Yin-chih as the greatest of scholars of *hsiao hsueh.*[4]

Rather than being a narrow technical study, in the world of Ch'ing scholarship *hsiao hsueh* claimed a position as a kind of basic science, the essential method needed to understand all aspects of history, philosophy, and politics. In the hands of masters like Tai Chen and Chang himself, it verged upon becoming a linguistic approach to all philosphical and cultural studies. Chang judged other Chinese scholarship first of all on the basis of its grasp of classical linguistics, which stood in his mind for the linked fundamental issues of truth and meaning.

By these standards the movement judged most severely was the New Text school, the late and novel revival of a long submerged apocryphal tradition of Confucianism which was actually an indirect response to the political crisis of imperialism. Although study of these texts had been pioneered by the eighteenth-century Ch'ang-chou group of scholars, interest in the New Text tradition first acquired an aura of political dissent in the hands of nineteenth-century individuals like Kung Tzu-chen and Wei Yuan. In Chang's day New Text studies had become a full-blown and highly polemical "school" almost totally dominated by K'ang Yu-wei.[5] Depicting Confucius as the personal author of the Five Classics and as a semidivine prophet of a future utopian age, K'ang made him seem both a political reformer and a potential world savior—a figure to serve as the model for innovating "practical statesmen," and also as the cult hero of an inspirational movement which might become China's answer to Christianity. Impatient with the philologists, New Text partisans accused them of sterile, apolitical, and conventionalized scholasticism. They did not want study to be confined to the mere history of words, but looked for "hidden and subtle meanings" (*wei yen ta i*)—those deeper levels of interpretation which revealed the prophetic purposes for which the classics had been composed, they said, and for which they might still be used.

Nevertheless, because their movement was so thoroughly Confucian in spirit, they felt it needed canonical authority. In defending the validity of *Kung-yang* and *Ku-liang* New Texts they were led to claim that the versions over which the philologists had been laboring for two centuries had all been A.D. first-century forgeries by Wang Mang's minister Liu Hsin. In this way they were drawn into debate on the home ground of *Han hsueh*—questions of the history and authenticity of texts—where their case ultimately proved to be weak.

Chang Ping-lin's first important work as a scholar, written to expose New Text historical and philological errors, was "On Liu Tzu-cheng [Liu Hsin] and Master Tso," and he was just completing it in 1896, on the eve of the great reform movement.[6] By then, of course, the controversy over texts had become intimately associated with that over K'ang Yu-wei's institutional innovations. In the complicated crosscurrents of the reform movement, K'ang Yu-wei's leadership briefly made it seem as if the New Text school was the one which offered a means of integrating Confucianism with Western learning and a formula for political modernization under the monarchy. Those partial to the far older and more widely based *Han hsueh* movement could choose either to sidestep the issue of interpreting the classics or assume a conservative position on reform. Like many others, Chang Ping-lin chose to join the reform coalition, even though the decision displeased his old master, Yü Yueh, and meant a personal break with him. However, as Chang said later of himself and the reformers, "From beginning to end I never agreed with them about the old text and new text versions of the classics."[7] Though for educated Chinese the world was never again the same after the 1890s, *Han hsueh* scholarship survived and proved more adaptable to the needs of the new nationalism than did that of the New Text movement. Over the next fifteen years Chang's scholarly career formed a bridge between *Han hsueh* and the post-Confucian nationalist and scientistic historical revisionism of republican scholars.

Late Ch'ing thought in general had gradually come to be no respecter of texts. Philological inquiries which focused on the classics in the seventeenth century soon branched out to analyze the language of the ancient noncanonical philosophers (*chu tzu*), and from these to study all manner of Chou-Han documentary remains. The evolution of this scholarship has been aptly described by one analyst as having begun with the study of the philosophers in order to illuminate the classics and having ended with the substitution of the philosophers for the classics.[8] But where New Text advocates undermined the special position of the classics by declaring that the historically accepted texts were forgeries and by claiming that Confucius and the philosophers of the rival schools were alike in being the founders of original and didactically conceived systems of thought, they did not say these things in a spirit of rationalist analysis. For K'ang Yu-wei, Confucius' creation of the classics was a cosmic act—heaven's revelation of human norms and of the course of history.

In this setting, Chang Ping-lin claimed that his sort of scholarship fostered a more critical and modern approach to history. His wide-ranging attack on the new text interpretation of history was based on philological precedent, but it also showed that thinking on historiography was changing fundamentally in the 1890s. For Chang, the central task of historians was to analyze the fundamental alterations of institutions over time, and their absolute obligation was to base such analyses upon the sole foundation of verifiable fact, drawn from the widest possible range of ancient sources viewed, without special reverence, as documents.[9] Chang never carried out his ambition to write a comprehensive history (*t'ung shih*) which, while maintaining the formal structure of the accepted historical genres, would provide an analytical exposition of the general principles of institutional change.[10] But he left a clear account of his idea of historical method. In place of the mechanistic historical schema of the "three ages" offered by New Text scholars, he asked for skepticism about history's ability to predict the future and careful search for causal patterns in the past:

From vague and distant [documentary] traces of the society of ancient times, its general outline may still be known. By studying them synthetically, change and progress are understood. By studying them analytically, conclusions are drawn about causal patterns.[11]

In place of New Text fondness for analogical reasoning, he asked for method modeled on the magistrate's sifting of evidence and for recognition that the gaps in the historical record could not be filled in by speculative theory.

Recently vulgarians have claimed that making "judgments"(*p'ing-i*) about history accord with science, and that those who do not make "judgments" are not scientific. Now where history is based on heterogeneous writings, the causation of events cannot be entirely determined.So however much you apply "judgments," how can that be scientific?[12]

In this way his claim for the Ch'ing scholarly tradition of *Han hsueh* anticipated that made later by the historical revisionists of the May Fourth period: They were the ones who had been careful students of the historical record, and whose methods "developed the shoots of science."[13] In turn, although historians of the 1920s followed iconoclastic fashion in saying that their predecessors had used only the old-fashioned "method of schoolmen" (*chia fa*), "reorganizers of the national heritage" like Ku Chieh-kang, Hu Shih, and Ch'ien Hsuan-t'ung either recognized Chang as their teacher or acknowledged their considerable intellectual debt.

But when Chang looked at New Text historical scholarship it seemed to him that its failings were the result of something more serious than just sloppiness or mystical obfuscation. By contrast, the Ch'ing historical scholars had not only been "strong in the search for truth," but they had also practiced an admirable negative virtue: "they did not use skills based on the classics to clarify questions of political order, or did they use yin-yang theory to judge men and affairs."[14] To Chang the ideal was "disinterested history," the antithesis of the politically motivated utilitarianism (*chih yung*) of the New Text literati. Intellectually, disinterested history implied that there is an objective historical truth and that obstacles to knowing it lie simply in the prejudicial use of evidence. Socially it was a protest against two thousand years of scholarship in the service of the state — including that of scholar-officials in the service of the Manchu dynasty — as gentlemen made careers through mastering the classics for examinations and made public policy by manipulating the canon to support their plans. The apolitical character of Ch'ing scholarship which had brought it into disrepute in the 1890s was to Chang its greatest glory. The ideal literatus was not a scholar-statesman but a detached and bookish specialist.

Moreover, disinterested history was secular and rational, and not canonical. It revealed humanity and affairs, and focused on change and its causes. It did not project the "transmission of the *tao*" through the ebb and flow of historical circumstance. Chang Hsueh-ch'eng, the greatest eighteenth-century historian, had devoted much thought to the "six arts" of antiquity, but the difference between his view and Chang Ping-lin's is an index of this alteration of outlook.

These "arts" — or departments of knowledge comprehending all the accomplished person of feudal times was expected to know — were associated by the earlier Chang with the branches of ancient

government. The original classics were conceived of as public documents recording the activities of early courts. Such a society, where
scholars automatically were public officials, where learning was integrated into everyday life, and where there was no distinction
between private and public activity or private and public writing,
enjoyed a perfect and harmonious collectivism, a unity between
thought and action. For Chang Hsueh-ch'eng, this was the ideal of
the "*tao* in history." Around the time of Confucius, however, personal authorship emerged, and with it the separation of learning
from public affairs, rupturing the original unity. The "*tao* in
history" persisted as an ideal, as a metaphysical reality, perhaps, but
never again as a perfectly actualized social whole.[15]

Chang Ping-lin accepted his predecessor's historical judgment on
the largely public character of the early documentary record, contrasting this interpretation with K'ang Yu-wei's extreme view that
before Confucius there could have been no documents because Confucius had had to invent them. But his idea of the change that had
taken place in Confucius' own day was quite new. The six classics
were indeed public documents, collected and transmitted by Confucius, but the "private" life and work of Confucius had brought
about a highly desirable divorce of historical studies from the political functions of the aristocratic courts. Confucius was neither a
political sage or a religious prophet, but the independent "transmitter" who began the all-important tradition of scholarship for its
own sake. In this view, the classics, in the hands of the Confucian
school, became documents, sources for knowledge of real history.[16]
History, though certainly not lacking in lessons for men of affairs,
was the source of a kind of knowledge analytically separable from
both practical politics and ethics.

The vocation of "disinterested scholar" came to seem increasingly
attractive to Chang and to many others in the early twentieth
century. It was part of the general loosening of the historical
relationship between literatus and government, and the accompanying new view among intellectuals that "cultural" life occupied a
separate autonomous sphere. In Chang's own career revolution and
politics were interludes, while scholarship was a lifelong calling. At
the same time, this scholarship was neither as totally disinterested

nor as totally divorced from all possible moral significance as his arguments for skeptical and rational historiography would suggest. After all, if history no longer revealed the *tao*, the historical record defined the nation, and such a modern historical consciousness had utilities and values of its own.

In writing nationalist history Chang was capable of discussions as tendentious and as politically inspired as anything a New Text partisan ever conceived.[17] Indeed his denigration of the achievements of the Ch'ing dynasty and exaggeration of its presumed crimes against the Han people set the pattern for later Kuomintang interpretations of the regime their revolutionary movement had overthrown.[18] Further, he repeatedly recommended the study of history for its value in stimulating patriotism and a sense of common ethnic and political community among the Chinese people.[19] Yet if Chang could be passionately partisan and if he could insist upon the usefulness of scholarship to the revolutionary cause, actually for him that utilitarianism itself was more nearly a means to his own "disinterested" ends. Rather than instrumentally manipulating history to serve nation, he valued the nation because the cultural "essence" depended upon it for existence. "Awareness of the past and future is what distinguishes people from beasts. To say sweep away the past is like saying we may also do without a future!" he cried.[20] Here Chang was not just assuming that nationalism rests first of all upon the psychological foundation of a type of human consciousness, and that there could be no effective nationalist movement without the inspiration of the historically rooted native culture; he was also expressing his further and more fundamental belief that the preservation of Chinese culture gave the nation its mission and meaning.

Yet something lay even beyond culture, though it required a cultural form to become accessible. Chang's own practice of "disinterested history," divorced from all practical entanglements, revolved around the minute, specialized inquiries of the antiquarian and philologist. Of the meaning to be grasped from such pure knowledge Chang, as an old man, spoke only in hints: "To take the measure of my whole life's study: in the beginning I turned away from the commonplace to attain the True (*chen*); but in the end I turned back from the True toward the commonplace."[21] Chang did not believe this devolution was a retreat. Rather, the explorations of

Buddhist and Taoist philosophy which had fascinated him in his middle age were seen as not so far removed from the solid scholarship (*p'o hsueh*) he had practiced all of his life.

As a modern nationalist historian Chang had broken quite thoroughly with the earlier Confucian notion that history records the "transmission of the *tao.*" But in his cryptic suggestion that the experience of exploring Chinese culture through historical scholarship could have personal spiritual significance, there lingered some echo of the structure of the earlier historiography. Such an echo sounded quite clearly when Chang turned to the historical subjects which he believed revealed most about China's particular national essence. The most subtle and perfected manifestations of the essential China were to be found, Chang thought, in the history of the people themselves and in their unique language.

More than any other cultural product, it was the Chinese language which embodied in itself the entire history of Chinese culture and revealed its organic unity over time.[22] In legend the sage emperor Fu Hsi received the Eight Diagrams in the form of carvings presented on the back of a magical tortoise. For Chang this story symbolized the unitary nature of the Chinese language, much as that of the Yellow Emperor evoked the ethnic unity of the Chinese people. Even though the myth remained metaphor for him, he was a person for whom metaphors were images to conjure with. In the study of language, as in the study of history, the new historical consciousness made Chang sensitive to the fact of evolution and so ready to discuss the primitive stages of China's past with comparative realism. In his mind the essential spirit of the Chinese language did not depend literally upon specific acts of creation in antiquity, as conventional sage-king lore would demand. As a philologist Chang broke new ground because of his working assumption that the formation of the spoken language far antedated the use of written characters, and, even further, that in many cases the former actually determined the structure of the evolution of written forms. Moreover, he saw the gradual evolution of this archaic language as a process which directly corresponded to the development of human powers of conceptualization and reasoning. In this way language, he believed, appeared side by side with the appearance of the human intellectual faculty of making distinctions — beginning with the distinctions of physical form and of "fact," and extending to those of logical relationship. Where earlier Ch'ing philologists traced the evolution of characters pictographically, Chang insisted that new vocabulary arose from the associations of meanings and sounds.[23]

Nonetheless, in spite of this flirtation with what could be called a genetic method, like that advocated later by Hu Shih, Chang spoke as if a developmental perspective was not incompatible with an essentialist reality. Divorced from point of origin, essences were nonetheless real, even if only historically realized. The meaning of each word related to a core which had to be understood in terms of the unique properties or virtue (*te*) of the thing "named." Moreover, though Chang did not feel himself philosophically required to do so, as an antiquarian he was always happy to emphasize the historical roots of meaning in archaic forms. Basing himself on these principles, Chang saw the modern and ancient languages as a single total system.[24] By a process of analogy and association of ideas, words branched out historically to encompass widening layers of nuance and additional meaning, spawning in the process new vocabulary which revealed its links with earlier stages through phonetic family resemblance and ideographic form alike. The study of the ideograph was the key to understanding the archaic stages of the process, while modern regional dialects showed that the diverse modern tongues went back to a single language of antiquity and that the vulgar speech of illiterate common people was often more faithful in preserving orthodox idioms than the language of contemporary mandarins.

From the logic of this followed Chang's own proposals for language reform. First of all, he dismissed debates over literary versus vernacular style as the product of limited minds which did not recognize the organic interaction that had been taking place all along between colloquial and written forms of Chinese. (He noted, for example, that speeches in the *Shang shu* were in the ancient vernacular, and that lexicons like the *Erh ya* were designed to explain early Chou colloquial.) Of course his principles required that everyone study the classical written language, including the seal styles (in order to appreciate archaic forms) and the Han dynasty lexicon, the *Shuo wen,* the only dictionary, Chang believed, which authoritatively traced the historical evolution of characters before the Han dynasty. The neologisms necessary in modern times had to be created by sensitive students of *hsiao hsueh,* for, he said, "in changing language, we must make words flow properly from their origins."[25] The idea of creating a new, totally unified written and spoken language fascinated him, because he saw the possibility of building it out of those written and spoken forms which philological research would select as the purest and most appropriate representatives of essential ancient and modern orthodoxy. In keeping with the spirit of this enterprise, Chang wrote a series of complex studies of the origins of the Chinese language and of its modern dialects, which he and many of his followers evaluated as perhaps his most brilliant contributions to scholarship.[26]

Such a view of language was well suited to express the national essence ideal—that for Chinese supreme value must be assigned to certain cultural products of their civilization. Moreover, he implied that the Chinese language was not just a cultural product in some secondary or derivative sense. By associating the origins of the Chinese language with the emergence of a kind of psychological activity—abstract reasoning—which could be considered the unique property of human as opposed to animal nature, he implied that the basic evolutionary leap from nature to a properly human condition must have had integral links with the origins of linguistic forms of Chinese culture.

To most reformers, Chang's view was daring most of all in its lofty refusal to consider the practical problems of communication. Moreover, out of a serious, philosophically conceived, mystical theory of language came literary habits which made many others, even in his own generation, regard Chang himself as obscure, cranky, and unreadable. In his own writings, Chang refused to use any character which was not also part of the pre-T'ang literate vocabulary. This, together with other antiquarian predilections, made his style perhaps dazzling in its own way, but so erudite that most younger people read only his polemics. Lu Hsun, Ku Chieh-kang, and Kuo Mo-jo all recalled later that as young men before the revolution they admired Chang more than they studied him. His philological theories, while suggestive and original, kept to the spirit of the *Shuo wen* in their habit of farfetched etymologies, and his refusal to accept the authenticity of oracle-bone inscriptions cut him off from advances in the field long before his death.

On the other hand, his classical learning gave him a glamour and prestige possible only in a society still impregnated with literati values, yet also beginning to be conscious that here was one of the last great masters, exercising a ritual- and mystery-laden craft. Because he was read less, his writing was perhaps revered the more. As a keeper of the cultural essence, his art of manipulating the emblems of the mystery was often enough by itself, and Chang's literary influence must be weighed in terms of what he symbolized as well as in the light of what he failed to communicate.

Race and Evolution

Chang Ping-lin's theory of racial revolution (*min-tsu kuang-fu*) — or perhaps more accurately "Chinese people's renaissance" — was developed during the aftermath of the 1898 reform movement and expounded formally in the *Ch'iu shu*. It is best understood as the outgrowth of reflections on the problem of nationhood, change, and the nature of the Chinese people, for which his most important inspirations were works of Wang Fu-chih[27] and Herbert Spencer. By an odd congruity, the seventeenth-century Chinese philosopher and the nineteenth-century British social scientist offered somewhat complementary theoretical frameworks for the analysis of race and society, and so together stimulated the Chinese social Darwinism of the reform period. In 1898 Chang was recommending Wang's *Yellow Book* (*Huang shu*) to other reformers; and late that year, in the journal *Plain Speech* (*Chang yen pao*) appeared a Chinese version of several essays by Spencer for which Chang was cotranslator.

Like the other seventeenth-century Ming loyalists, Wang Fu-chih's popularity surged upwards in the 1890s. Though the record of their opposition to the Manchu conquest was a common element in the appeal of them all, Wang enjoyed a special place as a precociously nationalist thinker. Written specifically as a protest against barbarian rule, the *Yellow Book* described China as an ethnically exclusive, geographically based community of people all descended from the Yellow Emperor, with a heritage of imperial greatness dating from the postclassical native dynasties of Han, T'ang, and Ming. Correspondences between his thought and Darwinism derived first of all from the fact that Wang saw human as well as animal kinds (*chung-lei*) in a hierarchy of species-like groups, and perhaps more fundamentally from the fact that he complemented this with a theory of change and its agents which made it easy to conceive of these groups naturalistically altering gradually over time. Such a way of thinking, developed by a highly original mind out of the tradition of Taoist phenomenalism as applied to the observation of nature, lacked the unilinear concept of historical change which would suggest a standard theory of evolution. At the same time, it also lacked the fixed, taxonomic concept of "species" which made evolution so philosophically shocking to many in nineteenth-century Europe. If for Wang the existence of a grouping principle is cosmically ordained, the form which particular groups assume was determined through the adaptation of creatures to cosmic forces which are also forces of environment. The pattern is a heavenly one and not a human one, but one sign of a group is its own consciousness of solidarity—a consciousness which depends for existence on the maintenance of group integrity and is also a defining principle of that integrity. Since they adapt to changing environment and are conscious of cultural norms, human "kinds" are not fixed into permanently lower and higher orders. Rather they exhibit great malleability, and by implication there is no general, universal human nature, but only culturally and environmentally specific natures. "Circumstance" may lead to civilization overcoming barbarism, or to barbarism defeating civilization.

So for Wang Fu-chih as for so many other Chinese, the role of the barbarian in Chinese history remained perplexing. A theory conceived in protest against the Manchu conquest proposed on the one hand that ethnic exclusiveness must be part of the natural order of things. Yet on the other it introduced an idea of the adaptation of creatures to the forces of circumstance which suggested the fundamental changeability of human nature and cultural patterns, including presumably those of Han and Man. For the 1898 generation, both sides of Wang had great appeal — the side that claimed an ethnic and territorially based national identity for the Chinese; and the side that suggested that for human beings and other creatures alike adaptation to changed situations was a necessary law of nature and history.

In the 1890s Herbert Spencer's laws of nature and of history, transmitted to the Chinese through Yen Fu,[28] suggested a dynamic and purposeful evolution of human societies toward greater heterogeneity, increased specialization, and higher culture — the social extension of the biological evolution of species. For Chinese facing imperialism the idea of a global competition of cultures was a stimulus to public mobilization, and the Spencerian theory that the social organism thrives best when it gives free play to the diverse creative struggles of its independent "cells," individuals, suggested a pattern of statecraft that shocked people out of Confucian ways of thinking. However, the most important essay by Spencer, which Chang Ping-lin helped to translate in 1898, did not stress the role of strife and competition in natural evolution, or the importance of liberal political institutions for the development of the highest and most successful societies. "Progress, Its Law and Cause," which Spencer wrote in 1857, and which he said exhibited the "form under which the General Doctrine of Evolution made its first appearance," was an effort to formulate the universal principles of change itself.[29]

The essay illustrated at its most sweeping Spencer's underlying monistic cosmology — his tracing back of all existing geological, biological, and social phenomena to an original homogeneous point of generation. The direction of change is toward heterogeneity, and its agents are described in terms of gross physical phenomena. In the case of the development of the solar system, there is the cooling of matter, the slowing of motion, and the condensation of particles into denser conglomerations. In the case of the development of organic life, there are the variations of climate, topography, flora, and fauna — all interacting to create more and more complex and specialized forms of life. This is a biological frame of reference closely resembling that of Wang Fu-chih, and therefore nothing very surprising to Chinese interpreters. From the point of view of modern biology, Spencer's account of adaptation to environment as the agent of evolution has a Lamarckian flavor, which had been one basis of criticism of Spencer in the West.[30] Not only Chang but many other Chinese of the reform generation gave a Lamarckian twist to their accounts of evolution. The reason for this lies deeper than the existence of a Western model. The fact is that in discussing the evolution of human societies as opposed to animal species the cultural inheritance of characteristics "acquired" through socialization and education is an obvious reality. Chang, like other Chinese exposed to Darwinism, focused first on social rather than biological issues and followed Wang Fu-chih in seeing the acquisition of culture as a key to group survival.

These views formed the background of Chang Ping-lin's concept of *min-tsu* as outlined in the *Ch'iu shu*. As a Meiji Japanese neologism, *min-tsu* (*minzoku*) had never been part of the vocabulary of Wang Fu-chih. It first began to appear in the writings of Liang Ch'i-ch'ao and other Chinese nationalists around 1901. My present hypothesis is that *minzoku* was Kato Hiroyuki's 1873 Japanese translation for the German word "nation" in J. K. Bluntschli's *Theory of the State* and that the term caught the attention of Chinese through Liang's essays on Bluntschli which were based on this translation.[31] "Nation" in Bluntschli's usage denoted a human group united by ties more fundamental and organic than simple political association—a sense of common identity based on blood, history, and custom. Far more than that of Liang Ch'i-ch'ao, Chang Ping-lin's conception of *min-tsu* was thoroughly in this spirit.[32] The later common Chinese Nationalist claim that Chang Ping-lin provided the theoretical basis for Sun Yat-sen's famous "Principle of the People" may not be accurate, but it is likely to be the opinion of those who wished to see Sun's Chinese nationalism defined primarily in terms of organic historical group consciousness.

In his five essays on race and evolution in the *Ch'iu shu*[33] Chang tried to trace the biological and cultural strands which have bound the Chinese people together since earliest times and made them a unity. Although Chang knew the outlines of Darwin's theory of the evolution of the species, still for him as for Wang Fu-chih the important story began with the entry onto the scene of primitive people and their subsequent differentiation into Hsia and Jung. As before, the agents of change were described primarily in terms of adaptation to environment on one hand, and conscious civilizing effort on the other.

With the differentiation of dry and wet, and hot and cold, skin color altered. With the differentiation of sex and mating habits, bone structure altered. With the differentiation of social hierarchies, customs and manners altered. With the differentiation of ordinances and contracts, language altered.[34]

Eventually this process led to the formation of the particular Chinese people:

Before the nation (*kuo*) was established on our great continent the territory was vast and teeming with black-haired people. In the beginning they were not one people (*tsu*). Beginning with T'ai Po, there were numerous efforts: through the power of government and sustained plans the various tribes were gathered together; races and names were made to harmonize, and so people followed the way of kings. Once script and customs became unified, what had been heterogeneous in the beginning in the end was purified. For this reason the Ch'un-wei, the Western Jung, the sons of Hsi Ho and of Yü all slunk away and became different. In fact this differentiated them.[35]

In keeping with Wang Fu-chih's claim that all Chinese were descended from the Yellow Emperor, Chang attempted to demonstrate how the ancient record, with its conflicting welter of legendary sage heroes and tribal ancestor deities could in fact be fitted into one genealogical scheme. At the same time he tried to harmonize the *ur*-history of the Chinese with what he knew of prevailing Western theories that placed the origins of human civilization in the ancient Near East. Following the French historian Terrien de Lacouperie, who had originated the theory in the 1880s, Chang claimed that phonetic analysis of certain Babylonian king lists showed that the sages Fu Hsi, Huang-ti, and Shen Nung were leaders of Bak tribes which had migrated from Mesopotamia to the eastern slope of the Kunlun mountain range.[36]

Concerning the lineage of the Yellow Emperor, the most important problem he saw was to explain how the mythical Huang-ti could be established as the ancestor of the emperor Shun, who, together with Yao, begins the dynastic succession for which there is documentary record in the *Shang shu*. Chang concluded that gaps and inconsistencies in the record might be explained by assuming that the ancient Chinese, like other early peoples, were ceremonially matriarchal, transmitting family names through maternal uncles and nephews.[37] Chang believed that the character *hsing* referred to the original matriarchal lineage names, and that *shih* were first posthumous grave names, and gradually were taken over to indicate patriarchal lines. In this way the emperor Shun's "paternal" family name of Ying could be linked back through the generations to one of the twelve "matriarchal" lineages descended from the Yellow Emperor.[38]

Here Chang was carrying on the tradition of speculative historical genealogy which had been a feature of Chinese recordmaking ever since the Spring and Autumn era, when the expansion of Chou culture first created the need to integrate the more recently sinicized regional groups into the dominant culture by the myth of common ancestry. When he claimed that the people of Wu and Yueh were descended from T'ai-po, a legendary ancestor of the Chou royal house, he was following the *Tso chuan;* and when he said that the courts of the "barbarian" Yangtze valley states of the South had all received a "testamentary charge" from the Emperor Yü he was following the *Shih chi*. These were late Chou traditions born out of an anxiety as vivid as his own to deny the barbarian past of people now part of the Chinese cultural heartland.

Like the chroniclers of Chou, however, Chang was more ritualistically concerned with lineage than genetically concerned with stock. He did not claim that the people of the far south, or the "naturalized" descendants of invaders and immigrants between the Six Dynasties and the T'ang were not now in some sense Chinese.[39] He cared most about the transmission of the heritage of the Yellow Emperor via unbroken clan and family records "for one hundred generations without a change."[40] This record, over the centuries, had become obscured because of the carelessness of Chinese in clan record-keeping, and the custom, common among barbarians throughout the imperial age, of adopting Chinese surnames. The remedy would be a work of historical philology in the spirit of Ku Yen-wu's unfinished *Book of Surnames* (*Hsing shih shu*) to strip away distortions and reveal the underlying unity of the Chinese family state.[41]

Nevertheless, as long as the all-important ritual lineages could be transmitted without interruption, Chang was not worried about intermarriage. He was knowledgeable about the biological mechanisms of inheritance, and he even had something to say about eugenics. Yet his discussion of the presumed eugenic marriage practices of antiquity focused upon the importance of health and intelligence in offspring, and not on the issue of racial purity. His language was free of the sexual innuendo or anxiety about "pollution" commonplace in racialist writings of the West. Intermarriage on the female side did nothing to disrupt lineages, and so was not objectionable. A crime of the modern Mongols and Manchus, in fact, was that they refused to integrate: "Today in China only the Manchus and the recently immigrated Mongols marry exclusively among themselves and do not ask for names from the Chinese."[42] For Chang, racial purity lay in a name.

A specifically biological definition of race is lacking in Chang Ping-lin's characterization of what it means to be either a Chinese or a barbarian. However, the categories which appear vague and contradictory as biology are clearer when seen in terms of psychological consciousness. The distinction between Chinese and barbarian is one between beasts (*shou*) and people (*min*), that is, between those whose natures do not delight in culture and those who have a self-conscious civilized collective life. The differences are known, he said,

not by bodily form, not by speech, not by homeland, not by social position, not by ordinances and commands. If the "kind" do not have a cultured nature, the Chinese do not call them human (*jen*). If the "kind" do have a cultured nature, though they are dismembered for their crimes, still they are human.[43]

Moreover, these differences are no more static and fixed than evolution itself, which is capable of reversals as well as advances, and almost assumes the cast of a phenomenological flux. As apes may become human beings, and vice versa,[44] so "beasts" may become "people" and vice versa. Chang observed that many of the southwestern Miao, historically a particularly unregenerate lot, had become civilized over time, and "could be considered gentlemen of the empire."[45] In the other direction, there existed in the remote Shou-ling district of Szechwan a tiny seemingly aboriginal community, the Ma-liu; but according to a tradition in the T'ang history they were thought to be descended from a detachment of Chinese soldiers who had settled there in the Han dynasty. "Today their skin is swarthy, their understanding limited."[46]

Linking psychology and biology, Chang came to the conclusion that a major agent of human evolution is the active effort to acquire culture, which is strengthened and passed on from generation to generation through the Lamarckian agency of use. Outlining the lessons to be drawn from the degeneration of the Ma-liu, he spoke of social and biological evolution as a single process involving the inheritance of acquired characteristics:

With gradual increase in knowledge, people change to become tall, broadbrowed, and full of spirit; with gradual loss of knowledge, they change to become stupid like "limping turtles." The nature of the changes I cannot know. The important fact is that the old use is sloughed off and the new use is acquired . . . Look down into the lower depths where the fish and crayfish are all blind, not because they have never had eyes, but because they have no use for them any more . . . So we know that human beings (jen) who are slothful in the use of their intelligence will atrophy into long-tailed monkeys and wild pigs.[47]

From racism, Chang had argued his way back to culturalism. His "kinds" were not fixed or taxonomic and could not be identified with the concepts of either "species" or "race." They were malleable and adapting beings, capable of changing their fundamental nature through conscious effort and receptivity to environmental influences. Culturally freighted, Chang's definition of what it is to be human circled back on itself. The truly human are those with cultured natures, and by means of these natures they both know themselves and make themselves. It was as Wang Fu-chih had said: What Heaven's pattern establishes, human beings by their actions complete.

Altogether considered, in Chang Ping-lin's mind the racial

renaissance could not be separated from the revival and enrichment of the cultural heritage as well. The nation, however much it received revolutionary definition through opposition to the Manchu imperium, was not seen in line with the common Western biological model of social Darwinism, as the creation primarily of blood and soil. Rather it was a dynamic organism, continually nourished and transformed by those national essences which from the beginning had shaped its being. If racialist thinking in modern China reached a high point in the anti-Manchu ideology of late Ch'ing militant nationalists, Chang's interpretation of race both echoed the more traditional culturalism of Wang Fu-chih and provided an opening toward that extreme idealization of culture which was a leitmotif of later republican conservative thinking.

Such an account of the evolutionary origins and development of the Chinese people and their culture had further implications for any Darwinian-inspired analysis of the role of struggle in national history. Interacting with the forces of environment, ancient leaders in their wisdom had guided the cultural-ethnic development of the Chinese, leading to the interrelated refining of stock and perfection of civilization. A process which involved the active sage-like effort of the ancient kings could not have been simply a ruthless competitive drive for survival. In antiquity, then, the evolutionary process must have had a benign and "public" character — "Though it was struggle for existence, it was not of a selfish kind," Chang said.[48]

However, the patterns of change which in the past had seemed the reflection of a dynamic yet stable cosmos could not maintain such a benign character when transposed to the present. Even faced with the Manchu conquest and all the horrors it held for him, Wang Fu-chih had imagined that the sage-like energies of human beings could once again make themselves the instruments of heaven's impersonal yet beneficent purposes and did not really conceive that barbarism might obliterate Chinese culture forever. For Chang the realities of imperialism made contemporary patterns of change appear in an altogether more sinister light. In 1898 he had translated Spencer's essay presenting change as a unilinear process of natural and social differentiation. In Spencer's scheme of things such a model of change had a positive value because an individualistic, liberal society could seem to be the outgrowth of such a process in its higher stages. Yet even when translating Spencer, Chang had communicated his source's facts about the nature of change while subtly altering Spencer's conception of its value and of the character of the metaphysical necessity behind it. Rather, the Englishman's words provided a skeletal structure through which to resonate the haunting vocabulary of Taoist cosmology:

In the beginning heaven and earth together with the original basic particles of all other things were all one body. Over time there arose changes (*pien*) endlessly surpassing one another in complexity. As one force spent itself, further changes arose, teaching us that the fundamental transformations of things (*pien-hua*) cannot be caused by forcible action.[49]

The changes which in Spencer's nineteenth-century mechanistic frame of reference were necessary laws of nature, in Chinese language were spontaneous and so "free." The progressive direction which Spencer called a "beneficient necessity" was simply an inexorable, impersonal multiplication of things and events.

Years later in the *Min pao* Chang interpreted Spencer's theory in the light of his more recent understanding of Buddhist thought, and came up with conclusions which subverted the idea of progress altogether.[50] Believing that Spencer's theory of "progress as differentiation" was very close to Buddhist conceptions of change, Chang drew the Buddhists' conclusions. As the world evolves, both good and evil must evolve with it; since all good and evil proceed from ego consciousness, the higher and more prolific the forms of consciousness in the universe, the greater the capacity of creatures for both joy and pain. Compared to an imperialist power, a weak country like China suffers less and has less power to do harm, just as a creature of limited sensibility like an insect has a minimal capacity for injury or pain. While superficially neutral concerning the value of the process of differentiation, Chang actually reflected the Buddhist's existential pessimism — the multiplication of consciousness and the products of its activity in itself enmeshes human beings deeper in the illusory world of phenomena. Good itself is the last illusion.

It is interesting that Chang's few brief discussions of industrialization took place in the context of these and other statements that progress is a delusion and belief in it a kind of modern superstition.[51] In the economy of pains and pleasures the convenience of steamships must be balanced against the horrors of coal mining, the pleasures of goods against vexations of work, which he believed people did not by nature enjoy for its own sake. Sociologically, his attitude suggests the proud frugality of the scholar, whose greatest class privilege in old China was not possessions but leisure. Chang's ideal economy was agrarian and simple; he believed that peasants were on the whole happier than people of great social power and position, and that China's economic problems came from official corruption, not from poverty itself. In his economic thinking, Chang was assigning value to an agrarian style of life which seemed to fit the Buddhist-Taoist moral ideal that less is more. In answer to early revolutionary talk of national industrial progress Chang replied with a sketch of "the spiritual East."

If progress is an illusion, for people to imagine themselves bound to engage in a Darwinian struggle for survival would appear futile, immoral, or both. Here an ethnocentric nationalist was trapped between two opposing consequences of his love of country and its past. Chang questioned the Spencerian association of "survival of the fittest" with the inevitable triumph of civilization by pointing to historical instances of successful barbarian invasions, to the extinction of many ancient civilizations, and by implication to China's own situation. At the same time China's survival *was* important, and it would be won or lost in a predatory world of rival national and imperialist powers, making the idea of the "struggle for existence" a powerful political metaphor.

The conflict between the need for national survival and inherited morality was, of course, a central preoccupation of the whole reform generation. Almost everyone experimented with some form of an instrumental interpretation of ethics. Yen Fu offered a statist version of liberalism; Liang Ch'i-ch'ao called for a "new people" morally dedicated to the collective good of the national community; even K'ang Yu-wei suggested that the universal cosmic-moral value of *jen* operated as a principle of utility, naturally inclining human beings toward those social choices most productive of the long-term happiness of humanity. Chang Ping-lin's solution to the problem was distinguished by his refusal to consider such compromises, and hence by its pessimism. The requirements of China's struggle for existence led him back to Legalism, the ancient theory of statecraft which asserted that public and private standards of morality are incompatible, and that the political "good" must be defined as survival itself.

Politics and Morality

Legalism, as a tradition of administrative practice designed to satisfy the needs of the autocratic state, was of course a perennial feature of the imperial government, including that of the Manchus. But since imperial sovereignty as a theory depended upon the deeply moralistic Confucian ideal of the ruler as an ecumenical sage, keepers of official orthodoxy always branded Legalism as nothing but a tyrannical and amoral statism. Nonetheless, Chou Legalist texts, particularly *Han Fei-tzu*, admitted different interpretations. Han Fei had argued that an autocratic government disassociated from the sagely virtues of a ruler or the mediation of "good men" in fact best served the public interest (*kung*). He defined "public interest" holistically, as the antithesis of the private interests of members of the society, whether considered individually or collectively, including the interest of the ruler himself. Ideally, the public interest was expressed in a system of comprehensive, impersonal laws. Where Confucianists considered public and private morality indistinguishable, Legalists asserted that political acts reprehensible by the standards of Confucian ethic had their own different standards — the survival and prosperity of the political organism conceived as a whole. Without sharing a social Darwinist's historical dynamism or naturalistic frame of reference, the ancient Legalist, like the social Darwinist, suggested the irrelevance of conventional ethical norms to the issue of social survival and defined survival itself as the political "good." Both were theories of politics which could not be assimilated into any Confucian imperial ideology.

In the late nineteenth century, as the emperorship came under critical scrutiny and the movement for institutional reform gathered momentum, it was hardly surprising that many reformers began to take a new look at the Legalist tradition. Kuan-tzu's phrase, "wealth and power" (*fu chiang*), was the best-known slogan of the self-strengtheners; Wei Yuan called on the literati to learn to bridge the gulf between hero and sage, tyrant and king. But in the reform generation itself, Chang Ping-lin was the one who most boldly pioneered a modern rehabilitation of Legalism. He went beyond Liang Ch'i-ch'ao's interest in Kuan-tzu's economism and nationalist message to advocate the principles of Han Fei himself, and to defend the reputations of the Legalist archvillains, the Ch'in minister Shang Yang and the emperor Ch'in Shih-huang. His study of administrative issues, while far more superficial than that of K'ang Yu-wei, took the form of a preoccupation with the improved administration of criminal justice and a tendency to favor Ch'in-Han precedents of centralization in administrative geography (the "prefectural" or *chün-hsien* system) over K'ang's proposals for a modern development of traditional ideas emphasizing local autonomy (the "feudal" or *feng-chien* system).[52] As Chang himself said of his thinking in 1898, "When I looked for techniques (*shu*) that would save the political situation and explored ancient history, the only words I could fully accept were those of Han Fei and Hsun Tzu."[53]

Once again Chang's predecessors in many ways had been the Ming loyalists who, though they still called themselves Confucianists, had first come to see new and critical ambiguities in the relationship between political authority and moral norms. In 1898 Wang Fu-chih and Huang Tsung-hsi were looked to by many as complementary precursors of modern institutional reform. Both disapproved of personalized autocracy and insisted upon the naturally public (*kung*) character of the empire. "Though a king be a son of heaven, how can he take heaven and earth as his own possession, or presume to swallow up their natural riches and divide tham as his own land?" asked Wang,[54] closely echoing Huang's famous declaration that in ruling the empire the people must be considered the "hosts" and the ruler the "guest." Both in some sense accepted the finality of the institutional changes which had created the empire. But Huang was more restorationist in temper, idealizing what he saw as the spirit of the pre-Ch'in feudal (*feng-chien*) system, and believing with Mencian optimism that it might be possible to recapture this, and so satisfy people's needs while according with their

desires. His basic proposals for an expanded role for enlightened
consultation in government through both the public bureaucracy
and private educational institutions were bedded in a Confucian
faith in "good men" quite unlike Fu-chih's philosophical insistence
that the mark of the sage was his capacity to adapt to historical
circumstance, a capacity which eluded interpretation simply in
terms of ethical formulas. Without himself approving of the harsh
laws of the ancient Legalist alternative, Wang was much further
away than Huang from the optimistic moralism of a more familiar
kind of Confucian reformer.[55] In the 1890s Huang Tsung-hsi
appealed especially (though not exclusively) to K'ang Yu-wei and
the constitutionalists, who hoped to accommodate new laws and
institutions without bringing about the fatal secularization of politics which would follow if the monarchy was detached from Confucianism altogether.

Chang Ping-lin, who hated the existing monarch, sacred Confucianism, and Confucian bureaucratism, and who thought that the
Han dynasty theory of imperial sovereignty was New Text contrived
nonsense, saw Huang's ideas as a perversion, not an application of
the sound principles of law, which in his mind were those of Han
Fei.[56] Confucianized, law became the instrument for private
advancement, not public good, Chang thought — an unwitting if not
hypocritical invitation to a government of special interests and
personal favoritism. As examples he pointed to Huang's key proposals for formalizing the consultative function of literati through
the establishment of schools and for eliminating yamen clerk abuses
through restoration of the early Sung system of local government by
an unpaid service corps of gentry and elders. If ideas like these were
seen by their admirers as close to the spirit of Western constitutionalism, this just confirmed for Chang the dubiousness of foreign-style
innovation:

Those who truly follow the law concentrate power of supervision at
court, while everywhere among the people they make royal inquiries
and establish mutual responsibility groups. How can they judge
matters on the basis of the opinion of private schools?[57]

In the *Ch'iu shu* Chang stated explicitly that the basis of a sound
revival of Chinese politics lay in making use of the councils of the

"later kings" admired by Hsun-tzu and of the skills of the school of law. His own suggestions for administrative reform, drawn from a variety of imperial precedents, were economically equalitarian and politically autocratic. His discussions of administrative innovations showed a persistent preoccupation with central control, in contrast to K'ang Yu-wei, who believed that the best long-term guarantee for public welfare was a properly designed local government infra-structure giving room for grass-roots initiative. Throughout Chang emphasized the strict and detailed administration of law as the sole bulwark against the ever-present corrosive manipulations of those with criminal intent or material interests to defend.[58] He offered two suggestions for guaranteeing the essential public character of the rulership: first, the ruler should be accountable to the criminal justice system; and second, his office should be separated from those other institutions of government, such as the military or a state church, which might serve to entangle it with "interests"—religious or aristocratic.[59]

To drive home his views, Chang offered a defense of one of the great villains of Chinese history, Shang Yang, the Legalist prime minister of Ch'in. Though unceremonious and even harsh, Legalist government under Shang Yang had tried to curb all of the special privileges of feudalism in a spirit that was impartial, public spirited, and free of capriciousness. "This was to use punishment to uphold the law, not to make it the basis of law," Chang said.[60] Legalism, he concluded, was the system of government most likely to provide for "the people's welfare" (*min sheng*). It was the exact antithesis of the private, interest-ridden Confucian government, which for so much of imperial history had catered to the greed of officials and the whims of autocrats.[61]

Carrying his analysis to modern times, Chang came to the con-clusion that constitutionalists in China and abroad were also "private" governments of "interests." Under a false facade of modernity, the "new parties" of constitutionalists were bureaucratic factions, responsive to traditional officialdom's personal ties to family, colleagues, and fellow-provincials.[62] In the West, Chang noticed that parliaments historically had been seats of elite opposi-tion to the monarch; in Japan and America the key role of money in elections and of bribes in political decision-making were clear to him. These did not seem to him accidental corruptions, but a built-in feature of any political system which allowed legitimacy to private interests. The parliamentarians, representatives of specific districts and the special views of their constituents, were in principle servants of partiality, incapable of standing for the indivisible, organic political body. Chang's political ideal of total unity and total impartiality was best embodied in an autocrat.[63]

Historically the polarity between "laws" and "men" in Legalism had been full of tensions. On the one hand Han Fei had conceived of his system in the most abstract and depersonalized way: the autocrat was a still, unmoving center of power, a Taoist sage "who sits in darkness to observe the light."[64] The content of the laws was seen as self-evident, dictated by the natural structure of society and the unavoidable necessities of the times. Their scope was seen as comprehensive, supplying a regulatory pattern for human social relations as totally formal in structure and as seemingly spontaneous in action as nature itself. Such a system of laws would be totally impartial were it indeed possible for it to function, like nature, without any human intervention, but in fact, "men" were needed to make the system work. However "men," in Han Fei's theory, were precisely those natural egotists, driven by their instinctive drive for personal gratification, who had no rational interest outside personal self-advancement. The gulf between "laws" and "men" was unbridgeable: administered by mere human beings, the dis- interested and public character of the laws was certain to be com- promised; except as applied in a real theater of human action, the ideal of an impartial system of laws patterning society in accordance with public ends was a dream conceived in a spirit of Taoist mysti- cism. Han Fei's "enlightened ruler" could only be a Taoist sage.

As a philosophical hermit, Wang Fu-chih could solve the problem with the reflection that evil leaders can be instruments of history's purposes. Chang, for whom the question was linked to the real and present struggle for national survival, had to think in terms of his own personal choices and live out the contradictions in the theory. His solution was to advocate a revolutionary countermorality detached from all private and particularistic Confucian social obligations and from all pacifist scruples which might erode a fighting spirit, but which would internalize as the sole moral norm the ideal of impersonal dedication to the public good—national survival. This was the morality appropriate in a time of crisis when the ordinary mechanisms of impersonal law did not function. It was a morality that thought of conventional virtue in purely instrumental terms: in a struggle with one who will commit any treachery, the Confucian-style gentleman, like Hsiang Yü, will certainly lose. Yet in an age when all cheat or deceive, even treachery may lose its usefulness, and virtue appear as clever strategy.[65]

When Chang admonished his revolutionary comrades that "public and private morality are one," and begged them to keep the faith, he played upon the ethical association between personal unselfishness and revolutionary disinterestedness. But his message did not lose its instrumentalist implication. Chang went beyond Han Fei in demanding that in a revolutionary situation "men" rather than "laws" be the vehicle for attaining public goals. As a consequence he faced Han Fei's dilemma in an acute form: as an internal quality of persons rather than an externally imposed pattern of laws, the public good required a suppression of human feelings such as is seen only in martyrs, sages, and saints, while giving people no *reason* to reject partiality for an ideal that did not grant them the dignity of being treated as ends. In the real world of the revolutionary movement around him, Chang saw a few martyrs, like Ch'en T'ien-hua and Wu Yueh, whom he honored; but mostly he saw contentious, faction-ridden, scheming, and irresolute human beings with whom one by one he quarreled, and who fit all too well Han Fei's theory that people are by nature egotistical and self-indulgent, ingenious and perseverent only in contriving their own advancement.

When "revolutionary morality" was seen as an impossible ideal, there was no way left to reconcile nationalism and ethics, or to deny the harsh terms on which humanity participated in the struggle for survival.[66] As competing organisms on a planetary scale, societies struggled against one another, and as a "natural principle of common existence" (*kung li*) individuals had to contribute to their own group on the assumption that groups without such a spirit of collective effort would be extinguished. Yet on the individual level as on the collective the natural competitive struggle for survival made people creatures with an "instinctive love of superiority" (*hao sheng chih hsin*). A truly social morality therefore was impossible.

What remained was the road of introspection and withdrawal — the effort through private meditation to eliminate desires and to dissolve the ego itself. The social Darwinist laws of group survival which governed the world of politics were themselves part of the phenomenological flux — a product of human egotism and therefore in a metaphysical sense illusory. Sometimes in the language of "consciousness only" (*wei shih*) Buddhism,[67] and sometimes in the language of Chuang-tzu, Chang asserted his right to abandon politics and nation and to look at the world from the point of view of what lies behind and beyond the differentiated phenomena of natural and social existence. From that perspective alone a person might hope to experience the spiritual ease of one unconstrained by human judgments of social necessity:

What Chuang-tzu means by "the equality of all things" (*ch'i wu*) is that there is no measure of the "right place," "right taste," or "right color," but that everything follows its own natural inclinations. This immeasurably transcends "the natural principle of common existence" (*kung li*). When Chuang-tzu says, "nothing is not the way it is, nothing is impossible," he means the same thing Hegel did when he said that all events are in harmony with principle and that all things are beautiful. Only the first believed that because people's minds are unlike, it is hard for a state of general equality to happen; and the second believed that [the equality of things] is a stage on the road to a definite goal. Therefore, on the basic level, the two are very different.[68]

Chang Ping-lin's apparent sympathy for anarchism should be seen in the context of this view of the nature of reality from the point of view of religious truth. The term "anarchism" (*wu cheng-fu chu-i*) smelled Western to Chang; it was a political philosophy peddled by his old enemy Wu Chih-hui; and Chang's best-known essay on anarchism was a scathing reductio ad absurdum of the anarchist's arguments.[69] In thinking about politics he continued to insist that laws, governments, and national strength were essential, and to recommend *min-tsu chu-i* in their name. But from the point of view of religious truth, the fundamental barriers to the equality of all things were not the superficial social barriers of caste, government, and nation, as anarchists would have people believe. They were rather those imposed by the structure of consciousness itself, which divides the world into the discrete units of ego and object, time and space, cause and effect. In language heavily indebted to Chuang-tzu's "On Seeing Things as Equal" (*Ch'i wu lun*), he replaced the notion of social equality imposed by public and impartial systems of laws with that of a phenomenological continuum of the perfectly "equal" (because finally undifferentiable) universal whole.[70]

Chang had moved from Legalism to Taoism, two poles whose complementary assumptions had lent such unsettling ambiguity to the thought of Han Fei and Lao-tzu before him. The ego that one asserted and the other denied was for both an ego of essentially selfish and private impulses. The equality of the laws was contrasted with the more perfect equality of the natural order, but both alike were inalterable, fixed patterns since neither humankind in society in the first case nor humankind in nature in the other could reasonably expect it was possible not to follow them. For both the gulf between public and private morality was unbridged, since the first asserted the social utility of an egotistical realpolitik; while the second denied any possibility of "goodness" to all the necessarily ego-entrapped acts of political actors. Neither allowed the comforts of the old Confucian synthesis of heaven, earth, and humanity whereby human beings could live in society on the same terms as they lived in the universe as a whole, and sagehood could seem to be a fulfillment of one's social human nature and not the negation of it.

In this way, even in the Legalist-Taoist spectrum Chang may have seen a synthesis of a kind. As a scholar he followed Chuang-tzu in believing that all of the contending schools of antiquity descended from that of Lao-tzu. Moreover, he claimed that the most perfect account of Lao-tzu's political philosophy was to be found in the two chapters of Han Fei in which the minister's insight into the shifting circumstances of affairs is compared directly with the sage's far-seeing comprehension of the Way, and statecraft, like sagehood, is made to lie in the mysterious art of riding the pattern of things.[71]

Arcane stuff, this, which served Chang Ping-lin as it had served Han Fei before him to come to terms, however unhappily, with an age of fundamental institutional change. Han Fei may have been more fortunate, however, for at least he had believed in the new post-Chou imperial order even as it killed him. But for Chang the republic was only a stratagem, accepted without conviction, and the briefest of excursions into party politics after 1911 was enough to confirm him in the conviction that they did not suit the times. Yet Legalism offered no workable institutional models for the twentieth century, and Chang's post-1911 political career was spent, like that of so many others, drifting from the *mu fu* of one strong man to another chasing the will-o'-the-wisp of effective power. Thus, though he lived as if Legalist political action went hand in hand with Taoist private belief, his Legalism failed by its own pragmatic standards, while there was in his Taoism a quality of revolt against life itself—more detached than Han Fei, more dynamic than Chuang-tzu—that marked him a person of the modern world.

Chang's story, then, is part of the familiar one of the twentieth-century breakup of the Confucian intellectual synthesis. K'ang Yu-wei, as a radical Confucian, made a remarkable, final effort to imagine a way to integrate monarch, great tradition, and reform; while Chang might be seen as one of the first post-Confucians disguised as a throwback to the age of the Warring States. As a historical thinker, K'ang tried to maintain a universalistic view of China at the center of world evolution; Chang, on the other hand, evoked a more tribalized China, whose essence was seen as based on the singularity of Chinese history, people, and language. These were the ideas of two men who were both using the past against the present, and were therefore more ideological and less truly conservative in the Burkean sense than those who believe in the primary importance of the process of transmission from generation to generation and derive their ideas of the content of tradition from the latest point in that chain—the present state of affairs.

In China, Chang Chih-tung was the latter sort of person — loyal to his monarch, ready to moralize about neo-Confucianism and the five relationships to suit the ear of any patriarchal gentry house-holder, preaching a *t'i-yung* formula for preserving the Chinese essence which itself was a forty-year-old adjustment of tradition now become respectable. Chang Chih-tung was less interested in history, either as a counterideal or as fact, than either K'ang Yu-wei or Chang Ping-lin. As far as he was concerned, the noncanonical philosophers of antiquity were hardly less subversive than New Text Confucianism was, and the intricate scholarship of the late Ch'ing philologists largely a waste of time.[72] But this pragmatism of his, of course, showed that the Burkean kind of conservatism had its ambiguities too. Where the ideological conservatives identify a particular interpretation of the idealized past with the idealized future, the conservatives who focus on the process of transmission fall into the habit of pragmatically adjusting existing arrangements and so make their own compromise with change. As a reflection of the larger rate of intellectual change taking place within a given generation, none of these varieties of conservatism is pure, and analytically there is little to choose among them.

However, such a neat conclusion, which sees the two Changs and K'ang Yu-wei as all alike in degree, makes nonsense of the political controversies of their time, where these three men were identified with important groups of bitterly opposed opinion. In China between 1898 and 1912 almost everybody for the first time began to understand politics within the framework of the new nationalism, and political conflict could be said to be structured around rival conceptions of the nation. Chang Ping-lin was the only one of the three whose idea of the nation broke with both the existing monarchy and with Confucianism as an ethicocosmic system of belief. This put him in the revolutionary camp.

Nonetheless the substitutes he offered for sage and throne were *kuo ts'ui* and *min-tsu,* both of which became important themes of cultural conservatism in the postimperial context — a context in which political innovation was generally seen as inevitable, and traditional culture appeared to occupy a new and special realm. The *kuo ts'ui* movement, which Chang did so much to foster in the years after 1905, not only crystallized modern Chinese opposition to Western models in culture, but also introduced a critically altered Chinese attitude toward the idea of culture itself. In a revolutionary world where the cultural-moral and the sociopolitical orders were no longer perceived as united, culture became an essence, detached from sociopolitical forms; and the scholar, as its guardian, became a socially and politically disinterested student of pure truth. As an ideal set apart from society, culture symbolized values which prevailing political practice was not really expected to match — an ideal historically born of social reality yet in present fact unsullied by it. The conservative republican apotheosis of Chinese culture documented elsewhere in this book carried on the pattern set by the *kuo ts'ui* movement even as it repudiated the formal classicism in terms of which individuals like Chang Ping-lin expressed it.

Chang Ping-lin's interpretation of *min-tsu* was not simply nationalist but ethnically nativist. Looking for the organic roots of the nation in history and language, land and people, Chang pioneered the republican conservative's search for value in a "Chineseness" defined in terms of the concrete, special circumstances of China's historical culture and race. As such he must certainly be counted one of the parents of Kuomintang ideology. Moreover, his ideas reflected some important characteristics of Chinese Nationalist nativism, as opposed to ethnically oriented modes of neotraditional thought elsewhere in the world. Chang, and Kuomintang spokespersons after him like T'ao Hsi-sheng, Tai Chi-ta'o, or Ch'en Li-fu, were neither successfully populist nor theoretically anti-intellectual. They did not identify Chinese racial consciousness with the rural, presumably backward, and traditional masses, nor did they interpret the wisdom of tradition as something best expressed in nonrational forms of popular religious or communal sentiment. Mandarin, erudite, their nativism did not depend upon narrowly biological conceptions of racial groups, but rather turned to the historical culture more than to the people themselves, and to the abstract products of culture rather than to the body of customary practice favored by ordinary individuals. The consequent elitist and rationalist assumptions about the Chinese nation and national essence were used by Chang to serve anti-Manchu

revolution before 1912, and continued to be used by later Nationalists concerned with the newer issue of technocratic modernization of
China.

There remains the question whether Chang's very personal kind
of Legalist-Taoist sensibility played a role in recent Chinese conservatism. As an alternative tradition in politics pointing to an
authoritarian statism, the Legalist heritage did not have only conservative implications for postimperial Chinese, as the recent
linkage of Mao and Ch'in Shih-huang well illustrates. Nonetheless,
in the republican period it did hold special attraction for those
Nationalists like Chiang Kai-shek, Ch'ien Mu, Ch'en Li-fu, and the
Blue Shirts, who were anxious to find native historical precedents
for modern systems of centralized authoritarian government based
on formal law. However, these later interpreters most typically
understood the tradition in terms of a Confucian-Legalist synthesis,
rather than following Chang's more eccentric and original Legalist-Taoist outlook. It was as a Taoist that Chang tried to go beyond
the issue of China's survival as a culture and to take a stand outside
of history and all of its categories, including conservatism. Here,
although his refusal to moralize spiritual experience was unpalatable to the later neotraditional mainstream, he was making claims
most parallel to those of the "new Confucianists": that even revolutions leave the basic human situation unchanged, that all social
existence is at best a reflection of something else, and that what
people must finally rely upon cannot be spoken of.

6 The Suicide of Liang Chi: An Ambiguous Case of Moral Conservatism

LIN YU-SHENG

On November 10, 1918, Liang Chi, an obscure and minor former official of the Ch'ing and father of the famous philosopher Liang Sou-ming, drowned himself in Chi-shui T'an in the northern part of Peking. In the letters that he left to his family, friends, and compatriots, he said that if his suicide was to be understood in concrete terms, it was "for the Ch'ing dynasty."[1] This event immediately created a great stir across the spectrum of public opinion in the captial of China.

Comments concerning the meaning and effect of Liang's suicide differed but many were moved by Liang's resolute act. The deposed Ch'ing emperor promptly issued an "edict" conferring upon Liang a posthumous title praising his loyalty and uprightness. No less a radical intellectual than Ch'en Tu-hsiu, although he thought that Liang's suicide had been undertaken in order to defend the traditional "binding constants of Confucian morality" (*kang-ch'ang ming-chiao*),[2] paid respect to Liang's integrity in an article published in the *New Youth* (*Hsin ch'ing-nien*) shortly after Liang's death. T'ao Meng-ho (L. K. Tao), a well-known sociologist, looking at the case from a purely functional perspective, considered Liang's suicide a result of his mental confusion and ignorance of modern concepts of political science. As for the social effect of the act, T'ao thought it could have very little. The awakening of consciousness and rectification of morals, he argued, can only be carried out by persons living in the world rather than by a person who cut his life short.[3] T'ao's views were taken to task by Hsü Chih-mo, a famous poet, when the latter came to read Liang Chi's *Collected Works* posthumously published in 1925. The suicide of Liang Chi, Hsü pointed out, was a self-conscious act inspired by a spiritual imperative. Liang sacrificed his life because he had followed the calling of something—"be it called the principle of heaven (*t'ien-li*), *i* (roughly, the sense of what is right), faith, ideal, or, if one wishes, the Kantian categorical imperative."[4] To him, to follow this calling was more important than to keep himself alive regardless of whether or not his act could produce the social effect he hoped. Hence, the meaning of Liang Chi's suicide, Hsü maintained, cannot be understood in terms of functional perspectives of sociology.

None of the contemporary comments on the suicide of Liang Chi has really reached a true understanding of the meaning of Liang Chi's act. Even Liang Sou-ming at the time expressed opinions that were apologetic, confusing, and quite remote from the heart of the matter. He admired his father's moral ardor and resolute independence but attributed his decision to commit suicide to a weakening of spirit and to intellectual mistakes resulting from his lack of new knowledge.[5] Hsü Chih-mo rightly pointed out the spiritual side of Liang Chi's act but failed to grasp its complex ambiguity.

Contrary to what may be imagined, Liang Chi was not a diehard reactionary or a Confucianist blockhead. As a matter of fact, he was a reformist deeply concerned about the fate of China well before the Sino-Japanese War in 1894-1895.[6] In 1892 he wrote in his diary that "although the newly published books about foreign affairs and Western learning are despised by 'gentlemen,' I must read them, for there is no such thing as an unchanging state of affairs. I must be realistic and must not avoid ridicule from others."[7] On the eve of the Sino-Japanese War, amidst clamor for war by many Peking officials he was knowledgeable and realistic enough about China's situation to maintain that military confrontation with the Japanese should be avoided. In 1898 he wrote that "to send one's children to study abroad is an urgent matter for which one should not be blamed even if one spends half of one's fortune."[8] Liang Sou-ming began his education this year and Liang Chi asked the tutor not to assign the Four Books to his son to recite. Instead, Sou-ming was given a book entitled *World geography in rhyme* (*Ti-ch'iu yün-yen*) to study. Thus, Liang Sou-ming was never able to recite the Four Books by heart — an interesting exception to the educated Chinese who began their education at the turn of the century and a rather curious fact about one of modern China's most famous neotraditionalist philosophers.[9] When the first modern primary school was opened in Peking, Sou-ming was among the first group of students enrolled.

Liang Chi approved of the Reform movement of 1898, but being merely a clerical secretary in the Grand Secretariat (Nei-ko chung-shu) at that time, his position was too remote from the center of the actual politics of the Reform movement for him to be directly involved. His approval of the Reform movement was not inspired by the particular doctrine of the New Text school, for he had no connection with it or any other scholarly movement. Since he did not know K'ang Yu-wei, Liang Ch'i-ch'ao, or any other prominent reformers, it was also not due to personal association. His approval of the Reform, then, had resulted from realistic assessments of the social and political situation and his patriotic wish to see China strengthened. As to his stand on specific reformist policies, he agreed with K'ang and Liang's institutional reforms, such as the abolition of the examination system and the establishment of modern schools; but he was worried that the multiplication of reform decrees issued from the court within such a short time might be rash. He was preparing a draft of a memorial in which he suggested prudence and patience in the implementation of the reform programs when the coup d'état occurred.[10] In this draft he also stressed rectification of the mind and conscientiousness of the officials as the foundation of politics. This intellectualistic-moral approach to political problems was quite compatible with K'ang and Liang's basic outlook, although their proximity to the center of political power at this time made them more conscious of the need to utilize the opportunity to implement institutional reforms.[11]

At the height of the Boxer Rising in 1900 Liang Chi, at the risk of his own life, urged two censors who were in change of inspecting the capital to arrest the Boxers. In 1902 he helped his friend Peng I-chung to launch the publication of the *Pekingese Daily* (*Ching-hua jih-pao*), the first vernacular newspaper in Peking, with the purpose of enlightening the Chinese people. For the first few years their enterprise met with public indifference and even hostility, and they struggled through grave financial difficulties.

The foregoing outline of Liang Chi's domestic and public activities gives the impression that Liang was a resolute reformer who, in some areas, stood at the forefront of the Reform movement during the last years of the Ch'ing. It does not give us the slightest hint that Liang was prepared to die for the Ch'ing if it should be overthrown. Even on the eve of the downfall of the Ch'ing his attitude toward the revolution was ambivalent but not antithetical — a rather common reaction among many erstwhile reformers. When he realized in 1911 that Liang Sou-ming was involved in the activities of the Peking branch of T'ung-meng hui, he admonished his son not to engage in subversion because many generations of his family had served the Ch'ing, but he also took a detached attitude of waiting for what would happen: "Constitutionalism [that is, transforming the Ch'ing into a constitutional monarchy] should be sufficient to save our country. Why should there be a revolution? Nevertheless, if revolution is inevitable, who does not hope that it will bring the fate of China to a new turning point?"[12] Here his admonition to his son to avoid revolutionary activities indicated not so much a loyalty to the Ch'ing as a disapproval of his son's sharp departure from the family tradition. As his statement suggests, his overall outlook gave nationalism priority over loyalism, while showing certain preference for gradual change.

Underneath Liang Chi's zeal for reformist activities during the last years of the Ch'ing and his surface equanimity in the face of the rapid changes in 1911-1912, however, there had lurked a profound disquietude. He was seized by the idea of committing suicide for the fallen dynasty within a few days after the formal abdication of the throne on February 12, 1912.[13] On June 16, 1912, when he joined his fellow provincials at the Kwangsi *Landsmannschaften* in Peking to sacrifice to the god of literature and the god of war and their ancestral tablets (among which stood that of his father) he confirmed his decision to commit suicide for the Ch'ing dynasty in his secret vows to the gods and his father's spirit: "so as to make the manifestation of rectitude and righteousness save the degenerating customs of the country."[14]

Liang's decision was surprising and puzzling in a number of ways. As we have seen, the external style of his life up to this point did not at all suggest the likelihood of this decision. Secondly, as Liang Chi himself observed with disbelief, unlike what usually happened at the end of a dynasty in earlier times, none of the Ch'ing officials, royalty, aristocrats, or bannermen, let alone erstwhile reformers, had felt compelled by the traditional Chinese precept of loyalty to commit suicide for the fallen dynasty[15] — a fact indicating, among other things, the complete breakdown of the mystique of traditional Chinese universal kingship. Why was Liang Chi an exception — a minor and peripheral official at that? Or was his suicide really committed for his fallen dynasty as he claimed?

This study will show that Liang Chi actually did not die for the Ch'ing in the manner of a traditional minister's suicide for his fallen dynasty; yet there were intelligible reasons for Liang to claim that his suicide was committed for the Ch'ing. No attempt is made here to search for the ultimate psychological cause of Liang Chi's suicide, nor shall I try to exhaust the infinite possible factors that might have led to his fateful decision. The purpose of this essay is threefold: first, to define the ambiguities of Liang Chi's thought; second, to weigh the bearings of such an understanding of Liang's thought on the nature of his fateful decision; and third, to explicate the implications of Liang's thought in the context of historical change. I hope not only to render Liang Chi's decision and his view of its meaning understandable, but also to portray a kind of Confucian conscience at work in the midst of deep cultural crisis. Liang Chi was in touch with the spirit of Confucian morality in an age in which that morality was under grave stress. An understanding of ambiguities involved in his justifications for his suicide is significant because these ambiguities reflected the disintegration of the traditional cultural-moral order. They also serve to underline several of the intellectual tensions that challenged many Chinese in the early Republican period, and exhibit the historical built-in difficulties for Liang Chi's moral conservatism after the collapse of the universal kingship.

Liang Chi was born to a concubine of a middle ranking scholar-official in 1859 in Peking. When he was seven years old his father died after two years in office as a local magistrate in Shansi. The family had been burdened by debts incurred by Liang's grandfather, a retired local official known, as was Liang's father, for his integrity. The grandfather was still alive at the time of the death of Liang's father, and he and the other family members returned incognito to Peking and stayed in a relative's house in order to avoid their creditors. Under these lonely and impoverished circumstances Liang began his education under the supervision of his formal mother (the principal wife of his father), who came from a scholar-official family and had studied the classics and poetry. Liang Chi, as the only child of the family, was naturally expected to prepare for and pass the civil service examinations so as to redeem its social and economic status. His formal mother, while not an unloving person, was a stern Confucian moralist who disciplined him severely in matters of both learning and personal behavior.

Liang did not obtain the *chü-jen* degree until he was twenty-six, however, and he failed twice in the metropolitan examinations. He was never awarded the *chin-shih* degree. For a number of years he taught small children at private schools and sometimes served as a tutor to the children of a Manchu grandee. Between 1895 and 1898 he was on the personal secretarial staff of Sun Yü-wen after Sun was dismissed from the Grand Council. Liang entered into the Ch'ing officialdom at the age of thirty-nine in 1898 and served, as noted earlier, as a clerical secretary in the Grand Secretariat. He remained in that position, drafting routine imperial endorsements and rescripts until 1906, when he transferred to the Ministry of Civil Affairs and appointed commissioner in charge of establishing the Bureau of Prisoners' Education. However, he resigned this position a year later and remained through the last years of the Ch'ing as an expectant vice-director (Hou-pu yüan-wai-lang) without salary.[16] (He supported his family throughout the years primarily by careful management of his wife's modest dowry.) Such an undistinguished career bred frustration, which Liang felt deeply.

Liang Chi's commitment to Confucianism did not stem from any particular Confucian school of thought, nor was it derived from a scholarly study of any particular text of the Confucian classics or of any special neo-Confucian philosophical theory. Of course, Liang was familiar with the Four Books, the Five Classics, and some generally used commentaries on these works since they comprised the main curriculum for any educated Chinese in nineteenth-century China. But being uninterested in literature (except popular drama) and philosophy, Liang was an educated Confucian but not an active scholar. On the contrary, he had great contempt for bookish and literary activities and attributed China's weakness partly to the empty talk of the literati.[17] Liang acquired his Confucian sensibility mainly from childhood training and examples available in his family tradition.[18] He became a Confucian by breathing the air of Confucian culture in his environment.

At the heart of Liang Chi's Confucian religioethical sensibility lay the firm belief that humanity innately possesses moral resources (or energy) and judgment. Implicit in the belief was the notion that innate moral resources, being naturally endowed, are in harmony with the true nature of heaven and,when cultivated to the highest level of moral excellence, allow human beings to form a unity with heaven. This belief resembled the Lu-Wang school more than the Ch'eng-Chu school. The metaphysics of the Ch'eng-Chu school, while still formally assuming the innate goodness of humanity, shifted away from the Mencian characteristics of this belief through the development of the conception of the "investigation of things" as a means to gain knowledge of principle. The metaphysics of the Lu-Wang school had strengthened this belief by confirming the innate origin of moral judgment. The idea of the innate origin of moral judgment within the Confucian framework did not imply that one was entitled to create a new moral system; most traditional Confucians who shared this belief took for granted, on the general level, the validity of the traditional Chinese political and moral order. Nevertheless, the belief in the innate origin of moral judgment did mean that one should evaluate specific rituals and customs in terms of whether they were in line with the essence of the Confucian tradition as one personally understood it. Accompanying this belief was the ardent desire to see one's moral nature actualized in society, not only for personal fulfillment but also for the ordering of society. In this Confucian ethos, especially in its Mencian and Lu-Wang development, personal and social goals, although analytically separable, were conceived as being holistically related. Indeed, the peculiar characteristic of this ethos, which dealt with social problems primarily as problems of the individual person,[19] had received a living reconfirmation in Liang Chi's religioethical sensibility.

Immersed in his Confucian faith Liang viewed the demoralized social and political situation of the last years of the Ch'ing as a personal challenge to put forth more conscious effort in actualizing his moral nature in society. As a Confucian, he believed that moral nature was of course to be actualized through observing *li* (norms of social and ritual conduct) in society. But observance of *li* did not necessarily mean conforming to all prevailing official etiquette and ceremonials. It was precisely by using one's own moral judgment regarding the propriety of a certain ritual or social custom that one could observe *li*. As Mencius said, "Acts of *li* which are not really *li* and acts of righteousness which are not really righteous the great man does not do."[20] If on the basis of one's understanding of the essential meaning of the Confucian tradition a certain *li* was known to be improper, one should not observe it, since it would be impossible to do so with sincerity.

While most minor officials in the capital flocked after powerful officials for personal favors, in his dealings with colleagues and superiors Liang was literally obsessed with considering the appropriateness of various prevailing customs in Peking official circles. After he was transferred to the newly established Ministry of Police, in order to preserve his sense of propriety he deliberately gave up possible chances of personal advancement by refusing to pay a visit to the minister.[21] "Although I have lived in the capital for many years and had daily contact with the world of fame and wealth," said Liang Chi, "I have never paid attention to the intrigue of getting wealth and status. I feel especially at ease with my conscience for the fact that I did not climb onto the coattails of Jung-lu and Prince Su [when opportunities offered themselves].[22] Nothing would have been wrong had I asked my father's old friends to recommend me for a better position. But my nature is not clever and I have not been well versed in worldly affairs. I may point out myself that I have never been helped by the rich and the powerful. When I said earlier that 'I had requested a few old friends of my father to do me some favor[23] but had never in my life sought to advance my career by ingratiating myself with the rich and the powerful,'[24] I was beating my breast with delight."[25]

By means of such obsessive scrupulousness in conduct, Liang Chi both expressed his indictment of the times and consoled himself for his own obscurity and lack of influence. But significantly, his sense of moral integrity went hand in hand with a deep sense of failure. A pervasive theme in Liang's diary and notebook written before the downfall of the Ch'ing was his profound sense of responsibility for redeeming his family's fame and status through the civil service examination. He constantly reminded himself of his duty to study hard in order to win the highest degree. Although he despised the eight-legged essays, he knew he had to practice them in order to fulfill the expectations of his formal mother and natural mother.[26] He recalled in vivid detail the domestic scene on nights when he was studying for the examinations: his natural mother usually sat near him carefully mending the bindings or covers of some of his books, while his formal mother supervised with intense attention his review of lessons by the dim oil lamp. Sometimes his formal mother sobbed over his lack of progress and over the inapt replies he often inadvertently responded to the question she usually asked him as to what he wanted to be in the future. She would say to his natural mother that she feared their son would probably disappoint their hope to see him redeem the family's fortune.[27]

It should be noted that material success and moral achievement were not differentiated in Liang Chi's education. His formal mother couched his education in moralistic terms because she regarded personal moral discipline as a means as well as an end. She believed that her son's personal moral discipline would make him not only a good man but also a success. Although she did not differentiate beween material success and moral achievement for her son, it is clear that the goal of making her son a successful official loomed very large in her mind. In fact, she wanted Liang Chi to become an official so badly that after he failed the metropolitan examination in 1890 she even urged him to borrow money to purchase a title. Liang Chi replied that since he was not yet forty he still hoped to win the degree on merit in the future.[28]

To a large extent, Liang Chi failed to attain the material success he and his family longed for. He never won the highest degree, nor did he ever gain a high office in his life. After deciding to commit suicide he said that throughout his life he had wished to make a contribution to the world but never succeeded in doing so and that he deeply regretted his failure to fulfill his formal mother's expectation of him.[29] It is apparent that he felt that his suicide would be an act of contribution to the world, an act which would fulfill that expectation of him. On another occasion he said that his decision to commit suicide was a direct consequence of the moral education given by his formal mother.[30] But, his formal mother had desired of him both moral achievement and material success, and it cannot be denied that the latter was the dominant part of her expectation.

Painfully aware of his lack of material success, Liang Chi was also deeply disturbed by the lack of social influence of his ethical endeavors. It cannot be said that his ethical efforts were made for the sole purpose of social influence; nevertheless, for a true believer in Confucian faith moral self-cultivation necessarily had to be socially relevant. The highest ideal of Confucianism—inner sagehood and outer kingliness (nei-sheng wai-wang)—commanded a Confucian both to engage in internal moral self-cultivation and to exert external influence upon others for the construction of the universal moral community. The dual commitment of this complex ideal, at least for certain Confucians, did not entail two distinct courses of actions, each following its own logic, that would eventually coincide at the highest level of their respective developments. Rather, it meant that outer kingliness was to be gained by the radiation of sagehood attained from within. At the root of this Confucian ideal lay the fundamental thesis that moral self-cultivation was not only an end in itself[31] but also a social-moral means (in terms of the effectiveness of moral example) to bring about the universal moral community. Hence, the social problem was primarily a personal moral problem. Accepting this ideal, some Confucians could never feel fulfilled unless their moral endeavors generated a proportionate influence upon society.

In actuality, however, one's moral achievement could hardly have a corresponding social impact. There were problems of times and fate for the morally superior man (*chün-tzu*). Historically these problems had certainly been recognized and within the range of the Confucian polarity of moral self-cultivation and the ordering of the world some realistic schools did stress the roles of institutions and laws in society.[32] But, such a Confucian as Liang Chi was not permitted by his faith to deal with the problems of times and fate squarely. The tension between moral self-cultivation and the ordering of the world, although emerged in the history of Confucianism, was, personally, quite remote to him precisely because of his prior commitment to moral self-cultivation as a means no less than as an end. If moral self-cultivation had not been very effective for the attainment of the good society, what other means should be employed to achieve it? A Confucian, if he was faithfully committed to this strand of Confucianism, would have no viable answer and could only revert to the emphasis on the function of the transforming force of moral example. It is not surprising that Tseng Kuo-fan's essay, "Yüan ts'ai" (On talent), which elaborated on the idea that social custom could be transformed by the examples of a few morally superior men, was a cherished piece of reading for Liang, and one to which he referred on numerous occasions.[33]

In this way, Liang's realization of the practical futility of his moral self-cultivation did not lead him to give up his desire to exert moral influence on society, nor did it invalidate his belief in the charisma of virtue. Apparently it only intensified his desire for moral influence on society, which now would have to take an extraordinary form to be realized. In death as a suicide "for the Ch'ing," social recognition would be gained without jeopardizing his theory and practice of self-cultivation, and moral influence would be achieved without losing social recognition.

Liang Chi was "suddenly" possessed by the idea of committing suicide for the Ch'ing almost immediately after the Ch'ing's formal abdication of the throne. Nonetheless, Liang made clear he was not motivated either by personal loyalty to the fallen dynasty nor by monarchist sentiment. "I am not opposed to republicanism," said

Liang, "I heartily welcome it."[34] Unlike some conservatives who supported Yuan Shih-k'ai's monarchic movement, Liang Chi despised Yuan and was opposed to his scheme. Contrary to some remnants of the Ch'ing who rejoiced in Chang Hsun's restoration of the last Ch'ing emperor, Henry Pu-yi, in 1917, Liang wrote long letters to Chang trying to persuade him to give up his plans.[35] However, he was also deeply pained and frustrated by the aftermath of the revolution: the rise of Yuan Shih-k'ai's dictatorship, the exacerbation of the suffering of the common people, and the chaos and demoralization in almost every area of activity.

After his original resolve to the gods and the spirit of his father in 1912, however, Liang did not carry out his decision for six years. During these years he took great pains to articulate his justifications for his suicide as fully as he could in writings to be released upon his death so that his act would not be in vain. In fact, on the very eve of his suicide he was adding new supplementary statements to what he had already written during the previous six years. He explained that many things had delayed his action. He had originally wanted to wait for the convening of the unprecedented provisional parliament and turn his open letters over to the representatives of the people. Later, he decided not to do so because he was greatly disillusioned by the corruption of these representatives. Liang loved his children and grandchildren and enjoyed family life. He was deeply saddened by the thought of leaving his family. Nonetheless, in 1913 he reconfirmed his vows to die,[36] and during the rest of his life repeatedly said to himself that he had to keep his solemn pledge before his "witnesses."[37] It seems plain that his very human hesitations and delays between 1912 and 1917 did not shake his original intention. Rather, his decision to commit suicide was further strengthened as the accelerating demoralization in Chinese society after the founding of the Republic led him to think the warning he could issue through his suicide was all the more necessary and urgent.

If the reasons for Liang Chi's suicide are so understood, how do we explain his insistence that his suicide was for the Ch'ing in its concrete sense? It should be noted at the outset that he did not say that his suicide was committed for the fallen dynasty pure and simple. He merely said that if it was to be understood in *concrete* terms, it should be understood as for the Ch'ing. Liang wanted to use his suicide as an example of his devotion to the ideals he had learned in his early education in order to inspire others to devote themselves to the ideals they had been taught. It was futile, he believed, to engage in empty talk of the ideals of republicanism. The important task was to work sincerely for the realization of the ideals of republicanism in substantive forms. In other words, his insistence that his suicide be understood as a concrete act of devotion to the Confucian precept of loyalty was not for the Ch'ing as such but was for the purpose of inspiring others to act in accordance with their own ideals.

On the formal level the combination of Liang Chi's positive attitude toward the recent historic change and his concern for the realization of republican ideals indicated that he was quite open to the future. There is nothing particularly conservative about this aspect of his thought. However, his singular stress on sincerity reflected a traditional Confucian category of analysis. Like most Confucians, he assumed that morality rather than social arrangement was the foundation of society. For Liang, the form of society might change but the foundation of society could not. Hence he believed the *most* crucial factor leading to the success of republicanism in China was sincerity on the part of republicans. Without it, he was convinced, the new society could not be created.

In considering the question of how to lead people to be sincere in their work for republicanism, Liang began to advocate preserving the Chinese national character (*kuo hsing*). According to his own testimony,[38] this idea was influenced by Liang Ch'i-ch'ao's "On National Character" ("Kuo-hsing p'ien") and Wu Ting-ch'ang's "The Future of China" ("Wei-lai chih Chung-kuo"), published respectively in December 1, 1912, and September 1, 1913, issues of *"The Justice"* (*Yung-yen pao*). The life of a nation, said Liang Ch'i-ch'ao, depends upon the strength of its national character, which consists of national language, religion, and custom. Some nations might be powerful but short-lived because their national character had not fully developed. The Chinese nation had existed for more than five thousand years owing to the strength and solidity of its national character which has long since evolved into maturity.

But, Chinese people nowadays are doubting their national heritage
and traditional social and moral norms. Thus the common faith
and the common behavioral standards are being eroded. Liang
Ch'i-ch'ao concluded his essay with a plea to his compatriots to save
their national character. He warned that should it once be destroyed, not even a sage could create it anew; for it had to evolve
through history. Although he claimed that there were many good
and beautiful things in the Chinese national character, the main
thrust of this piece was its pragmatic concern: a nation without a
common moral tradition to rely on could not survive.[39]

Wu Ting-ch'ang went further than Liang Ch'i-ch'ao's warning,
bluntly predicting that the Chinese nation would definitely perish
from the earth if the present trend of demoralization continued. To
talk of political reform was useless. The fate of China was to be determined by the advancement or degeneration of the virtue of the
Chinese people.[40] These two essays came to Liang Chi's attention
when he was actively looking for formal justifications for his suicide.
The tenor of these two pieces fitted well with his basic orientation
and convictions.

In Liang Ch'i-ch'ao's essay, national character was defined, as
noted earlier, in terms of three elements. Liang Chi had no such
taste for scholarly enumeration. For him national character contained essentially the moral tradition of the Chinese people as he
understood it, the major elements of which were *jen, i, lien, ch'ih,
ch'eng, ching, chung,* and *hsin* (roughly translatable as "humanity,
righteousness, incorruptibility, sense of shame, sincerity, respectful-
ness, loyalty, and faithfulness").[41] In another context he defined the
national character as justice, sincerity, conscientiousness, and fair-
mindedness and added that "they are, in other words, heavenly
principles and innate human nature (*min-i,* the 'people's con-
stancy'), being the source from which the sage has derived his Way,
the original character of our nation, and the foundation upon
which our nation has been established."[42] Here, Liang Chi defined
the moral tradition of the Chinese people in terms of Confucian
moral values at their most general level. He claimed they were universal human values, being the manifestations of the principles of
cosmic reality.

Liang's argument for the preservation of a particular tradition in terms of its universal claims involves grave intellectual difficulties and points to problems in the type of conservatism held by many Chinese in this period. If Chinese moral tradition contains nothing but the universally human, what is particularly Chinese about it? Or, was Liang interested at all in preserving the moral tradition that is particularly Chinese? In his practical goal of providing something to hold Chinese society together he was indeed hoping to preserve the particular Chinese moral tradition, and he recognized that the moral tradition of China was different from that of other people. Later on under the influence of an article published in the *New Youth* Liang began to call the essential elements of Confucian tradition (*cheng-t'ung ssu-hsiang*) the Chinese moral tradition and to emphasize its historical function as a centripetal force in Chinese society.[43] He did not offer an analysis of the relative importance of the main Confucian values or of the relationships among them. For example, while Confucian moral values can be said to be ultimately founded on universal principles, their relative importance was, by and large, defined in terms of their relation to the central virtue of filial piety. As early as in Book I, chapter ii of the *Analects* filial piety and brotherly respect (*ti*) were regarded as the "roots of humanity" (*jen*). In other words, the first basic referent of humanity was filial piety and the second basic referent brotherly respect.[44] Significantly, "filial piety" never appeared in any of Liang's definitions of the cardinal Confucian virtues, and he tacitly dissociated himself from the specific Confucian social referents — the three bonds and the five relationships — in spite of his claim that his suicide was committed in the name of the traditional minister's loyalty to the throne.

When Liang defended Confucian moral tradition, his argument stressed its universal claims. But was this claim of universalism a useful means for conserving traditional values in modern China? In Confucian tradition, universal values were embodied in behavioral norms conceived as also universally valid. The relationship between universal ideals and values and their manifestations in concrete behavioral norms was stable. Owing to the close integration of the moral and sociopolitical orders in traditional China, the abstract ideals and values had definite and concrete referents. When the traditional sociopolitical order disintegrated, could the understanding of these abstract and universal ideals and values remain the same? To put it another way, to follow heavenly principle is the duty of humanity, traditional or modern, but the nature and referents of heavenly principle are now open to different interpretations.

Liang wanted to leave the future open because of his forward-looking attitude toward historical change. He did not want to argue that the past behavioral norms be preserved. Since he did not specify the relative importance of Confucian values and the relationship among them — he had in fact reduced them to the most abstract and general level of human values — they were seen as universally human, no longer particularly Chinese. His universalistic claim for them turned out to be counterproductive because the Confucian moral tradition could not be preserved in this fashion at all.

Liang Chi regarded morality rather than social arrangement as the foundation of society. He meant his suicide to demonstrate the relevance and efficacy of Confucian theory and practice, and he was especially influenced by the Confucian imperative of exerting moral influence on society. In these respects Liang Chi's thought can be described as unconsciously traditional but not consciously conservative. However, Liang Chi also consciously desired to preserve Confucian moral tradition as a means to provide the foundation for a new Chinese society. Here his means was conservative while his end was not.

At the same time Liang defended Confucian moral tradition in general terms. By claiming that the "heavenly principles" of Confucian moral values were applicable to all ages and places, he had shifted his definition of Confucian moral values from the substantive Chinese level to the formal universal level. As a result, important problems of coping with historical change while preserving the Confucian moral tradition simply did not occur to him. He did not ask whether Confucian moral tradition (in its substantive sense) could be useful and meaningful to the new society without undergoing fundamental change. Nor was he concerned with contributing to a creative transformation of Confucian moral tradition through which the Confucian system of symbols, ideas, and values would be so reconstructed as to provide seeds for change and simultaneously maintain cultural identity in the course of change.

Elsewhere I have suggested that the crisis of modern Chinese consciousness, as reflected in the May Fourth period by the radicals' totalistic rejection of Chinese tradition, resulted in part from the legacy of traditional China's organismic integration of the sociopolitical and the cultural-moral orders. Because of this historically indivisible integration, the breakdown of the sociopolitical order which was effected by the collapse of the universal kingship inevitably undermined the traditional cultural-moral order as well. All aspects of traditional culture and morality lost their credibility to radical Chinese intellectuals.[45] This crisis of modern Chinese consciousness was also reflected in Liang Chi's effort to preserve Chinese moral tradition. The collapse of the traditional sociopolitical order led to the simultaneous breakdown of traditional culture and morality (in their substantive sense) and a loss of their moorings in specific social referents. Thus Liang reduced Confucian moral values to their most general level and issued a universalistic claim for them. But a moral conservatism that is viable in the social sense assumes or is able to create a stable relationship between traditional or traditionalistic concrete channels of behavior (through which abstract ideals and values are supposedly expressed) and abstract ideals and values. Hence to preserve the traditional or traditionalistic concrete channels is to preserve the abstract ideals and values. When advocates of traditional Chinese morality abandoned the specific social referents of their abstract ideals, a socially viable moral conservatism could no longer be assumed or established.

Later on, some neotraditionalist philosophers undertook a conscious search for meaning which was quite different from Liang Chi's unconscious assumption of meaning. But in many ways the problems of Liang Chi's "conservatism" were shared by these later men, such as T'ang Chün-i and his kindred spirits, who also tended to argue for the preservation of Chinese moral tradition in general terms without being able to create new social referents for traditional or traditionalistic moral ideals and values. The case of Liang Chi demonstrated the early emergence of a central difficulty underlying the efforts to find a socially viable moral conservatism in modern China.[46]

III POLITICAL MODERNIZATION AGAINST REVOLUTIONARY POLITICS

7 The Hung-hsien Emperor as a Modernizing Conservative

ERNEST P. YOUNG

In the latter half of 1915, Yuan Shih-k'ai, president of the Republic of China, sponsored a campaign of agitation that aimed at his own enthronement as emperor. Although formal investiture never took place, some of the traditional aspects of Chinese monarchy, including the adoption of a reign title (Hung-hsien), were revived for a few months in early 1916. This monarchical attempt proved fatal, both to Yuan's political power and to his subsequent reputation. A timely death in June 1916 rescued him from the ignominy of expulsion from Peking, but it could not save him from the obloquy of history. By his dynastic ambition, Yuan won for himself the name of traitor to the Republic.

Yuan Shih-k'ai's monarchical movement was essentially an event of political rather than intellectual history. Intellectuals participated only marginally. Nevertheless, a style of political thought is clearly discernible among the debates, pronouncements, and exhortations surrounding the movement, and whatever else one might want to call it, the style was surely conservative.

Indeed, a central definitional problem regarding Yuan's monarchical movement is just how modern was the conservatism informing it. How much of Yuan's urge to revive the monarchy derived from what Karl Mannheim has called a natural conservatism, "a tendency to cling to vegetative patterns, to old ways of life," and how much from modern conservatism, "a countermovement in conscious opposition to the highly organized, coherent and systematic 'progressive' movement,"[1] a style of thought that admits of reform and has been predominant among the political leadership of some modernizing societies (for example, of Bismarck and the mid-Meiji oligarchs)? Joseph Levenson has emphasized the retrograde side to the conservatism of the monarchical movement. The effort was "undertaken deliberately as an antimodernist counterthrust." Reestablishing the Chinese monarchy was "incompatible with modernization."[2] This judgment is characteristic of much Chinese literature on the subject.

The problem before us, then, is to determine whether or not Yuan's monarchic movement represents the kind of post-1911 conservatism which may be called a response to new issues, in which redefinitions of Chinese tradition were linked to competing models for change. I shall approach the question through an examination of Yuan's uses of tradition in 1914 and 1915.[3]

Yuan's Traditionalistic Revivals

By mid-1914, Yuan had a strong grip on the administration of the country and its provinces. Inherited institutional obstacles to the exercise of his power, such as representative assemblies, had been swept away. The prospects for achieving fiscal solvency on the basis of domestic resources were promising. Although sometimes dubious about the methods Yuan had used to accomplish these things, an important body of Chinese leaders who were not Yuan's close associates had supported the establishment of the dictatorship after the Second Revolution in 1913 as a necessary preliminary to reform. Among them were Liang Ch'i-ch'ao and Ts'ai O. But the question remained whether Yuan would convert the painstakingly accumulated administrative power into strength, dignity, and progress for China. Perhaps even among Yuan's old entourage this question hovered in the recesses of minds overtly unconditional in loyalty to the chief. Judging from subsequent behavior, one might conclude that in several cases it did.

Yuan's first concern in 1914 and 1915 was to articulate an administrative system and consolidate control over the country's revenues. In the process, he cut back several reform programs. He was not opposed to some directions that reform had taken in the late Ch'ing (especially the years 1901-1911) and in the provinces during the early, liberal phase of the Republic (1912-1913). He pressed for a continued expansion of the modern educational system at the elementary level. Even as he suspended representative institutions, he planned for their revival in different forms. He pruned the structure of the new judiciary that had been started in the last years of the Ch'ing; but he held parts of it in reserve as a basis for a later reconstitution. A variety of reformist programs — economic development, the suppression of opium, the further articulation of administrative specialization and training — were on the agenda of Yuan's dictatorship in 1914 and 1915. He believed in caution but insistently professed his commitment to reform. He was still ready to entertain ideas remarkably progressive for the period, such as literacy campaigns in alphabetized Chinese. But the main impression left with his compatriots was one of marking time and the restoration to authority of the bureaucracy of the late empire. Yuan in no way made up in domestic dynamism what he lost in setbacks in foreign affairs — particularly regarding Mongolia, Tibet, and Japan's Twenty-one Demands.

As a consequence of slowing momentum, Yuan was soon losing his audience. He demanded much from the country and gave little. The desire for national unity, which had induced the country to offer him the presidency in 1911 and early 1912 and which had kept a sizable proportion of political leaders with him in 1913, was wearing thin as the justification for all policies. Perhaps Yuan sensed the steady erosion of support among the politically active and the socially dominant — the people who had made the Ch'ing reforms, the 1911 Revolution, and the provincial governments of the liberal Republic. In any case, he drew increasingly on symbols out of the past as props for his sagging political appeal. While at every point attempting to win elite assent to his revivals by "modernizing" them, he sought to broaden his base in the population, not by new social policies, but with ceremonial. Strike the right poses, he seemed to think, and the people would show the wonderful reverence for authority that he imagined they had before the revolution. Had it not worked in Meiji Japan?

If not personally attracted to some of the old forms, he would not have had confidence in their political efficacy. We cannot dismiss the elements of belief and choice. For example, he surely believed in the moral effect on young minds of reading Mencius, whom he had introduced into the primary school curriculum, though he sent some of his own sons to England for their schooling. The revolutionary leaders may have been inconstant in their advocacy of equal rights for women; Yuan, with some fifteen or more wives, appeared sincerely committed to the opposite view when he spoke of the idea as destructive of morality, family, and the nation.[4] But in most instances the manipulative intent of his traditionalistic revivals was conspicuous and probably decisive. The premise underlying them was that the mass of the people had no idea of the meaning of republicanism, equal rights, and representative government, and were only confused by it all. In this Yuan was undoubtedly correct. How could they have learned, in a society where these matters belonged only to the privileged? He also seemed confident that the general population would respond to the emission of familiar political signals out of the past and that the sensibilities of the westernizing, nationalist elite would be unoffended or could be ignored. In this he was disastrously wrong.

The question of the relevance of Confucius to the Republic was complex but less contentious than one might suspect. The name of Confucius was used by all sorts of people for all sorts of purposes. There was a nationalist overtone to the late Ch'ing and early Republican effort to transform the veneration of Confucius into something it had never been, a formally established state religion. The leaders of the movement were not obscurantist scholars nostalgic for the past, but the idiosyncratic reformer K'ang Yu-wei and Ch'en Huang-chang (1881-1931), a Columbia Ph.D. In any case, Yuan Shih-k'ai explicitly rejected this tack. He announced that in order to establish moral standards and in acknowledgment of the reverent regard in which Confucius' doctrines were held by millions of Chinese, officials high and low, including himself, would preside over rites in honor of the sage. "Although one must reform the system of administration according to modern methods, ceremonies and customs should by all means be preserved." The distinctive quality of China should be acknowledged. But this "is not at all the advocacy of a religion," Yuan emphasized.[5]

The honoring of Confucius, particularly on his supposed birthday, was a common custom during the early days of the Republic. In the fall of 1912 in Canton, for example, the city's schools celebrated the birthday with schoolroom exercises and suspended classes, although more traditional Confucian rites were banned from the schools by the education commission of the province. In Suchow in that same year, a school holiday was declared and ceremonies performed.[6] A prorevolutionary Eng-lish-language journal in Shanghai, under Chinese management, combined extravagant praise of Sun Yat-sen with welcome to the movement for the promotion of Confucianism. It disputed the idea that the study of Confucianism fed reaction: "We shall certainly lament if our people in aiming to be strong and wealthy, lose our moral greatness."[7] The same parliamentary committee that in October 1913 produced a draft constitution reducing the power of the president also ruled that Confucianism should be the basis for national education in ethics.

By ordaining official sponsorship of rites venerating Confucius, Yuan was going further. Though the rites were modernized with newly composed song and dances (one is reminded of the Meiji refurbishing of *gagaku*) and though in Nanking officials led the ceremonies in Western-style frock coats, Yuan was attempting to draw on old responses for present political and social purposes.[8]

Yuan's revival of the worship of heaven, an ancient ceremony previously performed only by the emperor, served the same purposes. The argument was expressed in early 1914 in the Political Conference, a task force of prominent citizens commissioned in the fall of 1913 to refashion the Republic. They stated that the mass of the people were unenlightened and the revival of old ceremonies would be a practial measure designed to check the moral decline evident since the revolution.[9] The worship of the Yellow Emperor, the mythical progenitor of the Han people, was considered as an alternative, but was rejected on the grounds that the other four "races" of China would be excluded (indeed a Mongol delegate sought to inject Chinghis Khan into the act for balance). Further, it was argued, the worship of heaven need not be an imperial prerogative, since, if one pursued the records back far enough, the ceremony was once broadly shared. In fact, what could be more republican than taking what had belonged only to emperors for thousands of years and inviting the whole population to participate? The subcommittee of the Political Conference recommended: "We have now entered upon a new era, an era in which all marks of inequality are obliterated, and therefore the worship of Heaven should be made universal."[10] The president would represent the people, but local authorities in the provinces should follow suit. Every family should be allowed to perform its own little ceremony. What had been a reaffirmation of the cosmological centrality of the emperor was converted into a device for piecing together a dissolving polity, with a manipulative intent openly discussed. In this fashion, using old ideas to make new political patterns, Yuan on December 23, 1914, led a ceremony adapted from China's oldest public cult.[11]

Yuan's grasping at symbols was at once more catholic and discriminating than a concentration on his attention to Confucius and heaven implies. On October 10, 1914, after his first public ceremony for Confucius and shortly before his first trip to the Temple of Heaven, he reviewed troops and received school children at T'ien-an-men, while Peking was bedecked in honor of the anniversary of the Wuchang revolutionary uprising of 1911. He ordered protection and restoration for the temples of Ch'ing officials who had helped suppress the Taiping Rebellion (some had been destroyed after the 1911 Revolution). His main argument stressed, not the justice of their cause, but the innocence of their error, since "Euro-American civilization" had not yet reached China at that time and the old moral imperatives of ministerial loyalty toward the sovereign still pertained. He also ordered that sacrifices should be offered for those who had given their lives for the 1911 Revolution. In June 1914, the Peking government embarked upon a queue-cutting campaign. The police removed the queues of anyone arrested, and the minister of internal affairs ordered that all officials and their servants, as well as rickshaw haulers and carriage drivers, had to abandon the Ch'ing style or lose their jobs. Merchants were to be exhorted in public lectures to follow suit.[12] Like Charles de Gaulle, Yuan saw himself as inheritor of both the conservative and progressive past.

Yuan also exercised selectivity in considering past precedents and rejected those that he felt were incompatible with the new age. A censorial suggestion in late 1914 to revive the kotow was rejected by Yuan, who continued to bar the ceremony even when he entered upon his emperorship late the following year. When the discovery of a fossilized dragon was reported from Ichang in Hupeh in early 1916 as an omen favorable to the new imperial era, Yuan dismissed the interpretation as superstition. "Science is steadily advancing," he announced, "and everything must be thoroughly probed for its truth value." He refused to send the object to the Office of History (*shih kuan*) and declared that his only concern was the happiness and well-being of the mass of the people.[13] Yuan had traditional and modern reasons for whatever he did, with arguments drawn from both Chinese circumstances and Western or Japanese precedent. He believed he was making a new, reformist product from a mixture of old and modern elements.

There is no evidence that any of this produced the intended effect. To the progressive element, the old ceremonies reeked of reaction and suggested preparations for an imperial restoration. Truly traditional scholars could only be offended by the ersatz quality of these patchwork revivals. And the mass of the people were surely unaware or indifferent.

The Decision for Monarchism

As we look back from some distance, the 1911 Revolution seems not only to have unseated the Manchu monarch but also to have mortally wounded the monarchical principle. Republicanism in some form or other decisively triumphed, despite the youth of the idea among Chinese. In the first years of the Republic, however, the permanence of the victory was not obvious. The gentry were schooled in millennia of monarchical history and the countless tales of imperial heroes, imperial achievements, and imperial villainies that gave the history substance. The consciousness of monarchy had not been nullified by the recently acquired knowledge of the Western republican model; it had only been overlaid. Among the nonelite portions of the population, where monarchical song and story were embedded in the culture, even the overlay was absent. As Mao Tse-tung was reported to have said in another context in 1970,

"It was hard . . . for people to overcome the habits of 3,000 years of emperor-worshiping tradition."[14] Among republican partisans, the possibility of a monarchical restoration was a source of great anxiety.

The prime monarchical candidates during the years of Yuan's presidency were the deposed Manchu court, which continued after the revolution to have some few domestic and foreign supporters, and Yuan Shih-k'ai himself. From the moment that the seriousness of the 1911 Revolution became apparent, agitation by some in Yuan's entourage for his enthronement emerged and recurred intermittently until Yuan adopted their goal as his own in 1915. In November 1911, Yuan K'o-ting, Yuan Shih-k'ai's eldest son, explored with important foreigners in Peking their reaction to the possibility that after a transitional republican stage, the revolution might acclaim his father as emperor.[15] Yuan Shih-k'ai himself did not indulge in these explorations; if he had been surreptitiously floating trial balloons, he acknowledged their failure by sending his son home to Honan in early December 1911.[16] Tuan Chih-kuei, an intimate military associate of Yuan's, and Chang I-lin, a literary secretary, seem also to have favored Yuan's enthronement at the time of the revolution.[17] Although prorepublican sentiment predominated among Yuan's aides during the 1911 Revolution, the obvious alternative of Yuan's own emperorship was present from the beginning and never failed to find advocates.

The continuing life of the monarchical alternative was best demonstrated, however, by the fear of it among republicans. Much more common than the occasional advocacy of monarchy among a minority of Yuan's entourage was the constant warning against its reemergence among the makers of the revolution. When the 1911 Revolution was not two months old, Ts'ai Yuan-p'ei, a veteran Shanghai revolutionary intellectual, wired from Berlin his suspicion that Yuan Shih-k'ai would use the occasion to make himself emperor.[18] During January 1912, when the negotiations between Yuan and the revolutionaries seemed bogged down, the thought that Yuan was aspiring to imperial honors was frequently expressed in Nanking. After the abdication, there was worry that Yuan might cooperate in a Manchu restoration.[19] Actually, serious consideration seems to have been given in 1914 in Peking to the possibility of a Manchu figurehead monarch with Yuan as prime minister or regent. The idea was publicly broached, and the American-educated Liang Tun-yen, minister of communications at the time, espoused this course.[20] But the primary fear, and the real possibility, was that Yuan himself might assume the throne. In Kwangtung in late 1912, opposition to policies of centralization was justified partly in terms of thwarting Yuan's presumed imperial pretensions.[21] Huang Hsing in Shanghai, a couple of weeks before Sung Chiao-jen's assassination, understood Yuan to be striving to become emperor.[22] Sun Yat-sen from his exile in Japan in early 1914 was warning Japanese of Yuan's imperial eagerness.[23] Many more instances of this sort could be cited. Monarchy remained a plausible option: feared by many, but much alive.

Why did Yuan try to exercise that option? The question cannot be answered definitively. Perhaps Yuan himself could not have explained it to our satisfaction. An aide observed that he had never seen Yuan, who was given to quick decisions, so uncertain and "torn with conflicting emotions" as when he was deciding for the monarchy.[24]

Certainly Yuan had ambition. That quality would seem to be essential to a career that had gone so far. The question remains: why did his ambition assume an openly monarchical form in 1915? We cannot exclude the element of dreams of imperial glory for himself and his progeny. Few people within reach of exploiting the august imperial tradition of China would be entirely indifferent to its temptations. But those who were close to Yuan at the time and who recorded their impressions have not stressed the element of vainglory or preoccupation with personal fulfillment. Being unable to follow Yuan very far into this intimate psychological area, I can only convey my sense that an infatuation with images of yellow robes and dynastic splendor was at most a minor factor in his decision.

The public power of China's ruler and his government, however, was very much at issue. In the aftermath of Yuan's submission to the Japanese ultimatum in May 1915, an aide spoke of the president's concern "at the mess he is making of things" and his desire to do something "theatrical."[25] As the monarchical movement was launched in August 1915, Yuan spoke privately of his frustations as president, of how he had been less beset by restrictions on his authority when he was governor-general under the Ch'ing.[26] Although the reach of his political power had in fact never been greater than it was in mid-1915, he was dissatisfied with what he had accomplished and feared for the future stability of the government.

The belief that the revival of monarchical forms would succeed where a republican dictatorship had failed rested on assumptions about the "real conditions" of China. Yuan had never been persuaded of the suitability of the Republic. Even as he was maneuvering toward a republican posture during the 1911 Revolution, he held that the "masses of the people . . . were intensely conservative and monarchical."[27] Peking officials and old China hands entertained new foreign arrivals with stories of popular ignorance regarding the Republic, of how only a few miles from the capital the common folk took the title of president as a new name for the emperor. Advocates of monarchy often said that the republican system had not engaged the feelings of the ordinary people, and that it was premature in China.[28] In expounding the new presidential election law of December 1914, which reduced the process of election to a very limited ritual, Yuan asserted: "The fundamental laws of a nation should reflect the country's history and the sentiments of its people. This is definitely not a situation where the people's welfare and the national need can be served merely by legal theories and abstract speculations."[29]

In the formal defense of monarchy inaugurating the movement in August 1915, the argument was made that the Republic, loose talk about freedom and equality, and low levels of education among the people had combined to diminish respect for the state and to dissipate the power of the central government. Even Peiyang soldiers had become disobedient.[30] From this point of view, the Republic, with or without representative institutions, spelled instability. The Latin American cases were often cited, particularly the contemporaneous Mexican upheavals. Unwilling fully to face his own failures of leadership and blind to the fundamental flaws in his strategy of bureaucratic centralization, Yuan opted for monarchy as an accommodation to popular psychology and as a means of gaining public order and greater power for the central government.

In effect, Yuan was appealing to the sanction of popular will. How could he reconcile this appeal with his hostile attitude toward assertive representative assemblies? In this aspect of the matter, Yuan was operating in a field of political ideas that shared more with the modern West than the nineteenth-century Chinese empire. Like subsequent Chinese political leaders, Yuan had to pay deference to the theory of popular sovereignty. Both in establishing his dictatorship and in aspiring to the emperorship, he was exercising power within a new, "postimperial" political order, where the leader was directly accountable to the popular will. Hence, like other modern politicians, he had to adopt an operational understanding of the popular will that would suit his purposes. In late 1913, for example, he said that "the term 'national will' only possesses value when it represents the will of the majority of law-abiding citizens. The one desire of law-abiding citizens is to pursue their respective avocations in peace and quietness: I am absolutely certain that they have no sympathy with that minority of turbulent demagogues who only delight in making mischief. So too with public opinion."[31] This was propounded when his government was about to suspend all institutions of representative government and when a campaign of terror against the largest political party was in full swing. Proceeding from these attitudes, Yuan could see his monarchy as an effort both to represent and to reach the "intensely conservative and monarchical" masses. And he could dismiss as self-interested or narrow-minded the swelling opposition.

It is important to note that in one sense Yuan was right. There often exists an inarticulate, politically inert majority, who may not feel represented by the society's active organizations and spokespersons, including its elected officials. But Yuan did not intend to break down hierarchical social and political structures in order to reach mass sentiments and organize it on its own terms or give it power. Rather, the very powerlessness of the unorganized masses, lacking effective voice, seems to have attracted this practitioner of bureaucratic politics. Almost any opinion could be ascribed to the people. Accordingly, claims to legitimacy could be based on such ascribed sentiments and on manipulated elections.

The monarchical movement in China in 1915, then, was an effort designed to express the presumed preferences of the mass of the population and, by appealing to ingrained attitudes, to win greater responsiveness to the government. The result would be a stronger and more advanced country, with a better chance for stable constitutionalism. Or so the movement's defenders insisted. In October 1915, Liang Shih-i and Chou Tzu-ch'i, leading members of Yuan's entourage, argued that a reversion to monarchy would facilitate reforming the land tax, which was the ultimate test of China's ability to survive. They did not envisage simply the revival of Ch'ing levels of taxation; in their view, basic modernizing programs would require that the agrarian sector bear a heavier burden than ever before. The sanction of national traditions, "a form of authority with which the people are more familiar," was necessary, they said, to meet these new requirements.[32] Wellington Koo, who was appointed minister to the United States in 1915 at age twenty-eight, had worked closely enough to Yuan to be familiar with his thinking. Perhaps he expounded Yuan's views when he explained the new monarchy to the American Academy of Political and Social Science in January 1916. The Chinese were divided internally, he said, between the old literati and the foreign-educated, leaving "the problem of striking a middle course of action between the conservatives on one side and the radicals on the other." But only a strong and unified government could handle China's impaired freedom of action under the treaties, he argued. The decision for the monarchy reflected the need for "a government able to hold the country together, develop its wealth and strength, and help realize the intensely patriotic aspirations of its people."[33]

The major weakness of the monarchical argument in 1915 was not the assertion that republican sentiment among the mass of the people was shallow. Ch'en Tu-hsiu, dean at Peking University and later head of the Communist Party, wrote in 1917 that Yuan had been quite right in thinking that "most people still believed in monarchy and had no faith in the Republic."[34] His mistake was in thinking that this "belief" meant support, in the absence of any political links with the masses, and in thinking that the educated elite would cooperate.

To win support of the social elite and to bridge the gap between the "conservatives" and "radicals" of Wellington Koo's analysis, Yuan's monarchical movement stressed the modern character of his

projected empire. Although the process was blatantly rigged, Yuan
had himself *elected* emperor. He referred frequently to his emperorship as arising from the will of the people (an interpretation that
also served a convenient excuse for violating his republican oath):
"Our country's sovereignty is founded upon the whole body of the
people. How could I oppose their desire?"[35] The name of the new
order was to be the Empire of China (*Chung-hua ti-kuo*), an alteration of one character from the name of the Republic (*Chung-hua
min-kuo*) rather than a traditional dynastic appellation (such as *Ta
Ch'ing-kuo*).[36] The kotow, certain servile forms of address, the use
of eunuchs as palace attendants—"all the worthless features of
monarchy"—were rejected.[37]

Most important of all, the monarchy was to be constitutional.
Indeed, those who publicly launched the monarchical campaign in
August 1915 argued that a monarchy was an essential precondition
to constitutionalism. Because of the disorder attendant upon republicanism under Chinese conditions, the Republic led inevitably to
despotism, they said. Ironically, they cited the character of Yuan's
dictatorship to demonstrate the need for his monarchy. They held
that the dictatorship contained merely the forms of constitutionalism (and little enough of them, one might add), but was governed
by the spirit of despotism. Only a monarchy could bring true constitutionalism; and only constitutionalism could bring wealth and
strength to China.[38] The argument was ingenious and self-serving.
Everyone was supposed to be appeased by the blending of
traditional and contemporary, Chinese and Western, monarchical
and constitutional.

American Technical Assistance

One indication that the monarchical idea was not simply a peculiar
Chinese atavism was its endorsement by representatives of Western
social science. Yuan's most conspicuous foreign advocate in this
enterprise was Frank J. Goodnow, who had been the first president
of the American Political Science Association and who left a
Columbia professorship in 1913 to serve as Yuan's constitutional
adviser. He took up the presidency of Johns Hopkins University in
the fall of 1914 but returned to China by previous agreement for six

weeks during the summer of 1915. Recently, Goodnow's contributions to political thought have been hailed by a leading
theorist of political modernization. Between the Federalist Papers
and the 1950s, Gabriel A. Almond has written, Goodnow's "systematic and creative leads" were unrivaled insights into the functional
theory of politics.[39] The application of these insights to China — an
aspect of Goodnow's work to which Almond understandably does
not address himself — has not enjoyed such a good reputation.

Goodnow believed that institutions, in their multifunctional
complexities, must accord with realities if they were to prosper. He
was willing to work with a definition of reality given him by ingrained Western notions of Chinese incapacities, by the views passed on
by the restricted circle of his Chinese acquaintances (including
Yuan Shih-k'ai), and by the *faits accomplis* of the Peking government (his employer). His functionalism became, in practice, an
instrument for justifying a flight from liberalism.

Not long after his arrival in 1913 he became a participant in
Yuan's moves toward a dictatorship. When the national assembly
proposed a constitution with clear legislative supremacy and Yuan
outlawed the Kuomintang in response, Goodnow took Yuan's side.
Just before the crackdown, Goodnow published an attack on the
assembly's draft, and soon after the crackdown he published an article arguing Yuan's case regarding presidential rights in constitution-
making.[40] He had not given up on some sort of representative
government but started proposing highly limited forms. He urged
Yuan not to dissolve the national assembly completely.[41] When that
happened anyway, he and the Japanese adviser Ariga Nagao developed a scheme for an assembly partly appointed and partly elected
on the basis of the functional representation of certain classes
(literati, merchants, and landowners).

As Goodnow's commitment to representative government for
China attenuated, he became an apologist for Yuan's dictatorship.
He chimed in with others in pronouncing the former national
assembly unfit. In May 1914 Yuan's government fashioned and pro-
mulgated the so-called Constitutional Compact, a ratification of
Yuan's dictatorial powers. Although Goodnow and Ariga
reasonably disclaimed full responsibility for this document, they

probably influenced aspects of it. At any rate, they met frequently in subsequent weeks with the president and his staff to discuss its implementation. In a report to the Carnegie Endowment, Goodnow made this comment on the Constitutional Compact: "Most of the ideas which I recommended in the draft I made about a year ago have been adopted, although they have given the President somewhat greater independence of the legislature than I had proposed. I must confess, however, that on the whole I approve of what has been done."[42] In an article published in America that year, Goodnow concluded that "for quite some time to come the function of a Chinese representative body should in large measure be consultative and advisory."[43] In the guise of prescription, Goodnow was describing, and implicitly endorsing, the institutions by which Yuan had decided to rule for the time being, that is, advisory councils.

Goodnow returned to the United States in the summer of 1914. He reported the findings of his experience not only to the American press but also to the American Political Science Association at its annual meeting in Chicago in December 1914. In an address entitled "Reform in China," he described a China which, like the rest of Asia, was bound to lose out to Western efficiency in the emerging conflict between East and West. To remedy her lack of the institutional and psychological preconditions for industrial development, China must in these matters "rely very largely on foreign management and submit to foreign control." In the political and social sphere, Goodnow reported, she was without the concept of political authority (but relied instead on ethical and customary notions), without the rule of law, without the idea of individual rights, without discipline, and without the concentrations of property and organized classes characterizing the European societies where parliaments began. He counseled his audience that "a form of government which has many of the earmarks of absolutism must continue until she develops greater submission to political authority, greater powers of social cooperation and greater regard for private rights."[44]

One of Goodnow's closest associates during 1914 had been Yuan K'o-ting, who in 1915 was a leading agitator on behalf of the monarchy.[45] Goodnow was a known quantity to the monarchists. He was asked soon after his return to Peking in July 1915 to write an essay on the suitability of a Chinese monarchy. He agreed and came out privately and publicly for a monarchical restoration.[46] What moved him to this action was probably a combination of honest conviction and a cultural and professional arrogance that permitted him to regard his intervention as appropriate.

His famous essay began with the thought that "the form of government which a country usually possesses is for the most part determined by the necessities of practical life." His analysis, as in the earlier years, stressed the uneducated state of the people, their low political capacity, and, because of the global character of European capital and its enterprises, the growing Western intolerance of disorder anywhere. His weighing of these factors led him to this conclusion: "It is of course not susceptible of doubt that a monarchy is better suited than a republic to China. China's history and traditions, her social and economic conditions, her relations with foreign powers all make it probable that the country would develop that constitutional government which it must develop if it is to preserve its independence as a state, more easily as a monarchy than as a republic."[47]

With the formal launching of the monarchical movement in mid-August, much was made of the scientific basis provided the movement by Goodnow, a distinguished scholar of a leading republic. His essay was widely circulated. It is true that he soon regretted his temerity and began to emphasize the conditions (foreign and domestic toleration, arrangements for the succession, and plans for a constitution) that he had attached to his monarchical prescription. On the other hand, he believed that the conditions would be readily met.[48]

Goodnow and the monarchical advocates around Yuan Shih-k'ai spoke the same language as far as political modernization was concerned. The dictatorship, they agreed, had been a necessary response to the anarchy of the liberal Republic but did not promise sufficient stability. Constitutional monarchy (the German and Japanese models were cited by Yuan's spokesmen) would weld the country together, provide the foundation for national wealth and strength, and fend off foreign domination. Yang Tu, the leading

Chinese theoretician of the movement, went so far as to predict the consequences of rejecting this course: warlordism, followed by foreign intervention and a puppet monarchy, perhaps built around the deposed Manchu emperor, under foreign control.[49] Goodnow and the Chinese advocates of Yuan's monarchy were no doubt influencing each other, but their analyses were not merely manufactured for the occasion. In America, Goodnow was a Progressive. Transplanted to China, his approach blended easily with that of the monarchists: modern and reformist, but conservative with respect to Chinese politics.

The modern conservative voice was not the only one heard in Yuan's monarchical movement. In the formal petitions of December 1915, asking Yuan to accept the throne, there was much reference to the will of heaven and Yuan's extraordinary virtue. That such aspects should be present was, of course, part of the conservative design. The monarchy was useful precisely because it could appeal to old, ingrained attitudes of a benighted population. It would be wrong to conclude that the heart of the movement lay in nostalgia and in unreconstructed commitments to old cosmologies and political theories. Measurements such as the frequency of use, the forcefulness of presentation, and the source of the varieties of rationales for the movement force me to reject that possibility. Rather, as Mannheim says of conservative thought, the monarchical movement raised "to the level of reflection and conscious manipulation those forms of experience which [could] no longer be had in an authentic way."[50] Yuan's monarchy represented the manipulation of symbols, not commitment to their inherited meaning. Those who were still committed to the old meanings, it turned out, were among those who rejected Yuan's version of the monarchy.

Some other elements present in the movement and important in its timing lay quite outside the realm of political thought. They included the role of Japan and the practical politics of Yuan's situation in 1915. For the purposes of this essay, I must leave them aside. Rather than filling in details, I wish to put the issue of Yuan's conservatism in a broader context.

The overarching problem that all Chinese political movements had to address from the 1890s until 1949 was the recovery of a dignified measure of national autonomy. The entrenchments of the foreign imperialists in China had to be rolled back. The requirements for leadership in these circumstances included militancy in dealing with the imperialist powers. And they included attaining the wherewithal — in energy, organization, and matériel — to sustain the militancy.

Borrowing Mannheim's imagery, we can identify three major progressive assertions or movements that addressed the need for national autonomy. The first was the drive for reform along advanced Western lines, beginning in the 1890s and culminating in the 1911 Revolution and the decentralized, parliamentary order of the succeeding two years that I call the "liberal Republic." The social base of this movement was mainly gentry, or major elements from the gentry who had become responsive to nationalist issues. The second progressive assertion was the revolutionary nationalist movement of the 1920s, which drew some of its inspiration from the May Fourth movement and culminated in the defeat of warlords in the central and lower Yangtze regions in late 1926 and early 1927. The social base included a variety of urban classes and portions of the peasantry. The third assertion was the Communist movement as it was reorganized under Mao's leadership in the 1930s. It culminated in a new social and political order in 1949, and the largest part of its social base was peasant.

Each of these three progressive movements elicited committed participation from a larger portion of the society than had its predecessors. (In the first case, there was no immediate predecessor but rather an environment where the ideology of nationalism had not been fully formulated and where politics was kept largely in the hands of bureaucrats.) Furthermore, each political movement improved on any previous efforts at recovering national rights from foreign hands. Finally, the first two were followed by domestic movements of conservatism. (In the third case, the progressive movement triumphed with a thoroughness previously unmatched. Although one may speak of an international reaction, the nationalist problem was fundamentally solved soon after 1949. Any domestic reaction focused on other issues.)

The domestic conservative attitude in the first two cases saw the progressive movement as destructive in its effects on the social fabric and on the drive for national unity. The politically significant expositors of this attitude were not the purist adherents of tradition but defectors from the progressive movements. Such were both Yuan Shih-k'ai and Chiang Kai-shek. The conservative responses, as led by Yuan and Chiang respectively, were not simply efforts to turn back the clock. Rather a compromise was sought between change-inducing reforms and the retrieval of symbols, values, and behavior that seemed to support the social order. Conservatives in this situation were not denying the reality of the nationalist problem. On the contrary, they were convinced that they had better and more reliable answers to it. Further, the symbols and the values need not necessarily be sought in the Chinese past. Like the progressives, the conservatives could draw on either Chinese or foreign justifications for their programs.

A central feature in both conservative programs was that participation in politics be brought strictly under control. Although this move was not portrayed as a reduction in participation, it had that effect. The vision was still a nation of citizens, but the citizen's role in the conservative conception was one of deference and obedience, not autonomous engagement.

It is in this framework, then, that I see Yuan's monarchical movement as an example of "modern conservatism." It was a response to new issues that had been formulated since the 1890s. It was an effort to redefine elements out of the Chinese past and the experience of other countries and use them in order to move China gradually into the modern world. It was not deliberately antimodernist, as Levenson and others have argued, unless one wishes to limit the meaning of "modern" to "progressive." Indeed it shared with much American modernization theory a bias toward stability, equilibrium, compromise with forces for change rather than endorsement of them, and a celebration of gradualism. Balance was Yuan's guiding principle. He put it this way as he was consolidating his dictatorship in the spring of 1914: "Generally speaking, most of the young men who have just acquired influence are inclined to theories unsuitable for the circumstances of the country, while the more steady and experienced class are not farsighted and are too conservative. Should we desire to utilize the services of both and to amalgamate these two forces, it is necessary that we should be careful and progressive at the same time."[51] The monarchical movement, in the particular form it took under Yuan's aegis, was a natural consequence of this approach.

8   The Kuomintang in the 1930s

LLOYD E. EASTMAN

Conservatism is one of the less precise terms in the social science lexicon.[1] As often as not, the term is used in the vague sense of implying opposition to something that is positive, progressive, and good. Some scholars, in an attempt to gain a degree of precision, imbue the term with specific political or philosophical connotations, such as a preference for authoritarian rule, a belief in human irrationality, or opposition to class struggle. While doubtless useful in some cases, these refinements are generally misleading, because the added connotations are usually peculiar to a specific historical setting rather than being inherent in conservatism itself. In this essay, following Roberto Michels, I choose to remove all value and philosophical implications from the term, and to define political conservatism simply as "a tendency to maintain the status quo regardless of what that may be."[2]

The period of Kuomintang rule during the Nanking decade, 1927-1937, has been viewed as a time when conservatism reigned supreme. Mary C. Wright, in an essay that has deeply influenced a generation of American students of China, contended in 1955 that Chiang Kai-shek and the Kuomintang sought to restore the Confucian system, that they gave "full and uninhibited adherence . . . not only to the values of the traditional society but to the specific institutions in which these had been embodied." Wright did perceive that the Kuomintang's commitment to Chinese tradition was not a pure conservatism. It was, she believed, a "distorted echo" of true Chinese conservatism, for a "romantic nationalism" had crept in that clashed with the rational universalism of the traditional doctrine and system. The emphasis in the Wright interpretation was, however, that Chiang Kai-shek and other Kuomintang leaders were essentially backward-looking. They were prepared to adopt certain surface manifestations of modernity, but they sought to conserve for their own sake the old ways, the old values. In the end they failed to revitalize the principles and policies of the Chinese conservatives of the 1860s, but — Wright has led us to believe — not because they did not try.[3]

This interpretation has, I believe, distorted our understanding of both the character of Kuomintang rule and the intent of the Kuomintang leaders, for the dominant leaders perceived that China had changed, and realized that their task was to forge a new, modern state. They were not, as Mary Wright argued, conservatives by intent. Rather, the conservatism of the Kuomintang — insofar as it was indeed a conservative force — resulted in large degree from the persistence among the officials of the Nationalist regime of unarticulated traditional attitudes and behavioral characteristics.

The Kuomintang, having come to power in 1927, was confronted with the challenge of reinvigorating a nation that had been declining at an accelerating pace for over a century. China was enfeebled, vulnerable to the whims and insults of both Western and Japanese imperialists. It was divided, riven since the collapse of the Manchu dynasty by autonomous and politically ambitious regional hegemons. It was moving without any clear sense of direction, for it had broken loose from the solid moorings of its traditional institutions and culture.

During the 1930s, the leadership of the Kuomintang sought a strategy that would restore stability, strength, and a sense of pride to the nation. The three dominant policy-formulating elements of the leadership — Chiang-Kai-shek, the CC clique, and the Blue Shirts — each articulated variant strategies to attain those goals. Significantly, however, none of them proposed a strategy for restoring the traditional order, for they all perceived that the ultimate solution for China lay in creating a wholly new political, economic, and cultural system.

The Blue Shirts and Fascism

The Blue Shirts were secretly organized in the spring of 1932, at a time when the very existence of the Nanking government was imperiled.[4] Five years previously the Kuomintang had seized national power, proclaiming its triptychal program of national unity and independence, democracy, and economic betterment. During the ensuing years, the Kuomintang, rather than diverting the course of China's history, had been swept up in the current of national decline. Its administration had become no less ineffective and corrupt than that of the preceding warlord regimes; it had been unable to impose any real unity, politically or psychologically, upon the nation; and it had lost the popular support that had helped sweep the party to power. As a member of the Blue Shirts observed in 1932, "The revolution [during the period 1927-1931] not only did not progress but it gradually floundered; it not only made no new achievements but lost even its previous achievements . . . so that the hopes that the people had placed in the Kuomintang were gradually dissipated, and their faith in the Three People's Principles was shaken."[5]

After 1931, the situation had worsened. In that year Central China was struck by the most destructive floods within memory; the world economic depression hit the country in the winter 1931-1932; and, at the same time, Japanese armies attacked Manchuria and Shanghai. At no time in its modern history had China's prospects appeared bleaker than during the first years of the existence of the Blue Shirts.

The Blue Shirts were formed by a group of young military officers who only a few years previously had graduated from the Whampoa Military Academy. Staunchly loyal to Chiang Kai-shek, these officers proclaimed that the revolution had failed because the vehicle of the revolution, the Kuomintang itself, had been immobilized by capitalism and bureaucratism. The party was merely an arena, therefore, where warlords and bureaucrats fought for power and the harvest of corruption. Ideally, they thought, the Kuomintang should be abolished and replaced by a wholly new organization. This was not politically feasible, however, and they therefore proposed to seize control of the old party and to instill in it a new spirit of dedication and sacrifice that would regenerate the faltering revolution.

Acting with the approval of Chiang Kai-shek, the Blue Shirts — also widely known as the Regenerationist Society (Fu-hsing she) — soon controlled political training in the army, the schools, and the Boy Scouts. They attacked the inefficiency and corruption of the governmental bureaucrats. And they terrorized political enemies with tactics of secret arrests, bombings, and assassinations.

Fascism provided the core of the Blue Shirts' ideology. Only one of the founding members of the Blue Shirts had studied in Germany; most of them had received training in either Japan or Russia.[6] But there had been ample literature on fascism for them to read, and there was a strong Nazi influence among the German military advisers and diplomatic corps in China.[7] Moreover, the Blue Shirts had been impressed by the apparent decline of democracy throughout the world since World War I and by the accomplishments of first Mussolini and then Hitler. To the Blue Shirt leaders, fascism appeared to be the most modern system for the creation of a strong and great nation. As one of the former Blue Shirt leaders told me in 1969, "Fascism is now thought to be backward, but then it seemed to be a very progressive means of resurrecting the nation."[8]

Dictatorship, exaltation of the nation, total abnegation of the individual — these were the goals of the Blue Shirts. To attain these goals, the Blue Shirts believed that they would have to transform Chinese society. They would root out elements of Western culture that had become a dry rot on the Chinese soul. They particularly execrated Western liberalism. Liberalism to the Blue Shirts meant political freedom, humanism, and — worst of all — individualism, which caused the people to emphasize personal welfare to the exclusion of the overriding needs of society at large.

At the same time, the Blue Shirts also attacked China's traditional society and culture. A Blue Shirt publication proclaimed for example, that "in order to create a new culture, Lenin, Stalin, Mussolini, and Hilter launched an unfeeling, cruel attack on the old culture, replaying the drama of the First Emperor [of Ch'in], burning books and burying scholars alive. Naturally this cannot but be done!"[9] One is initially incredulous that the Blue Shirts wished to emulate the First Emperor, who for nearly two thousand years had been regarded as the archvillain of Chinese history. But the Blue Shirts' praise of the First Emperor was consistent with their general rejection of the nation's traditions and the humanistic values of the past. As Chang Yün-fu declared, the self-satisfaction, superstition, passivity, and individualism that characterized the traditional society were unsuited to the current age. He admitted that the four traditional virtues of *li, i, lien,* and *ch'ih* (then espoused by Chiang Kai-shek) were forever valid. However, "everything else in our traditional culture . . . must be changed, corrected, or reformed."[10]

Some indication of the extent to which the Blue Shirts aimed to transform the existing social system is found in their educational policies, epitomized by the slogan, "Nationalize, militarize, productivize." The goal of the "nationalization" of education, for example, was to create students possessed of a single-minded love for the nation and a readiness to sacrifice even their lives for it. How radically this policy would break with Chinese tradition is seen in the words of Yü Wen-wei: "The children that we educate are the nation's children, *not children of the family or clan.* The ultimate goal of educational policies must be the nation."[11]

"Militarization" of education would transform the educational system so that "future teachers will train students to be fighters in a great war." Military indoctrination would therefore begin in the kindergartens. Youngsters would be given guns and warships for toys, and pictures of battle scenes would be placed on the walls "so that from childhood they would develop an interest in military equipment and battle situations." Throughout the school years, students would be nurtured in a military environment—with a particular stress on physical development—so that the "frail and bookish" youth of the past would be replaced by a generation of warriors.[12]

The educational goal of "productivization" similarly represented an attack on the old and accepted social system. The Blue Shirts deplored the "long-gown" tradition in education, believing that the schools perpetuated an arrogant elite that performed no useful function in society. The new system of education, they urged, must eliminate the prevalent stress upon study of "dead books" as a means of preparing for government office. Instead, all students would devote part of their time to manual labor on farms or in factories. The traditional disdain for manual labor and the working classes would in this way be removed, and intellectuals would become producing members of the nation.[13]

The Blue Shirts were therefore in large part indifferent to, and often outrightly contemptuous of, Chinese traditions. The leaders were military officers who valued action, discipline, and efficiency. The corruption of the self-seeking bureaucrats who ran the civil administration of the Nationalist regime outraged them, but no more than did the empty ritualism, the effete culturalism, and the enervating individualism of traditional society. The Blue Shirts were, in other words, radical in their discontent with tradition and with the status quo, and they advocated measures that would have changed the nation profoundly.

The CC Clique and Modernization on a Chinese Basis

The chief rival of the Blue Shirts for paramountcy within Chiang Kai-shek's coterie of supporters was the CC Clique. Formed in the midst of the purges of 1927-1928, this clique was identified with, and some thought named for, the two Ch'en brothers, Kuo-fu and Li-fu.[14] As a result of Chiang Kai-shek's trust in them, and through their administrative prominence in the party, Ch'en Kuo-fu and Ch'en Li-fu by 1929 dominated both the civilian wing of the party and the governmental bureaucracy.

Initially this clique adhered to no ideology that distinguished it from the Kuomintang generally. During 1934, however, probably in response to the political challenge of the Blue Shirts, the CC Clique began to stake out its own ideological position. CC Clique dogma shared none of the Blue Shirts' iconoclasm toward the traditional culture, but it too admitted the necessity of farreaching changes.

The attitude of the CC Clique was first defined in 1934 by the younger of the Ch'en brothers. Ch'en Li-fu, although United States-trained as a mining engineer, enthusiastically proclaimed the greatness of Confucianism and of China's past. "China's culture," he declared, "is indisputably peerless in all time and throughout the world." He also maintained that one could understand the doctrines of Sun Yat-sen only after having thoroughly absorbed the ideas of Confucius. "Therefore," he wrote, "although the two plans [of Confucius and of Sun Yat-sen] are different, the value of the two is eternally the same."[15]

Subsequently the CC Clique's tendency to uphold tradition was clarified, and its views received national attention when ten professors closely associated with it issued a "Declaration of Cultural Construction on a Chinese Basis." This declaration, published in January 1935 and reportedly based on a preliminary draft by Ch'en Li-fu, proclaimed the thesis that modernization in China would have to be accomplished through a selective syncretism of the best elements of Western and Chinese cultures.[16]

Few social scientists today would dispute this thesis. S. N. Eisenstadt, for example, contends that "however great in principle the contrast between a traditional and a modern society may be, successful modernization—the successful establishment of a viable modern society—may greatly benefit from some elements within the traditional setting from which modernity develops or which respond to the impact of modernity."[17] Even Mao Tse-tung has proclaimed the syncretic principle, urging the critical acceptance of "good things" from foreign countries, but rejecting "total westernization." In the end, Mao insisted, "Chinese culture should have its own form, its own national form."[18]

The "Declaration of Culture Construction" appears, therefore, to have been a reasonable formula for change in modern China. Its authors were, however, immediately subjected to the scorn and recriminations of the nation's more politically liberal intellectuals. The novelist Shen Ts'ung-wen, for example, declared that the Declaration's emphasis upon the past was utterly unrealistic, and that the proponents of this view either were ignorant or were using the policy to preserve their own rice bowls.[19] And Hu Shih claimed that the ten professors were actually hiding their conservative intentions "under the smoke-screen of compromise."[20]

Without doubt the members of the CC Clique did not share the political predilections of Shen Ts'ung-wen and Hu Shih. They were not democrats out of the Anglo-American mold. They defended the one-party rule of the Kuomintang, and supported the personal leadership of Chiang Kai-shek. But we ought not conclude that they were conservatives simply because they were authoritarian and anti-Leftist in their political views. Indeed, their stated purpose was less to conserve the cultural traditions of China than to create a new culture that would be neither traditionally Chinese nor Western.

Ch'en Li-fu himself unambiguously rejected the conservative label, declaring that the goal of commemorating Confucius was not "restoration of the past" (fu-ku) but "restoration of glory" (fu-hsing). Speaking in metaphor, he attempted to clarify his distinction between the two terms. Suppose, he said, that this lecture hall had been demolished. If we were to attempt to reconstruct the hall using the original plan and the same pieces of bricks and lumber that had made up the old structure, that would be "restoration of the past." But such an attempt would be foolish and even impossible, Ch'en stated, for the reconstructed hall would certainly not be as good as the original structure. If, by contrast, we were to throw away the old, broken building materials and supplement the old but still useful materials with new bricks and lumber; and if, in addition, we built it in accordance with a design for a new, more functional, and more beautiful building, then that would be "restoration of glory."[21]

Like the lecture hall described in the metaphor, said Ch'en, China's traditional culture had already been demolished, for it had suffered from two major shortcomings. First, China—which during the ancient period had discovered the source of a truly spiritual life—had since the Sung dynasty overemphasized the spiritual aspects of life. As a consequence, Chinese culture had evolved abnormally, failing to develop the powers of material creativity. This failure had led to the second cause of China's decline: because of China's material shortcomings, the Chinese people during the past sixty years had come to suffer a national inferiority complex.

To reconstruct the nation's culture, Ch'en Li-fu continued, China must make use of both the original and imported building materials:

If we wish to regenerate the nation, we must first restore the nation's self-confidence and promote material creativity . . . To restore national self-confidence, we must first examine China's ancient culture in order to realize the brilliance of the nation's past . . . To promote material creativity, we must absorb Western culture in order to realize the creative powers of natural science.[22]

According to Ch'en, therefore, Chinese culture and the morality of Confucianism were not ends in themselves, but were means with which to regenerate society and to facilitate the task of modernizing the nation. They were, as Ch'en also remarked—employing the technical jargon that he had acquired during his engineering studies—a "propellant force" in the modernization process, because the people, if made aware of the nation's past glories, would be motivated to strive for a national renaissance.[23]

The concept that the past could serve as an instrument of change was expressed also by Fang Chih, a leading member of the CC Clique. According to Fang, "The reason that our nation's thought is so confused, our determination so discordant, our actions so anarchic, and our minds so disordered is, at base, entirely because we lack the power of belief." An awareness of China's traditions, Fang argued, would provide the necessary "power of belief," and was therefore an essential ingredient in the struggle for survival. For, without a "central belief" to unite the people, they all sought their private benefit without regard for the welfare of society or for abstract principles such as Truth.[24]

Ch'en Li-fu and other members of the CC Clique seem to have been genuinely convinced that modernization could be a vital process only if rooted in Chinese traditions. This conviction differentiated them from the Blue Shirt leaders, and could perhaps be construed as an essentially conservative position. Their position did not, however, coincide with classical Western conservatism. It differed because, first, the CC Clique leaders expressed themselves as being deeply discontented with the current situation; second, they perceived that change forward, not backward, was both necessary and desirable; and, finally—and this point separated Ch'en Li-fu from Benjamin Disraeli just as the other points set him off from Edmund Burke—they valued social and ethical traditions not as ends in themselves, but as the means to create a modern state.

The CC Clique's emphasis upon traditional morality, and the way that it differentiated traditional Chinese culture from Western culture, led some observers to the conclusion that Ch'en Li-fu and his adherents had merely revived the distinction made by conservatives of the nineteenth century between *t'i* and *yung*. As Chang Chih-tung had invoked that concept, *t'i*, or the essence of Chinese culture, had at all costs to be preserved, whereas *yung*, or Western implements (technology and institutions), were merely tools to be employed to preserve the *t'i*.

In fact, however, the CC Clique's theorists claimed that they rejected completely Chang Chih-tung's formula of "Western learning as implements, Chinese learning for essence." They did not believe, as did Chang Chih-tung, that elements of a culture—even those of Confucianism—were isolatable, or that they could be preserved intact within a changed environment. Instead, these writers premised that the culture of China and of the West would inevitably be combined in a "dialectical" process. Thus, the cultures of China and the West would be melded into "a new Chinese culture" that would be neither traditional nor Western.[25]

Chiang Kai-shek and the New Life Movement

Chiang Kai-shek has been styled an "old-fashioned Confucian," and the New Life movement has been regarded as the hallmark of his conservatism. Neither generalization is true.

The New Life movement, inaugurated on February 19, 1934, was Chiang Kai-shek's fundamental answer to the question of how to "reconstruct and regenerate the nation."[26] China, thought Chiang, was weak and was despised by foreigners because the Chinese people lacked "virtue and knowledge." He had been profoundly impressed by the recent rise of Italy and Germany to the stature of major world powers. He observed, for example, how Germany, despite the terms of the Versailles peace settlement, had finally spurned the Allies' demand for payment of the war indemnity and had acquired military equality with the foreign powers. China, by contrast, albeit many times larger and with a greater army than Germany, had been unable even to discard the unequal treaties. The explanation, he reasoned, "was entirely because the knowledge and virtue of most of our citizens are not equal to that of other peoples . . . Therefore, we know that the regeneration of the nation and of the race does not depend on the size of the military force, but depends entirely on the eminence of the people's knowledge and virtue."[27]

In Chiang's thinking, the means by which to elevate the Chinese people's knowledge and virtue was to reform their attitude and behavior in the most mundane activities of daily life — in the way they ate, dressed, and housed themselves. The Chinese people, he thought, would do well simply to emulate the life-styles of the Westerners. "The foreigners," Chiang declared, "whether with regard to eating, dressing, living, walking, or in whatever aspect of behavior, always act in accordance with the requirements of a modern citizenry, revealing a spirit of love for the nation and loyalty to the race. In sum, everything is in accordance with *li-i-lien-ch'ih.*"[28]

These four vague virtues — *li-i-lien-ch'ih* (loosely translated as propriety, justice, integrity, and self-respect) — provided the ethical base of the New Life movement. It was a Confucian base, but it was a Confucianism that possessed no philosophical richness. It was rather a sloganized Confucianism, encapsulated for mass consumption in simple dicta regarding personal conduct and hygiene:

> Don't smoke or eat when walking!
> Keep to the left when walking!
> Look straight ahead!
> Don't recklessly throw away garbage!
> Don't go whoring or gambling!
> Keep your buttons buttoned!
> Sit up straight!
> Don't make noise when drinking!
> Don't quarrel or fight with others!
> Don't interrupt others when they are speaking!
> Be prompt![29]

Many of these rules made good sense in the Chinese context, and they have in fact frequently been echoed by the communists. What made the New Life movement appear ludicrous to some observers was that these rules were not incidental to Chiang's scheme of national reconstruction but lay at its very core. "If we are to have a new life that accords with *li-i-lien-ch'ih*," Chiang asserted, "then we must start by not spitting heedlessly." "If we are to restore the nation and gain revenge for our humiliations, then we need not talk about guns and cannon, but must first talk about washing our faces in cold water."[30]

Chiang's remarks may sound naive, but he reasoned that rigid adherence to such rules of behavior as promptness and neatness would result in a change in the inner person, and that if all the people could be thus transformed, then society and the nation would likewise be created anew.

Chiang found the models for his ideal society in the specifically militaristic aspects of Japan and Europe. He recalled his student days in a Japanese military academy, convinced that the moral fiber of the cadets had been strengthened by the rigorous observance of barracks discipline. "They did not speak about *li-i-lien-ch'ih*," Chiang said of the academy life, "but the spirit of all conduct, whether with regard to eating, clothing, housing, or walking, was in every respect in accordance with *li-i-lien-ch'ih.*"[31]

The fascism of Germany and Italy likewise provided Chiang with an image of the future society. "In fascism," he declared, "the organization, the spirit, and the activities must all be militarized . . . In the home, the factory, and the government office, everyone's activities must be the same as in the army . . . In other words, there must be obedience, sacrifice, strictness, cleanliness, accuracy, diligence, secrecy . . . And everyone together must firmly and bravely sacrifice for the group and for the nation."[32] This image of fascist society was incorporated essentially unchanged into the New Life movement. "What is the New Life movement that I now propose?" Chiang asked rhetorically. "Stated simply, it is to thoroughly militarize the lives of the citizens of the entire nation so that they can cultivate courage and swiftness, the endurance of suffering and a tolerance for hard work, and especially the habit and ability of unified action, so that they will at any time sacrifice for the nation."[33]

Soon—with the Blue Shirts serving as leading cadre[34]—the fascist principles of the New Life movement were being transformed into fact. In Wuhan, for example, the New Life movement reportedly "set in motion forces that would organize the man in the street and the literati each in a separate organization, but with fascist ideals as a foundation." "Mass meetings are frequently being held in the public parks of Wuchang and Hankow. School children of all ages parade through the streets and are taught to march in very orderly fashion. Sometimes a lantern parade is organized."[35] Also in accordance with the plans of the New Life movement, government officials, teachers, and students began wearing uniforms and receiving military training. A group of YMCA leaders concluded, correctly I think, that the New Life movement was "really a blue-shirt movement, looking forward to the regimentation of the country under a sort of Fascist regime."[36] And an American re-marked in 1935 that "a Fascist utopia has been let down from heaven upon the spot. It's all very neat and wonderful but gives me a slightly shaky feeling inside."[37]

Chiang Kai-shek's strategy of national development, particularly in its relation to traditional values, lay midway between the strate-gies advocated by the CC Clique and the Blue Shirts. Further research on the differences between the philosophic outlooks of Ch'en Li-fu and Chiang remains to be done. It may be sympto-matic, however, that Chiang laid special stress on *li,* or social propriety. *Li,* he contended, was the most important of the tradi-tional virtues, and was the basis of all morality. Significantly, too, *li,* was the virtue that (in Chiang's interpretation) contributed most specifically to social order, to organizational discipline, and to the loyalty of the people toward the state and the race.[38] Ch'en Li-fu, by contrast, placed primary emphasis on the virtue of *ch'eng* (sincerity or, as translated by Ch'en, "sophi-conscience"), which was first and foremost a virtue pertaining to personal moral cultivation.[39] *Ch'eng,* as discussed by Ch'en, would necessarily have social conse-quences. Nevertheless, the fact that Ch'en placed primary stress on an ego-regarding ethical concept (*ch'eng*) suggests that he may have been more committed to the existential verities of Confucianism than was Chiang—whose stress on a sociobehavioral virtue (*li*) implies a commitment to Confucianism because of its sociopolitical utility.

Although Chiang's strategy of national development emphasized social order and political control, he did not entirely agree with the Blue Shirts' brand of an amoral, fascist totalitarianism either. Like a true Confucian he professed to believe that the ultimate source of social order lay not in external political controls but in the moral cultivation of individuals. And nothing that has occurred since the 1930s gives one reason to doubt that his attachment to at least certain elements in Confucianism was anything but sincere.

Yet his Legalist-style use of force and terror seemed often to contradict his Confucian-inspired assumptions about behavioral psychology. And his political goal—a thoroughly regimented society in which each particle of the social mass would immediately respond to the wishes of the governmental leader—bore no resemblance to the society of the past. He aspired to extend political control farther into the fabric of the nation, and to subordinate the individual and all of society to the state to an extent that the Manchu rulers had not even thought possible. Chiang's ideal of the future Chinese state featured a government that would perform an active role in all aspects of society and that would weigh directly on all individuals in that society. This was not a conservative ideal. On the contrary, it was an ideal that differed profoundly from either the realities or the ideals of the past.

How the leadership elements in the Kuomintang interacted to produce policy is a problem that awaits study. It appears that the Blue Shirts and the CC Clique were frequently at odds with one another, with neither acquiring preponderant power in the regime. Chiang Kai-shek benefited from—indeed, he encouraged—these intraparty struggles. As a consequence, at least after 1932, he was the Kuomintang leader *non pareil*. "The shadow of Chiang Kai-shek extends over his whole scene," Clarence Gauss wrote in 1934. "Sitting at Peiping, I would have been unwilling to believe that he dominated the Government set-up here to the extent that is now so apparent. Where his interest touches, there you will find a certain governmental activity; elsewhere, if not paralysis, at least a policy of drift."[40] Chiang, in short, was the supreme arbiter of policy, and his strategy of national development presumably had more effect on policy than did the strategies of either the CC Clique or the Blue Shirts.

The Conservative Face of the Kuomintang

China, particularly in the cities, changed markedly during the decade of the Nanking government. Modern-style office buildings sprang up, and paved boulevards ran through what had been dense warrens of humanity. Electrical and water-supply systems were extended to many major areas, and sanitation in some cities noticeably improved. The growing presence of radios and rolled cigarettes, of movies and automobiles, of cabarets and foreign dress, testified to the impact of Western ways.

More significantly, the central government's political and economic control was reaching far across the country. The most troublesome of the regional warlords had by 1936 been replaced by more docile, though often sulky, provincial commanders. Railways were nearly doubled in length with the addition of 6,592 kilometers of new tracks, and the highway system grew from 28,000 to 82,000 kilometers during the decade.[41] And, for the first time in China's history, the currency of the nation was unified.

Despite these and other indicators of modernization, the Chiang regime did display a conservatizing tendency. Its conservatism was not, however, as Mary Wright suggested, a conscious, articulated conservatism. It was rather a conservatism that resulted from a lack of executive vision, from a purblindly traditional concept of political method, and from a persistent administrative inability to implement policies of change.

The Kuomintang leadership's lack of vision was most signally apparent in Chiang Kai-shek's incomprehension of the means of creating a modern state. Chiang was, in many respects, a man of preeminent qualities. He was dedicated to the nation, personally forceful, and a master of the art of political manipulation. But he had virtually no understanding of economics; he has in fact been called "an economic ignoramus."[42] He had little sense of the importance of institutions: he disliked delegating responsibility, and under his aegis institutions withered and initiative died.

Chiang also had an incredibly shallow understanding of human motivation and mass psychology. He believed that robbery, banditry, and the communist scourge resulted not because the masses were hungry and ill-clothed, but because they were infected with a "degenerate spirit." His primary solution to the poverty and disorder in the countryside lay, therefore, in teaching the people the virtues of frugality, diligence, and discipline, and not in promoting programs of land reform.[43] In some ways, his agrarian policies were even restorationist in character. In areas recaptured from the communists, for instance, the Nationalist authorities attempted to undo the effects of communist land redistribution by returning lands to the original owners.[44] Chiang also rejected force as a means of attaining the proclaimed goal of "equalization of land-holding." His plan was to encourage the formation of farmer cooperatives, which would purchase land whenever it was offered for sale. In this way, he thought, all farmland would gradually be owned cooperatively. More drastic solutions to the problem of land tenure, such as expropriation of the landlords, were, he asserted, "sheer robbery" that subverted the morality of the common peasants.[45]

To what extent Chiang Kai-shek was responsible for the shortcomings and conservatizing tendencies of Kuomintang policy remains a question for future research. There are indications that the secondary leadership of the regime also lacked adequate comprehension of the scope and nature of the problems that beset the nation. It has been shown, for example, that T. V. Soong and H. H. Kung were skilled financial technicians, but that they comprehended neither the problems nor the fiscal potential of the rural areas. As a consequence, the policies they supported during their respective tenures as minister of finance had, as Y. C. Wang contends, "adverse effects on Chinese economic development."[46] And Franklin Ho, who joined the Nanking government in 1936, has remarked that "One can only be surprised to know just how unaware people at the top were of what was going on, how little they knew of the actual conditions in the country, and how they were even less aware of the theoretical basis of those conditions and what had to be done."[47]

No less an obstacle to change than the leadership's myopic perception of the means of modernizing was the patrimonial concept of political leadership. Political power was narrowly concentrated at the very top levels of the regime. Not only were the masses and the non-Kuomintang elites of the nation excluded from a political role; even within the party itself the vast majority of members were reduced to passive subservience. By the end of the Nanking decade, therefore, as much as 90 percent of the party's nominal two million members had ceased to be active.[48] And the regime had failed utterly—despite its ideological commitments—to institute constitutional rule, to convene a National Assembly, or to breathe life into the district level assemblies.

In other ways, the Kuomintang leadership sought to create a monopoly of political power. Rival parties or factions were outlawed. And the execution of Teng Yen-ta (head of the Third Party), the assassination of Yang Ch'üan (secretary of the Chinese League for the Protection of Civil Rights), and the incarceration without trial of the "Seven Gentlemen" (*ch'i chün-tzu*—leaders of the National Salvation Movement) bespeak the awful vengeance with which the regime suppressed those who tried to challenge it. Using similar methods, the regime worked to purge newspapers, periodicals, and books of dangerous thoughts, and to cow the intellectual community into submission.

Authoritarianism, of course, is not the same as conservatism, and the dictatorial aspirations of the Kuomintang were not inherently antagonistic to change. The authoritarian regimes of Ataturk, Hilter, Stalin, and Mao wrought farreaching changes in their respective nations. In Kuomintang China, however, authoritarianism imparted a weak stimulus to change. For, as noted above, the dominant leadership poorly understood how to cope with the problems of national development. And the patrimonial character of the leadership tended to prevent the infusion of fresh and progressive ideas. Thus, not only did the leadership obstruct the masses' desires for change; soon even the slightly innovative impulses of T.V. Soong and Sun Fo ceased to affect the policy decisions of the top leadership.

This is not to contend that the Kuomintang leadership made no attempts to effect change. In agrarian policy, for example, the regime lent support to land reclamation and water control projects

of the National Economic Council. But the chief of the League of
Nations' advisers, Ludwig Rajchman, bitterly complained that the
effectiveness of the council was undercut by the regime's penchant
for dominating and interfering with the reconstruction projects.[49]
The government also promoted the rapidly growing rural cooperative movement — but it permitted the local "gentry" rather than the
poorer elements of rural society to govern and profit from the
cooperative associations.[50] Indeed, the Kuomintang leadership had
been badly frightened by the peasant movement during the
Northern Expedition, and it therefore opposed any social and
economic innovations in the villages that might encourage the lower
classes to revolt against the political status quo. As even an apologist
for the government admitted in 1936, the Nanking regime had done
little to benefit the peasants, because it "preferred to follow a slow
and gradual policy that would *avoid too great a disturbance* in the
country."[51] This statement epitomizes the leadership's determination to allow no change that it did not itself control.

Finally, we turn to the governmental administration as a conser-
ver of the status quo. Nanking's bureaucrats were, in fact, prodigal
in producing plans and regulations. The Legislative Yuan churned
out new land laws, labor laws, marriage laws, and constitutional
drafts that — if implemented — would have revolutionized the
political, judicial, and social life of the nation. And governmental
ministries drafted multifarious schemes of development that envisioned swift modernization of the national economy.[52]

The striking fact was, however, that few of these laws and plans
were related to the actual problems of the nation or to the capabili-
ties of the government. T. V. Soong, after witnessing the prolifera-
tion of rarified and impractical plans, remarked patronizingly that
"we have seen each department of the government proposing its own
pet projects, all of them involving huge expenditures. Doubtless
many of these projects are in themselves sound but they must be
unrealizable because of the known lack of funds, and the fact that
they are not coordinated with the projects of other departments."[53]

If few of the bureaucratic schemes of development were realistic
or practicable, even fewer were actually put into effect. For the
Nationalist administration was clogged with paperwork, and the

bureaucrats themselves were committed less to the attainment of policy goals than to the operation of the bureaucratic machinery. Chiang Kai-shek complained in 1932 that "In China, when something arrives at a government office, it is *yamenized*—all reform projects are handled lackadaisically, negligently, and inefficiently."[54] Later he scolded the bureaucrats for their refusal to *shih-kan*—that is, to act so that there are real results. "Our work," he declared, "consists almost solely of the passing back and forth of documents. Stated simply, the documents sound good, but they are written negligently without regard for the true facts of the situation. With regard to practical work, Chinese either do not know how, or—if they know—they are slow in the extreme. It is not simply a matter of not completing today's work, but of putting off this week's work until next week, and indeed often putting off this month's public affairs until next month, and even of not doing this year's work until next year. The amassing and delaying of documents in this way can ruin everything, causing deadly suffering for the common people."[55]

These characteristics of bureaucracy were not peculiar to China. In Kuomintang China, however, they were extraordinarily pronounced. Explanations of the administrative ineffectiveness of the Nationalist bureaucracy are too complex to be examined here, but that it contributed to the absence of dynamic change in the 1930s is clear.[56]

Conservatism—in the sense of a conscious desire to maintain the status quo—was rare during the Nanking period. However great their material stake in the established order, few could remain undisturbed by the conditions of instability, decay, and humiliation that afflicted the Chinese nation. In fact, any educated Chinese living in the 1930s had to choose between reactionary nostalgia for a lost order, and commitment to some model of reform or revolution. Clinton Rossiter has perceptively commented on the dilemma of persons of conservative temperament in countries such as China that are in the process of rapid modernization. "Genuine conservatism as a political force," Rossiter contended, "can hardly be said to exist, and persons who might make excellent conservatives in more ordered societies must choose between the nihilism of 'standing pat,' the frustration of trying to recreate a dead past . . . , or the cryptoradicalism of riding the tiger of revolution."[57]

The dominant leaders of the Kuomintang — as exemplified in this essay by Chiang Kai-shek, the CC Clique, and the Blue Shirts — viewed their task not as the perpetuation of the established order, nor even as the restoration *for their own sake* of traditional values. Rather, they sought to create a new and modern order. Yet they could not attain this goal because, first, they possessed no adequate comprehension of the means of creating a modern state; and, second, they lacked the cadre that could effectively implement whatever reform programs they did conceive. Their goals, in other words, were modern; yet their methods tended to be traditional. This is why the Kuomintang was conservative only in a limited sense, and why the Nanking decade appears in historical perspective to be so starkly transitional. Whether the forces working for the modernization of the Chinese state would in the long term have preponderated over the conservatizing forces is a question that must remain forever unanswered, because the war with Japan prevented the drama from being played to the end.

IV THE NEW CONFUCIANISM OF THE POST MAY FOURTH ERA

9   The Conservative as Sage: Liang Shu-ming

GUY ALITTO

> The integrity crisis [of a *homo religiosus*] is a life long chronic crisis
> . . . [Such a person] focuses in a precocious way on what it takes
> others a lifetime to gain a mere inkling of: the question of how to
> escape corruption in living and how in death to give meaning to
> life. (Erik Erikson, *Young Man Luther*, p. 261)

Most Republican-period intellectuals, conservative or not, were concerned primarily with China's profound cultural crisis.[1] A few, however, oriented themselves to universally human questions rather than to their own specific historical situation. Such "choice spirits" concerned themselves more with the perennial problem of the meaning of human existence than with the immediate problems of their environment.[2]

One of these temperamentally transcendental personalities, Liang Shu-ming, emerged from a period of personal crisis and contemplation with a messianic sense of identity as a man with a message of universal significance. He projected his own encounter with meaninglessness onto China's cultural dilemma, joining his conception of universally human concerns with the immediate concerns of the particular Chinese situation.

Such an experience in the West is usually subsumed under the rubric of "religious experience." Prophets and saints, however, are sages and worthies in China. Chinese sagehood of all varieties (Confucian, Buddhist, Taoist) involves a merging of the transcendent external with the particular temporal. The sage rises to the sublimity of the universal transhistorial *tao* and then returns to the common world to teach how the ultimate reality relates to the mundane problems of men and women. He succeeds in synthesizing in himself the contradictions inherent in the human condition, and so joins the sublime and the common, the universally human with his particular historical situation. Perhaps only in the Chinese concept of sagehood does Liang Shu-ming's complex life, which weaves around and through almost all major events in twentieth-century China, emerge as a congruous whole.

His compatriots have assessed him in other ways. To most of his iconoclastic comtemporaries of the May Fourth generation like Hu Shih or Wu Chih-hui, he was a muddleheaded defender of Chinese spirit against Western matter — a sort of Chinese Tagore.[3] Some of his foreign-trained confreres in the Chinese rural reconstruction movement of the 1930s patronizingly considered him dedicated but "unscientific."[4] Some of his Marxist contemporaries saw him and his programs as the agrarian feudal clan society's ideological Parthian shot at the inexorably advancing bourgeois industrialization.[5] Under the communist regime he has been characterized as the subjective idealist who tried to anesthetize the revolutionary masses with feudal morality, wanted to keep China weak by opposing industrialization, and worked hand in glove with Western imperialism.[6] In Taiwan he is both quoted in textbooks and condemned as a fellow traveler.[7]

There is some agreement on him, however. The hundreds of Chinese interpretations and opinions on Liang which I have seen or heard have almost invariably singled out two qualities for special note. Even his bitterest critics feel compelled to praise his personal character, moral rectitude, and selflessness.[8] Ubiquitous too are words like "old-fashioned," "traditional," and, of course, "conservative." The reasons given for the latter designation vary from Liang's opposition to violent revolution to his insistence on wearing a long scholar's gown even in the sweltering heat. Obviously, what makes Liang (or anyone for that matter) "conservative" depends upon the sphere of activity analyzed — political, social, or moral — and on what is conceived of as nonconservative in these spheres. In the case of Republican China, we find extremely varied nonconservative phenomena going on simultaneously in all spheres within a short period, which makes identification of what is conservative particularly problematic.

Liang Shu-ming and Chinese Cultural Conservatives

If we narrow our focus to the still quite general category of cultural conservatism, Liang's thought and action seem *prima facie* just another expression of Chang Chih-tung's familiar *t'i-yung* dichotomy — "Chinese learning for fundamental principles; Western learning for practical application." This theoretical distinction between principles and practical application provided cautious Chinese reformers with a convenient formula for conservative modernization in the last years under the monarchy. They could uphold their commitment to China's cultural essence (*t'i*) and still in good conscience copy Western factories and firearms in order to achieve national wealth and power. Early references to the nature of the Chinese essence were vague, usually mentioning some fundamental principle of Chinese moral philosophy and social usage. When in the last years of his life, Chang Chih-tung felt compelled by events to take more concrete measures to preserve the *t'i*, he moved to promote the study of traditional literature — indicating that whatever he considered the ultimate nature of the *t'i*, it was somehow inseparable from classical and historical scholarship.

At the same time, some of the anti-Manchu revolutionaries — Chang Chih-tung's political and ideological opposites — began using the same basic concept, "national essence," for their own purposes. They adopted the Japanese neologism *kokusui* (*kuo-ts'ui*) instead of the word *t'i*, but even Chang Chih-tung himself used *kuo-ts'ui* on occasion to refer to the general concept of Chinese essence. The *kuo-ts'ui* coterie, led by such figures as Chang T'ai-yen, Liu Shih-p'ei, and Huang Chieh, persisted until the May Fourth era, when Wu Mi and Mei Kuang-ti of the *Critical Review* group took on the mantle. In the hands of the *Critical Review* people, Chinese essence became just another classical "cradle" culture — equal to, but not necessarily superior to Western classical culture. The genealogy of the national essence idea may be extended forward in time

to the more instrumental and politicized Kuomintang neotraditionalism of Tai Chi-t'ao and Ch'en Li-fu in the 1930s, and even on to
the recent Cultural Renaissance movement in Taiwan.

In all of its various reincarnations, the National Essence school
was devoted to the preservation of Chinese spirit, which adherents
believed was embedded in the literary heritage. Thus, their specific
activity on behalf of national essence concentrated on classical and
textual scholarship, history, and belles lettres, and they often drew
parallels between their own endeavors and the revival of Western
classical studies during the European Renaissance. Like Chang
Chih-tung, they welcomed Western social, political, and economic
forms as means for protecting China's national essence. Liang Shu-
ming, too, was dedicated to the preservation of the Chinese cultural
essence (or, more precisely, Confucian ethical values) while
accepting, albeit with substantial qualifications, Western political
forms and technology. He too sought to create an authentically
Chinese cultural renaissance.

In the pre-May Fourth phase of this general thought current, the
ancient antagonism between the Old and New text schools of historical interpretation again flared up—this time over the issue of the
establishment of Confucianism as a religion. K'ang Yu-wei, the last
great exponent of the New Text school, felt that the Chinese soul
would be best safeguarded through the institutionalization of
Confucianism as a formal state religion, a position perfectly consistent with the New Text school's attitude toward Confucius. The Old
Text school opposed the idea of a Confucian religion and maintained that the principal function of scholarship was transmission of
the transcendental *tao*—the absolute set of values valid for all
people and for all times—which was discovered by the ancients and
transmitted through time by sages and worthies. Liang Shu-ming
relates most specifically to this tradition of *tao-t'ung* (transmission
of the truth). He had "no respect" for K'ang Yu-wei and the Confucian church made him "nauseous."[9] Possessed of a sage identity,
Liang felt that in the present age he and he alone had fully comprehended the *tao*, and so was under the awful imperative of transmitting it: "The former worthies had a phrase, 'to carry on for the
past sages their learning which has become extinct, and to open an

age of universal peace for all ages.' This is the mission of my whole life."[10]

Yet there are fundamental dissimilarities between Liang and others identified with the National Essence persuasion. In the first place, Liang was not a member of any scholarly clique, and his knowledge of China's traditional canons, commentaries, and chronicles was infinitely inferior to that of a dazzling scholar like Chang T'ai-yen.

In direct contrast to the central thrust of post-May Fourth cultural conservatism, Liang attached little importance to the literary heritage and textual scholarship. He dismissed academic rummagings through traditional literature as misdirected energy and regarded fiction, belles lettres, and poetry as a lamentable waste of time. He was, if anything, a proponent of the written vernacular.[11] He wrote almost all of his own dozen books and hundred-odd articles in *pai-hua*. Finally, Liang explicitly rejected the National Essence group's efforts at cultural persistence, describing it as "nothing more than simply piling up obsolete curios" and "lifeless rotten goods."[12]

The dilemmas we face in identifying the conservatism of Liang Shu-ming exemplify the broader problem of conservatism in the Republican period. Liang is a tangle of complexity and contradiction. He was a scholar of Buddhism who denounced the twentieth-century Chinese Buddhist revival as the baneful work of "selfish bookworms playing on psychological weakness to gain influence."[13] He was a lifelong antimilitarist who was friend and adviser to four warlords. He was a reactionary who classed Chiang Kai-shek with Yuan Shih-k'ai and Mao Tse-tung with himself, who thought that the Kuomintang was conservative and that the communists were meeting the real needs of China. What kind of conservative could have been close to Li Ta-chao, Mao Tse-tung and Chou En-lai but have only a nodding acquaintance with the Kuomintang neotraditionalist ideologue Ch'en Li-fu?[14]

A Worldwide Conservative Response?

Perhaps we can see Liang's real significance as an instance in a worldwide response to a common universal nonconservative, nontraditional phenomenon—modernization. For purposes of this discussion, we shall generally use the term in the sense of Weber's "rationalization" (*Zwecksrationalität*). The main thrust of this ongoing critique of modernization has been an emphasis upon the limits of pure rationalism is solving all problems of the human condition. It might be called a tradition of awareness of certain flies in the cure-all ointment of modernization, or an uneasiness about the brave new world of unlimited technological salvation. The reaction has transcended conventional political categories and has included both pessimistic conservatives and optimistic revolutionaries. Because they share a common opponent, certain types of conservatives resemble Marxist social critics. As Mannheim points out, both the Marxist and Vitalist concepts of reality originate in a common romantic opposition to pure rationalism.[15] This elusive antimodern sensibility has never been satisfactorily defined, although some historians have tried to describe its manifestations with such terms as romanticism, irrationalism, cultural conservatism, critique of modernity, and even literary modernism. When the smoke has cleared from the West's most recent expressions of the modernization critique, savants might add a few more terms.

No definition is ever likely to be definitive. Personal circumstances, the positive content of each premodern tradition, and the specific historical situation shape each conservative's total response. Yet I would suggest that there are certain common themes, regardless of historical circumstances or individual concerns. Conservatives all seem to take, and then idealize, a traditional form of society as the touchstone for social excellence. They share a common enemy in political and economic liberalism (although their own political stances may be classified as liberal) and a common antipathy toward individual material self-interest. They are suspicious or outrightly hostile toward the results of industrialization, especially modern urban life. Such a posture emphasizes society over the individual and organic group relationships over artificial legal relationships and individual rights. In addition to their stress on organic physical community, these conservatives seek, or long for, common values and a common truth. Most important, they highly value the nonrational, nonutilitarian aspects of human existence.

A second related yet distinct element in this conservative response to modernization may be discerned in those areas which are outside the Western European cradle of modernization. When such cultural units were confronted with modernization they conceived of it as foreign, and thus productive of that tension between "history" and "value" which Joseph Levenson has identified. Accordingly, formulations similar to the Chinese *t'i-yung* dichotomy, or the later "spiritual" versus "material" distinction, appeared in other traditional societies such as India, Japan, and the Muslim world. These areas were directly menaced by the West's superior military and economic power and so were compelled in self-defense to borrow culturally from their aggressors. The making of a distinction between unique native "spirit" and useful foreign "matter" might be interpreted as an emotional response resulting from feelings of inferiority.

In the non-Western societies undergoing these transformations, culture came to be understood in an important new way. Indeed, within the heartland of bourgeois utilitarian society itself, the idea of culture also appears and performs a function quite similar in some respects to its role in the more traditional societies. As Raymond Williams says in his classic study of the English term:

Culture emerges as an abstraction and an absolute; an emergence which, in a very complex way, merges two responses — first, the recognition of the practical separation of certain moral and intellectual activities from the driven impetus of a new kind of society; second, the emphasis on these activities as a court of human appeal, to be set over the processes of practical social judgment and yet to offer itself as a mitigating and rallying alternative.[16]

Of course, the English did not conceive of the modernizing process as coming from the outside. It evoked no crisis of identity or feeling of inadequacy. But Germany around 1800 was decidedly backward, economically and politically, in relation to the well-established nation-states of England and France. And it was the Germans who most systematically developed a concept of culture which focuses on people's interior feelings in opposition to the social and economic rationalizations which were changing Europe's exterior.

The distinction between interior and exterior is often expressed as a distinction between culture and civilization.[17] The first, culture, is qualitative, organic, normative, emotional, subjective, and particularistic (and includes custom, religion, and art), while the second, civilization, is quantitative, mechanistic, intellectual, accumulative, and universal (and so includes science and technology). The idea of a spirit-matter or spirit-nature dichotomy which so thoroughly permeates post-*Aufklärung* German thought is comparable to the dichotomies constructed by conservative romantics and idealists in the non-West. The Russian Slavophiles, sometimes borrowing directly from the German Romantics' fund of ideas, devised similar dichotomies—Russian *sobornost* and spirituality versus Western legalism and rationalism. We could also view the culturally regenerative reform movements of the late nineteenth-century Muslim brotherhoods, such as the Sanusiya, in the same way. In India, China, and Japan, formulas such as harmony with nature versus control of nature, and intuition versus intellect, were commonplace.

In all of these formulations there are explicit or implicit claims both to the superiority of indigenous spiritual culture as well as for the progress made possible by a selective borrowing from the Western material culture. The result of such a combination of the best from East and West would provide the "backward" people with the nature-mastering equipment of the West, and also enable them to retain their higher spirituality (*Kultur, âme slave*, and so forth). Thus a distinguishing element in the response of backward areas is the crisis of collective identity. The cliché "Chinese (or Indian, Japanese, or other) spirit with Western technology" in all its myriad forms arose from a fear of spiritual and cultural deracination and frequently culminated in the fundamentally modern emotional and intellectual response of nationalism. For example, German romanticism was inextricable from German nationaliam and Pan-Germanism; Pan-Slavism incorporated Slavophile ideas; and the Pan-Islam movement absorbs the spiritual-cultural revival of the Muslim brotherhoods. The ideas of Pan-Asianists became the underpinnings of Japanese imperialism, and even such a man as Gandhi became a nationalist leader. In China, the ideas of the National Essence group became part of the Kuomintang's neotraditional nationalism. In all of these cases culture came to be seen as a unique, nonrepetitive essence, national in origin and significance, and set apart from the sociopolitical realities of modernization. Cultural renaissance based on the pristine national or people's spirit often became a central concern of intellectuals associated with these movements, creating great interest in linguistic, historical, literary, and folk studies.

The Education of a Conservative

In order to see just how the "instance" of Liang Shu-ming relates to this vaguely identified conservative response, we must first look to his particular historical situation and his own personal experience. The declining patrician family, a familiar theme in modern Western literature and in the lives of many of its writers, often produces children of marked sensitivity or spirituality. Both Lu Hsun, Republican China's greatest literary artist and most trenchant critic of traditional society, and Liang Shu-ming, its saintlike champion of traditional society, seem to provide examples of a relationship between declining family fortunes and spiritual sensitivity. Liang Shu-ming's father, sometime metropolitan official, Liang Chi,[18] was the last of seven centuries of Liang family scholar-bureaucrats. Yet he knew shabby gentility in his youth and the pawnshop in his maturity. A man in the statecraft (*ching shih*) tradition of the nineteenth century, Liang Chi was pragmatic, had little regard for China's literary culture, and made the crucial transition from culturalism to nationalism earlier than most of his contemporaries.[19]

Shu-ming's childhood and early education reflected his father's cultural iconoclasm. Liang Chi consciously cultivated a friendly, spontaneous relationship with his children, urging them to talk freely with him of their problems and opinions, and to develop a spirit of independence. Liang Chi was similarly progressive in the formal schooling he gave Shu-ming. While other children began their education chanting the Four Books, young Liang studied a primer of world history and geography. In 1899, when Peking's first Western-style primary school opened, Liang Chi enrolled his son.[20] Liang Shu-ming also attended a modern-style middle school, so he never seriously studied the Confucian classics until adulthood. It is significant that traditionalist Liang Shu-ming's early training was far less traditional than that of any of his future progressive antagonists.

Liang's youthful concerns reflected the nationalistic awakening in the decade preceding the revolution. He sought to save the nation through nationalistic reforms and political activism. He was, like his father, a disciple of Liang Ch'i-ch'ao, and saw the key to wealth and power in English-style parliamentary government, rule by law, and gradual reform. Liang's adolescent philosophy of life was classic Benthamesque utilitarianism. (He himself describes it variously as utilitarianism, pragmatism, instrumentalism, and hedonism). Human activity of whatever kind had no inherent value, he felt, but could be judged only by how far it contributed to "the greatest good of the greatest number." Virtue and morality had merit only insofar as they made the individual a more effective instrument in achieving his or her ends. In the best, or worst, utilitarian tradition, he considered art and philosophy as self-deceiving nonsense. Toward the end of middle school, Liang gradually awoke to the difficulties in his position and began to wonder: if the sole criterion of good was hedonistic calculus, what actually constituted pleasure and pain. These meditations led him to Buddhist studies and to the conclusion that desire is the source of pain.[21]

The 1911 revolution marks the political parting of ways between Liang and his father. Liang Chi viewed the 1910 opening of the Provisional National Assembly with a jaundiced eye, convinced that moral decadence in government and society, and the representatives' lack of talent would prevent the assembly from accomplishing anything.[22] He considered moral reform more critical than piecemeal political reform and so busied himself with proposals for mass education and mass moralizing[23] while his son skipped school to attend all the assembly sessions.[24] By October 1911, Liang Shu-ming had concluded that revolutionary methods had more utility than gradualist constitutionalism, thus climaxing the rift with his father. He joined the Peking-Tientsin T'ung-meng-hui in direct opposition to the wishes of his father,[25] who counseled him: "the establishment of a constitution is sufficient to save the country. Why must [you insist] on revolution? Wait for the Mandate of Heaven. Don't follow [the revolutionaries]."[26] But Shu-ming could not wait. He set about to hasten the mandate on with bombs and bullets.[27] When the Manchu abdication was announced on February 12, 1912, Shu-ming was mingling with the joyful crowds in the streets of Peking, while his father remained at home muttering, "So it has really come to this! A fine affair indeed!"[28] Shortly thereafter Liang Chi made a vow before the gods and their ancestors to defend the principles of Chinese culture to the death.[29]

It is precisely at this juncture — his revolution triumphant and his father bitter but still refusing to interfere — that Liang Shu-ming suffered a cataclysmic depression and attempted suicide. In another year he attempted suicide again and finally retired to his father's home in early 1913 to "escape the world" through Buddhist meditation "behind closed doors." This late adolescent psychosocial moratorium lasted until late 1915, when he gradually started writing on Buddhism.[30] In the summer of 1916, he took a position as personal secretary to a relative who was the minister of justice.[31]

The nature and resolution of this spiritual crisis is the key to Liang Shu-ming's subsequent conservative ideology and programs. On later occasions throughout his life, Liang wrote of this period of "madness" and near suicide, and his explanations for it were numerous.[32] Sometimes he described himself as acting upon his earlier Schopenhauerian conclusions about pleasure and pain and retiring to negate his painful will by means of a calm ascetic life. Elsewhere he ascribes his collapse to disappointment with the failure of revolution to achieve its aims, or to his disgust with the corruption of republican politics, or to disgust with himself.

In the terms of Western clinical psychology, Liang undoubtedly suffered a psychosis, and he continued to bear the psychological stigmata through life. The crushing guilt which he felt toward his father was certainly related to his illness, and his gradual recovery during the years 1915 to 1918 from the complete psychotic withdrawal of 1913-1914 was marked by an increasing interest in his father's areas of concern — Chinese culture and Confucianism.[33]

On a wintry blue dawn in 1918, Liang Chi fulfilled his vow of seven years before and drowned himself in the icy waters of the lake

Chi Shui in Peking. It was after this that Liang Shu-ming devoted his life to fulfilling his father's will—perpetuation of the absolute moral values embedded in Chinese tradition which were being destroyed by Western influence.[34]

We may also view Liang's experience as a protracted late adolescent crisis of identity (integration). As Erik Erikson has observed:

The youthful crisis of identity and the mature one of integrity makes the religionist's problem of individual identity the same as the problem of existential identity . . . This concentration in the cataclysm of the adolescent identity crisis of both first and last crises in the human life may well explain why religiously and artistically creative men often seem to be suffering from a barely compensated psychosis, and yet later prove superhumanly gifted in conveying a total meaning for man's life . . . The chosen young man extends the problem of his identity to the borders of existence in the known universe . . . He acts as if mankind were starting all over with his own beginning as an individual, conscious of his singularity as well as his humanity.[35]

Immediately upon emerging from his period of transcendental meditation, Liang identified his own "return to the world" with that of a bodhisattva from Nirvana.[36] This "delusion of sagehood" was the basis of Liang's personality integration, which withstood failure after failure in the external world. When circumstances were bleakest, he could still state: "I cannot die now, for if I do, heaven and earth will change color and history will change its course . . . Not only would China perish, but the world itself would perhaps be on the edge of extinction."[37]

Liang also saw his crisis as a reflection of the "modern condition," the devaluation of all value by critical rationalism, the disintegration of traditional beliefs and absolute standards into relativism, which results in tension between intellect and emotion.[38] He seemed particularly disturbed that the scientific view of humanity turned persons into biological mechanisms indistinguishable from lower forms of life. The critics who labeled Liang a "spiritualist" or "religionist" were not mistaken, for his commitment to his Confucianism as the one enduring truth unassailable by critical rationalism, as an irreducible absolute which could survive in the modern world, is certainly what the existentialist theologian would term "a leap of faith."

Chinese and Western Cultures: Theory

The year 1921 was a critical one for Liang Shu-ming. He published his first book, became a national figure, publicly abandoned Buddhism for Confucianism, and first met the man who eventually led him to rural reconstruction.[39] His philosophy of life, history, and culture and his theoretical solution to China's cultural crisis were all first systematically presented in the book *Tung Hsi wen-hua chi ch'i che-hsueh* (Eastern and Western cultures and their philosophies). Although he would later alter the terminology and points of emphasis, his essential analysis and conclusions would not change through the many years and books to follow.

The book gained Liang his national reputation as a conservative and he was accordingly attacked by both liberal and socialist wings of the New Culture movement. The New Culturists did not seem to consider Liang as important a danger to progress as "metaphysicians" like Chang Chün-mai, who were involved in the 1923 debate on "philosophy of life"; yet Liang's book galloped through seven editions in four years, and attracted an audience far out of proportion to the attention it received from the intellectual establishment. That Liang's theories had such a powerful appeal in 1921 suggests the limits of the New Culture movement's impact outside the scholarly circles in the large coastal cities. But the real nature and sentiments of this large, undefined, and generally more conservative sector of society, which responded to Liang's book, are difficult to study for China's middle-brow masses leave almost as little written record as the peasant masses. Liang's book seems to have resonated the structure of sentiments in the literate silent majority. Unlike those of his contemporaries who lived and worked primarily in Peking or Shanghai, Liang was at his best in the provinces, and these were the places where he was in greatest demand as a lecturer. Even his disciples were less cosmopolitan, less articulate types who attached themselves to Liang as their spokesman. That nearly thirty-five years later the communist regime devoted almost as much time and energy criticizing Liang as they spent on a Western-educated liberal like Hu Shih gives a further indication both of the appeal of Liang Shu-ming's ideas and of their durability.

Liang's 1921 book is usually categorized as a part of the westernized conservative response to the antitraditionalist New Culture movement, with Liang Ch'i-ch'ao (*Reflections on a European Journey,* 1919) and Chang Chün-mai ("Philosophy of Life," 1923) as Liang Shu-ming's partners in obscurantist reaction. *Eastern and Western Cultures* does share with these other works an impulse to preserve ethics itself from the determinism regarded as implicit in positivism, and an effort to find, under the encrustations of tradition, the core significance of Chinese culture.

How Liang identified the essence of Chinese culture as an absolute value is a complicated process. In his *Eastern and Western Cultures,* his starting point was a concept of a monist universe in eternal flux, which he identified as common to the thought of Schopenhauer, Nietzsche, Bergson, and Wei-shih Buddhism. The life process is a continuous sequence of problems presented to individual expressions of a Schopenhauerian Will.[40] It has no inherent meaning, and at the outset human beings are just another expression of the Will, no different from animals or plants. Culture is the means by which humanity resolves the contradictions between the Will's demands and the obstacles presented by environment. Liang posited three cultural ideal types, which are expressions of three distinct directions the Will may take, and which should succeed each other in a historical continuum. These phases are portrayed by Western, Chinese, and Indian cultures.

In the first phase, represented by the West, basic problems of physical survival are not yet solved. The Will goes forward to conquer the environment and satisfy primal desires. In the second phase, represented by China, the Will moves sideways to adjust and harmonize itself with the environment, thus gaining inner contentment, and *joie de vivre.* In the third phase, represented by India, the Will turns backwards onto itself seeking self-negation. By way of illustration, Liang imagined that the archtypical Westerner would resolve the contradiction between the Will's demand for shelter and the obstacle of a dilapidated house by completely demolishing the house and building a brand new one. The Chinese would repair the old house, and the Indian would attempt to extinguish the desire for housing.

Each of the directions is an equally valid preoccupation of humanity at the appropriate stage of its evolution: "The present victory of Western culture lies only in its being appropriate for the immediate problems of humanity, while the reason for the present defeat of Indian and Chinese culture lies not in any inherent goodness or badness which can be spoken of. It lies in nothing more than the fact that they are unsuited to the times."[41]

Yet this relativistic metahistoricism did not prevent Liang from finding an absolute value in life itself interpreted in Vitalist terms as pure dynamism. Mannheim has traced the German conservative romantic origins of Vitalism and "philosophy of life" and has shown it to have been a defense of absolute value against pure critical rationalism. Liang's Vitalist interpretation of Confucianism derived from the Wang Yang-ming school and suffused with Bergsonian images and terms performed the same function. We might summarize his theory as follows:[42] If the universe is a ceaseless flux of life, and the only reality is pure change, then to comprehend change is to comprehend the essence of life. According to Liang's interpretation, Confucius had grasped the nature of pure change (and so of life) from the *I ching* (Book of Changes), which like the metaphysics of Wei-shih Buddhism describes the universe as life in ceaseless flux. From this flow of life one underlying universal principle emerges: harmonization of all elements of existence. For Liang this basic concept provided the connecting thread in all of Confucius' thought. Expressed as a philosophy of life, it is *jen* (benevolence), the ultimate expression and essence of Confucianism. Like Bergson, Confucius saw intuition as the human finger on the pulse of the ever-changing cosmos and intuitive feeling as the infallible guide to a life of harmony with nature. Through the Buddhism and Bergsonianism we can make out the outline of the venerable old concept of the *tao,* the Way of the Universe, which has been intuitively grasped by the sages and transmitted to the sage of the modern age, Liang Shu-ming.

In the late 1920s Liang gradually discarded Buddhist metaphysics, Bergsonian Vitalism, and the whole metahistorical

continuum, and fashioned a new theory around the term
li-hsing[43] — a word certainly not translatable by the usual English
equivalent "reason," except perhaps as Coleridge distinguished it
from "rationality." In this new theory, *li-hsing* functions much like
other vague terms which served as cornerstones in the thought of
Liang's spiritual brothers: Matthew Arnold's "culture," Cardinal
Neuman's "illative sense," or Gandhi's "truth." Liang described
li-hsing as "the normative sense which directs moral action . . . the
sense of right and wrong which makes man human." People are not
animals precisely because they can achieve this "sphere of disinterestedness" or "impersonal feeling" which transcends biological
instinct or self-interest.[44] While *li-hsing* is "actually the distinguishing characteristic of humanity, it is also at the same time the special
feature of Chinese culture."[45]

Liang admits that possession of intellect, too, marks human from
beast, and intellect is indeed a prerequisite of *li-hsing*. But, while
"the two are intimately and inseparably connected" they are distinct. "For example, in the calculation of figures, the mind which
does the calculating is intellect, while the mind which seeks
accuracy [in calculating] is *li-hsing*."[46] Significantly, at times Liang
explains *li-hsing's* relationship to intellect with a *t'i-yung* formula:
"*Li-hsing* is life itself, it is essence (*t'i*); intellect is a tool for [main-
tenance of] life, it is ultility (*yung*)."[47]

Thus we see that in both of his schematizations of the history of
culture, Liang implied that because of the great insight of her early
sages, Chinese culture made a premature leap, as it were, in the
evolutionary process, and achieved human ethical perfection while
bypassing the basic task of mastering the physical environment
through intellectual calculation. It is as if the "literary intellectuals"
whom C.P. Snow decries appeared in China some 3,000 years ago,
and before their people had developed the capacity to completely
satisfy their primal needs, turned the direction of their whole
culture toward, in Coleridge's famous phrase, "the harmonious
development of those qualities and faculties that characterize our
humanity." The Chinese had discovered the generic essence of
humankind prematurely, and while evolving a more human existence than the West, suffered materially because of it. Although he

never says so directly, Liang infers that non-Chinese, having developed only functional intelligence and not the moral essence of humanity, are simply lower on the evolutionary scale.[48]

Liang Chi's suicide notes—his "Warning to the World"—had proclaimed that he was dying to preserve Chinese national character (*kuo-hsing*) and the heavenly principles (*t'ien-li*).[49] His thought harbored a contradiction—how could the particularistic Chinese tradition (national character) relate to universal human values (heavenly principles)? All of Liang Shu-ming's cultural theories are designed to show how the heavenly principles (expressed in human beings by intuition—*jen* and *li-hsing*) could be universal to human-kind and still be particularly Chinese. Chinese culture was good for everyone, not just the Chinese. He accorded to China a privileged role in the total cosmic-historical process. A historical community, the Chinese people were unique in history in having a cultural and spiritual life which represented the culmination of human moral possibilities. Underneath the corruption of externals, this moral community still lived in the present, at least in the rural villages.

To Liang, Western culture was based upon two fundamental attitudes: that of intellectual calculation directed at the external world, which led to the development of science, and that of individual self-interest, which led to democracy, and later to the collective selfishness of communism. Liang uses the word "intellect" in much the same tone as the nineteenth-century European Romantics. Like Shelley's "calculating faculty," it could dissect and so destroy life. An attitude of selfish calculation, Liang claimed, led to one's very life becoming a means to ends external to oneself, with the result that one's interior vital force was dissipated in the external world. He belived that what Marx called the "icy waters of egotistical calculation" was the very life blood of Westerners, and that it drowned not only ecstasies and enthusiasm, but life itself.

Industrialism, the theory continued, is a logical consequence of the wedding of the two tendencies of self-interest and material calculation. The Faustian spirit's drive for knowledge of the external world united with Promethean Will to produce gave birth to the Machine, which, much in the tone of a Gandhi or a Ruskin, Liang termed the "devil of the modern world." Liang's critique of capitalism is in that area where the conservative and Marxist traditions overlap:

When machines were invented . . . small scale industries were destroyed in succession . . . Society virtually bifurcated into the two classes [of workers and capitalists] . . . The relationship between the capitalists and their workers appears to be a free contract . . . Actually the capitalist has the power to oppress the workers and control their existence completely. And the workers have only the freedom to starve, because if they don't work they don't eat . . . There are continuous crises of unemployment; on the one hand they accumulate production surpluses of food and clothing, and yet on the other people are still starving and freezing.[50]

In his various anticapitalist animadversions, Liang was actually talking about alienation, believing that Westerners are compelled by their social and economic environment to act in a way destructive to their real human nature. Liang thus provides another example of how a conservative's groan of despair could sound, to use Durkheim's phrase, like a socialist's "cry of pain." But Liang believed all classes of Westerners were equally alienated: "The present economic predicament and its destruction to human nature . . . is just intolerable. It makes no difference whether the people are workers, those who are better off, or even capitalists. The vital force of all of them is just about exhausted; life is unnatural, mechanical and insipid for all in the same way."[51]

Since the alienating social and economic environment is the inevitable result of the Western cultural attitudes, Westerners would achieve true humanity not via the proletariat but by some vague evolutionary process which would develop their *li-hsing,* their truly human "reason." Liang predicted that, having already provided for their material needs, the Westerners were on the verge of liberating themselves from their slavery to the external world.[52]

While Liang was aware that traditional Western society had been similar to that of China in certain respects, and that premodern Western culture had some of those virtues which he ascribed to Chinese culture alone, he could not make the comparison (even to himself), for this would have reduced his commitment to Chinese values to mere nostalgia and would have implied that China was not qualitatively different but simply quantitatively less rationalized. Like Western conservatives, he idealized a traditional society in his polemics against innovation, but could not, as they did, attribute alienation to the recent changes involving increased rationalization. To do so would imply that China's only virtue was its traditional nature. He repeatedly argued against both the liberal bourgeois and the Marxist assumption that China was merely a bit behind on some common course of human development. If not forced by contact with the West, he said again and again, China would never in a thousand years have developed industry, science, and democracy, or a nation-state. Thus the central thrust of all his theory-building was to demonstrate that the Chinese and Western cultures had taken different directions or had been on different levels from their beginnings.

As Liang became cognizant of the growing influence of Marxism on Chinese intellectuals, he responded by concocting his own social theory in which Marxist categories figured prominently. With this new theory he sought to explain China's stagnation and weakness, to show the unsuitability for China of all Western-style political and social institutions, and to prove the historical inevitability of his own solution to China's modern crisis — rural reconstruction. Marxist historical materialism, Liang declared, is perfectly valid for the West.[53] Having not yet evolved *li-hsing,* Westerners' actions are determined solely by their material self-interest. Like simple biological organisms, their lives consist of the interaction between their body's demands and their external physical and human environment. In order to satisfy their demands on nature or protect their rights against others, they organize into groups, a habit acquired early from organized religion. The national and class contradictions between groups constitute the internal dynamic of Western history. Competition between groups results in increasing social and economic rationalization as well as political revolutions and wars. Any government is only a class tool of exploitation.

Chinese society, on the other hand, has been based not on force and self-interest, but on ethics and self-abnegation. While the Westerner's selfishness has always been kept in check by external forces (either God through the priest, or armed force through law),

Chinese humanity has been governed by internal force — moral obligation, mutual respect and yielding, etiquette, and custom. All Western-style political and social schemes are thus unsuited to China, which has developed neither classes nor government in the Western sense. For Liang, *Homo Economicus* has been extinct in China for over 2,000 years, so both bourgeois capitalism and proletarian communism were equally irrelevant. From his perspective, Liang saw in the West only the Enlightenment assumption common to both Marx and Smith — that any reform can succeed only if based on material self-interest.

Rural Reconstruction: Practice

It was Liang's discovery in 1927 that communism did not seem so irrelevant to peasants and young intellectuals that prompted him to produce his own reform program — rural reconstruction — which would not be based on material self-interest.[54] In the rural discontent underlying communist successes,[55] Liang saw a spontaneous social force on which he hoped to build his own revolutionary movement, one that would revitalize China's ethical fabric as well as remedy her political and economic backwardness.

Liang conceived of rural reconstruction as a quasi-religious mass movement which would reintegrate China's crumbling political-social community by creating an underlying moral consensus and spiritual solidarity. The small face to face group, built around the traditional teacher-student relationship, was to be the central agency of spiritual transformation. Through mutual criticism and encouragement group members would cultivate their moral character and spiritual capacities, thus energizing themselves for action. They would also develop habits of cooperation and organization for united effort to achieve common goals.

This fundamental concept of moral and intellectual improvement through the intimate group was the heart of Liang's philosophy of education, which he began developing soon after his father's death. It is, in fact, quite similar to his father's Confucian ideal of moral influence through education for the preservation of Chinese values. Liang Chi's concrete reform proposals had called for small-scale application in the capital district first, on the Mencian assumption that the people of other areas would "with their necks stretched out, rush like a torrent" to follow the lead of virtue.[56] In the same faith, Liang Shu-ming, sage to all humankind, would content himself with initiating his program in one small county in Shantung.

In 1922, while still teaching at Peking University, Liang Shu-ming tested his theory with practice and organized a commune-cum-academy with a small group of students.[57] For the rest of his life he continued this teacher-student communal life-style. In 1924 he left the university in disgust over its stress on mere utilitarian instruction to the neglect of the whole person, and went to Shantung to found a school based on his own educational theory.[58]

It is important to note that the common focus of both his educational and rural reform was not the masses but the young intelligentsia, upon whom he quite obviously projected the crisis of his own youth. He saw the new generation influenced by Western mechanistic thought as he had been and felt compelled to provide them with a satisfactory philosophy of life and program for action, lest they suffer the same existential despair and impulse toward self-destruction that he himself had experienced. It was natural that "youths of courage and spirit," like some of his own disciples, would be attracted to the communists. The irresponsible Kuomintang, the soulless liberals like Hu Shih, and the irrelevant conservatives like Chang T'ai-yen provided them, he felt, with no other path.[59] Indoctrinated first in the small intimate group, Liang's Confucian cadre would then merge in the same way with the masses. Both Confucian and expert, they would cultivate the masses' inherent goodness through moral leadership and guide rationalization of economic and social processes and organization.

The basic building block of the new society was to be the local village, which would be organized around a school, very similar to Dewey's scheme of dividing up the country into wards organized around the local school. But Liang's school, managed by the cadre and local notables, would be a multifunctional, socioeconomic-political education center. It would simultaneously disseminate agricultural technology, create peer-group pressure against bad customs like footbinding and opium smoking, organize cooperatives and local militia, spread literacy, and undertake a hundred other modernizing functions; at the same time it would revive Confucian customs and practices, promote public interest in community problems, and mold the villagers into economic, political, and spiritual collectives. It would be the center for transforming the entire Chinese countryside into a great school of Confucian collectivist thought. Governments would relate to the people through the organizational structure of schools, and officials would relate to them as teachers. Through village-level participatory democracy, political power would rise from the people instead of flowing down from a distant bureaucrat ignorant of local conditions.

Liang's philosophical thought might be described as a twentieth-century elaboration of Wang Yang-ming's Confucian intuitionism, and his rural reconstruction program could be interpreted as a modern refurbishment of the traditional *hsiang yueh* (village compact)[60]—a rural community action institution originated by Lü Ho-shu, a Northern Sung official. Although there is little evidence to indicate that the *hsiang yueh* ever functioned exactly as its theoreticians intended, the two main pillars of neo-Confucian thought, Chu Hsi and Wang Yang-ming, also constructed their own versions of Lü's original design. Like Liang's rural reconstruction endeavors, the *hsiang yueh* was to have been a comprehensive, spontaneously generated mutual aid collective through which villagers would work together to meet common economic, military, and educational needs. At the same time they would scrutinize and perfect each other's moral character.[61] Liang himself acknowledged that the *hsiang yueh* furnished some inspiration for his program, but emphasized that old institutions could not solve new China's modern problems; tradition did not provide for progress, which was to be one of rural reconstruction's most important products:

The general aims [of *hsiang yueh*] are similar to those of village schools and district schools which we are establishing; one could say that we are imitating the ancients. But today's world is different from that of antiquity. In addition to imitating the ancients' method of encouraging one another to do good, we must put the pursuit of progress uppermost in our minds.[62]

Liang's progress was certainly different from the sort sought by rival "agrarian reformers" under the leadership of his old acquaintance Mao Tse-tung;[63] yet Liang's "conservative" rural reconstruction affords some interesting points of comparison with certain aspects of Maoism. Liang seems to share with Mao a peculiarly Confucian faith in the influence of the human environment and the efficacy of intimate group contact in moral and intellectual improvement. They both conceived of internal virtue (rectified heart, proletarian consciousness, and so on) as linked to external political, military, and economic success. To both, the good society would be achieved by continuous spiritual transformation of the whole society, a never-ending moral drama, which would solve China's economic and political backwardness, and, at the same time, avoid the dehumanization of urban bourgeois society. Both were apprehensive that selfish, mundane desires might extinguish the spirit of self-sacrifice. But for Mao, the nationalist, the purpose of sacrifice was the nation-state. For Liang, self-sacrifice was an end in itself, an expression of the true nature of the human being, not a means to an external end. Self-abnegation was primarily an expression of the *tao,* and only secondarily for the material benefit of the collective.

Both Mao and Liang had broadly conceived programs based upon their synthesis and systematization of those inchoate demands and inherent wisdom of the rural masses. Both relied on small group education and discussion to stimulate mass participation and to forge a *gemeinschaftlich* unity of leaders and led. Both men hoped that in the continuous moral scrutiny of small groups, a new elite of selfless moral paragons would emerge to maintain unrelenting revivalist fervor. Both movements had an earnest populist dedication to "serving the people," yet Mao moved the peasants in a way that Liang admitted he had always sought but never found.[64] Do the reasons lie in the traditional content of Liang's program? Was it ever possible for Liang to achieve, as he hoped, authentic traditionalism and authentic modernization? In his theory, Liang abstracted from the past those basic values he wished to preserve in order to achieve a humanized (that is, Chinese) modernization. In practice he seems to have found that the life values were embedded in a cultural reality which was decidedly inimical to his modernization goals, and conversely, modernization itself seemed to undermine the values he wished to preserve.

Liang's ultimate political inefficacy was directly related to his traditionalism. In 1927 both Mao and Liang heard a cry of pain issuing from the countryside. Mao perceived in it a motive force for an armed political movement and immediately set about developing an army. Liang heard it as a call for the leadership of virtuous men and immediately set about designing a program which would fill the countryside with *chün-tzu*. His idealist Confucian *Weltanschaaung* precluded an understanding of the nature of power relationships and the necessity of having an independent power base in order to realize his goals. Throughout his life Liang thought all politicians — communists, nationalists, and warlords — were unprincipled opportunists. While even the post-1911 Liang Ch'i-ch'ao conceived of himself as at least a crafty Chu-ko Liang, making puppets of the warlords he had in fact sold himself to, Liang Shu-ming thought and expressed himself politically in the images and categories of a Confucius or Mencius, a sage with a vision. He saw modern Chinese political disintegration in terms of the Spring and Autumn period and believed, like Mencius, that his reform program would attract the people of the whole nation once one of the local power holders put it into practice.[65] By contrast, if Mao identified himself with any figures of the Chinese past, it was not with Confucius and Mencius, but with Ch'in Shih-huang and Han Wu. Mao remembered how the Warring States were in fact united.

It was not that Liang was unaware of the basic problem. The major difficulty of rural reconstruction, he said, was its connection with and reliance upon the government. He saw too that the only path to independence of the government was an armed political movement.[66] But his traditional values would not allow him to draw the logical conclusion — that rural reconstruction could succeed only as a part of an armed political movement.

Liang's rural reconstruction efforts were hampered by his traditionalist views in other ways. For instance, the type of men who were apparently attracted to Liang's neotraditionalism were also prone to such faults of the traditional scholar class as bureaucratism and petty factionalism. While Liang himself sought a union of theory and practice and an integration of peasant with intellectual, he could not achieve these aims using traditional men in traditional ways. Those closest to him in his rural reconstruction work did not seem to share his commitment to the joining of theory and practice. These men were still acting and thinking in a world of a "government of literati," where an essay or a report was a task accomplished and where there was an unbridgeable gap between the labor of mind and the labor of muscle.

Similarly, Liang wanted to develop a politically active and aware peasantry but he also hoped to use the natural leadership of the organic community, the gentry, as the agents for this transformation. Unfortunately, China's modern gentry operated on principles quite foreign to Liang's and they refused to compromise on the hard matters of economic and power interests for the sake of Liang's programs. He sometimes came close to admitting that perhaps the communists were right after all: "Although the communists' methods are bad, there are some useful aspects . . . If it were really possible to overthrow the local bullies and bad gentry and redistribute the land equally, short and sweet just like that, it would be pretty good too."[67] But he could never abandon the idea that Chinese culture was founded on reason, and thus, moral influence and education would have to do the job.

While both the communists' and Liang's movements were, in the end, fundamentally elitist, the communists' objectives and work style were more truly populist. At Liang's projects the cadres did not live in comparative luxury and lack any feel for the real life of the peasant for whose benefit they were ostensibly working (as was the case at the projects of the central government and those of various returned students like James Y. C. Yen). Liang and Mao, for example, were both simple and hard-working in their life habits. But in hot weather Mao could casually remove his pants while Liang always insisted on wearing the long scholar's gown regardless of the work he was doing. Mao drank, smoked, and talked saltily while Liang always maintained the life-style and demeanor of a contemplative monk.

These style differences reflected two quite distinct life experiences in Chinese society, personified by Mao's peasant background and Liang's scholar-official background. While the "big and little traditions" in China were more integrated than in other premodern societies, there was a palpable distinction in concrete life-styles and experiences. For instance, the *chiang-hu* (literally, "river and lake") folk tradition of bandits, secret societies, and itinerant bully boys had values, standards of conduct, and ideals which seldom found their way into the Chinese written literature, but it was a more vital part of peasant life than the classics. Liang, brought up in a Peking scholar-official family, knew a very different world and was incapable of comprehending such fundamental aspects of Chinese rural life. He himself admitted that his background made it difficult for him to relate to rural life.[68] For example, he failed to see any particular significance in the prevalence of banditry in Ho-tse county, Shantung, even though the problem was so severe that most of his work in this district was devoted to local militia organization. Liang never indicated that he saw any connection between the bandit problem and the fact that this area also had one of the highest landless peasant rates in the province. To a peasant the relationship was obvious.

On a small scale, Liang's projects did succeed in that area in which he had least interest—technological diffusion and economic improvement. His research stations, farm extension work, and schools raised the level of agricultural technology and efficiency. His introduction of certain cash crops and improvement of the marketing system also raised farm income. However, Liang himself could not find much satisfaction in these modest successes as they fell so far short of his real objectives. In the end it was the communists who realized his final goal—the revival and reintegration of China based on an impassioned mass commitment to a common ethic—a "religion which was not a religion," as he often described Confucianism. But the revival was not based on the traditional values which were Liang's central concern.

Some Conclusions

Whether or not the values of China's inherited culture were compatible with modernization was the pivotal question of Liang's entire life. Was *Zwecksrationalität* reconcilable with the Tao? His answer—the whole thrust of rural reconstruction and of his thought in general—was that China could indeed eat the cake of modernization and retain the core of her traditional values too. She could preserve that priceless gift of her sages — the discovery of true humanity — and still acquire wealth and power sufficient to provide for her people's material well-being and protection against the morally inferior foreign aggressors.[69]

Yet at the core of his many ways of putting the question and answering it there lay an absolute and inescapable contradiction. If the essence of Chinese culture was directly responsible for China's material inferiority in the first place, how could renaissance of that essence solve the problem of material inferiority? Ever since the sages perfected it, *li-hsing* had kept the Chinese from wealth and power. How could *li-hsing* now abruptly permit them to achieve it? Conversely, percisely those elements in Western culture which Liang saw as the antithesis of Chinese culture were responsible for Western material success. There was no way that Liang could have both bear paw and righteousness. Although he refused to admit that any choices were necessary, he had opted for the latter.

Finally, we should distinguish between the agrarian reform aspects of Liang's rural reconstruction and its underlying agrarianism. In the prewar decade, hundreds of local rural reform programs appeared in China, most focusing on only one specific problem such as education, credit, irrigation, or health. Liang's own projects in Shantung were distinguished by their attempts to solve all such problems and effect a total cultural renaissance as well. While Liang did indeed emerge in the 1930s as the national spokesman for rural reform in general and during the war headed a quasi-political party, the Rural Reconstruction Group (Hsiang chien p'ai), not all rural reformers shared his philosophical agrarianism, which claimed general superiority for rural Chinese life and society.

Agrarianism has been a common attitude among antimodernist conservatives, going hand in hand with abhorrance of one or several aspects of industrialized urban life. Indeed, it might be more accurate to speak of antiurbanism or anti-industrialism rather than agrarianism.[70] Liang's agrarianism also had a negative quality, but it had none of that almost pantheistic regard for nature, that aesthetic delight in the bucolic which has characterized Western agrarianism. The pristine primitiveness of village life held no particular charm for Liang, and in his way of thinking nature was no specially charged moral metaphor. After his 1936 trip to Japan, for instance, he observed, with considerable admiration, that the Japanese rural areas differed little from the cities.[71] The goal of rural reconstruction was to achieve a kind of reverse *rus in urbe* rather than a primeval Taoist utopia. What he hoped to preserve was community, morality, and human relations, which is why he often sounds more like community oriented urban reformers such as Robert Park and Jane Addams than like Thoreau or Calhoun.

It was war with an industrialized nation which forced America's outstanding theoretician of agrarianism, Thomas Jefferson, to reluctantly abandon in part his cherished vision of an agrarian state unspoiled by that "sore on the body politic," the industrialized city.[72] Jefferson too was committed to what he considered universal human values which were inseparable from an agrarian form of society, but upon weighing them against national survival, he hedged.[73] What was Liang's response when confronted with a similar conflict between agrarianism and national power at the time of the Japanese invasion of Manchuria in 1931? He pointed to what he felt were suitable models for China — India and her unarmed but united moral resistance to British imperialism, and Denmark, which instead of struggling against its shrinking international position, concentrated on improving the quality of life for its people.[74] Confronted with full-scale war in the summer of 1937, Liang's answer was fundamentally unchanged — spiritual solidarity not industry and military hardware would save China.[75]

When pressed to make a choice, Liang could not, as Jefferson did, allow the interests of national power to destroy the culture, for he was *au fond* a culturalist, intent on preserving the Way and not a true nationalist dedicated to the Chinese state. The Chinese nation could be a means to preserving the Way, but it could not be an end in itself. To be sure, Liang often presented his case to the public in nationalistic terms, saying in effect that only through revival of China's heritage could the nation-state prosper. But for Liang that heritage possessed not just historical but transhistorical significance. It must not be merely a museum piece which would serve the interests of national identity and pride, but the basis for present action. Like premodern Chinese, Liang believed that China was not just a culture among cultures but the only truly human one. Because he lived in the twentieth century, however, this conviction was hard-won, being reached only after a difficult spiritual odyssey; it was not a mere stubborn clinging to an assumption he was born to. Liang once drew a revealing parallel between himself and Gandhi:

Originally English rule of India was very severe but the people's movement which Gandhi leads has virtually forced the British . . . to acknowledge his superiority. Here we should note that Gandhi was not always a traditionalist but only slowly rediscovered [Indian spirit] . . . [From Gandhi's *Autobiography*] we know that as a student he abandoned his religion in disgust . . . In order to assert his rejection of the old, he intentionally ate meat and drank wine. When he was studying in England he worked hard at learning to be an English "gentleman." At the start he was not a religionist in form or spirit, and had no traditional thought; he was completely alienated from the spirit of India. Only later did he gradually come back . . . [His] movement is a new invention, but its spirit is still truly that of the Indian ancients; it is just that after Gandhi discovered the spirit, he used new methods to develop it . . . I read Gandhi's *Autobiography* with special insight because I am like him. On the basis of my book, *Eastern and Western Cultures*, a lot of people have taken me for someone who likes to talk about "Eastern spirit" or "Eastern culture." Actually that is not so. At the start I too abandoned Eastern culture and the Chinese people's spirit in great disgust. Only afterwards did I slowly find my way back . . . I am not a conservative person.[76]

Whatever the ultimate nature of that crisis through which he "found his way back," it has transformed a modern nationalist "in search of wealth and power" into a culturalist "man of destiny." The destiny of modern China fell to other hands, for the situation did not call for a Chinese Gandhi. A sage, however, does not calculate the possibility of his success, for he is one who "knows it's no use, but keeps on doing it."[77]

10 Hsiung Shih-li's Quest for Authentic Existence

TU WEI-MING

Confucianism in Modern China

One of the pitfalls in studying Confucianism in general and its modern transformation in particular is that of oversimplification. This may take the form of a conscious attempt to impose a preconceived category upon a vast body of Confucian literature or of an indiscriminate use of the word "Confucian" to cover a large group of unknown entities in Chinese cultural history. Both tendencies are equally disturbing. The former approach tends to ignore the whole area of human experience which is concerned with spiritual values; the latter tends to explain complicated motivational structures in terms of unrefined sociopsychological models. Genetically, Confucianism has been closely associated with an agriculture-based economy, a patrimonial bureaucracy, and a family-centered society; but to reduce the Confucian point of view to an expression of agrarianism, familialism, or bureaucratism is to overlook its ethicoreligious character.

To be sure, as the mainstream of Chinese thought in the last millenium, Confucianism has deep economic, political, and social roots in traditional China. However, even if those roots are completely destroyed, we cannot conclude that Confucianism has thereby lost all of its human relevance. Indeed, it is not inconceivable that some contemporary Chinese intellectuals find in Confucianism not a fixity of past wisdom but a reservoir of humanistic insights, mean-

ingful to their own existence and relevant to their perceptions of the
vital issues of the modern world.

Joseph Levenson in his *Trilogy* pronounces the fate of Confucianism as follows:

The orthodox Confucianists, standing still, had been moving
towards oblivion. In the beginning, their idea was a force, the product and the intellectual prop of a living society. In the end it was a
shade, living only in the minds of many, treasured in the mind for
its own sake after the society which had produced it and which
needed it had begun to dissolve away.[1]

This line of thinking does not begin and end with Levenson; it is
often followed by students of modern Chinese intellectual history.
The decline and fall of Confucian China is now no longer debat-
able; it is a historical reality. Only the specific event that best symbolized the end has yet to be determined. Some scholars would consider the abolition of the examination system in 1905 the single most
important blow to the Confucian tradition. Others would choose the
collapse of the Yuan Shih-k'ai regime in 1916, the May Fourth
movement in 1919, or the debate on science and metaphysics in
1923. At any rate, since the Confucian tradition definitely ended
before the emergence of the republican era, any attempt to salvage
it afterwards is usually labeled neotraditional.

If we follow this practice, we inadvertently subscribe to the belief
that the modern world, presumably dominated by the rationality of
science, and Confucian humanism are incompatible. The rise of the
one entails the decline of the other. To be sure, Levenson warns us
that the dichotomies he offers are not "stark confrontations really
'there' in history," but "heuristic devices for explaining (not
conforming to) the life situation." He further contends that his
categories are used to explain "the overlapping, intermingling, non-
categorical quality of minds, situations, and events." He is quite
aware that "antitheses are abstractions, proposed only to let us see
how, and why, their starkness in definition is mitigated in history."[2]
In his analysis of the fate of Confucianism in modern China, however, the "starkness" of his dichotomy seems to resist even the possi-

bility of historical mitigation. The incompatibility of the traditional, humanistic Confucian China on the one hand and the modern, scientific West (no matter how narrowly defined) on the other is considered such an absolute that even the rise of scientism in China fails to lessen the fundamental conflict.

"What was weak about China," Levenson states, "was not just the paucity of science which the scientism coterie detected. It was what the scientism reflected, as something ostensibly universal, but merely historically significant in the end: too banal as disembodied *thought* to be anything more than an index to Chinese *thinking*."[3] As a result, "cosmopolitan in the Chinese imperial world, Confucianists struck a provincial note in the wider world of the nations, and they passed out of history, into history."[4] Levenson is said to have bled for the decline and fall of the Confucian tradition. The source of his agony seems to lie in his conviction that "the way back" is never "the way out." And yet when Confucian humanism enters the modern world, it cannot but suffer the fate of being alienated from its sociopolitical roots.

Levenson's lament for Confucian China is reflected in his vision of the plight of those modern Chinese intellectuals who are emotionally attached to their *history* but intellectually committed to imported *values*. In other words, their emotional identification with Confucian humanism is a futile, nostalgic longing for the past; their intellectual identification with Western scientific values is merely a cognitive understanding of the necessity of the present. In their identification with the past an intellectual justification is absent, and their identification with the present is devoid of an affective strength. These intellectuals seem to accept the notion that truly original insight in the philosophical sense cannot be generated from within themselves, but must be stimulated from outside. In other words, great ideas in contemporary China must be delivered by a midwife from the Western world.

While in the seventeenth century "a syncretism was necessary to western thought to effect its entrance into the Chinese mind," since the time of Liang Ch'i-ch'ao in the 1890s, "a syncretism [has been] necessary to the Chinese mind to soften the blow of the irresistible entrance of western thought." Levenson continues, "In the first case, the Chinese tradition was standing firm, and the western in-truders sought admission by cloaking themselves in the trappings of that tradition; in the second case, the Chinese tradition was disinte-grating, and its heirs, to save the fragments, had to interpret them in the spirit of the western intrusion."[5]

In the terminology of *t'i-yung*, once the "substance" is alienated from the "function," the former becomes a useless identity and the latter a groundless adaptation. What actually happened to Chinese intellectuals, in Levenson's view, was that they were gradually per-suaded to shift from an unquestioning loyalty to China's cultural identity, which was at the time dynamic enough to accept foreign ideas in terms of its own inner logic, to a complete betrayal of the Confucian tradition, which was neutralized to the extent that it became totally subordinated to the urgent need for adaptation.

However, Levenson's perceptive analysis of the plight of the Chinese intellectual in the world dominated by values alien to Chinese culture was never intended to exclude the possibility that an original thinker in modern China might still find meaning in the Confucian tradition not only for emotional gratification but also for intellectual identification. Liang Shu-ming's (1893-) ability to "champion Confucian moral values and to arouse the Chinese to a degree seldom seen in the contemporary world"[6] in 1921 was not just an isolated instance. Nor should it be understood purely as an expression of nationalist sentiment. The generation of Fung Yu-lan (1895-), Ma I-fu, and Chang Tung-sun (1886-) shared with Liang a level of intellectual sophistication hardly explainable in psychosocial terms alone.

However, the question is not whether or not a creative minority existed but what kind of cultural resources they tapped to formulate their intellectual orientation. If a significant number of them pro-fessed to be Confucian in their approach, the answer would seem to entail not only the availability of Confucian symbols for imaginative adaptation but also the continuing validity of Confucian ideas as a vehicle for original thinking. On this basis, the notion that the Confucian tradition has passed out of history into history[7] must be reconsidered.

If the tradition is thought to have been inseparably linked with the imperial state, or a residue of that system, then Confucianism as a political ideology must either have totally lost its efficacy or fundamentally altered its power base. From this perspective, its great moment would appear to be over and its political message would seem an archaic irrelevance.[8] Similarly, if the tradition is thought to have been indivisible from either the agriculture-based economy or the family-centered society, the inexorable changes in the social and economic structures of modern China must inevitably have led to the disintegration of the Confucian value system.

An alternative position envisions Confucianism not merely as a form of political ideology, or a kind of socioeconomic ethic, but primarily as a tradition of religious philosophy. Confucianism so conceived is a way of life which demands an existential commitment on the part of Confucians no less intensive and comprehensive than that demanded of the followers of other spiritual traditions such as Judaism, Christianity, Islam, Buddhism, or Hinduism. The suggestion may seem innocuous, but actually, it is still problematical to characterize Confucianism as either a religion or a philosophy, for the Confucian *tao* is a secular way par excellence.[9] And the degree to which Confucianism has been intertwined with the Chinese polity is a phenomenon rare in any other cultural tradition. Many students of Chinese intellectual history have been led to believe that since Confucianism was so intimately a part of imperial China, the fall of the latter must necessarily have brought about the decline of the former. To a large number of social critics of the May Fourth generation, their attack on "Confucius and Sons" was an integral part of their struggle against the remnants of the ruling elite in imperial China.[10]

In the light of the above, it is understandable that any discussion of Confucian personality in modern China seems to smack of antiquarianism. While there is no compelling reason to characterize a Martin Buber, a Paul Tillich, a Suzuki Daisetz, or an S. Radhkrishnan as "neotraditional" in their respective cultures, a modern Confucian, no matter how creative and innovative he or she may be, is likely to be labeled "conservative" or "reactionary" with more or less negative connotations. We have yet to develop a new (and much needed) vocabulary to account for the emergence of a small coterie of sophisticated thinkers in the post-May Fourth generation,

Confucian in character, alienated from centers of political power, relatively limited in immediate social influence, but pregnant with ideas of far-reaching implication. Similarly, we have yet to study their ideas in an ethicoreligious dimension. Consequently, they are apt to be called "cultural conservatives."

As Benjamin Schwartz has pointed out, while in the West "conservatism as a conscious doctrine emerges as an inseparable component of the triad conservatism/liberalism/radicalism," the issues raised by those called conservatives in China are "problems of such an order of generality that they transcend the "conservative/liberal/radical" trichotomy.[11] However, he notes that the bulk of the essays in this volume have given him the impression that the "nationalist component of the conservative syndrome is unusually powerful and the other components weak."[12] This leads us to the question whether nationalist sentiment is also a defining characteristic of cultural conservatism in China. Since "the enormous identity crisis of the articulate classes in modern China caused by the loss of cultural confidence added a sharp edge of intensity to nationalism in China,"[13] one can easily observe that nationalist sentiment was so ubiquitous that it underlay all forms of political persuasion, from ultraconservatism to extreme radicalism. Even the most liberal-minded intellectuals, stung by the burning desire to save China from total disintegration, were in a sense nationalistic, while the cultural conservatives, intent on stressing the importance of preserving or rediscovering a sense of spiritual identity with China's past, added a strong layer of ethnocultural pride to their way of attaining the common goal, namely, arousing the nationalist sentiment of the people. However, the cultural conservatives further believed that the task of saving China involved much more than a quest for wealth and power. Any attempt to manipulate cultural symbols merely for the sake of political integration could neither revive the glory of the past nor create a sense of pride in the present. What could be achieved by this one-dimensional approach would be no more than an emotional attachment to a system of values without a social base, indeed "a shade, living in the minds of many . . . after the society which had produced it and which needed it had begun to dissolve away."[14]

Admittedly many of the cultural conservatives themselves were involved in a romanticization of China's past. Their efforts to universalize Chinese cultural traits such as the monosyllabic language, the bureaucratic state, and the family-centered society were sometimes grotesque. But their approach to national survival was not confined to the political arena. Despite their nationalist sentiment, they raised issues of such magnitude that they must be appreciated as sharing in the concerns of modern individuals generally, and not merely as Chinese responding to the specificities of the Chinese situation.

To some of the cultural conservatives, notably Liang Shu-ming and Hsiung Shih-li (1885-1968), the search for wealth and power as a prerequisite for national survival had to be predicated on a sense of community, which in turn could only result from the fiduciary commitments of the people involved. Accordingly, the most urgent task of the educated elite in China was to sensitize the people and to raise their level of cultural awareness. This could be done only if the intellectuals themselves were resolved to face the challenge of the West not only as a clash of economic strength and military might but also as a confrontation of basic human values. Therefore, the way to save China as a sociopolitical entity was not to imitate slavishly what was believed to be the obvious superiority of the West. To deliver China from its miserable state of inertia, the intellectuals must first try to overcome the false belief that its internal cultural resources had dried up, and that the saving grace had to come from outside.

In this light it is understandable that what really struck Hsiung Shih-li in the Confucian tradition was not its historicism, its holism, its sociologism or "culturalism," but its ontological vision and its philosophical anthropology. To be sure, Hsiung philosophized from a Confucian perspective, but he did it with a universal intent. He responded to the pressing issues of his time not only as an agonized Chinese intellectual but also as a concerned thinker dedicated to the quest for authentic existence. His cultural conservatism involved an ethicoreligious dimension, which both transcended narrowly defined nationalism and informed his national concerns. Thus, at a time when the search for spiritual ideas was thought to be of a limited significance, Hsiung perceived that the survival of China as a national community could not bypass the route of cultural reconstruction. While the majority of his contemporaries were obsessed with China's weaknesses, Hsiung opened up a new line of inquiry by examining the philosophical basis on which the modern world as well as the future of China was to be judged. To be sure, his value orientation was Confucian in character, but the issues to which he addressed himself were of such a level of relevance that they must be recognized as perennial problems of human existence.

Hsiung's Career as Teacher and Scholar

To study Hsiung Shih-li the man, as reflected in his career as a teacher, is to confront a number of seemingly incompatible images. When the news arrived in Hong Kong of his death in the early summer of 1968 at the age of eighty-four, he was unanimously hailed by Chinese scholars outside of mainland China as one of the most original thinkers in the last century.[15] But his lonely demise seems to have had little impact on the intellectual scene in the People's Republic. He is said to have been one of the most dynamic teachers at Peking University in the late 1920s, but the record seems to show that because of poor health he could not handle more than one lecture course per semester, and he never attained the rank of professor there.[16] Although he is considered one of the most consistent and persistent critics of Chinese communism, he was probably the only eminent idealist who never experienced the humiliation of self-criticism and public confession in the last two decades of his life.[17]

All evidence shows that he led a fairly secluded life throughout his career as a teacher, and his association with the academic community did not begin until he was in his forties. Nevertheless, his followers in Hong Kong and Taiwan outnumbered those of Fung Yu-lan and Liang Shu-ming. Partly because of his self-imposed intellectual isolation and partly because of his uncompromising character, Hsiung never gained in his lifetime a wide reputation; yet his views carried tremendous weight among a group of highly respected scholars, including the logician Shen Yu-ting, the metaphysician Chang Tung-sun, the historian Ho Ch'ang-ch'ün, the Buddhologist Jen Chi-yü, and the Confucian master Ma I-fu.[18]

To study Hsiung Shih-li as embodied in his philosophical treatises is to witness the unfolding of a profound vision, deeply rooted in the Chinese tradition and yet singularly relevant to some of the vital issues of the modern world. Even in a brief survey of his major works one is struck by the perspicacity of his observations and the originality of his ideas. Although his ideas have far-reaching implications, they are centered around a single concern: to live authentically as a Confucian thinker amidst depersonalizing forces in contemporary China.

A brief comparison of Hsiung's public image with that of Hu Shih (1891-1962), probably the most well-known intellectual of the May Fourth generation,[19] is instructive, for these two symbolized two basically different modes of thought in contemporary China. While Hu attempted to conceptualize Chinese problems in terms of categories he had acquired from the West, Hsiung tried to appreciate what he believed to be the strength of Western learning from the perspective of Confucian humanism. And though many of Hu's provocative ideas have long become outmoded in the intellectual world, Hsiung's imaginative vision only now begins to find a sympathetic echo in the minds of professional philosophers.[20]

Hu came from a fairly affluent scholar-official family. He was a cosmopolitan scholar with a broad educational background, a wide intellectual horizon, a high reputation, and an influential position. Hsiung came from a poverty-stricken family. It is doubtful whether he had been exposed to any formal education at all. His scholarly background was limited to the Three Teachings (Confucianism, Taoism, and Buddhism), and his knowledge of Western learning came from translated works. He led a marginal existence as a part-time lecturer, and his social influence was negligible. Hu as the champion of democratic liberalism and pragmatic scientism was the center of attention for more than a decade. He was urbane, eloquent, and gregarious. The large halls where he lectured were constantly filled to capacity. In sharp contrast, Hsiung was a lonely fighter for his own vision of the Confucian *tao*. He was earthy, arrogant, and even eccentric. He had only a small but dedicated following. Others occasionally drifted into his lectures mainly out of curiosity. Hu was closely in touch with the mainstream of ideas. His teacher, John Dewey, during his two-year visit in China (May 1919-July 1921), aroused wide interest in pragmatism. Hsiung, on the other hand, limited his teaching either by choice or by default to an extremely small coterie of scholars. Their concern for the great spiritual traditions of the East was like that of the Indian poet Rabindranath Tagore, whose message of universal human kinship in 1924 generated little enthusiasm among the young.

On the intellectual plane, Hu, despite his early training in the classics, was a great supporter of the campaign to overthrow Confucius and Sons. He advocated the scientific method and a piecemeal solution to well-defined problems, and was intellectually committed to Western learning. With the possible exception of Chu Hsi's notion of *ko-wu* (the investigation of things), he saw very little contemporary significance in the entire tradition of neo-Confucianism. He believed that the Indianization of China in the form of Buddhism had made only negative contributions to the rationality of the Chinese mind. His involvement in the study of ancient Chinese logic, vernacular literature, Mohism, and Ch'ing scholarship was intended to demonstrate the applicability of his new method of investigation. Hsiung, by contrast, devoted himself to the creative reformulation of the Confucian position. He propounded a philosophical inquiry into the ontological basis of the Chinese tradition and a complete reexamination of the value system existing at the time. He was deeply committed to the Confucian personality-ideal and his involvement in the study of Buddhism was profound. In fact, contrary to Hu's rational, pragmatic approach to restructuring Chinese society, Hsiung was so much an integral part of it that he could only feel his way from within. While Hu was able to look at China's major problems in a relatively disinterested manner, Hsiung totally identified with and felt victimized by them. While Hu achieved a measure of detachment in examining some of the specific social and intellectual issues confronting China at the time, Hsiung was deeply agonized and totally overwhelmed by the spiritual bankruptcy of the Chinese value system.

It is not surprising that their conflicting perceptions actually led to some personal animosity between them. As Hu Shih's associates, presumably members of the credentials committee, began to wonder why and how Hsiung had been hired as a college teacher in the first place, Hsiung and his three or four disciples became so disgusted by the "superficiality and vulgarity" of the so-called *ming-liu hsueh-che* (famed scholars)[21] that Peking University seemed to them a place full of sound and fury signifying nothing.

In fact, one of Hsiung's most serious campaigns was to expose the insubstantiality of the famed scholars. They might spend hours debating on a philological point or the true authorship of the *Dream of the Red Chamber*, which to Hsiung only added a bizarre aspect to the spiritual disintegration of the Chinese intelligentsia. Issues of profound ethicoreligious significance seldom crossed their minds. Their claim that the scientific method could open up new horizons in classical learning Hsiung regarded as irresponsible. What they actually accomplished, he felt, was no more than a continuation of the least creative Ch'ing scholarship,[22] and under their influence, students had no inclination to establish an experiential link with their own cultural heritage and no interest in probing the intellectual foundations of Western thought. In his view, the marriage of scientism and scholasticism blocked the way to either scientific thought or classical learning and deterred a sophisticated formulation of fruitful ideas.

Challenging the general view that the two decades following the outbreak of the May Fourth movement (1919) had fostered a great release of creative energy in appropriating new ideas, Hsiung criticized the fragmented approach to Western learning as a series of short-lived fads. He remarked that new literature, pragmatic philosophy, and applied science had each in turn become fashionable. When new literature was in vogue the students all wanted to become writers. Then philosophy became their favored field. Later they believed that only applied science could satisfy their dedication to real learning. Hsiung charged that despite massive translation of works by Spencer, J. S. Mill, Huxley, Darwin, Schopenhauer, Nietzsche, Bergson, Dewey, and Russell, and despite the tremendous potential for introducing new insights and visions into China, philosophical ideas from the West had produced little impact on the Chinese mind. Instead, impressionistic notions about them had actually caused obscuration, confusion, superficiality, and other problems in the intellectual world.[23]

While most historians would explain the phenomenon as inevitable in an early phase of cultural assimilation, Hsiung charged that the scholars who assumed the role of transmitters of Western learning had failed to appreciate the complexity of their self-assigned task. Although they were motivated to render some of those fascinating ideas into Chinese, they were not prepared to present a systematic treatment of any of them. Hsiung contended that the only way to absorb the insights of a philosophy which had become a dominant intellectual force in the West was to make a continuous effort to understand its root concepts. Only then could one really enter into the tradition and develop it as an integral part of one's "own thing" (*chi-wu*). However, Hsiung noted, the pursuit of Western learning as it had been carried on in modern China, like the aimless searching for strange smells on the sea by the eccentric in *Lü-shih ch'un-ch'iu*, was not only futile, but also damaging to the visions China already had.[24]

Hsiung argued that a more serious attempt to understand the West required a willingness to probe deeply into the philosophical bases of Western ideas. If those who advocated new ideas did it only for propagandist purposes and those who followed the fashion made no effort to comprehend the ideas, "how could the spirit of the [Western] philosophers ever set foot in China?"[25] Hsiung seems to suggest that Western learning, far from being what the westernizers in China professed it to be, involved a profound ethicoreligious dimension which could only be apprehended by a systematic inquiry into its philosophical import. Any sporadic effort to encapsulate it in a simple-minded formulation would seriously inhibit further attempts to study Western ideas. Dewey's lecture tour in China was probably just the kind of phenomenon Hsiung had in mind. Even though Dewey's pragmatism took the intellectual world in China by storm, Hsiung might have argued, so long as his propagators such as Hu Shih failed to form an integrated vision of pragmatic philosophy, the possibility for Dewey's ideas to take firm root in China was slim.

Underlying Hsiung's argument was the conviction that genuine learning from the West required a particular kind of intellectual disposition, a willingness to go beyond the apparent manifestations of wealth and power, and a courage to confront issues at the deepest level of human existence. In keeping with this line of reasoning, Hsiung devoted himself to philosophical inquiries with a profound sense of urgency. To him the real choice that was thrust upon each Chinese intellectual at the time was whether to live by values created through experiential learning or merely exist by timidly following ideas to which there was no way to meaningfully relate. It was a choice between a creative process of self-assertion and a static prolongation of identity diffusion.

Philosophical inquiries so conceived are much more than pure analyses. They are aimed at the establishment of a structure of meaning in which human activities can be accounted for not as fragmented occurrences but as an integrated process of transformation. However, Hsiung made it clear that his route to philosophy was not a speculative one. Instead of being a series of painless reflections on existing insights, Hsiung's philosophical journey was an agonizing quest for authentic existence. This quest was most intimately revealed in his *Dialogues*.

Hsiung's Self-Image

Although the complete version of Hsiung's *Dialogues* did not appear until 1947, the first part of it was published in 1935 and most of the rest had been completed by 1939. The book contains short articles, essays, lecture notes, recorded sayings, and letters to friends, acquaintances, students, and relatives. Comparable in style to some of the *yü-lu* (recorded sayings) of the Sung-Ming Confucian masters, the book is a series of reflections on a variety of life situations. The bulk of the book involves what Hsiung frequently refers to as *chiang-hsueh,* or philosophical inquiry in the neo-Confucian sense. Occasionally we find glimpses of his worries, frustrations, anger, despair, and indeed an autobiographic account of his life history.[26]

We learn that he was born in a poverty-stricken family in the Huang-kang area of Hupei. His father, a follower of the Ch'eng-Chu school, was a village teacher who died of tuberculosis when Hsiung was only ten years old. By then Hsiung had read the *Three Character Classic* and the *Four Books*. His father's death forced him to support the family by serving as a cowherd for his neighbor. From then on the only formal teacher he had was a certain Ho Shen, who taught him parts of the *Five Classics*. Ho was said to have been active in the revolutionary movement toward the end of the Ch'ing dynasty; and having been influenced by the ideas of the Reform movement, he advocated the establishment of local schools and the liberation of women. When Hsiung was in his early twenties, he became fascinated by the new subject of science. At that time, his only access to the world of ideas was to borrow books from a member of the local gentry in a neighboring district. Later he managed to read articles and memorials of the Reformists and became aware of the impending revolutionary change. He then chose Fan Chung-yen's (984-1052) maxim, "To be concerned (*yu*) before the whole world becomes concerned," as his own motto (*tso-yu ming*).[27]

Hsiung confessed that as a young man he was utterly unrestrained. In the summer, he would frequently live in a deserted temple, hike nude in hills, and smash Buddhist icons as a pastime. By then he had read some of the works of the late Ming loyalists such as Ku Yen-wu (1613-1682) and Wang Fu-chih (1619-1692). Deeply touched by their cultural loyalism he decided to take part in the revolution. He first joined the army in Wu-ch'ang as an infantry-man. Later he entered a special army training school. His revolutionary activities aroused the suspicion of the commander, Chang Piao. Although he escaped before the order for his arrest arrived, an award was offered for information leading to his capture. After the 1911 Revolution and a sojourn back home, he joined an expeditionary team to cultivate the land in the northwestern frontier of Te-an. This move was prompted not so much by a yen for adventure as by the necessity of earning a living for himself; however, because of an intense fear of accidental death, he withdrew from the expedition. In 1918 he joined the Kwangsi army, but again soon changed his mind, and went with a friend to Canton. He reported that it was in 1920 that he finally set his mind on learning. He described this existential decision at the age of thirty-six as a "great transformation" and a "rebirth" in his life.[28]

His first period of concentrated training in rigorous thinking and spiritual cultivation was at the Nanking Institute of Buddhism under the directorship of Ou-yang Ching-wu (1871-1943). However, after he thought he had grasped the philosophical position of the

Wei-shih (Consciousness-only) doctrine, he found himself much more in sympathy with the Confucian "learning of mind and human nature" (*hsin-hsing chih hsueh*).[29] In retrospect he remarked that he suffered from a serious illness in his late thirties, and it was then that he vowed to devote his life to the study of the Way of the sages. The only two books he wrote and published in the last two decades of his life, *Yuan-ju* (On the essence of Confucianism) and *Ch'ien-k'un yen* (An exposition of the two primordial hexagrams), together with all of his works printed prior to the founding of the People's Republic of China, seem to bear out the seriousness of his decision.

What was the nature of Hsiung Shih-li's decision? Was it an emotional attachment to a traditional ideal which had long since faded away? Was it an apologetic assertion of his cultural identity as a desperate attempt to meet the challenge of the West? Was it his idiosyncratic way of creating an area of meaning for his own existence regardless of the main thrust of the intellectual momentum of the time? Or was it merely a belated manifestation of Chinese culturalism?

To answer any of the above questions presupposes an analysis of Hsiung Shih-li's philosophical argumentation and his underlying intention. Hsiung made it clear that his intention to become a true Confucian was predicated on an inner decision, which he described as the "effort of self-reflection and self-mastery" (*fan-shen k'e-chi chih kung*).[30] The nature of his philosophy is thus linked with his self-image as a Confucian thinker.

Violently reacting against what Levenson calls "syncretism" and Munro terms "token integrationism,"[31] Hsiung believed that the gravest danger confronting modern Chinese intellectuals was their willingness to adapt themselves to forces from outside, while lacking the courage to face squarely the intrinsic problems of their existence here and now. What he saw in modern China was the collapse of the value system, the disintegration of the meaning structure, and more seriously, the loss of the self—not the self as a psychological ego but that which is, in the Mencian terminology, the real basis of human existence.[32] Once that sense of the self is lost, we may add, human beings are no more than an aggregate of biological, physiological, and psychological processes. To become a true Confucian in this connection means to be an authentic person, which entails a genuine awareness of the true self.

This explanation is loaded with ambiguous terms which require some elucidation. Hsiung's concept of the self is reminiscent of the Mencian line of Confucianism and especially of the Wang Yang-ming school in the neo-Confucian tradition. Indeed, the self so conceived is not only an irreducible reality but also the ontological basis for the attainment of sagehood. It should be pointed out that sagehood in this sense refers to true selfhood, which means the full manifestation or complete realization of the humanity (*jen*) inherent in each human being. The tendency toward a subjective point of view is quite obvious, but Hsiung, and for that matter his spiritual predecessors, clearly differentiate self-mastery from self-centeredness and true self from selfishness. Leaving aside technical issues in Hsiung's thought such as the egocentric predicament and the problem of intersubjectivity, it should be clear in the present context that Hsiung's emphasis on self-realization as a precondition for human communicability is not a form of intuitionism, and it is in basic conflict with, if not diametrically opposed to, many familiar forms of subjectivism.[33]

Although Hsiung Shih-li repeatedly stated that his philosophical intention was in complete agreement with that of Wang Yang-ming, as a situational response to the challenges of his time he departed from Yang-ming's teaching in a fundamental way. While the Ming philosopher refused to put his ideas in a systematically developed form for fear that the experiential dimension would be relegated to the background, Hsiung devoted years of his life to a rigorously constructed presentation of his philosophical position. His deep commitment to self-realization was thus manifested in his intellectual passion to deliver the Confucian message in a systematically reasoned form.

Ordinarily a Confucian by moral conviction must serve the state and assume the burden of social responsibility as an official. Such a person's spirit of *engagement* is commonly reflected in political participation. However, the lives of many historical personalities point to another possibility, which has also been fully accepted as a legitimate demonstration of the Confucian Way, namely the purification of the self in a time of chaos. Hsiung's role as a philosopher dedicated to the task of systematic inquiry is thus compatible with Confucian teaching. In a deeper sense, however, the purification of the self in Confucianism is never conceived as an isolated act or a self-imposed political moratorium, because a transformation in the meaning-structure is thought to entail a reshaping of the existing state of affairs. After all, in the Confucian perception, political participation is always predicated on a structure of meaning, which is considered an independent variable. It can be further argued that politics is here viewed as a function of moral education rather than as a system of bureaucratic control. Therefore, the Confucian enters into politics for the purpose of what the *Doctrine of the Mean,* one of Hsiung's favorite classics, calls "realizing one's own human nature as a way of helping others to realize theirs."[34]

Confucians believe that self-realization, inasmuch as it conveys an ethicoreligious meaning, necessarily affects the course of action in the world, even though it should not be seen simply as a means to a social end. It is precisely in this sense that Mencius defines the role of the moral leader (*chün-tzu*) as the guardian of the cosmic process as well as of the social order.[35]

It would not be far-fetched to suggest that Hsiung actually tried to philosophize in the capacity of a *chün-tzu*. Of course he appreciated Liang Shu-ming's efforts to actualize Confucian values in village reforms and Fung Yu-lan's efforts to incorporate Confucian values in a new political ideology, but he believed that his own philosophical efforts to revitalize the Confucian persuasion as an integral part of his quest for a new ontological vision were more fundamental. He felt justified in exploring his ontological vision purely as a concerned thinker, devoid of any direct involvement in political and social action. To a majority of Chinese intellectuals under the spell of scientism, his struggle might appear as rather distant from the burning issues of his times, but he was convinced that doing philosophy as a form of ontological inquiry was intrinsically meaningful to himself and demonstrably significant to his generation.

Implicit in Hsiung's writings is, therefore, an awareness that one's temporal existence is closely linked with a structure of meaning which transcends the immediate historical present. This awareness is predicated on the belief that a person is not a self-sufficient entity isolatable from his or her historical roots, but a center of relationships derived from the past but continuously relevant to the present. Intellectuals, as reflective persons who are consciously responding to the situations of their times, cannot afford to ignore those processes which have conditioned their way of thinking, molded their patterns of behavior, and shaped the direction of their spirituality. For the sake of self-realization they must penetrate deeply into the nature of those forces that have contributed significantly to their being what they are. According to this line of thinking, even if one is absolutely convinced that the tradition is on the verge of fading away, a sophisticated understanding of it is still necessary as a precondition for creative adaptation. Hsiung's perception of the problem was not apologetic; an intellectual appreciation of Confucianism, he felt, especially its ontological vision, was a fruitful way of restoring self-respect among modern Chinese intellectuals. However, a critical examination of the fundamental discrepancies in terms of value-orientation between China and the West was absolutely essential for the absorption of new values and the preservation of old ones.[36] From this perspective, the greatest fault of the intelligentsia was their unwillingness and inability to probe deeply into the underlying structures of ideas they espoused or rejected. Superficial denunciation of traditional China and wishful appropriation from the modern West had only led the intellectuals to fickleness.

Alienated from the predominant intellectual trends of the time, Hsiung had to be content with a limited circle of friends and a very small group of followers. It was probably this hostile intellectual environment that prompted him to write in an extremely forceful style. Although, as Hsu Fu-kuan has pointed out, elegant phrasing and felicitous diction give a classical tenor to his language, a salient feature of his works is the virility of his presentation — an urgent, sometimes indignant tone.[37] To those familiar with the prose style of the Confucian classics, whether his philosophical followers or not, his literary strength is all but overpowering.[38]

Hsiung the Thinker

It is true that the majority of the May Fourth intellectuals never felt that China's ability to westernize actually depended on a willingness to abandon its cultural burden in total. Even the most ardent supporters of Western learning recognized the need to make China's past relevant to the urgent concerns of the present. But since they all felt that the survival of China was at stake, many were absolutely convinced that strengthening the nation had to take precedence over any other consideration, and problems of meaning, such as the search for spiritual values, were deliberately suspended. Few perceived that ethicoreligious ideas might be essential to nation-building.

As a member of the post-May Fourth generation, Hsiung shared in the general desire of the Chinese intelligentsia to "save the nation" (*chiu-kuo*). He was acutely aware of the seriousness of the intellectual task and the urgency of trying to appreciate and internalize the dynamism of the West. However, he insisted that such an attempt must be based upon a high level of self-knowledge. He argued that the appropriation of Western insights must be made correlative to the reconstructing of Chinese values.[39] Hsiung believed that drilling deeply into the bedrock of the Chinese mind was not only of intrinsic value; it was functionally necessary for the successful absorption of new ideas. Hsiung's uneasiness with the May Fourth mentality arose not so much over its indiscriminate acceptance of the West as over its emotional attachment to the superficial manifestations of Western thought. Nevertheless, despite his sharp criticism of propagating Western ideas merely for public consumption, Hsiung apparently never displayed any revulsion toward Western thinkers. Although his *Dialogues* included only a few comments on Kant, Bergson, and Russell, he made perceptive observations on Greek culture as well as on Marxism, science, and ontology.[40] His knowledge of Western learning was certainly limited, but his imaginative vision enabled him to appreciate the meaphysical dimensions of Western culture, which were largely ignored by the westernizers at the time.

In the language of *t'i-yung*, what Hsiung realized was the necessity of reconstructing the Chinese *t'i* as an authentic way of understanding the *t'i* of the West. Similarly, he maintained that an appreciation of the Western *t'i* would in turn deepen the level of Chinese self-awareness. Only then would creative adaptation be possible.

Chang Chih-tung's formulation was a fallacy not because the dichotomy itself was inappropriate, but because in his wishful thinking he completely failed to appreciate the complexity of the relationships involved. The weakness of the westernizers was their one-dimensional approach to Western learning. Their determined effort to learn from the West brought no substantial change in the Chinese mind because they abstracted Western *yung* from its *t'i*. When the ideas were detached from their ontological structure, they became fragmentary opinions, useful only for propagandist purposes. Total adaptation was not a shortcut to westernization, but a blind alley. Hsiung was convinced that sporadic romanticization of Western ideas could never lead to a sophisticated appreciation of the underlying structure of Western thought. If the *t'i* problems in both China and the West were not even touched upon, any attempt to make use of borrowed ideas was bound to be futile.

One wonders what sorts of issues Hsiung envisioned as *t'i* problems. Rendered by the brilliant sinologist Peter Boodberg as "form" or "body," *t'i* certainly conveys the meaning of the basic structure.[41] However, as Wing-tsit Chan has pointed out, ever since Wang Pi's (226-249) commentary on Lao Tzu, in which he interprets the *t'i* of *tao* as *wu* (nonbeing), the term has assumed a metaphysical meaning in the sense of "substance" or "essence."[42] As one of the most prominent concepts in Buddhism and neo-Confucianism, *t'i* refers to the deepest sense of reality. Understandably, "ontology" has been translated as *pen-t'i lun* (the learning of the original *t'i*). Problems concerning *t'i* are therefore ontological issues.

To Hsiung, the main task of philosophy is to engage in ontological inquiries, and ontology, he claimed, is not a form of speculative thought or a search for external truths; the ontological quest, he insisted, is to make manifest the ultimate source of creative transformation in human culture as well as in the cosmos. Underlying his assertion is the assumption that ontology, often thought of as the intellectual game of a small group of professional philosophers, ought rather to be understood as closely linked with the welfare of the people. As a reflection on the ultimate source of creative transformation, ontology deals not only with the cosmogenic process, but also with the nature of human beings.

In Hsiung's philosophy, ontology is not a variable dependent on a given sociopolitical system. Rather, by its perception of what constitutes reality, it actually shapes the general direction of social change. Of course Hsiung can be labeled as an idealist, but to characterize his approach as idealistic is no more informative than to call Wang Fu-chih a materialist. Hsiung held that consciousness can determine the mode of existence; he further argued that human will molds as well as perceives the realities of the world. Ontology, in this connection, not only reflects but also creates the intellectual ethos, which in turn charts the general direction of social change. Thus, in a tortuous but substantial way, ontology affects the life of the people.

It is beyond the scope of the present essay to give even a synoptic view of Hsiung's ontological insights. Suffice it to say that Hsiung assumed that ontology can restructure existing reality in a fundamental way, and he undertook such a task with a profound sense of relevance. His undertaking should not be thought of as simply an action-oriented enterprise, for his main concern was not social thought or political ideology. However, he believed that the kind of ontological mission he was attempting was important for China's survival and that the continuation of Chinese culture as a dynamic, living tradition was dependent on it. Despite the hubris inherent in such a belief, it reflected a sincere and painful realization of what he himself had to do to participate in the national effort to save China. His ontological quest was thus colored by a strong nationalist sentiment, but the way he envisioned his task and the manner in which he carried it out defies a reduction to simple sociopsychological interpretation.

Hsiung's conscious response to the intellectual crisis of the post-May Fourth period can undoubtedly be explained in terms of his perception of the current historical situation. Of course Hsiung could not avoid the kind of psychological pressures that were felt by every thinking Chinese at the time. Indeed his works would be better appreciated if the effects of such pressures were noted and analyzed. His very style of writing and the format in which his books were printed vibrantly echo the sound and fury of his generation. Still it would be wrong to argue that his ontology is reducible to a sociopsychological need to search for roots. It would be equally wrong to interpret his quest as "seeking to avoid a conflict between historical affection and acknowledgment of value," for he clearly was not an example of what Levenson conceptualized as the "traditionalist" who "drained the contemporary value from what . . . [he] perpetuated."[43] Therefore, it is misleading to characterize him either as a stale syncretist or as a token integrationist.

Furthermore, given his ontological perspective, Hsiung not only outrightly rejected iconoclasm; he also regarded the common slogan of selecting the best from East and West as no more than wishful thinking. Serious selection, he maintained, depended upon experiential knowledge and critical examination. Hsiung's inclination was to probe the ontological dimension of Chinese culture as a way to arrive at a critical examination of the philosophical foundation of the West. He believed that only then could Chinese intellectuals really absorb wisdom from the West. What Hsiung tried to promulgate was more than an approach to Western learning. His intention was to formulate an ontological awareness which would serve as the ground for a mutual appreciation of cultural values between China and the West. One may very well ask whether Hsiung's "supposed commitment to value alone, to the generally acceptable, masks a concern with its special, historical origins."[44] Was Hsiung in the last analysis still caught in the Levensonian predicament: "the only motive which a Chinese could have in celebrating the beauty of blended values would be a desire — entirely foreign to the world of value — to see China and the West as equal partners"?[45]

If we accept the view that, in a cognitive sense, the only way for post-May Fourth intellectuals in China to relate themselves to their own cultural heritage was to measure it against the rules imported from the West, Hsiung's ontological vision must of course be subsumed under the category of psychological adjustment. According to this line of argument, the coming of the "brave new culture" compelled Hsiung to face a world which was basically non-Confucian. As a philosopher deeply rooted in Chinese traditions, he could not help being alienated by the westernizing process. His emotional attachment to China's past, a form of particularism, lingered on in his own mind and in the minds of his followers, and his universal intent in constructing a new ontology was no more than a philosophical strategy designed to make his nationalist sentiment intellectually respectable.

Such a line of reasoning is actually based upon a reductionist dogma; namely, that westernization is an irreversible, one-dimensional, linear progress. Once such an interpretive position is called into question, it is no longer plausible to assume that just because Hsiung's ontological insight was Confucian in character it was necessarily an attachment to history rather than a commitment to value. Nor does it seem proper to regard Hsiung's mode of thought as a form of particularism simply because he made a conscious attempt to philosophize from a specific point of view. Similarly, to characterize his universal intent as no more than an expression of nationalist sentiment is to rule out the possibility that in a confused and chaotic setting an original mind could still perceive fundamental humanistic values as such.

The Original Mind and Ultimate Reality

Although few attempts have been made to study the genesis of Hsiung's mode of thinking, it is generally accepted that "metaphysical idealism in the Vijñāptimātra (Yogācāra) tradition of Indian Buddhism" played a very important role in his philosophical training. He openly acknowledged his intellectual debt to Ou-yang Ching-wu, whose Nanking Institute of Buddhism (also known as the Academy of Inner Learning) was instrumental in the revival of systematic studies on the Vijñāptimātra school in modern China. This school, better known as the Wei-shih doctrine, is also referred to as the Fa-hsiang (Characteristics of the Dharmas) tradition.[46]

A salient feature of the school is the subtlety of its understanding of the mind (consciousness). The prominence of the mind in the whole tradition has yielded volumes of minute analysis on the subject. To begin with, the mind is divided into eight consciousnesses. The first five are sensory perceptions: sight, hearing, smell, taste, and touch. The sixth is the sense center (*manovijñāna*), the conscious mind or the general perceiving agency. The seventh is the thought center (*manas*), the self-conscious mind or the cognitive basis of thinking, willing, and reasoning. The eighth is the store-

house-consciousness (*ālayavijñāna*). Each of the eight consciousnesses is supposed to be a separable reality, demanding a type of
analysis suitable to its nature. While the first six sensory perceptions
can be readily understood in terms of ordinary psychology, the last
two require a much more complicated model of analysis.[47] Especially noteworthy is the idea of *ālaya*. Instead of being a mechanistic
interpretation of the unconscious, the Wei-shih teaching on *ālaya*
contains many insights reminiscent of psychoanalysis. The following
quotation is a case in point:

> A seed produces a manifestation,
> A manifestation perfumes a seed.
> The three elements (seed, manifestation, and perfume)
>   turn on and on,
> The cause and effect occur at one and the same time.[48]

An impression, a seed of act or thought by the human subject,
necessarily produces a manifestation in the external world. Thus
one's mental state is not an isolated private affair, but an active
agent inevitably affecting the world in flux. The manifestation is an
integral part of what we perceive as the universe. Simultaneously the
manifestation in turn exerts influence on the quality of the seed
through a perfuming (or polluting) process. However, the relation
between them is not a simple causality. Rather, in accord with the
principle of dependent origination, they occur "at one and the same
time." The kind of analytical method required for this doctrine is,
therefore, twofold: to differentiate entities as discrete for heuristic
purposes, and to integrate various levels of observation for a
comprehensive understanding.

Intent on "penetrating behind the veil of impermanence to attain
to the absolute knowledge that transcends all conditionality and
relativity," the school focuses its attention on the purification of
ālaya. This task involves, among other things, raising the level of
consciousness. This partly explains why the school has been considered the most intellectually oriented tradition in Chinese Buddhism. As Kenneth Ch'en has pointed out, while the Mādhyamika
School of Nāgārjuna conceives of two levels of truth, the Wei-shih
doctrine advocates three levels of knowledge, which refer to three

approaches to truth. The *parikalpita* view, based on "sole imagination," grasps truth in a distorted and fragmented manner. The *paratantra* view, based on the principle of dependence, recognizes only the temporary and impermanent aspect of truth. The *parinishpanna* view, based on the vision of ultimate reality, comprises the "rounded comprehension" of truth. Accordingly, the main purpose of the school is to teach the road to enlightenment through analytical inquiries.

What Hsiung learned in the Nanking Institute was not only the basic philosophy of Buddhism and the tenets of the Wei-shih doctrine. As the closest protégé of the Institute's master, who was one of the most brilliant Buddhist thinkers in modern China, Hsiung received a very special instruction, combining experiential knowledge with a rigorous method of detached analysis. Indeed, before his "conversion" to Confucianism, he had already established himself as a leading light in Chinese Buddhism. His *Buddhist Concepts Explained* (*Fo-chia ming-hsiang t'ung-shih*) and *Commentary on the Great Treatise on Buddhist Logic* (*Yin-ming ta-su shan-chu*) are important contributions to Buddhist literature. This perhaps explains why Father Briere, in his *Les courants philosophiques en Chine depuis 50 ans* (*1898-1950*), characterizes Hsiung as an original Buddhist thinker who synthetically reconstructed the philosophical school of "mere-ideation."[49] In fact, at the time when Hsiung, under the guidance of Ou-yang in the late 1920s, was engaged in a systematic inquiry into K'uei-chi's monumental work, *Notes on the Completion of the Consciousness-Only Doctrine* (*Ch'eng wei-shih lun shu-chi*),[50] he was already recognized as a potential successor to the master.

According to Hsiung's own recollection, only after a long process of spiritual quest did he decide to change his philosophical stance:

Some people have stated that my philosophy is an attempt to adduce Confucianism as an evidence to support Buddhism. This statement might appear to be true, for my personal experience in this matter is absolutely incomprehensible to an outsider. There was a period when I was inclined toward Indian Buddhist thought. My pursuit of Buddhist studies was certainly not motivated by a mere desire to broaden my knowledge and to display my erudition. It was really driven by a great wish to search for truth as a ground for "peace of mind and a meaningful existence" (*an-hsing li-ming*). I studied the teachings of Asanga and Vasubandhu with Master Ou-yang and was thoroughly converted. Later on, I gradually rejected the theories of various schools. Totally putting aside Buddhism and other systems (including even Confucianism), I searched within myself with single-ness of purpose. I thought that truth is not remote from us. We can never lay hold of truth by turning around under the spell of verbal and written words of others. Thereupon I completely trusted my own devotion and open-mindedness. I constantly maintained vigil-ance lest my selfish desires and prejudices deceive my (true) self. I was entirely engaged in what Ch'en Po-sha[51] termed "placing the mind in non-being" (*ts'o hsin yü wu*). It means to make a clean sweep of all kinds of "cognitive perception" (*chih-chien*) derived from bigoted opinions and implanted superstitions. The purpose is to make the mind large and dynamic without any trace of stagna-tion. Only then can we "experientially recognize" (*t'i-jen*) the truth in all places. After a long time, I suddenly awoke to the realization that what I inwardly witnessed agreed entirely with the idea of "great change" (*ta-i*)[52] in the Confucian transmission. Thereupon I completely destroyed the draft of the Wei-shih doctrine which I had written on the basis of Asanga and Vasubandhu and avowed to compose a new Wei-shih doctrine of my own in order to save myself from the defect of the old. Hence my understanding of Confucian-ism was not derived from book learning. Only after my inner experi-ence had already embodied it did I feel that my understanding of it was in complete harmony with what was recorded in the books. This kind of experience is extremely difficult to explain to the general public.[53]

Based upon autobiographical accounts like this, Wing-tsit Chan suggests that Hsiung's new exposition of Wei-shih was a critique of Buddhism from the perspective of the *Book of Changes*. Chan's interpretive position agrees very much with Hsiung's own justifica-tion: "I present my synthesis in the tradition of the *Book of Changes* by a critical examination of the main tenets in both the Buddhist schools of Being and Non-Being."[54] We may, on historical grounds, object to Hsiung's assertion that "both Confucianism and Taoism are based on the *Book of Changes*."[55] But it seems undeniable that, as one of the oldest and most characteristic expressions of the Chi-nese mode of thinking the book offers a "striking cosmology and a philsophy of human potential for creative action and freedom in the cosmic process."[56] In Jungian terminology, it is of uncommon significance as a way of probing the "inner person" and "personal wholeness" from a Chinese perspective.[57]

Among the profound insights in the book, that which most directly inspired Hsiung is the ontological notion of great transformation (*ta-hua*). Contrary to the Wei-shih theory that phenomena are temporary, tentative, transitory, and thus false, the *Book of Changes* asserts the reality of the great transformation. To be sure, Hsiung maintained that the external world, insofar as it is conceived as absolutely independent of consciousness, is nonexistent. Nevertheless by accepting the great transformation as the necessary manifestation of the original mind, he completely rejected the Wei-shih claim that *ālaya* is instrumental in producing phenomena. He believed that the ultimate reality, or the original mind, far from being a static substance, is a constant flux. The phenomenal world which is inseparable from the great transformation should thus be recognized as an integral part of reality.

As Wing-tsit Chan has noted, in Hsiung's new perception reality in the ultimate sense is understood as a "running current." Ultimate reality so conceived is not only a state of being but also a process of becoming: "It is changing because it manifests itself in countless phenomena, and yet it is unchanging because its self-nature remains unaltered in the process of change."[58] Indeed, the notion of *i* (change) in the *Book of Changes* connotes the meaning of both a constant structure of rudiments and a dynamic process of transformation. Understandably, ultimate reality is also conceptualized by Hsiung as constant transformation. Fundamentally different from the Buddhist idea that the phenomenal flux of change is impermanent, without self-nature, and thus illusory, Hsiung insists that it is a concrete manifestation of the ultimate reality. Therefore, the multiplicity of the phenomenal world, far from being the figment of the mind, is intrinsically meaningful. For it shows, in a tangible form, the creativeness of the ultimate reality. In terms of Hsiung's favorite analogy, the relationship is like that between the ocean and its waves. The ocean is perceived in terms of the waves, which are its inevitable manifestations. The waves are inseparable from the ocean, which is their necessary ground of existence. It is in this sense that Hsiung advocates original substance (*pen-t'i*) and manifested functions (*tso-yung*).

Undoubtedly Hsiung's ontological vision resembles the teachings of the Neo-Confucian masters, notably Chang Tsai (Heng-ch'ü, 1020-1077).[59] Indeed, Hsiung's cosmological duality, contraction (*hsi*) and expansion (*p'i*), is reminiscent of Chang's fusion and inter-mingling of material force (*ch'i*) wherein lies "the subtle, incipient activation of reality and unreality, of motion and rest, and the beginning of yin and yang, as well as the elements of strength and weakness."[60] Hsiung himself has acknowledged his intellectual debt to Chang, although his appreciation of Chang's cosmology was first mediated through the philosophy of Wang Fu-chih.[61] Contraction, to Hsiung, is "the congealing operation that produces apparently concrete objects of matter."[62] This tendency toward concretization is the ontological basis of the manifold world and the multiplicity of existence. However, contraction is ever under the discriminating and directing activity of expansion. As a defining characteristic of the mind, expansion compels, as it were, "this universal flux of seem-ingly contradictory tensions" to become "an orderly, constant trans-formation rather than a static equilibrium of interacting forces." This leads to the view that ultimate reality is "function or process, never completely passive but ever producing and reproducing a harmonious synthesis of heaven, earth, and human being."[63]

It is not difficult to pinpoint the influence of Wang Yang-ming in this formulation. Hsiung repeatedly acknowledged that Wang was the true transmitter of the Confucian way, and was thus a precursor of Hsiung's own philosophy.[64] It is interesting to note that Hsiung's exaltation of Wang Yang-ming's concept of mind, which was se-verely attacked by Wang's contemporary critics as Ch'an Buddhist, is indicative of the direction of his own thought, which was also characterized by his detractors as basically in the intuitive tradition of Buddhism. Hsiung's rejection of the Wei-shih theory of causation can probably be interpreted as a conflict within the Buddhist realm of intellectual discourse.[65] However, by stressing the unity and inseparability of the ultimate reality and its manifested functions, Hsiung significantly departs from the Buddhist claim of the insubstantiality of the world. Furthermore, in Hsiung's philosophy, human activities and relationships are integral parts of the highest expression of truth, a position difficult to support by any Buddhist teaching.

True to the spirit of Wang Yang-ming's dynamic idealism, Hsiung maintained that the mind is not only a cognitive knowing but also an affective acting. The unity of knowledge and action is so much a part of Hsiung's mode of thinking that pure intellectuality devoid of any existential implication is dismissed by him as nonsense or, at most, a playful game. According to Hsiung's contention, there should never be a bifurcation of the mind. Its indivisible unity manifests itself in a creative process wherein the separation of the external and the internal is completely transcended. Therefore, the mind acts and generates as well as comprehends. Actually it is in the sensitivity of the mind — its ability to feel and to care — that the creative potential of human beings truly lies. In a strict sense, the word "mind," used here as a translation of the Chinese character *hsin,* really stands for "mind-heart." It entails much more than what is usually envisioned in the philosophy of mind. Indeed, Hsiung argued that the human mind-heart, as the quintessence of human nature, interprets and directs the great transformation in the same way as the ultimate reality manifests itself. As an interpretive agent it gives meaning to the universe; and as a directing agent, it shapes its very reality. To intend, in this connection, is not merely to will, but to will in the sense of molding and creating. The mind-heart's power of direction, Hsiung observed, is "life-force," ever developing and changing, yet without losing its inner identity.[66]

Hsiung's highly sophisticated understanding of the mind is predicated on a strong belief in the malleability of the human condition through internal self-transformation. The mind, by its experiential comprehension, not only understands but also directs and masters. Implicit in this ontological insight is the conviction that the intellectual, by raising the level of consciousness of the people, necessarily shapes the direction of social change and influences the fate of the nation. However, this form of elitism is based on self-knowledge, indeed self-direction and self-mastery. It thus points to an open system of moral community, rather than a prescribed hierarchy of control. In the light of this line of argument, Mencius' notion of "those who labor with their minds" (*lao-hsin che*) actually refers to the moral leaders who are responsible for the integrity of the meaning-structure of the society.[67] It is their duty to see to it that the cosmic process as well as the legal and ritual order is in a harmonious state. Of course their central concern is not to preserve the status quo. In Hsiung's philosophy, stasis means degeneration. If ultimate reality is perceived as a dynamic process of great transformation, the courage to change and to create is a prerequisite for survival. Hence, the harmonious state can never be attained merely by balancing off conflicting forces. It can only be realized by undergoing a continuous process of creative integration, despite internal contradictions. The intellectual who refuses to endorse the simple-minded model of one-dimensional progress thus contributes significantly to the actual sequence of change. After all, human community is a dialectical interplay between what is and what its members insist ought to be. An ontological inquiry into the mind, far from being the pastime of metaphysicians, becomes an inalienable right and an unavoidable duty of the people. If the intellectuals fail in their task as guardians of the meaning-structure, in the terminology of Mencius, they will no longer be "fed" by "those who labor with their strength" (*lao-li che*).[68]

It is important to note that Hsiung's emphasis on the internality of the mind presupposes a sense of community as the basis of self-realization. To be sure, the value of the individual as an integral part of social welfare is recognized. However, since a person is perceived never as an atomized entity but always as a center of relations, human dignity is demonstrated as much by the elimination of selfish desires as by the struggle for civil rights.

Jen in Hsiung's Ontology

Consistent with the Wang Yang-ming tradition of neo-Confucianism, Hsiung observes: "Humanity (*jen*) is the original mind. It is the original substance common to people, heaven, earth, and all things . . . From Confucius and Mencius to teachers of the Sung and Ming periods, all directly pointed to humanity which is the original mind. The substance of humanity is the source of all transformations and the foundation of all things."[69] As one would expect, *jen* occupies a pivotal position in Hsiung's ontology. This enables C. B. Day to conclude that "throughout all his philosophizing, Hsiung-Shih-li placed *jen* at the center and thoroughly believed in the capacity of all men to possess a share of it, thereby proving himself truly Confucian in spirit."[70]

Hsiung's emphasis on *jen* as a life-force might have given Father Briere the impression that what he had accomplished was no more than an eclecticism: "fusing the classical doctrines of the [Wei-shih] school with the essential principles of the neo-Confucianism of Wang Yang-ming, and by drawing inspiration from Bergsonian idealism."[71] The reference to Bergson demands some explanation. Virtually all of the available sources on Hsiung Shih-li in Western languages that I have examined have made at least a passing reference to the fact that Hsiung was somehow influenced by Bergson's philosophy. Clarence H. Hamilton, in his contribution to the *Encyclopedia Britannica,* simply says that "from Western thought he gained appreciation of analytical method and the idea of evolutionary change (Bergson)."[72] In what sense was Hsiung a Bergsonian?

Actually, the question was raised by Hsieh Yu-wei in a long letter to Hsiung. Hsieh suggested that Hsiung's method of apprehending *pen-t'i* seems quite compatible with Bergson's intuitive approach to reality. Hsiung, however, rejected the comparison outright on the ground that his ontological awareness was fundamentally different from Bergson's philosophical assumptions, which, he believed, were based on a biological model. Hsiung's knowledge about Bergson was definitely secondhand. It seems that by the time he received Hsieh's letter he had only read a translated version of *Creative Evolution* by his friend Chang Tung-sun, the famous professor of Western philosophy. Hsiung emphatically denied that his ontological awareness had anything to do with Bergson's "intuition." He further argued that Bergson's notion of instinct really functions at the level of the perfumed (or polluted) mind (*hsi-hsin*) rather than at that of the original mind (*pen-hsin*).[73]

We must hasten to add that Hsiung's unwillingness to endorse Bergson's philosophy by no means suggests that other attempts to analyze his ontology in terms of Western philosophy were also dismissed. To him, comparative study of this kind, far from being objectionable, was of great significance. In his response to Hsieh Yu-wei's letter mentioned above, he accepted the interpretation that F. H. Bradley's *Appearance and Reality* contained insights quite similar to his own insistence on the unity of "original substance" and "manifested functions." However, he warned that his ontological method of "experiential comprehension," which he regarded as "the outstanding spirit of Chinese philosophy," probably differed from Bradley's intellectual argumentation in a fundamental way. Similarly, though cautioning that such an analogy might be misleading, Hsiung appreciated Chang Tung-sun's comparative observation that his *New Exposition of Consciousness Only* (*Hsin Wei-shih lun*) was congenial with Whitehead's philosophical intent in *Process and Reality*.[74]

It is possible that in underlining the importance of the cardinal Confucian virtue *jen*, Hsiung's primary concern was to construct an ontology of his own, rather than to give respectability to a Confucian concept in the light of new ideas from the West. Unlike K'ang Yu-wei, who tried to universalize *jen* to suit the demands of his times, Hsiung was not very much concerned about how new or how cosmopolitan his philosophy would appear in the eyes of those who were familiar with the most recent trends in Western thought.[75] His single-minded attention was focused on the seemingly impossible mission of finding "truth" and "value" through a long and strenuous process of experiential learning. Though he did not envision his work as the lonely struggle of an isolated thinker, he strongly believed that his philosophical quest had to begin with a probe of the specificity of his own culture and the particularity of his own existence. To use a Mencian analogy, the search for the spring of wisdom commences with digging the ground of one's true self. Yet the intention is to assert neither the strength of one's ethnicity nor the power of one's cultural heritage, but the universal relevance of "authentic existence." *Jen* so conceived is an ontological idea of humanity without its sociopolitical trappings. Hsiung's philosophy is, in this connection, a conscious attempt to demonstrate that such a task is not only experientially possible but morally imperative.

If, like Levenson, we speak of intellectual history as "the history

not of thought, but of men thinking," Hsiung's ontological awareness definitely does not point to a system of ideas forever meaning
what it means in itself, as a logical construction. Rather, as "thinking," a psychological act as well as a philosophical pursuit, it
"implies context (changing), not disembodiment, [for] men mean
different things when they think thoughts in different total environ-
ments."[76] One may very well argue that the social context in which
Hsiung philosophized as a Confucian thinker makes it clear that "a
set of Confucian attitudes, even if one could deem them uncor-
roded, does not sum up the *gestalt*."[77] The theoretical attempt to
celebrate history as the persistence of an "essential past" by obliter-
ating history-as-process is certainly untenable, but to raise the
fundamental issue of meaning as a way of understanding the seemingly inexorable process of history is the birthright of a thinking person. What is the meaning of "men thinking" if the types of thought
involved are reducible to a mere reflection on an irreversible trend
of social change? " 'Out there,' in the history men make, the web is
never rent, and intellectual, social, political, economic, cultural
threads are interwoven."[78] But an interconnected mode of explanation need not imply a fixity of relationships. The possibility of reorganization is always there, and the thinking individuals are never
"situated" in the status quo.

Unlike Bradley, who maintained that philosophy, as a form of
intellectual reflection, should not tamper with social affairs, Hsiung
believed that ontological awareness would inevitably reorganize the
constellation of given realities. True to the Confucian "one-ness of
knowledge and action,"[79] he believed that to think is not merely to
reflect but to orient, to shape, and to create. Underlying Hsiung's
study of *jen* is a basic conviction that awareness is not only an expression of reality or an evocation of truth, but also a reorganization
of the basic structure of affairs. A profound awareness of the human
condition is necessary both for the production of a compelling
understanding of historical specificity and for the creation of a new
order of social community. A systematic questioning of the deepest
insights in a given culture is therefore the authentic way of formu-
lating an ontology as a prior condition for fundamental change and
adaptation. Hsiung might have argued that if China was to survive

as an integrated nation, it would be in part because it had the courage to dig into its roots and drill into the very foundation of its *raison d'être*. Indeed, Hsiung assigned himself the task of such "digging and drilling." It is in this sense that his ontological awareness, far from being a happy excursion into a detached realm of ideas, was an agonizing struggle through the grounds of his own cultural heritage. And this was done with profound intellectual passion.

11 New Confucianism and the Intellectual Crisis of Contemporary China

HAO CHANG

In the beginning of 1958, *Min-chu p'ing-lun* (Democratic tribune), a popular journal of conservative persuasion published in Hong Kong, featured as the lead article a manifesto signed by four prominent intellectuals outside Communist China, declaring to the world their stance on Chinese culture.[1] Since the four people were generally regarded as the most active and articulate spokesmen for Chinese cultural tradition since 1949, the manifesto stood as an important synopsis of a conservative trend of thought still very much alive among contemporary intellectuals in non-Communist China. This brand of Chinese conservatism is popularly known as the *hsin ju-chia* (New Confucianism).

The New Confucianism is not a novel phenomenon which made its appearance on the intellectual scene only since 1949, but is an outgrowth of a long-standing trend of thought dating back to the May Fourth period. One of the signers of the manifesto, Chang Chün-mai (Carsun Chang), a long-time advocate of democratic politics and the leader of a small political party, previously called National Socialist, now called Democratic Socialist (Min-chu she-hui tang) on Taiwan, had been a zealous defender of the traditional civilization of China since May Fourth days. The other three, Mou Tsung-san, T'ang Chün-i, and Hsu Fu-kuan, all professors of Chinese philosophy and literature in Hong Kong and Taiwan, are devoted disciples and followers of the late conservative thinker, Hsiung Shih-li.[2] Their intellectual outlooks are also influenced to varying degrees by Liang Shu-ming, another leader of cultural conservatism and a close friend of Hsiung Shih-li. Both Hsiung and Liang, like Carsun Chang, reached intellectual adulthood in the early decades of the twentieth century and emerged as leading advocates of intellectual conservatism in the years immediately following the May Fourth movement.[3] Thus the contemporary New Confucianist thought as represented by the manifesto of 1958 may be seen as the development of a major trend of Chinese conservatism which had its origin in the early 1920s.

From the beginning the New Confucianism differed significantly from two other trends of Chinese cultural conservatism which had already become prominent in the pre-May Fourth cultural scene. Unlike the broad trend generally known as the School of National Essence (Kuo-ts'ui hsueh-p'ai), whose adherents tended to define the Chinese national identity in terms of general cultural or racial traits, the New Confucianists were inclined to identify Chinese civilization with one particular traditional trend, namely, Confucianism. Further, while the National Essence school was distinguished mainly by a particularistic striving to seek China's national identity in certain historical cultural-racial traits, the New Confucianism was characterized by a universalistic claim that Chinese civilization featured something of a transcultural intrinsic worth in Confucianism.

This emphasis on the universal significance of Confucianism calls to mind another early development of modern Chinese conservatism, namely, the movement for a Confucian church, which began with K'ang Yu-wei's campaign in the late 1890s for the acceptance of Confucianism as a national and world religion. This campaign, which K'ang and his disciples continued to wage in the early Republican years, was centered around the proposal to establish a nationwide organized Confucianist church largely for the purpose of countering the spread of Christianity.[4] Behind K'ang's movement for what he called "preservation of the faith" (pao-chiao) was of course K'ang's distinctive interpretation of Confucianism based principally on the nineteenth-century revival of the New Text school of Han Confucianism. Central to this interpretation was K'ang's image of Confucius as the founder of an organized religion (chiao-chu) comparable to Christianity.[5]

Like K'ang Yu-wei's movement for "preservation of the faith" there is also a prominent tendency among the New Confucianists to understand Confucianism as a religiomoral faith. But where K'ang promoted Confucianism by trying to build up its institutional underpinnings, the New Confucianists were inclined to put a premium on articulating Confucian religiophilosophical beliefs. Further, while K'ang's "religious" interpretation of Confucianism stemmed mainly from his acceptance of the New Text interpretation of Han Confucianism, the New Confucianists' "religious" view of Confucianism was built on its identification with the principal opponent of Han Confucianism, namely, Sung-Ming neo-Confucianism. In fact, the distinguishing characteristic of New Confucianist intellectuals as compared with the other varieties of cultural conservatism in twentieth-century China was their self-image of being the modern defenders of the neo-Confucian ethicospiritual symbolism which they prized as the core of Confucian faith. This emphasis on the ethicospiritual symbolism of neo-Confucianism, as we will see, still lay at the heart of the cultural manifesto of 1958.

This neo-Confucian revival, emerging as it did in the context of the relentless attacks on Confucianism from all sides in post-May Fourth China, inevitably raises the question: What motivated the New Confucianists? One approach very much in vogue among cultural historians and social scientists is to answer questions of this kind with reference to the concept of cultural identity.[6] According to this approach, in a society undergoing rapid and drastic cultural changes, people are likely to become inundated by new experiences and to feel cut off from their own past. People begin to wonder where they belong, who they are, and where they are going. They become anxious to reestablish a meaningful continuity with their own past in such a way that the shock of changes can be absorbed and a compass be relocated within the self.

With the emergence of this anxiety people are undergoing a crisis of cultural identity. It is not surprising that in China, where radical change has swept the land for many decades, this kind of crisis has been widespread and acute among the intellectuals. But in China it has been further compounded by the fact that the impetus to change came mainly from outside China and that its source—the West—was also largely responsible for the many accompanying humiliations and frustrations. In consequence the crisis of cultural identity in China has taken on a character typical of such phenomena in non-Western countries. Its distinguishing feature has been an emotional complex resulting from humiliating contact with the West which has worked to compel Chinese intellectuals to find psychological compensation, often subconsciously, in asserting China's cultural equivalence with or superiority to the West.[7]

The concept of cultural identity does shed light on some aspects of the New Confucianists' thinking. They have tended to interpret the Chinese intellectual heritage in ways that could accommodate modern Western values such as democracy and science. They have repeatedly — even compulsively — stressed the uniqueness of Chinese civilization, in comparison with other major civilizations in the world, most notably, Western civilization, and they have tirelessly insisted on continuity and longevity of the Chinese cultural tradition.[8]

On the other hand, the concept of cultural identity, though useful, also has some serious limitations. As an explanatory device it is at once too broad and too narrow. It is too broad because, while some important aspects of the New Confucianists' thinking certainly may be seen as a reflection of their need for cultural identity, the need by itself cannot explain why it is expressed in the specific forms found in New Confucian thought. In other words, since the crisis of cultural identity was felt by Chinese intellectuals of all stripes, reference to it does little to illuminate the particular forms it took among the New Confucian thinkers. Furthermore, given their preoccupation with defining Chineseness, there remains the problem why people of New Confucian persuasion identify as they do with one set of cultural ideals among many within the Chinese cultural tradition.

At the same time the concept is also in a sense too narrow, especially when applied to explain the tendency among New Confucian scholars to center their intellectual identification around the moral-spiritual symbolism of Confucianism. Such an explanation would require an underlying assumption that Chinese intellectuals can only concern themselves with their own cultural tradition out of particularistic preoccupation with Chineseness. This assumption feeds the tendency to overlook the possibility that Chinese intellectuals may concern themselves with their cultural past on some universalistic, transcultural grounds. After all, it is likely that some Chinese intellectuals may perceive some of their problems not as particular to them as members of the Chinese cultural community but as universal to all members of human community. Furthermore, it is also possible that the problems which they conceive as universal to the human condition may lead some of them to seek directions or answers in the cultural source with which they are most familiar, namely, their own tradition. In short, Chinese intellectuals, like other people, are most apt to fuse in their thinking universalistic and paternalistic concerns.

To understand this distinctive dimension of New Confucianist thought, I propose not so much to forgo the concept of cultural identity as to go beyond it by looking upon the New Confucianism as a response to the intellectual crisis which began with the closing years of the 1890s and reached its height in the May Fourth period.[9] While certain aspects of New Confucianist thought may need be seen again against the background of the crisis of cultural identity, its moral-spiritual thrust and its neo-Confucian orientation must be understood in the context of other problems facing the May Fourth generation, that is, the crisis of meaning and the reaction against scientism.

The crisis of meaning is a dimension of the intellectual crisis in modern China which has not received as much attention as it deserves. To be sure, the source of this crisis is probably as old as human history, for in China as in other lands the fundamental meaning of life and the world has always been an absorbing question for sensitive spirits. But it became a widely disturbing one as new world views and new systems of value flooded into China and broke the protective canopy which the traditional *Weltanschauung* and *Lebensanschauung*—or what Susanne Langer calls the symbols of general orientation—provided to shield people from the threat of outer chaos and inner anxiety. With the traditional symbols of orientation eclipsed by the variety of conflicting new ones, the Chinese were plunged into a spiritual disorientation of a magnitude perhaps unprecedented since the influx of Buddhism in medieval times.

To understand the crisis of meaning among Chinese intellectuals we must begin by examining the different dimensions of this disorientation. We may start with moral values. Between 1895 and 1905, when the onset of a large-scale Western intellectual impact coincided with the resurgence of unorthodox trends in indigenous thought, some central moral-political values of the Confucian tradition were for the first time called into question.[10] The disorientation reached its climax in the late 1910s when the May Fourth zealots called for the transvaluation of all values, especially the whole Confucian moral tradition.[11] The scope of their moral iconoclasm is perhaps unique in the modern world; no other historical civilization outside the West undergoing modern transformation has witnessed such a phoenixlike impulse to see its own cultural tradition so completely negated. This radical iconoclasm, which created in its train a widespread sense of moral disorientation, naturally produced anxieties of the acutest kind.

Closely related to moral disorientation is existential disorientation. The insights provided by the studies of both religion and existentialism call our attention to the fact that there are anxieties built into the structure of human existence which are occasioned by the existential predicaments of suffering, death, fate, and the like — experiences that Karl Jaspers calls the "boundary situations" — and which are encountered inevitably in the process of life.[12] In the modern world the existential predicaments of human life may not necessarily be more acute than before. Yet to the extent that the symbolic shelter of traditional religious beliefs has been crumbling in China, these predicaments inevitably constitute a source of new anguish for Chinese.

Between the late 1890s and the May Fourth period the moral crisis was widely discussed, but a sense of existential pessimism was also spreading. This mood pervades much of the poetical literature of the period, and it is particularly apparent in the literary thinking of Wang Kuo-wei. It is also seen in the large number of Chinese intellectuals who were existentially involved in studying Mahayana Buddhism. In fact, two of the seminal New Confucianists, Liang

Shu-ming and Hsiung Shih-li, both grappled with existential problems through their study of Buddhism early in life before the conversion to Confucianism.[13]

Underlying the value and existential disorientations there was still another dimension to the spiritual crisis, which for lack of a better term may be called the metaphysical disorientation. Chinese intellectuals in the past lived in an intelligible world thanks to the all-embracing metaphysical world view of traditional religion and philosphy. The most powerful modern dissolvent of their traditional world views undoubtedly came from the introduction of science. For many educated Chinese, the impact of science, to be sure, was not entirely disturbing; for science also constitutes a new way of making the external world intelligible. But the intelligibility provided by science is bound to be limited. For science may be able to answer many of the questions of "what" and "how" but has to remain silent about the "ultimate why." Thus science by its very nature could not serve as a substitute for the all-inclusive world views of tradition.

Historians who study the intelligentsia in twentieth-century China have often observed their intriguing susceptibility to totalistic philosophies and ideologies. This propensity for intellectual totalism certainly has something to do with the widely felt desperate need to find an all-embracing solution to China's vast complex of sociopolitical problems. However, it also reflects a certain metaphysical need to find some all-inclusive world view, a cognitive map on a cosmic scale by which to anchor and orient oneself, spatially as well as temporarily, in this bewildering new environment.

The distinctiveness of the spiritual disorientation in modern China, however, lay not so much in the emergence of any one of these disorientations as in the coincidence and merging of the three together — the moral, the existential, and the metaphysical. It is the fusion of these three kinds of disorientation which lies at the root of the modern Chinese crisis of meaning. Much of the way the New Confucian scholars relate themselves to the tradition must be grasped against this background. Much of their thought may be seen as a quest for meaning — an attempt to overcome the spiritual disorientation felt by many sensitive souls among Chinese intellectuals. Of course, spiritual disorientation was not unique to New Confucian circles; it was a crisis that faced Chinese intellectuals of all persuasions. The factors which led them to identify specifically with Confucian religiomoral symbolism must be sought in the context of their reaction against scientism.

Scientism as it took shape in China in the early decades of the twentieth century refers first of all to an inflated conception of science as an all-inclusive system of nature which not only informs us of objective reality concerning the physical universe but prescribes an outlook on human life and society as well. Secondly, it involved a conviction that science represented a mode of thinking, a methodology which promised to be the only valid way of understanding life and the world.[14] While such extravagant claims about science continued to gain widespread acceptance among Chinese intellectuals after the May Fourth days, they also ran into a strong reaction. In fact, a visible reaction had already occured in the immediate post-May Fourth years with the publication of Liang Shu-ming's *Tung-Hsi wen-hua chi ch'i che-hsueh* (Eastern and Western cultures and their philosophies) and the opening of debate on "science" versus "metaphysics" in the early 1920s.[15] The revolt against scientism marked the emergence of the New Confucianism as an identifiable trend of thought.

Both Liang Shu-ming and the principal protagonist of metaphysics in the debate, Carsun Chang, accepted the conception of science as a system of nature. Both, however, had serious misgivings about the scientistic outlook on human life and society. From Liang's standpoint, science inherently involved such deleterious life views as crass utilitarianism and excessive activism, which needed to be corrected by developing the Chinese spiritual culture centered around the Confucian ideal of *jen*. In Chang's view, science bred a mechanistic and deterministic world view which had to be countered by fostering the moral idealism in the Chinese cultural tradition, especially in the Confucian philosophy of Wang Yang-ming.[16] But underlying these misgivings was a deeper objection to the claim that science represented the only valid way of getting at the total reality. Liang believed in a higher cosmic-moral reality which only could be captured by an intuitive and spiritual mind.[17] For Chang the whole sphere of human life was distinguished by an organic and spiritual uniqueness not amenable to scientific analysis. Thus he saw the world broken down into two realms of reality: the realm of nature and the realm of human affairs. While science provides the key to knowledge of the former, it has little value when applied to studying the latter, where what is essential to understanding is a personal, immediate, and sympathetic mode of comprehension: namely, intuition (*chih-chueh*).[18]

In New Confucianist circles a closely related but more important impetus to the revolt against scientism was provided by Hsiung Shih-li, who was more influential than any other of the first generation of New Confucianists in shaping the minds of those active in the post-1949 intellectual scene. Indeed Hsiung, whose major philosophical writings appeared largely in the 1930s and 1940s, may be seen as the single most important spiritual link between the early New Confucianists and those still active today in Hong Kong and Taiwan.

A creative self-made scholar, Hsiung began his intellectual career as a devoted student of Buddhism but later became converted to Confucianism. He undertook his religiophilosophical studies not so much from an intellectual interest as from an existential passion to search for spiritual wisdom with which he could, in his own words, develop peace of mind and lead a meaningful existence (*an-hsin li-ming*). Thus underlying all his major philosophical endeavors was a deeply felt concern for meaning which became crystallized in what Tu Wei-ming called an ontological vision.[19] This ontological vision, which he developed by drawing heavily upon both the idealistic philosophies of Confucianism and the Yogacarian thought of Mahayana Buddhism, consists in envisaging the ultimate reality of the universe as a dialectical process of creation by a cosmic mind which is seen not merely as the numinous beyond but also immanent in all the empirical concrete existences as their inner essences. Although Hsiung insisted on his philosophy as a metaphysical monism, his intellectual outlook in fact contained a dichotomous view of the world which emphasizes the division between the phenomenal realm and the realm of metaphysical reality. Regarding the former realm the goal of human knowledge is scientific truth. As for the latter the efforts to seek for scientific truth would be misdirected since, according to Hsiung's belief, in the realm of metaphysical reality the subjective and the objective, the intellectual and the moral all fuse together and merge into an undifferentiated whole of experience, which eludes the analytical distinctions and discursive reasonings of science. This "noumenal" whole, or the ultimate reality, could be only seized by an exercise of intuitive and empathic mind. The truth seized in this way is what Hsiung called "metaphysical truth" (*hsuan-hsueh ti chen-li*) as opposed to "scientific truth." The exercise of the intuitive and empathic mind Hsiung described with such terms as "experiential recognition" (*t'i-jen*) and "understanding through personal witness" (*cheng-hui*), which have connotations strongly reminiscent of the Buddhist and Confucian emphasis on the personal, immediate, transcendent experience of ultimate reality.[20]

In terms of intellectual approach, Hsiung Shih-li, as well as Liang Shu-ming and Carsun Chang, typified a general tendency among New Confucianist intellectuals not so much to deny the usefulness of scientific discourse per se as to complement the objective logical-causal mode of thinking with an approach which promised to yield a subjective, direct, and empathic comprehension of the world. In this sense the New Confucianists constituted a revolt against scientism rather than against science.

This revolt against scientism came to a head in a protracted debate begun in the early 1920s about the value of scientific method in interpreting the Chinese cultural heritage. In twentieth-century China this debate ran parallel to and often became intertwined with the other more sensational controversy over the value of Chinese tradition as a whole. The central issue underlying the latter controversy was primarily an evaluative one: What is the value and relevance of the Chinese cultural tradition in the modern world, and where should one take a stand? At issue in the former, however, was the intellectual-methodological question: Whatever the value of the Chinese tradition, how can one understand it? New Confucian intellectuals in the post-May Fourth period took their stand against the popular historical movement led by Hu Shih, Ku Chich-kang, and other scholars under the influence of scientific positivism to "reorganize the national heritage" (*cheng-li kuo-ku*). Underlying this popular movement was an effort to study cultural-historical questions "objectively" on the model of the natural sciences. Dominated by this objectivism the adherents of the *kuo-ku* movement tended to look upon China's cultural past as no more than a mass of verifiable data waiting to be reconstructed through the application of scientific method.[21] In the view of the New Confucian philosophers, a positivistic and objectivistic mode of thinking may reconstruct external facts concerning tradition but could never bring people to grasp the spiritual-moral meaning that lay at the core of it. The vital spiritual-moral meaning, they believed, could only be captured by an intuitionist, experiential approach.

The controversy between the New Confucianists and the intellectuals of positivist persuasion reminds us of the long-standing debate in the Ch'ing period between the so-called schools of Han learning and Sung learning. At issue in that debate was also a disagreement over the approach to understanding the teachings of Confucius in particular and the Chinese cultural heritage in general. Where scholars of the Han learning stood for an objective, empirical, textual-philological (*k'ao-chü*) approach, those of Sung learning espoused a "subjective," moral-metaphysical (*i-li*) approach.[22] Little wonder a sense of continuity with their recent past was felt by both sides in the post-May Fourth controversy. The New Confucian scholars often took pride in being the modern champions of the neo-Confucian moral-philosophical approach, while people in the opposite camp frequently saw themselves in the images of the Ch'ing "empiricist" scholars. However, the continuities were far less significant than the discontinuities that separate the two debates. For one thing, the post-May Fourth controversy took place in the context of modern intellectual crisis, whereas the debate in the Ch'ing period occurred as a result of internal developments within the tradition. In consequence, foreign influences which had no part in shaping the debate among Ch'ing scholars affected the New Confucianists and their adversaries in a most fundamental way. This foreign influence was obvious among the advocates of scientific study of Chinese tradition, who owed their position largely to the influx of the Western scientisim and positivism.[23] As for the New Confucianists, Western thought seemed to have little impact on Hsiung Shih-li, whose philosophical training consisted mainly of his study of the spiritual literatures of Confucianism and Mahayana Buddhism. But in fact Hsiung's acknowledgment of the value of scientific methodology in understanding the empirical world and his revolt against scientism testified to the fact that he was not immune to Western influences.[24] In the case of Liang Shu-ming and Carsun Chang, imprints of Western impact were far more patent. Liang Shu-ming admitted that Bergsonianism had significantly influenced his intuitionist approach. Carsun Chang, in emphasizing the limitations of scientific methodology and in accentuating the usefulness of the intuitionist outlook in humanistic studies, explicitly acknowledged his indebtedness to the thought of Rudolph Eucken and Henri Bergson as well as to the Kantian philosophy.[25] Clearly, among the New Confucianists, revolt against scientism was fueled as much by the Western impact as by the traditional influences; the approach which led to the affirmation of tradition was no less fed by contacts with Western thought than by study of traditional philosophies.

The New Confucianist battle against scientific positivism continued in the post-1949 years. One major reason was the undiminished dominance of scientism in the academic circles. Another factor was the increasing interest in the West in studying Chinese civilization. On top of these was the Chinese communists' radical attack on the Chinese cultural tradition. In the eyes of the New Confucianist intellectuals all these developments shared an unsympathetic attitude toward Chinese tradition which they believed resulted largely from the objectivistic, scientific outlook in vogue. Thus one is not surprised to see a reemphasis on the intuitive, empathic mode of thinking among the New Confucianists, as reflected in the cultural manifesto of 1958. The manifesto again stressed the conception of tradition as a historically accumulated objectification of the human mind. Tradition has a life, a spirit, and hence is not something inanimate and bloodless which can be studied impersonally and dispassionately. What can be so studied are only the externals of the tradition. But beneath the externals flow the spirit and meaning of the tradition. The latter cannot be grasped except through an act of sympathetic imagination and intuitive comprehension by the mind. This is especially true for the understanding of one's own tradition, where emotional involvement to a certain extent is inescapable. Thus according to the manifesto, any genuine understanding of tradition cannot involve the exercise of intellect alone. In their own words, what is needed is wisdom (*chih-hui*) which consists in the combination of intellect with feelings of sympathy and reverence (*t'ung-ch'ing yü ching-i*). The greater the feeling, the deeper the wisdom that brings us to the spiritual core of the tradition.[26]

It was this antipositivistic mode of thinking which from the beginning allowed the quest for meaning among the New Confucian intellectuals to develop in the direction of reaffirming the value of the Chinese cultural tradition. It was also this antipositivistic mode of thinking which faciliated the New Confucianists' central identification with the moral-metaphysical symbolism of Confucianism. Their characteristic perception of Chinese tradition as based on a form of Confucian religiousness can only be understood in terms of their search for symbols of spiritual orientation through an intuitionist, experiential mode of thinking.

The New Confucian scholars outside Communist China today are very conscious that their perception of the Chinese tradition is an exceptional one, placing them in opposition to the prevailing views among foreign visitors in China and many post-May Fourth Chinese intellectuals of iconoclastic persuasion.[27] The core of this conventional view is that historical Confucianism was nothing more than a cake of moral norms and a web of human relationships. Rejecting this view as simplistic and distorting, the cultural manifesto of 1958 announced in an emphatic tone: "With regard to Chinese civilization, for many years there has prevailed a view among many people both in China and abroad, that Chinese civilization put its emphasis on moral relationships between people and deemphasized religious belief in God. This view is not mistaken in principle. However, many people are of the opinion that the moral culture which is the focal point of Chinese civilization only seeks to order actual human relations so as to maintain social and political stability. They also think that there is no religious feeling of transcendence and that the Chinese moral thought does not go beyond prescribing norms for proper behavior and thereby fails to provide a basis for inner spiritual life. These views are seriously mistaken."[28]

According to the manifesto, the source of these mistaken views lies in a widespread tendency to misconstrue a basic characteristic of Chinese civilization, namely, its cultural undifferentiatedness. Admittedly, unlike in the West where religion has long been separate and distinct from the other elements of civilization, in traditional China religion was from the beginning fused with the political and moral orders. Mistaking this undifferentiatedness for a lack of religiousness itself is the serious error that underlies the prevailing tendency to identify Confucian culture totally with a traditional moralism.[29]

The important fact is that within the apparent undifferentiatedness there are cultural elements which point to the idea of transcendence and the belief in the numinous in Confucian thinking. One place where concepts of transcendence and the numinous can be found is that part of Confucianism which centers around the doctrine of mind (*hsin*) and nature (*hsing*) or what the manifesto calls the study of mind and nature (*hsin-hsing chih hsueh*).[30] This belief, according to Mou Tsung-san and his co-signatories, lies at the heart of Confucianism and neo-Confucianism and therefore constitutes the core of the Chinese cultural tradition. But unfortunately this all-important core is also that part of Chinese civilization that is most widely misunderstood.[31]

The misunderstanding stems partly from a tendency to construe what is called "nature" in Confucianism mainly in a naturalistic, psychological sense. In this sense *hsing* is understood to refer to the empirical constitution of the human mind. Another source of misunderstanding lies in the tendency to construe *hsing* in an intellectualistic sense. In this sense it is understood to refer to the mental faculty of reason. In the manifesto both senses are emphatically rejected in favor of a metaphysical view that considers *hsing* as the source of moral consciousness or what Mou calls the moral creativity of the human mind.[32] As the source of moral creativity *hsing* is asserted to be the real self, the inner core of what makes people human. Mou put this view most succinctly when he said: "What we commonly call 'self' can be understood in three senses, namely, physiological self, psychological self, and cognitive self . . . The self in either of these three senses however is not the concrete true self. The concrete, true self is the moral self which is realized only in the actual practice of cultivating the personality. This self is the true self and therefore the true subject of humanity."[33]

Thus, according to the Confucian doctrine of mind and nature, any individual human existence takes on a duality. On the one hand there is the inner, authentic self or what Mencius called the great self (*ta-t'i*). On the other there is the empirical physical self or what Mencius called the small self (*hsiao-t'i*). While the moral essential self is present in every human mind, the important fact is that it is something completely different in kind from the empirical self. Moreover it exists as something potential which can be actualized only by human effort through transforming the physical self. In this sense the inner moral self is a transcendental being as contrasted with the empirical self. In short, the Confucian conception of *hsing* implies a belief in an inner transcendence.[34]

In the framework of Confucianism, the manifesto points out, the idea of the inner transcendence of *hsing* is integrally linked with that of the outer transcendence of *t'ien* (heaven) or *t'ien-tao* (the way of heaven). For it is a central belief of Confucianism that *hsing* as the transcendent moral self is an endowment from heaven. In the Confucian tradition, *t'ien* is believed to refer to the metaphysical ground of being and source of meaning. As such it represents the numinous beyond, which transcends what is actually given in the natural world and human society. Along with the belief that *hsing* is an endowment from heaven, this conception of heaven constitutes the core of the fundamental Confucian world view — the doctrine of the unity of heaven and humankind (*t'ien-jen ho-i*).[35]

It is in this doctrine that the religiousness and the transcendental symbolism of Confucianism has its focus. As Mou Tsung-san points out, the formal characteristics of Confucianism as a religion, in comparison with those of other religions, especially Christianity, do not appear striking. First of all, although there is no lack of a conception of a transcendent personal god in the ancient Chinese thought, this conception became muted in the later development of Confucianism. Further, although Confucianism is not without its elements of supplication and prayer, these elements did not develop into the institutionalized rituals of prayer and worship as they did so strikingly in Christianity. All these, in Mou's view, however, do not imply the dearth of religiousness in Confucianism but mean only that the religiousness of Confucianism is channeled in different directions.[36]

According to Mou, it is in the direction of actualizing the way of heaven in human life that the religiousness of Confucianism is channeled. Since according to the doctrine of the unity of heaven and humanity the *hsing* directly partakes of the way of heaven, the problem of how to actualize the latter is also that of how to actualize the *hsing* or more specifically, how to make the inner moral self the controlling force in human life. In the Confucian frame of reference this problem is answered by the idea of self-cultivation (*hsiu-sheng*) which is centered around the belief that the only way to actualize *hsing* and thereby the way of heaven in human life is through engaging in an endless and rigorous process of moral-spiritual discipline.[37] In this sense the concern with self-cultivation, the leitmotif of Confucian moral tradition, takes on a significance more than moral. In a very essential way it also has religious significance, since to engage in moral effort is at the same time to fulfill one's inner real self and thereby also to follow the command of heaven. This is why Mou and his friends argue that Confucianism is never just a moral order or a system of ethical norms. As he said, it embodies "a high degree of religiousness."[38] In their view the doctrine of the unity of heaven and the human being holds the key to this high degree of religiousness in Confucianism.

Expounding on the religiousness of Confucianism, Mou Tsung-san, in his major work on the development of neo-Confucianism, terms Confucianism the "religion of moral cultivation" (*ch'eng-te chih chiao*),[39] which he describes in these terms: "The highest goal of moral cultivation is to become a sage, a man of *jen*, a great man. The real import of this moral cultivation, however, consists in achieving the infinite and the perfect out of the finite existence of humankind. Being both a moral system and religion at once, [Confucianism] has its purpose in establishing a 'moral religion' (*tao-te ti tsung-chiao*) for humanity."[40]

The religiousness inherent in the moral thought of Confucianism, according to Mou, is reflected clearly in the central ethicospiritual symbol, *jen*. In an ordinary sense, *jen* refers to a moral ideal signifying love or human-heartedness. In a deeper sense, however, *jen* embodies a world view which flows from the Confucian conceptions of nature and the way of heaven. Since according to these conceptions every existence in the universe has its inner essense in *hsing* and since every *hsing* partakes of the *tao* of heaven, these Confucian conceptions imply a belief in an essential union of every existence with every other and with the universe as a whole. In other words, Confucianism sees behind the apparent diversity of "ten thousand things" a spiritual unity which constitutes the ultimate reality comparable in its nature and function to God in Christianity.[41]

As such, Mou further points out, *jen* has two characteristics. First of all it contains the boundless capacity for empathy and compassion which, when extended to the utmost, would melt away any barrier among people erected out of indifference and animosity and allow an unimpeded flow of fellow-feeling in the human world. Secondly it generates an overflow of vitality which fuels incessant growth and regrowth of life in the cosmos. Together these two characteristics suggest that the actualization of *jen* would mean the whole cosmos merging into an organic oneness vibrant with vitality and feeling. This is the spiritual meaning which he thought many eminent neo-Confucian philosophers gave to *jen* when they defined the latter as "becoming one with the universe" (*yu t'ien-ti wan-wu wei i-t'i*). This spiritual meaning of *jen* is inherent in the doctrine of the unity of heaven and humanity.[42]

In the above view, *jen*, then, points beyond moral cultivation to spiritual transformation, beyond the finite to the infinite, beyond the mundane to the transcendent. It thus crystallizes for New Confucianists a moral-spiritual perspective through which life and the world are seen against a numinous, cosmic backdrop. Such a perspective implies that these New Confucian thinkers look at Confucianism not from outside but from inside. Seen from inside Confucian religiomoral symbolism functions for them above all as the value center.

As the value center this religiomoral symbolism projects a humanistic perspective which has the human world as its focus. Admittedly Mou Tsung-san and his colleagues place great emphasis on the significance of transcendental beliefs in Confucianism and thus see the ultimate source of meaning and value in the numinous beyond — the way of heaven. As seen above, however, the way of heaven, while transcendent, is also inherent in every individual person. In this sense value and meaning are also immanent in this world. True, in the framework of the Confucian doctrine of the unity of heaven and humanity, "immanent" must be understood in a special sense. For *hsing* as the repository of truth and goodness is something qualitatively different from the physiological and psychological constitution of the human self. But insofar as the empirical self and world provides the only context for the actualization of meaning and value, a this-wordly orientation is central to Confucianism. In the view of many New Confucianist intellectuals the unique value of Confucianism lies in its combination of an orientation to this world with an openness to transcendence.[43]

The this-worldly orientation of *jen* is specifically reflected in the Confucian vision of moral transformation of this world to achieve the universal humanization of existence. Flowing from the latter ideal are some social and moral implications contained in the Confucian life ideal of "sage within and king without" (*nei-sheng wai-wang*).[44]

In accordance with this ideal every human being has two commitments to fulfill. In the first place there is the commitment to the moral perfection of one's personality. This commitment is predicated on the assumption that the central dimension of human life is the moral. True, moral life is not seen as the only dimension of human existence. Confucianism recognizes the legitimacy of the intellectual, the artistic, or the physical dimensions. Yet Confucianism demands that the development of the other dimensions be ultimately controlled by the moral. The perfection of one's moral life constitutes sagehood — the goal of every human life.[45]

According to Confucianism the fulfillment of moral life and the attainment of sagehood is not adventitious and depends neither on the freaks of luck nor on the external grace of God. On the contrary, moral cultivation has an inner source within every human mind, and this inner source is the heaven-endowed *hsing*. T'ang Chün-i and his friends believe it is a profound insight of Confucianism that the attainment of sagehood is within the reach of every ordinary individual.[46]

Another profound insight of Confucianism is that the moral cultivation of any individual person cannot be self-sufficient. This insight is implicit in the very meaning of *jen*. For central to the realization of *jen* is the unimpeded flow of feeling between oneself and others. Given this character of *jen*, the fulfillment of one's moral life depends upon one's willingness to dedicate oneself to helping others achieve moral fulfillment. This dedication to the moral welfare of others is called *shu* (reciprocity) in Confucianism. As Hsu Fu-kuan said: "Only *shu* is the bridge to unite the self and others; only *shu* is the test of [the existence of] moral consciousness of *jen*."[47] Thus in addition to the self-regarding commitment to self-cultivation *jen* enjoins an other-regarding commitment to the moral fulfillment of others.

In Confucianism this other-regarding commitment leads to a recognition of the outer realm of reality as distinguished from the inner realm of the human mind with moral and spiritual capacities. A Confucian sage, while recognizing this dichotomy, however, must bridge the two realms. That is to say, he must go beyond cultivating his innate spiritual and moral capacities to actively concern himself with the outer world. Hence a sage must be a king, so to speak, who actively participates in the outer world.[48] However, according to the manifesto, although Confucianism is actively concerned with the outer world, this concern failed to develop over the centuries into an intellectual tradition equipped to cope with the problems pertaining to the latter. The recognition of this failure is the lesson they derive from comparing the Chinese civilization with that of the West.[49]

This comparison shows that to cope successfully with the outer world, both the natural and the social, a civilization needs to develop two cultural prerequisites which are the triumphs of the modern Western civilization, namely, science and democracy.[50] To be sure, as these New Confucian philosophers point out, before the modern era, China had long been ahead of the West in terms of scientific and technological developments and material standard of living. However, Chinese civilization lacked one essential ingredient which played a decisive role in the phenomenal development of science in the modern West: the long tradition in the West, dating back to ancient Greece, of emphasizing cognitive knowledge as a primary and intrinsic value. This valuation of knowledge for knowledge's sake made possible the development of mathematics, logic, physics, and other theoretical sciences. Since these theoretical sciences laid the foundation for the development of applied sciences and technologies, the distinctively Western emphasis on the primacy of cognitive knowledge must be seen as the "spirit of science." This spirit, however, was wanting in Chinese civilization largely because of Chinese overemphasis on a moral orientation toward the world.[51]

While Chinese civilization was short on developing science to cope with the natural world, it also failed to build up a modern state to cope with the social world.[52] To be sure, China had been the most enduring unified empire in the world before modern times. But as Carsun Chang and Mou Tsung-san pointed out, China in the past had been sophisticated in developing bureaucratic administration (*li-chih*, or *chih-tao*) but deficient in developing a sound political tradition (*cheng-tao*). The result was that China failed to become a modern state even well into the modern age, and the key to this failure lay in the inability of Chinese political tradition to develop in the direction of democratic government.[53]

The New Confucianists did not mean to say that there was no native potential for developing democratic institutions and ideology in China. They often pointed to the existence in Chinese political tradition of the institution of premiership whereby high ministers in government could share power with the emperor; to the censorial system whereby the censors had the right to remonstrate with the rulers over their behavior and policies; and to the system of bureaucratic recruitment by way of recommendation and examination, which kept open communication between the government and the society.[54] In terms of ideology the democratic potential is even clearer. To begin with, there was the belief in the doctrine of the mandate of heaven in which the conception of popular will as the reflection of heaven's will implied the idea of democratic legitimacy. This idea was reinforced by Confucian utopianism, in which the antipathy for any private monopoly of political power crystallized into the ideal that "all-under-heaven belongs to the public" (*t'ien-hsia wei kung*). In addition the Confucian notion that sagehood is within the reach of every individual person had the democratic implication that people are all entitled to equal status since every-one is recognized as having moral autonomy and dignity. All these democratically tinged ideals fed a long and unbroken tradition of moral protest against political despotism from Mencius to Huang Tsung-hsi. This combined tradition of ideological protest and institutional restraints did curb the growth of political despotism, but nevertheless failed ultimately to contain it. Herein lies the basic reason for the politically vicious circles of order and disorder, which succeeded each other throughout the long history of China.[55]

Together the failures to develop science and democracy in the Chinese tradition point to the inadequacy of the Confucian approach to the problems of the outer world. But the inadequacy of approach should not be taken to reflect any defect on the part of the basic Confucian value orientation. On the contrary it is the belief of these New Confucianist intellectuals that a broad and sound under-standing of such central Confucian ideals as *jen* and *nei-sheng wai-wang* would dispose the Chinese toward accepting Western science and democracy. As indicated above, in the framework of Confucianism moral fulfillment requires active involvement in the outer world. This involvement, they hold, would be facilitated by objective understanding of the outer reality both social and natural. Furthermore, there is a strong element of realism in Confucianism which recognizes the importance of material well-being for the moral transformation of people. Both in terms of developing objective understanding of the outer world and material well-being, science could make an essential contribution. In this sense the develop-ment of a scientific culture would not only enrich Chinese civilization by adding a new dimension to it; it is also a necessity dictated by the moral imperative to humanize life and society as enjoined by *jen*.[56]

From the standpoint of the New Confucianists, the establishment of a democratic state would be even more directly true to the spirit of *jen*. They view democracy as the most effective antidote to the bane of Chinese political tradition—despotism—which they see as nothing less than the crudest expression of human egoism (*ssu*). As such it goes against the spirit of public-mindedness (*kung*), which is essential to achieving moral solidarity. Democracy, conceived as the institution which takes political power out of personal hands and puts it under public control, is seen as the utmost fulfillment of the spirit of public-mindedness. Furthermore, democracy as an institutional device to insure political equality is in keeping with the Confucian belief that every individual has the potential to become a sage and hence should be respected as a morally autonomous being entitled to equal status with anyone else. In both ways democracy is regarded as an institution in tune with the unfolding of the moral ideal of *jen*. In short, the manifesto portrays both democracy and science as developments essential for the realization of Confucian moral idealism.[57]

While Confucian religioethical ideals inclined these New Confucian intellectuals to embrace science and democracy, these same ideals also accounted for their reluctance to accept without reservation some other elements of modern Western civilization. One such element is nationalism. It is true that they all prized the nation-state as an indispensable modern institution that was lacking in the Chinese tradition. They regarded traditional China either as a mere cultural unit or as no more than a network of social relations, and in view of all the threats to her political existence in the modern era, they considered her transformation from a sociocultural entity into a full-fledged nation-state to be a prime necessity.[58] To some like T'ang Chün-i and Mou Tsung-san, who to some degree believed in cultural nationalism, the nation-state had the added virtue of providing the only framework in which the national character of China could be fulfilled and the cultural individuality of the people articulated. But as T'ang and Mou emphasized, extreme nationalism can be a demonic force and no unmixed blessing for humankind. Furthermore, the ideal of *jen* inevitably impels them to look beyond the nation-state to a universalistic vision of all-under-heaven in one family. In short, their moral idealism could not allow them to commit themselves unreservedly to nationalism.[59]

A similar ambivalence is also seen in their view of what we may call the "spirit of modernization." This spirit can be described as a new mentality which centers around the belief in social progress through what Max Weber called the "rational mastery of the world." Toward this new mentality their attitude is of course not that of an explicit and simple rejection, for they know that this spirit constitutes the wellspring of the power and wealth of the modern West. However, their reluctance to be enthusiastic about it is clearly implied in their disapproval of what they call "the life ideal of heroism." The latter, as they define it, refers to the tendency to value any kind of remarkable achievement won by sheer force of powerful personality or by unusual talents or by a combination of both of these. Without the guidance of a spiritual-moral purpose, they feel, heroism in the sense of the raw will to struggle and to push forward is likely to turn into purely destructive force. Furthermore, without a spiritually and morally meaningful goal to sustain it, the untempered drive to achieve and to master is likely to end in a feeling of emptiness and despair.[60] Unqualified glorification of "progress" and the cult of nationalism are both of dubious value in building up an enduring civilization.[61]

Confucian moral and spiritual ideals, in addition to providing a value standard by which these New Confucianist scholars could define their position with regard to the new issues and novel experiences of the modern world, also supply a source of meaning, which helped them to come to terms with the existential situations of human life. In one of his works, T'ang Chün-i tried to drive home the value of Confucianism in this direction by envisaging the absurdity of human life without the guidance of a spiritual-moral ideal. Looking at the enigma of human existence in terms of whither and whence, he compares life to a small isolated light-tower standing in the middle of a vast sea in the night. Just as the light-tower is surrounded by boundless darkness, life beyond its beginning and end is also shrouded in unfathomable mystery.[62] If the beginning and end of life are seen as arbitrary and absurd, within the life process every phase is riddled with troubles and sufferings. The reason is that life is bound up with all kinds of cravings. Built into every kind of craving, such as the craving for the satisfaction of physical needs, for love, for honor, and even for the realization of lofty ideals and values, are unavoidable disappointments and frustrations. In view of the pervasiveness of sufferings and troubles in the life-world, it is no wonder that high religions such as Buddhism, Taoism, and Christianity almost all start with pessimistic premises about life. In T'ang's view, however, Confucianism provides an invaluable source of spiritual support enabling people to face the existential situations of life with equanimity and courage.[63] T'ang's view in this regard found an echo in an observation put forward by Hsu Fu-kuan and strongly supported by Mou Tsung-san, that Confucianism had its origin in a profound sense of sorrow and difficulty that was believed to have pervaded people's outlook on this world in the ancient Chou dynasty.[64]

T'ang Chün-i's claim that Confucianism is equipped to cope with the existential anxieties rests largely on his belief that Confucianism seriously comes to grips with the single most poignant source of existential anxieties—the problem of death. As he said, the key to overcoming the fear of death lies in the belief that there is something spiritual in a human life, which can survive the physical death of the body. Confucianism provides such a belief, and this belief stems again from the distinctive Confucian conception of moral cultivation. In the Confucian frame of reference, it must be recalled, moral cultivation is meant to be no mere compliance in behavior with the ethical norms, for in practicing moral virtues the Confucianists believe they are at the same time also fulfilling their inner true nature. As indicated before, this inner true nature of any person is essentially linked to that of everyone else by virtue of the fact that they are all endowments from heaven and partake of the same ultimate reality—the *tao*. Consequently in practicing self-cultivation one feels in unity with the minds of one's fellow human beings and engages in communion with the numinous transcendent. In short, through the practice of self-cultivation one loses one's physical self into the large spiritual unity of self and heaven. By merging into a larger whole one naturally transcends the fear of the extinction of one's physical self.[65] According to the manifesto, therein lies a key to the Confucian approach to the problem of death. The effectiveness of this Confucian approach is proven in the many instances where men of Confucian conviction in the past defied the fear of death and died as martyrs for their moral cause.[66]

So far we have seen how the Confucian religiomoral symbolism serves as the value center for New Confucianist intellectuals, providing them with moral orientation and a way to cope with the existential situation of the human being. By the same token, this value center also constitutes the focus of their loyalty and commitment. As such the spiritual and moral ideals of Confucianism are seen not as a system of abstract, theoretical ideas but as something to be expressed in actions and embodied in life. In fact, they emphasized that the meaning of these moral truths can only be grasped through devoted and persistent practice. In discussing the understanding of moral truths, they used the word "awakening" (*chueh-wu*), which has strong religious connotations. After rebutting the detached, theoretical attitude as a hindrance to awakening to moral truths, their manifesto explains the relation between awakening and moral action as follows: "We must rely upon awakening to fuel moral actions and moral action to increase awakening. Knowledge and action depend upon each other to go forward. This awakening can be expressed in language. However when other people read the language (which expresses this awakening), they have to understand this awakening through actions."[67]

From this perspective they argue for what they consider the unique profundity of Confucianism as a source of moral-spiritual wisdom. For in their view, Confucianism, especially that part centered around the belief in the inner transcendence of the human mind, is predicated on the precious insight that moral awakening is essentially a function of the "subjective" mind. They emphasized that Confucianism from the beginning assumes that moral awakening is not an intellectual understanding of an objective theoretical truth; nor is it a commandment from outside by God. An authentic moral awakening can only come from within—from the inner moral consciousness—and can only be enlarged and deepened through devoted moral practices.[68] With a long tradition of such concern, Confucianism, in their view, is a storehouse of moral wisdom and hence is uniquely equipped to cope with the universal human problem of how to become moral.[69]

The quest for meaning, then, has led these New Confucianist

conservatives to see in Confucianism not just a tradition which existed in the past but a living moral faith in which they are inside participants. They can thus appreciate the Confucian spiritual and moral ideals in a way that an outside observer cannot. Further, from the Confucian religiomoral ideals, they have derived a value center which, beyond functioning as a base for moral orientation, imparts a coherent meaning to life and the world. In this sense their identification with the ethicospiritual symbolism of Confucianism is above all a response to the crisis of meaning.

There is a general tendency to regard modern Chinese conservatism as a reaction against the "progressive" ideals of the modern West. Karl Mannheim may very well speak for a popular view when he defined modern conservatism broadly as a countermovement in conscious opposition to the progressive movement. In keeping with this popular view, Chinese conservatism would be seen as a response to the crisis of modernization.

Insofar as the contemporary New Confucian thought discussed above represents an important trend of modern Chinese conservatism, this view is too restricted. Admittedly the problem of modernization bulks large in the minds of these cultural conservatives. But as seen above, their stand on modernization is shaped largely by a religiomoral perspective which grew out of their reaction against scientism and, more important, their quest for meaning. To the extent that this religiomoral perspective constitutes a central dimension of their thought, discussion of New Confucianism or of cultural conservatism in general only in terms of a reaction against modernization is inadequate.

On the surface the reaction against scientism seems to be a response touched off by the spread of modernization. But it must be remembered that the New Confucianists' reaction is directed against scientism rather than science. Consequently their championing of an intuitionist, experiential mode of thinking is not so much a reaction against modernization as a response to the worldwide crisis of understanding provoked by the propagation of Western positivism.

As for the crisis of meaning, it arose, to be sure, partly because of the influx of that complex of modern Western values and ideas centered around the belief in social change through mastery of the world. Thus modernization, as far as its cultural dimension is concerned, certainly is a factor underlying the crisis of meaning. But other factors were also significant, especially the spread of Christianity and the resurgence of interest in the non-Confucian Chinese philosophies and religions, most notably Mahayana Buddhism. In view of these other factors, the crisis of meaning is a spiritual crisis which should be distinguished from the intellectual crisis of modernization, although the two are certainly related. Thus New Confucianism can hardly be explained by the intellectual impact of modernization alone. All these considerations serve to remind us of the complexity of Chinese conservatism, the various facets and different subtrends of which are yet to be identified, analyzed, and assessed. To examine it exclusively from the standpoint of its relationship to modernization is to fail to appreciate its complexity.

V MODERN HISTORICISM AND THE LIMITS OF CHANGE

12 T'ao Hsi-sheng:
The Social Limits
of Change

ARIF DIRLIK

T'ao Hsi-sheng is at first sight an unlikely candidate for a discussion of Chinese conservatism. When he first made his mark on the intellectual scene, in the years following the Northern Expedition (1926-1928), it was not as a defender of traditional values or of the extant social-political structure but as one of the first major Chinese Marxist historians, an advocate of revolutionary change. It is true that his close association with the Kuomintang leadership under Chiang after 1937 and his alleged participation in the composition of *China's Destiny* have given him an image of conservatism.[1] Even that portion of his career, however, provides insufficient grounds for defining him as a conservative in the usual sense of the word and is better explained in terms of his long-standing concern for the security of China as a national entity. To this day, he retains a revolutionary self-image which, if somewhat rhetorical, is nevertheless unconventional in a conservative.[2]

On the other hand, though T'ao was always a proponent of change, his view of desirable change did not extend to a total break with the past or the violent revolutionary transformation of Chinese social structure. In fact, he first emerged into the limelight as an opponent both of New Culture liberals and communist social revolutionaries. His Marxist sociologism played an important part in both cases. His perception of change as basically social rendered irrelevant the problem of culture, permitting him to undercut New Culture demands for cultural revolution. Similarly, he opposed liberal demands for political rights and legal government on the grounds that the transplantation of alien institutions onto a social structure not ready for them would be inefficacious, serving at best the interests of China's external enemies. Finally, his particular analysis of Chinese social history yielded conclusions which to him obviated the need for social revolution; he even construed it as contrary to China's needs. His "sociologism," in effect, served to place limitations on the extent and direction of desirable change even as it reaffirmed the necessity of change.

T'ao's conservatism, then, must be understood as relative; the antirevolutionary intention and effects of his thinking must be considered against a revolutionary environment. His case illustrates the complexity involved in employing the concept of "conservatism" with reference to twentieth-century China. The great majority of Chinese conservatives held complex attitudes toward the question of change, attitudes engendered by an ambivalence toward Western culture and institutions which intermediated China's past and future; they were conservatives largely within their immediate intellectual-political context. Not surprisingly, it is nearly impossible to find in China the specific commitments to institutions (such as the monarchy) and norms (such as religious values) that characterized European conservative ideology. Furthermore, few Chinese, especially in the twenties, gave serious consideration to the possibility or the desirability of preserving the cultural-political complex of the past in its entirety. In an environment of near total breakdown, even conservatives, one might venture, would have found little comfort in Lord Falkland's statement, "When it is not necessary to change, it is necessary not to change." The question in China at this time was not whether or not it was necessary to change but how radical the change was to be. What justifies the use of the concept of conservatism is the fact that many Chinese continued to insist that some ties to the past were necessary and opposed unqualified change into a future totally divorced from what had existed before.

The expressions of this conservatism took two major forms. One tendency, represented by the cultural conservatives, was to reaffirm traditional values without rejecting social and political change. These values were now abstracted out of their social-historical context into universals that were personally significant but had little immediate relevance to social and political organization. The second tendency was more explicitly political in its intentions and the conservatism it expressed took a more ambiguous form. It did not aim to preserve tradition or existing institutions but to arrest social and political upheaval and to bring change under control. Change was desirable, but only when it accorded with the historical tendencies of the society and met its particular needs. Here, historical continuity was the dominant issue. The demand for historical continuity may not by itself be sufficient to define conservatism, but it certainly has been a necessary component of the conservative attitude, gaining in importance especially in periods of revolutionary change.

T'ao Hsi-sheng's conservatism belongs to this second type. His major contribution to the discussion of politics in China was his argument that historical and social necessity imposed limits on change. He displayed no obvious commitment to the dominant values of the past; his work and that of his fellow Marxists represented, if anything, the full-scale historicization of tradition. Historicism, however, simultaneously implied the uniqueness of China's historical experience. When T'ao spoke of "native morality," it seemed to be a vague notion more important for its connotation of sociological necessity than for its value implications. He maintained that native morality limited the indiscriminate grafting of alien values onto it, but he neither stressed nor clarified its own intrinsic value. T'ao was predominantly concerned with the question of social and political change, in particular with the question of whether or not the need for change implied the necessity for social revolution. It was on this issue that he parted ways with fellow Marxists with whom he otherwise had so much in common. In the years after 1927, he engaged communist writers in a debate on this issue, emerging through the discussion as the foremost Kuomintang opponent of the communist advocacy of class struggle. His own historical and sociological arguments were derived from historical materialism, but the Marxist argument for revolution became in his hands a potent weapon with which to counter demands for social revolution in China. This, however, was not mere opportunistic use of historical materialism. His intellectual development indicates that

Marxism provided him with answers to certain questions that had arisen from his earlier intellectual experiences. These, in turn, had shaped the understanding of historical materialism that defined his standpoint in the debate over revolution.

T'ao's rise to prominence began with the "social history controversy" of the late twenties and early thirties. The controversy, which was the first large-scale Marxist discussion of Chinese social history, owed its origins to the breakdown of the United Front in 1927.[3] The feeling among many of the young participants in the revolutionary movement was that the split in the United Front and the resurgence of conservatism had been due to the failure of revolutionaries to assess correctly the historical stage of Chinese society, which caused them to miscalculate the forces and targets of revolution. These mistakes had perverted revolutionary goals, enabling counterrevolutionaries to gain control. The participants in the controversy undertook to define the evolution of Chinese social structure correctly, so that the revolutionary movement could be returned to the correct course. In fact, however, their discussions amounted to little more than the defense of the conflicting strategies of the left and right wings of the Kuomintang and of the Communist party, now divided internally between the Stalinists and the Trotskyites.[4] Kuomintang participants were mostly Wang Ching-wei's associates who at the time still retained their commitment to revolution when the party leadership had already turned sharply to the right. Their goal was to defend revolutionary "Sunist" strategy against both the right and the left by providing it with a social foundation, something that Sun Yat-sen and the major Kuomintang ideologues had failed to do. They included such prominent figures as Ch'en Kung-po and Ku Meng-yü, both members of the Wang group, but the most detailed and articulate analyses were provided by T'ao Hsi-sheng, hitherto relatively unknown in Chinese intellectual circles.

Until 1927, T'ao's involvement in politics had been at best marginal.[5] At the beginning of that year, he received an offer of a position from the Wuhan branch of the Central Military Academy, which he accepted readily. His experiences in Wuhan during January—November 1927 were to become a turning point of his life.

Up until May, T'ao's duties consisted of teaching political science at the academy. In May, in response to Hsia Tou-yin's revolt in Changsha, the academy was merged with the Peasant Movement Training Institute (*Nung-min yun-tung chiang-hsi suo*) as the Central Independent Division (*Chung-yang tu-li-shih*) with Yun Tai-ying (1895-1931) as the leading spirit. On orders from Yun, T'ao was sent to Hsien-ning district in Hupei to organize a *hsien* government and to lead its judicial section. Here he came into conflict with communist cadres who were "too enthusiastic" about the tasks of expropriating landlords and merchants and of mobilizing the peasants. He was recalled to Wuchang in early June as a result of complaints by these cadres, and he believed that his life was spared at this time only because of disagreements among the communists over the correct land policy. T'ao was then appointed secretary of the military academy's political department under She Ts'un-t'ung. He still held this position when the left KMT broke with the communists in July. He was offered a position by Yun Tai-ying in the political department of the academy, which was now headed by Kuo Mo-jo and preparing to move south. T'ao preferred to go into hiding and to break with the communists. In August, he associated for a while with Ku Meng-yü and Ch'en Kung-po when he served in the political and propaganda departments of the KMT, at the same time contributing to the *Central Daily*, advocating the continuation of revolution. After the establishment of the Special Committee in September 1927 at the initiative of the rightists in the party, he worked for a while with K'ung Wen-hsien and Teng Ch'u-min in opposition to this committee. With the movement of Nanking armies on Wuhan, he accepted an offer from Liu K'an-yuan in the Kiangsi party branch, which was controlled by the left KMT, to head the Nanchang Party Affairs School. But this committee soon fell apart and T'ao returned to Shanghai in early 1928.[6]

During the following three years, T'ao continued to move from job to job. Upon the invitation of his friends from Wuhan, Chou Fu-hai and Chou Ping-lin, he started working in February 1928 for the central propaganda department as well as teaching in the political department of the Central Army Officers' School. At the same time, he worked for the Central Mass Training Committee at the recommendation of another Wuhan acquaintance, Chu Ch'i-ch'ing. But he had to quit these jobs in December of that year because of his association with the "reorganizationists" headed by the Canton Committee under Ch'en Kung-po. For the next two years he continued to teach Chinese history in a number of schools in Shanghai.[7]

It was during these years that he wrote most of his works on Chinese social history in support of the left-KMT effort to formulate a revolutionary theory to counter that of the communists and to defend the revolution against the right. He became a regular contributor to *Hsin sheng-ming* (New life monthly), first edited by a number of people but finally under the sole editorship of Chou Fu-hai.[8] T'ao's essays here were historical in scope from the beginning, and they placed the journal in the vanguard of the discussion of social history in the ensuing years. These essays (and the books put together from them) met with immediate acclaim, making T'ao the representative writer of the left KMT position on Chinese society. Until he became a full-time politician in 1937, he remained one of the most important social historians in China.

The Origins of T'ao Hsi-sheng's Social Thought

T'ao entered the study of Chinese society through his studies in legal history, the field in which he had received his professional training. From his own account, a course on family law that he taught in the Anhui Provincial Law School at Anking after he graduated from Peita in 1922 inspired many of the questions that he later devoted himself to answering. In the previous year, while mourning for his father, he had embarked on a study of the writings of the historical and social schools of jurisprudence (*li-shih fa-hsueh p'ai* and *she-hui fa-hsueh p'ai*). One of these works, *Ancient Law* by Henry Maine, which he used for reference in his course, provided him with a "key to family systems":

Ancient Law pointed out that the characteristic of the organization of oriental society was the family system; the law of familistic societies was status law. Western society was individualistic, its law contractual. This made evident the difference between Western and Eastern societies and clarified the difference between Western and Eastern law.[9]

The influence on T'ao of Maine and other writers of the historical school was not restricted to an interpretation of differences between Western and Eastern law but went deeper to provide him with a whole new historical and sociological perspective. In the work of Maine, status and contract were not just different types of law:

Maine wrote in the intellectual climate of the eighteenth and nineteenth century social evolutionism and accordingly, he set his model in an evolutionary mold. His polar types were designed not only to represent extremes in a range of variable social forms but also describe development in the dimension of time. Hence the formula: "...we may say that the movement of progressive societies has hitherto been a movement from status to contract."[10]

Evolutionist though Maine was, however, it is clear from his quotation that he did not regard his evolutionary scheme as having been universally realized but only as applicable to the "progressive societies" of Europe. The moving force in these societies was social necessity, social opinion being "always more or less in advance of law."[11] By contrast he thought China had lacked this gap that served as the motive force of progress: "progress seems to have been there arrested because the civil laws are coextensive with all the ideas of which the race is capable."[12] This meant that Chinese law (and Eastern law in general) was not only a type of its own but was also a more backward type that had been arrested in the earliest stage of development. In T'ao's readiness to accept the scheme of development provided by Maine, with its implicit verdict on the Chinese past, one can perceive some influence of the ideas of the New Culture movement.[13]

The second important feature of *Ancient Law* (and of the historical school) was the establishment of a relationship between law and social institutions. The movement of law from status to contractual accompanied the change in society from patriarchal through feudal to democratic, a process which Maine regarded as universal though not yet universally realized. Status law corresponded to the first stage, contractual to the last. T'ao was quite willing to accept this trend and even noted that if the Chinese family did not give up its status differences and base itself on the principle of mutual respect and benefit (literally common life, *kung-t'ung sheng-huo*), the institution of the family would vanish.[14]

Although Maine and the historical school were committed to the idea of progress, their approach to law had its origins in the philosophy of the romantic conservatives, products of the early nineteenth-century reaction to the Enlightenment and the French Revolution. The historical school rejected both the rational and utilitarian notions of law on the ground that law was a natural outgrowth of "the changing social, economic and moral conditions of the people."[15] Change was the order of the day, but change could not be arbitrary; it had to follow the course of history. The same assumptions—that history determines legal institutions and that law is always a reflection of society—pervaded the legal studies of T'ao and became central to his thought.[16]

These ideas about the social background of law provided T'ao with a conceptual framework which he then applied to Chinese law. During the summer of 1923 he embarked upon a serious study of Chinese law and its relationship to the family system using the *I-li* and mourning practices as his material. These studies which continued during the ensuing years culminated in his first major work, *An Outline of Family Law* (*Ch'in-shu fa ta-kang*). The book is a survey of kinship systems and of legal principles based on those systems and utilizes modern sociological and ethnographic data that had proven Maine wrong on a number of points (primarily on his belief in the universality of patriarchal society). However, its approach is informed by the status-contract polarity suggested by Maine. From his analysis of mourning rules and the comparison of those rules with family law in China, T'ao concluded that Chinese law had been built on family law (*tsung-fa*) and was still heavily infused with the generational and sexual differentiations peculiar to that system. The family law of the ancient clan system had been dependent on hereditary emoluments and had disappeared with the end of the feudal period in Chou times. However, its standards had remained as the basis of Chinese law, its peculiarities idealized by Confucian philosophers and its features perpetuated in the new clan system.[17]

This created an obvious problem: if the social basis of *tsung-fa* principles had been lost, how had the law based on those principles managed to survive? To this Maine provided no answer because his "universal" scheme was quite independent of historical exceptions and he was quite content to leave China in the "childhood" of society. But for T'ao the question was more crucial. Even if he could accept the stagnation of Chinese law, he had to explain the reason for its stagnation. In the following years this problem occupied his mind, but it was not until the social history controversy that he was able to provide a solution.

Part of the explanation was provided by the work of F. Oppenheimer whose book, *The State,* T'ao translated into Chinese in 1930. In his memoirs, T'ao says that this book corresponded exactly to his own methodology of history,[18] and there is no doubt that Oppenheimer did provide him with a framework with which he could come closer to the solution of the problem raised by his legal studies.

By the time T'ao was writing his *Outline of Family Law,* he had become aware of the role of Confucianism in perpetuating the principles of *tsung-fa.* It would seem that while he was working on that book, the gentry, the social backbone of Confucianism, became increasingly important in his understanding of Chinese society.[19] This was probably where Oppenheimer's work proved to be relevant.

Oppenheimer criticized Marx (whom he otherwise admired) for having confused the distinction between politics and economics in society. He himself took the "economic impulse" as the "principal force" in human development but distinguished the means used to achieve those ends. "Economic means" were the use of "one's labor and the equivalent exchange of one's labor for the labor of others," while "political means" represented the "unrequited appropriation of the labor of others" for the satisfaction of needs that were basically economic.[20]

Oppenheimer's distinction became another important element in T'ao Hsi-sheng's view of Chinese society. As we have seen, his analysis of law in Chinese society had ended up with an anomaly wherein the ideas had been frozen in late Chou in spite of the social changes of that period. Now he could provide part of the answer to that dilemma. The Chinese society of the time had experienced important economic and social changes, but one class that had been the product of feudal disintegration had been able to establish its control over society and had imposed its ideology upon it, effectively obstructing the tendencies to change. This was the gentry group, which was closely related to landed economic interests but was itself a primarily intellectual-political group.

I say this was only part of the answer because given the prevailing mode of materialist historiography in the intellectual circles in which he moved, T'ao still felt uncomfortable with the idea of a ruling group without an economic basis. The missing economic base was finally provided by the idea of commercial capital, which was the chief contribution of Marxism to T'ao's social thought. With that, the elements of his social analysis were completed. In this completed form it was presented during the social history controversy, which, though triggered by immediate political problems, merged in T'ao's thought with his long-standing questions about the nature of Chinese society. And just as the Marxist approach to the controversy helped him solve his intellectual problem, the latter in turn colored both his Marxism and the final solutions he offered to the problem of change in Chinese society.

The Social History Controversy and T'ao's Contribution to the KMT Search for "Integrative Revolution"

In his introduction to a collection of essays by participants in the social history controversy, T'ao described six current alternative views: (1) China is a society with a feudal or semifeudal system; (2) In China, the feudal system has already disappeared but feudal forces remain; (3) China is a merchant-class society or a commercial capitalist society or a protocapitalist (*ch'u-ch'i tzu-pen chu-i*) society under the control of feudal forces; (4) China has been a capitalist society for the past hundred years; (5) China is a small landlord, merchant society under the control of feudal political power; (6) China is one of the Asiatic societies that Marx had talked about.[21]

The first and fourth views in this list were characteristic of communist participants and found few supporters in the New Life group. In spite of surface differences, the other four views represent collectively what we might consider the New Life view of Chinese society. Thus T'ao held the second view while Ku Meng-yü argued for the third. Advocates of the fifth standpoint were Ch'en Kung-po (China is a small peasant society under imperialism) and Liang Yuan-tung (China has been and is a petit bourgeois society). An advocate of the last and rarest view was Wang Chih-ch'eng.

In spite of the variation in their description of Chinese society, these authors all assigned a determinative role to commercial capital in the formation and makeup of imperial China.[22] Commercial capital had been the dynamic component of the Chinese economy since the Warring States period, long before Western intrusion in China. Having destroyed feudal society at that time, it had created a new social structure upon an economic foundation that represented the fusion of land and commercial capital. The descriptions above, though they stressed different aspects of society, all agreed upon this characteristic of the traditional economy. They also agreed that the ambiguity in the economic base, a combination of feudal landownership and nascent capitalism, had led to an ambiguity in class structure. The emergent bourgeoisie had destroyed feudalism but, because of its close ties with land, was unable to develop into a full-fledged capitalist class, capable of establishing its control over politics. The result was a vacuum in the political superstructure which had been filled by a group that represented economic interests but was itself primarily a political-intellectual elite, the gentry or *shih-tai-fu*. This group, though not feudal as such, preserved important feudal features, especially in its ideology.

The political dominance of the gentry had aborted the economic changes under way since mid-Chou and had resulted in a "special" society which, though subject to universal economic forces, had not undergone the same development as Western society because of the peculiar interaction of those forces. Chinese history was special not because the universal laws of development did not apply there but because the effect of those laws had remained unfulfilled. Since the peculiar economic foundation had not permitted the victory of any one class in politics, the older feudal forces had been able to perpetuate themselves in the political superstructure of society. T'ao Hsi-sheng described imperial Chinese society as "proto-capitalism under the control of feudal thought" (*feng-chien ssu-hsiang suo chih-p'ei ti ch'u-ch'i tzu-pen chu-i*).[23] Ku Meng-yü, criticizing those who re-

garded contemporary China as feudal, stated more unequivocally:
"This is a feudal system that has only a superstructure and no base.
[Chinese] feudalism has been like this since Ch'in-Han."[24] China,
then, was dominated by feudal forces, but it was not a feudal society.[25]

This view that commercial capital had been the single most
dynamic factor in China's development became the cornerstone of
the left-Kuomintang interpretation of Chinese history. It was most
fully developed in the work of T'ao Hsi-sheng and was called "T'ao
Hsi-shengism" by its opponents. Two corollaries of this interpretation are worth stating at some length because they were crucial to
T'ao's perception of change in contemporary China.

One was that the action of commercial capital lay at the root of
China's historically incomplete centralization and chronic economic
and political crises manifested in the form of dynastic changes. In
the Chou period, the destruction of feudalism had been partially a
result of commerce, which broke down the regional self-sufficiency
characteristic of feudalism. But the nature of this commerce prevented its unifying the country into one market. Commerce in
China came into being as a result of regional specialization of production and remained dependent on it. China's size and environmental diversity, in contrast to European countries, permitted a
large volume of trade which could flourish in isolation from production. As a result, commerce, instead of fusing with production,
remained outside of it and served as an intermediary between
regions. The independent development of commercial capital,
isolated from the production process, hindered rather than aided
the growth of productive forces. Commerce itself became an obstacle to economic development and contributed to economic disunity
and the "uneven development" of the various parts of the country.[26]

Moreover, excess commercial capital had no place to go but into
usury and land, and these kinds of investments both resulted in
negative consequences. Usury impoverished the peasant, while the
flow of capital to the countryside led to the concentration of landownership. Peasants deprived of their lands turned to vagrancy,
feeding the centrifugal tendencies of ever-present militarists. Concentrated landownership, on the other hand, cut into government

revenues and diminished central power. The result was periodic political upheaval and dynastic change.[27]

The second corollary of the "commercial capital" interpretation of China's history related the action of commercial capital to the social and political structure. As noted earlier, T'ao argued that the fusion of land and capital resulted in an ambiguous (partly feudal) class structure, with no one economic class able to assert its power over others. This situation permitted the domination of politics by the gentry, whose power was political rather than economic. The gentry were the vital link in a chain that consisted of the bureaucracy, the gentry, and landowners. To be sure, they had economic interests. Many of them were recruited from the landlord class and, when in office, they extended their landholdings in order to consolidate their power. But this only served to provide a commonality of interests between them and landlords; it did not identify them as an economic class. Gentry power was based on officeholding through the monopoly of education, not on the command of economic resources. As bureaucrats, it was even possible for them to come into conflict with landlords with whom they otherwise shared common interests.[28]

This political elite was economically parasitic and was the most exploitive element in the society. Its nature was essentially feudal. Its members differed from the feudal nobility of Chou in that they did not have a simultaneous economic and political control. Nevertheless, they bore a striking resemblance to the feudal nobility in their power relations with society: "Internally, the *shih-tai-fu* class was definitely not identical to the [nobility of the] feudal period [but] in its power relations with the peasantry, there was no difference from the feudal period."[29] Furthermore, as a political elite, they used the political means at their disposal to exploit the rest of society. The use of political means for the appropriation of economic benefits was to T'ao, as it was to Oppenheimer, an outstanding feature of feudal exploitation. Finally, the education that sustained the gentry, being a remnant of the Chou period, was feudal in its outlook. The feudal ideology of the gentry served both to perpetuate the values of the feudal period and also to suppress more progressive groups. Most important the gentry, dependent on the perpetuation of an agrarian society, used feudal arguments to suppress merchants whenever they became powerful.[30]

T'ao explained further that if Chinese society, subject to decentralizing forces in its economic foundation, had any hopes of achieving unification through political means, those hopes were betrayed by gentry domination of politics. The gentry-bureaucrats, along with the militarists who emerged especially in times of disorder, contributed to centrifugality by their constant attempts to maximize their power at the expense of the central government: "Summing up what we said above, the agricultural and handicrafts economy of China, as well as the products of such an economy such as poor communications, unreliability of money supply [literally, shortage and overabundance], the exploitation of landlords and usurers, the centrifugal nature of the officialdom and the military, all prevented the development of capitalism in China. China, all the way to the end of Ch'ing, remained a feudal society, and its politics remained those of a military feudal state."[31] This political arrangement, itself made possible by the economic characteristics of society, reinforced the tendencies of the economy. Local power to the end challenged the power of the central government.

The most important implication of this argument, one that brought T'ao into conflict with his fellow Marxists, was his inference that in China, political power had historically remained distinct from society. The political elite was above the classes of society.[32] Therefore, T'ao concluded, the most important question that faced China was not class exploitation but the exploitation of society by the state. This view was the concomitant of the argument that commercial capital was the formative force of the Chinese economy. Together they shaped T'ao's understanding of what revolution in contemporary China had to achieve.

Western intrusion had exacerbated both of these pernicious tendencies of Chinese history. Worse, now that China was no longer isolated from other nations, she was threatened by extinction through subjection to others if those tendencies could not be reversed. Economically, imperialism had strengthened the role of commercial capital in Chinese society. Imperialist economic involvement in China primarily took the form of finance capitalism. Native commercial capital was now subordinated to imperialist finances and helped the latter in its exploitation of the country.[33] Where native commercial capital had financed interregional trade in imperial times, it now served to link the remotest corners of China with the centers of world capitalism: the exploitation of the Chinese peasant now reached all the way from rural China to New York and London. The capital that did not flow abroad was diverted to unproductive enterprises within the country such as urban speculation. Thus although China became increasingly subject to the control and fluctuations of the world market, this did not in any way contribute to the development of a modern industrial economy; it only served to impoverish the country. T'ao did not deny that there was industrial development in China, but like many others, he made a distinction between Chinese and Western-owned industries. The available capital in China and the rapidly growing labor force (two conditions of industrial capitalism) helped not Chinese but foreign enterprises. As foreign industries continued to grow, Chinese industries stagnated. If this continued, China would soon turn into an economic colony of the developed countries of the world.[34]

Imperialism had likewise strengthened the hand of the old native elite. The gentry, who had earlier served landlord interests, now found new advantages in serving the imperialists. Some managed to become compradors, serving imperialists as their agents. The bureaucracy and the military in turn served these compradors and, indirectly through them, imperialism.[35] The result was: "Because of the intermediacy of the *shih-tai-fu*, the [Chinese] capitalist class has a strong *shih-tai-fu* nature and finds it very easy to ally with the military groups. Also, since the development of capitalism was not internal to the Chinese economic structure but was induced from the outside, the result is that although one sees the establishment of a capitalist class, one does not see the destruction of feudal thought or the success of the democratic revolution."[36] Ironically, even the introduction of modern economic methods contributed to the power of the older forces. China's growth under Western pressure was lopsided. Before industries had developed, the appendages of industry such as modern communications were built. The result was that whereas in industrialized countries communications served industries, in China they contributed to centrifugal tendencies by increasing the mobility of warlords. Consequently, the large "feudal" state of imperial times was not divided into small feudal states.[37] But the old political elite remained in power, exploiting the country even worse than before.

The correct revolutionary strategy, then, was one that would eliminate the twin economic-political forces that made for disunity. The interpretation above led to the inescapable conclusion that the greatest task of the Chinese revolution was to achieve economic and political integration.[38] Since the economy, given the pressures it suffered from, could not itself yield such integration, the task was a political one.[39] Only the unification of China under a party that represented the collective interests of the people could eliminate the centrifugal forces, economic and political, that threatened her existence. The revolution led by such a party would have two tasks, destructive and constructive.[40] The destructive aspect was the elimination of the "feudal" political leadership, warlords and bureaucrats inherited from the past. Their elimination and the establishment of a strong central government would put an end to imperialist political interference in Chinese affairs as well. The constructive aspect, on the other hand, required the elimination of the divisive role of commercial capital by industrializing the nation and establishing the control of production over capital and of urban centers over the rural economy. This would lead to the economic strengthening of the country and provide the foundation for unified politics as well as for the eventual achievement of socialism, which could only be based upon an advanced industrial economy.[41]

The implicit and explicit assumption of this view of revolutionary strategy was that China did not need a social revolution, or class struggle, as the communists advocated. In China, the problem of exploitation did not involve classes. The major question was the exploitation of society by the state and, through its agency, by outsiders. Economic crisis was due to the operation of an impersonal economic agent, commercial capital. Class struggle was not only unnecessary but, since it was not needed, it would only serve to undermine unity. What China needed most was a cooperative patriotic effort to develop the country. Struggle against native capitalists, as the Trotskyites advocated, would only destroy the small capitalist class, which was already oppressed by militarists and imperialists, and extinguish their potential contribution to the national revolution.[42] Struggle against landlords, on the other hand, would only contribute to peasant misery in general. Rural crisis was not due to feudal exploitation, as the Stalinists claimed, but was a consequence of exploitation by commercial capital. T'ao argued that landlords in China had no independent political power but derived whatever power they had from their encroachments on the bureaucracy. The latter, the root of the problem, did not base its power on landlords but existed independently of society. Economically, the landlords were themselves subject to the action of commercial capital. As T'ao put it, "Chinese society was not a feudal society but one controlled by the landlord class *under* finance and commercial capital."[43] The only relative advantage landlords had over peasants was their ability to pass exploitation on to the peasants. Peasants, on the other hand, depended for many of their needs on the landlords, who played a crucial role in the agrarian economy as merchants and credit agents. With the landlords gone, the peasants would only suffer, for many of their needs would remain unmet. Besides, many Chinese landlords were small owners and their expropriation would hurt a great number of the people in the countryside as well as workers and the small bourgeoisie in the cities who were still connected with the village. Finally, radical measures against landlords would hurt production in the countryside and place additional burdens on the flimsy resources of urban areas. It was "consumer socialism" to argue that the expropriation of landlords and the redistribution of land among the peasantry would solve China's agrarian problems.[44] Such a view concerned itself only with distribution, not with production. China's real problem, however, was not distribution but the low level of production, which condemned all to penury.

The Chinese revolution, then, was to achieve the following: (1) eliminate the militarists and bureaucrats; (2) secure economic independence (tariffs); (3) unify the country under a party that represented the whole people and secure economic development and justice under the aegis of that party in the national government. T'ao and many in the Kuomintang defined the task of the revolution as

political rather than social. The historical arguments provided by
T'ao helped justify this strategy of revolution. He believed that this
strategy was just what Sun Yat-sen had offered in the Three People's
Principles (san-min chu-i). The Three Principles directed a course
that was both integrative and revolutionary, with min-tsu aiming at
national independence, min-ch'üan at internal political equality,
and min-sheng at the development of production and equitable distribution.

Revolution, Change, and Continuity in T'ao Hsi-sheng's Thought

T'ao Hsi-sheng (and many KMT radicals) did not give up their commitment to revolution in 1927. On the contrary, much of the social
history of China written during the period was designed to show the
necessity of continuing revolution at a time when the KMT seemed
to be divorcing itself from the mobilization of the masses and the
anti-imperialist struggle.

At the same time, T'ao understood revolution differently from
the communists, even though dialectical materialism played an
important role in providing him with concepts with which to explain
the nature of Chinese society. KMT radicals in general saw revolution as the means to the unification of China; the advocacy of class
struggle seemed to them to counter this urgent necessity. This did
not mean they rejected the existence of classes or even the need for
class struggle under some circumstances. It was China's peculiar circumstances that made class struggle irrelevant there. Because of
imperialism and the inherent tendencies of the Chinese economic
and social structure toward disunity, what China needed most was
unity. Besides they claimed, echoing Sun, that though the Chinese
people suffered from the political oppression of feudal forces,
China's industrial backwardness meant that there were no sharp
class conflicts there. The ultimate function of the san-min chu-i was
to realize revolution in a constructive sense (simultaneous industrial
and democratic, political and economic revolutions) which would
prevent the rise of the social problem of class oppression.[45] Violence
was required only to the extent that it was necessary to overthrow
the feudal political superstructure in China, which not only op-

pressed everyone else but also stood in the way of the country's development. Once that was eliminated, the constructive tasks of the revolution could proceed gradually in peace, under the supervision of the KMT that represented all the people.

Sun Yat-sen's view of revolution is remarkable for its scope and for its simultaneous commitment to all the conflicting requirements of modernity as well as its claim to anticipate all the possible problems bound to arise from the meeting of those requirements. For our purposes, the most significant aspect is its assumption of the reconcilability of "peaceful evolution" and continuity with the past with the advocacy of revolution against one politically defined sector of society. The KMT interpreters of Sun Yat-sen deemed revolutionary violence necessary in the political arena because the holders of power would not give up their power without violence. Violence, however, was not only harmful but also without utility in the social and economic areas, which were subject to the evolutionary laws of development and largely immune to willful efforts to transform them overnight. As Chou Fu-hai stated it, "the method of *san-min chu-i* is to change politics through revolutionary means and use political means (peaceful methods) to change the economy."[46] T'ao had no difficulty in agreeing with this and most of his historical work was devoted to the resolution of the apparent contradiction.

T'ao believed that the forces that had been responsible for the development of modern society in the West had been operative in Chinese history but that they had led to different results in the two areas. In the West, the uninterrupted development of the forces of production had been accompanied by the establishment of the political power of a class that also controlled the means of production. In China, the development of productive forces had come to a halt with the end of the Chou dynasty when political power had been separated from economic power, and a group, a remnant even then, had managed to establish its power over the country and had put an end to all hopes of further development. Stagnation and the periodic breakdown of the economy (a consequence of the independent existence of commercial capital) had made it easier for this political group to retain its power, but it was the group itself and its reactionary ideology that had been the greatest obstacle to the natural evolution of society. Now that the West had intruded on China, threatening her existence, it was urgent to clear away the historical obstacles to development. Development was now possible, primarily by means of the new productive forces brought by the West which would enable China to break out of the vicious cycle of commercial capital. But it was still necessary to open a channel of advance, not following that of the West, but directed by the laws of history, universal and Chinese, at the end of which both China and the West would converge.

I think we can see from this analysis why T'ao's view of revolution did not preclude continuity with the past and how he could make continuity a condition of change to which he was also committed. Revolution was the means to political integration through the elimination of reactionary forces which were not an organic part of Chinese society but rather remnants of the distant past and obstacles to organic growth. In a sense, China had to pick up now where she had left off during the beginning of the imperial period two thousand years ago. The task of revolution, therefore, was to secure evolution in the historical sphere.

The direction such evolution was to take could not be selected arbitrarily, as both liberals and communists seemed to believe, but would be determined by the tendencies of Chinese history. Continuity with the past was a sociological necessity and guaranteed China a unique path of development, at least for the immediate future. That social institutions evolved organically from the historical experience of a society and could not be grafted at will from one society unto another was an idea that T'ao had first derived not from Marx but from Maine and the historical school of jurisprudence; historical materialism, divorced from class struggle, provided it with a deeper foundation. T'ao, however, was rather vague about the implications of continuity with the past; he affirmed the necessity of internal development without specifying what was to be preserved from the past. In the sphere of law, he was from the beginning an advocate of the view that the legal system had to be in keeping with the customs and traditions of Chinese society.[47] In the area of thought, he remarked that no matter how perfect a body of thought imported from abroad may be, it still required filtering through native traditions of thought if it was to take root.[48] Aside from these comments, there is little evidence that he placed any value on native traditions. His stress on historical process was not so much a consequence of commitment to tradition as a reflection of concern with change in the present.

This is not say that T'ao had little interest in China's national identity. But national identity was to him almost solely social and political, defined in terms of the Chinese people and their polity. The most conspicuous demonstration of this basic conviction was his joining in the Manifesto of the Ten Professors of January 1935 that touched off a controversy on native Chinese culture.[49] The manifesto made no attempt to define Chinese culture even though it protested the "disappearance" of China in the realm of culture. It attacked both conservatives who wanted to revive past culture and liberals and communists who advocated wholesale importation of one foreign culture or another. It reaffirmed China's spatial and temporal characteristics, demanding a compromise between modern needs and past traditions. It was wrong to revive the old because China was no longer the China of the past. The present China had new needs which had to be taken into account. The new needs, however, did not necessitate abandonment of native culture or justify complete disregard for it in the course of acquiring aspects of modernity. Thus, the professors argued, the Chinese need not give up the ideal of *ta-t'ung* (great harmony) but had only to make China the starting point of the long path to world unity, in which China would not be just a passive recipient but an active contributor to the end result.[50] The manifesto stated quite clearly that it was not Chinese tradition that defined Chinese culture. It called upon the Chinese people to assert control over the historical process and fashion a new culture for themselves that best suited their own historical and social needs. The components could be Chinese or Western but the synthesis, accomplished by Chinese, would be unique. This view, I think, was quite consonant with T'ao's views on contemporary China and its future.

The statement of the Ten Professors was directed at all westernizers, liberal and communist alike and perhaps more at the liberals than at the communists. It was criticized in strong terms by Hu Shih who attributed it to the "conservative tendencies" of the day.[51] T'ao's response to Hu was couched exclusively in political and economic terms. He made no attempt to defend Chinese tradition and even included among his antagonists the feudalist defenders of the past along with capitalists and socialists: "Once the feudalists open their mouths, one is reminded of the Three Dynasties, Han, and T'ang. The capitalists always have in their hearts something like the U.S.A. Among the socialists, there are some who openly defend the Soviet Union. *They all forget the China of the present* [my italics]."[52] The defenders of the past were obscurantists who tried to preserve what could not be preserved. The demands of the liberals and the communists, on the other hand, would only lead to the political and economic enslavement of China.

The communists, Stalinist and Trotskyite alike, agreed with T'ao that China's future had to be neither capitalist nor socialist but rather "noncapitalist." However, this divergence from the universal pattern of development was necessary to them not because it was natural to Chinese society with a past and a present of its own but because China was not yet ready to achieve the next stage, accepted by all as socialism. Their goal was to hurry along the development of China and push her into the universal stream somewhere beyond the point of capitalism. To them the past (the immediate past) was undesirable and relevant only to the extent that it stood in the way of revolution. I think this is the broader significance of the insistence that China was feudal or capitalist (depending on the observer), both of which translated the Chinese experience into one or another stage of a universal scheme of development. Whatever one thought the present to be, the goal was to make the transition to the next stage, with the totality of change that the transition from one stage to another implied.

Liberals like Hu Shih, by contrast, tended to assign universality to the values of the modern West and advocated the evolution of China in that direction. Compromise with tradition was necessary only to the extent that it was demanded by the requirements of peaceful change. Hu Shih valued certain aspects of the Chinese past, but it was no coincidence that those aspects happened to be tendencies in China toward what had been realized in the West but not fully in

China. What was particularly Chinese did not necessarily have value.

T'ao rejected both of these views. He accused the communists of converting Chinese history into a replica of the "foreign"[53] and turned the tables on them by reminding them of the immanence of dialectical change;[54] against the liberals he argued in terms of political and historical necessity;[55] and against both, as the Manifesto indicates, he could argue that not all that was Western was good and not all that was Chinese was bad. The ideal for China was to combine the best of both worlds and follow her own path until that day at the "end of history" when the two streams would meet.

Change conditioned by organic continuity with the past, advocated on the grounds of both historical necessity and general considerations of value, provided the sociohistorical basis of T'ao Hsi-sheng's acceptance of Sun Yat-sen's approach to revolution. Change was necessary, not only as a historical proposition but also for China's survival in the modern world, where isolation was no longer possible. But if China was to change, there had to be a China to change, both as a political and as a cultural entity. The task of revolution was to guarantee the political survival of China by paving the way for unity and development after which China could grow, to revise Joseph Levenson's statement, in a way of its own into a future not just its own.

Conclusion: Scientism, Historicism, and Conservatism

This essay has so far emphasized the ways in which the thought of T'ao Hsi-sheng differed from that of his contemporaries and opponents, the communists. However, while the two groups disagreed in their views on social change and revolution, they shared a common trait in contradistinction to liberals and to the basic assumptions of the May Fourth period: a sense of the burden of history and a conviction that change was historically conditioned. This viewpoint caused them to give greater weight to the Chinese past in the determination of the Chinese future, which T'ao did willingly and the communists did out of necessity.

Such a shift from the assumptions of the May Fourth period was not lost on native observers. Hu Shih, in his critique of the Manifesto of the Ten Professors, attributed that document to the conservative tendencies of the day. Kuo Chan-po, more neutral in his interpretation, distinguished the controversy on native culture touched off by that document from earlier discussions of China and the West by resorting to a dialectical explanation of the problem: the ten professors had presented a synthesis of the conservative attitudes toward the West represented by a stream of thinkers from Tseng Kuo-fan to Liang Ch'i-ch'ao (thesis) and the unconditional commitment to westernization of people like Hu Shih and Wu Chih-hui (antithesis).[56] Fung Yu-lan, dealing with the more general and more fundamental problem of historical attitudes, applied the same explanation to the dominant trend in historiography in the late twenties and early thirties, the "explanation of antiquity" (*shih-ku*).[57] He saw the "explainers of antiquity" (*shih-ku p'ai*) as a synthesis of the earlier "believers in antiquity" (*hsin-ku p'ai*) (thesis) and the May Fourth "doubters of antiquity" (*i-ku p'ai*) (antithesis).

The burden of all these statements (including Hu Shih's) is that the cultural revolutionism of the May Fourth period had somehow proven insufficient, making it necessary to revive ideas that had put value on China and Chinese history. The revised views did not call for a throwback to an earlier period; in this sense, the effects of the May Fourth movement had been irrevocable. They signified rather a modification of the cultural iconoclasm of the May Fourth period and the assumptions that had underlain that iconoclasm—that through a cultural transformation of outlook guided by universal principles of reason, the Chinese would be able to realize the values of universal validity that had been the product of Western civilization.

The West itself had come under attack simultaneously with the actual movement of May 4, 1919, when its integrity in upholding its own values had been called into question. But the major challenge to its values did not come until 1923, in the controversy on philosophy of life, when the challenge to the value of Western civilization was accompanied by the challenge to the omnipotence of science, seen as the chief creation of that civilization. This controversy, declared a victory by the advocates of a scientific outlook, who also reaffirmed their faith in the ultimate values of Western civilization, seems, in the long run, to have been the harbinger of trends to come, trends that indicate that the victory had been somewhat tenuous.[58]

The faith in the transforming power of science and democracy was further shaken by the rise of the Chinese Marxist movement, itself nurtured by a disappointment in the West. The claims of Marxism to be scientific may have fallen on receptive ears during the years following 1919, but the scientificity of Marxism was bound to have ambivalent effects on the scientism of the May Fourth period. Marxism claims to be a science of history, that is, it claims to offer a scientific understanding of the inexorable processes of history. Its scientism is vastly different from the empirical scientism of Hu Shih and the mechanistic scientism of Wu Chih-hui. It makes human beings prisoners of their own history, from which the only escape is provided by the scientific understanding of that history. In this area, Marxism ran counter to the dominant May Fourth ideology (with which it otherwise shared a common faith in science and progress). Increasingly, the attention of Chinese intellectuals was drawn from the symbols of civilization to its processes, social and historical, which had to be understood and dealt with before new modes could be realized.

Such tendencies of thought, concealed beneath the euphoria of the nationalist revolutionary movement of 1923-1927, required one final blow, the blow of disappointment, before they erupted to consciousness. The year 1927 provided it. The failure of the revolutionary movement led directly to the social history controversy. The new social thinkers still claimed to be scientific in methodology but their subject matter was dominantly historical. It was not possible in 1927, as it had been after 1911, to attribute the failure of revolution to individual reactionaries or ambitious militarists or even to poor organization. As the later generation of revolutionaries saw it, the explanation lay deep down in the social structure and in the history of that structure. It was not only that society had been conditioned by history, a platitude that does not require the historicist attitude for its acceptance.[59] More importantly, they felt that an understanding of a society could only be gained by determining its correct developmental location in time and in space—hence Wang Li-hsi's question in *Tu-shu tsa-chih* (Research magazine) in an article introducing the social history controversy: "What stage has Chinese society already reached?"[60]

The scientific solution of this problem became the focal point of the social history controversy. It is interesting that the experience of 1927, rather than discrediting Marxism and dialectical materialism, enhanced their value as the only methodology to offer a possibility of solution to that problem. The reason for this can perhaps be found in intellectual assumptions behind the Marxist approach to social analysis.

Marxism is at once historicist and rationalist; that is, while its immediate concern is to locate social phenomena in their historical context (which is individual and particularistic since the dynamics of change are provided by the unique internal and external historical circumstances of any society), it also aims at the discovery of general scientific laws that explain individuality through broad sociohistorical patterns. In the application of dialectical materialism, this paradoxical goal is reflected in the continuous effort to reconcile the mechanism of change (the dialectical relationship of the forces of production and the relations of production), which is universally applicable without necessarily leading to universal results, with a single pattern of historical development valid for many different historical situations. These contradictions, between universality and particularity, and between the mechanism of change and the pattern of change, were most probably behind the variety of periodizations which Marx himself suggested for Europe and which Marxists since then have been trying to apply, with slight success, outside of Europe.[61]

In 1928, Chinese intellectuals like T'ao Hsi-sheng, trying to place themselves with respect to the Chinese past as well as to the contemporary world, were drawn irresistibly to the metaphor of the dialectic. Rather than notice the contradiction, they simply ignored it by choosing what they thought best suited China's circumstances. T'ao, ambivalent toward revolution, regarded Marxism simply as a methodology and the dialectic as a mechanism of change. His rejection of class struggle as a necessary component of the dialectical process reduced Marxism to another evolutionist theory of society. The

effect was, on the one hand, to reaffirm China's historically determined particularity and, on the other hand, to refute the demands
for social revolution. In this sense, T'ao's Marxism was quite consistent with the basically conservative organic evolutionism of Maine
and the historical school of jurisprudence which had first provided
him with the tools of social analysis. Historical materialism helped
explain why China had failed to develop in the past. It also confirmed, by the economic arguments it provided, T'ao's basic belief
that social institutions are born out of the historical experiences of a
society and that social change was not arbitrary or rational but was
conditioned by history.

13 Chou Tso-jen: A Scholar Who Withdrew

DAVID E. POLLARD

In seeking to understand Chou Tso-jen's relationship to conservatism, one may ask two kinds of questions: first, what he was, or what influences in fact acted on him; and second, what he seemed, or what kind of image he has projected. In this essay, I deal with both aspects — more briefly with the latter first.

Though Chou has to be introduced nowadays as the younger brother of Lu Hsun, up to the late twenties he was probably no less prominent in the world of letters than Lu Hsun, even though he wrote no fiction. He established his reputation, like Lu Hsun, in *Hsin ch'ing nien* (New Youth) days, as the author of several essays which lent direction to the New Culture movement and thereafter kept his name in public view through contributing to major journals right up to the outbreak of the Sino-Japanese war in 1937. Over that period he brought out some fifteen collections of essays and several volumes of translations. Some of his essays appeared in school textbooks.[1]

Writers write in their own times for their own times. It is important therefore in assessing the nature of anyone's work, and the influence it might have had, to concentrate on contemporary reactions. This is especially true of Chou Tso-jen, as his World War II record of temporary collaboration with the Japanese has understandably colored his compatriots' subsequent views of him and has been used to prove him reactionary, backward, or whatever. Although it is clear from his frequent prewar warnings about Japanese militarism and colonialism that collaboration was not part of his philosophy and was undertaken from purely private reasons,[2] nevertheless, the stigma has led to general depreciation of the progressive stand he took on a wide range of social issues. In particular it has been alleged that even in his radical days, from May Fourth to his relinquishing the editorship of the *Yü ssu* (Tatler) magazine in 1927, the "spirit of resistance" to feudal culture was all supplied by Lu Hsun.[3] In fact Chou was very outspoken on his own account, even rash, and had no need to hang on to Lu Hsun's coat tails. But that story cannot be told here. What is relevant to our present concerns is that well before the war Chou had fallen far enough behind the revolutionary vanguard to be subject to attacks for his conservatism.

The substantial and well-informed critique of Hsu Chieh, published in 1934,[4] will serve as an example of the negative image Chou presented to his contemporaries. Hsu was repulsed by Chou's interest in popular superstitions, his antique collecting, his nostalgia for old country plays and pleasures, his attachments to leisure pursuits such as tea drinking in peaceful and unspoiled surroundings, his dislike of new foreign ways, and his reference to himself (in 1934) as a "stay-at-home monk."[5] All these, Hsu felt, betrayed a consciousness that was in every way "feudal." Chou's proclaiming himself a "follower of the mean" betokened a "shallow humanism" which may have had some relevance in the May Fourth period but was now past its usefulness. He had not realized that the New Culture movement was a manifestation of the transition from feudalism to capitalism, not, as he had come to see it, a repetition of something that had happened before in Chinese history. Chou had closed his eyes to what was going on in the outside world, and while other writers had seen a way forward and were working with a sense of purpose, he had taken to declaring that literature was "useless."

In sum, Hsu saw Chou as a typical member of the scholar-gentry who at first formulated all kinds of proposals embodying his ideals in the hope that they would be accepted by the ruling class, but later on, seeing that his ideals were not capable of being realized, became disillusioned. Still, catching at a straw, he took to grumbling and satire, in the hope of doing society the service of ameliorating its worst abuses. But when the state of society deteriorated even fur-

ther, he found it inopportune to even grumble anymore and re-
treated to merely making jibes without coming to grips with
problems. By this time he had taken on the identity of the "aloof
and incorruptible scholar" (ch'ing-kao ming-shih), the end of the
line.

This represents the core of the case against Chou Tso-jen as a
conservative, or antediluvian, and is valid as a reflection of the way
a section of the community received the signals he sent out, so to
speak. We can now look at these issues from what I judge to have
been Chou's own point of view; in other words, we will change the
focus from what he may have seemed to what he was, and what
made him so.

For a start, Chou would not have agreed that his antifeudalism
was ever "muted," as Hsu claimed, if by "feudalism" one meant that
social system, rigidly structured, in which landowners, and in the
Chinese case the scholar-gentry, have autocratic powers and special
privileges. Not that Chou ever seriously addressed himself to the
question of the economic infrastructure of feudal society and its
rights and wrongs; to him feudalism meant the traditional notions,
practices, and ethics which comprised the ideological superstructure
of that society and which lived on after the ground was cut from
under it: such things as concubinage, footbinding, female chastity,
superstitions, taboos, cringing before authority, mesmerization by
the literary ideal, and so on. These were common targets during the
May Fourth movement and they remained targets to him for the
next twenty years, though of course particulars varied and his tone
and mode of expression changed from the headlong assault to
probes and light skirmishing. He himself said on several occasions
that his basic thinking had not altered over the whole period, only
his delusions had been shed. In this one can readily concur. And yet
it is no accident that to Hsu's perception, Chou's spear had not just
been blunted but its shaft broken, for to many readers his critical
barbs were gradually lost from sight amid the masses of titles and
quotations, the recording of local customs and comestibles, the
notes on Japanese and Greek culture that filled his books.

To see how the balance shifted, let us look at the character of
Chou's successive collections of essays. Most of the essays in his first

collections were either discernibly related to questions of the day or carried the positive charge of introducing aspects of foreign culture. The *Yung jih chi* (Endless days) collection of 1929 still cited Western authorities almost exclusively, and while the tone was often ironical, still the subject matter was almost all serious—in fact didactic and educational. The quizzical and detached attitude that became his hallmark was more evident in *K'an yün chi* (Cloud-gazing, 1932), but there was no longing for the past, and Western savants still made a good showing; they were recruited for the wisdom of their views, while Chinese writers, who now began to appear in larger numbers, served simply to illustrate a point. *Yeh tu ch'ao* (Notes from night reading, 1934) was explicitly personal, consisting of thoughts and comments on books he had been reading. Understandably he took to reminiscing about how he acquired his interests. Western scholars were cast more in the role of old and trusted friends—people like Havelock Ellis, J. G. Frazer, Jane Harrison, Andrew Lang, and Henri Fabre, the entomologist. A few Chinese scholars were now recommended for their soundness of mind—the philosopher Yen Yuan (1635-1704), Yen Chih-t'ui (sixth century), and some of lesser fame; others were praised for their human qualities and their ability to write well. *Yeh tu ch'ao* set the pattern for the following collections: *K'u chu tsa chi* (Bitter bamboo, 1935), *K'u ch'a sui-pi* (Bitter tea, 1935), *Feng yü t'an* (In wind and rain, 1936), and *Kua tou chi* (Melons and beans, 1937), which varied in the proportion of essays on general topics to those of a scholarly nature, but which by and large were dictated by personal interest. When they turned on current depravity, they generally placed it in the gallery of national weaknesses, with the result that few people were offended and few feathers flew.

With such diversification of subject matter the impact of the one kind of essay which continued the indictment of feudalism naturally diminished, and this together with Chou's growing concentration on the artistic aspect of composition, his habit of turning away from the final thrust with a gesture of ineffectualness, and his depreciation of his own work, would together explain the impression of negativism he made on readers who did not share his priorities.

The weakening of morale apart, these trends were related to, if not determined by, the progress of Chou's career. When he first joined the faculty of Peking University in 1917 he adamantly refused to have anything to do with teaching Chinese literature (*kuo-wen*); he was given responsibility instead for European and Greek and Roman literature.[6] The decisive change appears to have taken place in 1925, when he accepted an invitation to teach traditional Chinese literature at K'ung-te (Comte) Middle School. Subsequently he undertook the same subject at Peking University, specializing in the prose of the Ming and Ch'ing dynasties.[7] He had long since recognized his incompetence in European literature and so dropped those courses. The complexion of his essays broadly reflected the changing pattern of his professional duties — in the beginning wholly Western-oriented, in the end absorbed in the *pi-chi* (miscellanea) of Ming and Ch'ing scholars, though he still maintained an interest in Greek literature. While his appetite for leisure reading continued unabated and extended to such extraordinary things as works on London street cries in the time of Addison,[8] it would have been surprising had he not exploited the field he knew most about.

Teaching in itself — not the fly-by-night variety that many writers practiced to tide themselves over difficult periods — nurtures an attitude that could have been expected to grow on Chou as his experience and commitment increased. In the effort to explain things it is usual to look for the universal in the particular, to find a framework to which individual phenomena can be related and according to which they can be better understood. The consequence of thus placing individual phenomena in some broad context of human history is to reduce their specialness, and so to blunt the sharpness of one's response to them. Chou was a teacher whose academic approach extended to his treatment of contemporary events.

Another aspect of professionalism in a teacher is objectivity, which is reached through detachment. Detachment is a quality in a writer that is highly valued by posterity, but less valued by contemporaries. Lu Hsun saw this clearly enough. In fact he regarded detachment as a threat to his life's work. As he was about to leave Amoy after resigning his post there, he faced the question thus:

Should I write or should I teach? For the two are incompatible: writing needs passion, teaching requires coolness. If the two are combined then both are smooth and superficial; or if both were to be pursued earnestly then at one moment the emotion would be at fever pitch, at the next you would have to be calm and dispassionate, which would lead to an unsupportable drain on your energies, and in the end you would lose out on both sides.[9]

Chou Tso-jen, for his part, was quite content to affect the tone of detachment in his essays, as well as, one hopes, embodying the quality in the execution of his duties. After the *Yü ssu* episode he had accepted a settled role and a life-style into which academic coolness blended smoothly.

Lu Hsun clung to his role of rebel as if it were his life, whereas to Chou two modes of living were possible, even natural. Chou referred to the duality in himself of "rebel" and "hermit";[10] or in another formula, "ruffian" (*liu-mang*) and "gentleman" (*shen-shih*).[11] Hsu Chieh made much of the latter identification with the gentry class in terms of habits and tastes, and he was right to do so, for if one's life-style is the externalization of one's conception of oneself, it lends a perceptible coloring to all one does and says.

When Chou originally spoke of his gentry style he referred specifically to "manners," but he also later linked "hermit" and "gentleman" with "idle essays," in opposition to "rebel" and "ruffian" and "serious essays."[12] It was in the idle essays that the "gentleman" disported himself. In Chou's own view his essay "Pi-hu tu-shu lun" (On reading behind closed doors, 1928)[13] marked the decisive shift in favor of gentlemen as opposed to ruffian, though the two were necessarily complementary, and the serious essays were always the main course on his menu.

Examples Hsu gives of the kind of feudal pleasures Chou prized and paraded in his idle essays include watching temple plays from a boat,[14] drinking tea under a tiled roof by paper-covered windows, using china of simple elegance,[15] and being drawn by the signboard of the I-fu-chai in Peking not only because it showed the shop dated from pre-Boxer days, but also because the faded writing conjured up for him the vision of a contemplative, leisured, and complete life.[16] Hsu's case that Chou did have a strong attachment to simple, old-fashioned ways and a corresponding dislike of brash and showy new ones is well founded. The question is, was he justified in calling it feudal? Not if that term of abuse was confined to the upper classes, since most of the pleasures Chou wrote about were enjoyed by the lower classes too: they both watched and played the plays, and they too had the knack of spinning out visits to teahouses. The types of food Chou wrote about also were items enjoyed by ordinary people either in their day-to-day lives or at festival times, not rare delicacies that the rich banqueted on. In contrast, the entertainment that Chou did regard as feudal, Peking opera, he thoroughly detested for its degenerate thought which elevated high office, personal wealth, and polygamy, for its prancing and posturing, and its sense-numbing caterwauling.[17]

Chou's own reply to the kind of criticism Hsu expresses was this:

Some colleagues who are zealous for social reform abominate ease, regarding it as a bourgeois pleasure, almost equivalent to being well fed, well clothed, and indolent. But not so. Ease is a very valuable state of mind; sad or happy, rich or poor, all can attain to it, but still it is not at all simple to master. It can be divided into two types. One is "little" ease. . . . The peasant, for instance, may have been working the water wheel, and suddenly stops pedaling to look at the western hills; there is a chill in the air as the sun goes down, the stream changes color. If he joyfully responds to this, then this too counts as ease. You are not required to be prostrate and inebriated.[18]

The "great" ease Chou goes on to talk about is that evinced in the face of death, illustrated by Wang Ching-wen's calm remark when proffered the poisoned chalice by Ming-ti of the Liu Sung dynasty that this wine was "not suitable to pass on to a guest." Observing that the ideal states one envisages for oneself are precisely those one is least likely to attain to, Chou disclaimed any aptitude in either category.

If we accept Chou's argument that human beings of all stations enjoy some sort of ease or relaxation, and further allow that Chou's own pleasures are not specifically feudal (or bourgeois), we might still ask what attitude informed them. Though he may have drunk the same tea as the ordinary laborer (indeed he did favor the plainest variety), his appreciation might differ, or, to be slightly more subtle, the simple fact of articulating the pleasure might indicate a divide between them. Since Chou never pretended to speak on behalf of any other class or individual, or even associate any other person with the point of view he expressed, his own attitude comes through plainly, and it is unmistakably that of a scholar. A number of his essays on plants and foods which draw on a variety of local records are indistinguishable, except for being written in a modified form of *pai-hua*, from the notes scholars had made for hundreds of years on the same topics. Even in recalling his own experiences he still writes as an observer trying to elicit the flavor of an occasion or of surroundings, rather than as a participant or a natural part of the scene. So even when he writes of common pleasures, he does not, in the spirit of camaraderie, join hands with the common people; and if coincidentally his response were the same as that of a laborer, say in swilling cup after cup of bitter tea leaning over the balustrade of a teahouse,[19] the affinity between them might be sundered rather than soldered by his stepping back and remarking on the habit as such.

Fellow intellectuals of a radical cast of mind were, it seems, alienated less by finding anything ideologically objectionable in his "idle" essays—though in a situation where the literary world was divided into rival political camps they naturally tended to argue on ideological grounds—than by the class of writing itself: theirs was not the time for inconsequentialities or irrelevancies. Chou was not only at a disadvantage in having wide personal interests, he was politically uncircumspect in advertising them and allowing the world to make what it would of them. When in addition he recommended that everybody else do the same, by advocating a "literature of taste," this could hardly go unchallenged. A literary doctrine which both insisted on taste as the only standard of criticism, with the corollary that no single criterion is valid, and proposed the human animal in all its variety as the proper subject matter of literature, was necessarily divisive: no united front could ever form under its banner, however liberal or progressive its individual supporters might be. Literature in this view may legitimately qualify as an "art of life," the formula Chou settled for fairly early on in preference to "art for art's sake" or "art for life's sake," but it certainly would not interpret "life" to mean its current social manifestations.

There is always a gap between the literature one likes to read and the literature one thinks people *should* read. When Chou gave up pontificating about literature and eventually gave his approval to the idea of a literature of taste, this represented a retreat to the first position; indeed it is no more than a rationalization of it. That does not mean that he had abandoned his opinions about what people should read,[20] only that he did not feel anyone would listen to them. Whether such opinions should be voiced or not is decided by the sense of being in touch with a body of opinion or with the trend of history, or, better yet, with both. Certainly after the Northern Expedition began, Peking ceased to be the place to which all roads led, and for Chou personally the exodus of the radical intellectuals in 1926 and 1927 seems to have cut the vital link.

Left to itself Peking has never been renowned for its excitement. By general agreement it was unmatched for its atmosphere of tolerance, civility, and humor, to which might be added complacency. The quality of manners that Chou himself particularly liked about Peking was "expansiveness," which embraced "tolerance," "liberality," and resistance to discipline and constraint—in contrast to the narrowness he found in other cities, where there was an atmosphere of suspicion and nervousness as if the neighborhood self-policing system were still in force.[21] Since he regarded himself as a "native by adoption" of Peking, Chou very likely tried to be more Pekingese than the Pekingese in these respects. On a more general and speculative level, there is usually in old capital cities a sense of superiority and stability that makes events in the provinces seem either slightly unreal or ephemeral, not of an order, certainly, to be able to destroy a way of life that seems so persistent as to appear almost synonymous with the civilization. Chou's continuing to harp on constant characterological themes and his neglect, on the other hand, of the real transformations that were taking place in the urban centers of the South, were at any rate consistent with such capital-city attitudes.

Mental barriers aside, Peking was physically remote from the new centers of revolutionary activity. This by itself would have made it difficult for Chou to get a realistic impression of the progress of communism in China. John Service has recently described how as late as 1937 Edgar Snow's report on communist strength was stunning news in Peking.[22] That Chou up until then had never given the communists much chance of succeeding is therefore not surprising; probably the wisest assessment of the best evidence available would have pointed in the same direction. But there was more to it than that: Chou was evidently predisposed to come to a negative conclusion. Already in 1925 he was lecturing Japanese and English observers on their foolishness in overestimating the revolutionary potential of the Chinese and their predicting that China would go communist — "they really do not understand a thing about China!"[23]

These depreciating remarks did not stem from hostility to communism. For capitalism, the chief modern alternative, he had a pronounced dislike, as Hsu Chieh recognized, but on moral grounds rather than because its brashness ruined old simple ways. Thus he had accepted, rather rashly, in 1921, the attribution of prostitution to women workers not being paid a living wage under capitalism,[24] and explained the continuing need to struggle for freedom and equality in Europe by the fact that the continent was still capitalist — a view which suggests a belief in the historical inevitability of some form of socialism.[25] There is no evidence though that Chou had any deep understanding of capitalism as a system, and he made no claim to understand economics. The aspect of the analysis of capitalism he did appreciate was the theory of property, because that could be applied to the society he knew. The unfortunate lot of women in China was, he thought, due to the dominance of the morality of the propertied class (yu-ch'an chieh-chi) which emphasized male superiority and the rights of ownership, with the result that women were chattels and differed simply in being classed as private or public property. Among other things this accounted for respectable women having to wear skirts and prostitutes being forbidden to.[26]

Communism he approved of for the most part — in theory. As he said in a comment on Ts'ai Yuan-p'ei's pronouncements on his return from Europe, everybody with a little bit of sense agrees with communism.[27] Its aim is the creation of a heaven on earth, and only those who rely on wealth to usurp special privileges would be against that. Ts'ai had said that he was no exception, only he preferred the methods of Kropotkin to bring it about and rejected the Marxist class struggle. Obviously irritated by this attempt of Ts'ai to run with the hare and hunt with the hounds, Chou argued quite realistically that the scope of Kropotkin's "mutual aid" is limited to situations of mutual interest; actually "the fact of the class struggle is incontrovertible; it is not something dreamed up by Marx."[28] To Chou the inadequacy of the philosophy of mutual aid and peaceful cooperation had been proved by the failure (through insolvency) of the New Village movement in Japan, to which he had been an enthusiastic convert.[29] It had seemed to him to satisfy his ideal of supplying basic human needs on the basis of cooperation while leaving maximum room for the exercise of individual talents and interests. Though he himself had been inept, Chou had found great happiness in the fields, where all worked together without distinction. At the same time, however, he stressed the aspect of individualism, each person making a contribution to the life of the community by developing his or her talents to the full. Perhaps he already felt misgivings about pressure to conform and invasion of one's private preserve. But still he was clearly convinced that communism as a form of social organization was a good thing. As he said in December 1926 when two girls lost their lives in a fire at the Women's College in Peking, hospital services should be equally available to all without question of ability to pay, and this would only be possible in a communist society.[30]

But if the theory was good, realization was another matter. It seemed unfortunate to Chou that communism appeared to put so much faith in the masses, for he had limited expectations of the majority of his fellow human beings—at least in their present state of darkness, whatever their ultimate educability might be. He felt there was no communication between the political activists on the streets and the masses to whom their message was directed, because their ideals were at odds.[31] This objection was inflated to the status of repudiation in his essay of 1928 entitled "The feminine question and Oriental civilization, et cetera":

In China those who have been expounding problems and ideologies in recent times are all, let us face it, rather too romantic. They dream their rose-colored dreams and will not on their lives admit that beyond their curtains there is darkness. Take, for instance, our friends who talk about revolutionary literature: what they fear most is the dark side of life; that it may exist they will allow, but they haven't the courage to look at it, nor the courage to speak of it.

They give themselves up to shouting about the light dawning, the peasants all awakening, tomorrow seeing the world revolution! As to how benighted, mean, and selfish the actual life of the peasants is, that one is absolutely forbidden to utter; and if uttered, then it is bourgeois vilification.[32]

Such a view of the "actual life of the peasants" in China did not augur well for the prospects of a beneficent system based on the consciousness of the working class. Chou was not ready to believe that the Soviet citizen was much improved either. In this same essay he seized on a short story by the Soviet ambassador to Norway, Alexandra Kollontai, called "Sisters," which showed that in Soviet Russia, too, women still had to put up with the abuses of their husbands; if they left home the only occupation open to them was prostitution.

Chou's skepticism went far beyond doubting the validity of a particular political philosophy. Its depth and scope were clearly exposed in many essays written over a number of years, but for convenience we will revert to one of 1925 already cited (see note 23). The burden of its message was that, *pace* Bakunin, history enables us to predict that what has happened before will happen again; human beings do not learn from past mistakes; the leopard does not change its spots. Hence China will never see what it has not seen before: on the stage of the future will be enacted the same old scenes; only the actors will change, and the clothes and audience along with them. So the May Fourth movement, which had seemed to usher in a new age, was itself nothing new. It had had predecessors in the factions of Han times, the academies in the Sung period, and in the Tung-lin party under the Ming. While people continued to glorify China there would be no improvement: there could be no revolution, though there might be a change of dynasty; there could be no communization, though there might be civil disorder. The precondition for progress for the Chinese, Chou maintained, was that they acknowledge their shame and repent their sins. A people who bound feet, smoked opium, and dealt in human merchandise, could not become strong however much they might worship strength.

If there was a faint hope after all, then it lay in moral renewal. What possibly made it so faint was the same stumbling block of the masses, for a renewal that did not affect the majority of the people was not much of a renewal. What made Chou's views on the subject so decided? When he stated in this same essay that he did not believe in "the masses," a view he repeated in the postscript to *T'an hu chi* (Talking of tigers) in November 1927, he pinpointed the influence of Gustave le Bon's works, *Psychologie des foules* (2d ed., 1896) and *Lois psychologiques de l'evolution des peuples* (9th ed., 1909), which he had read in English or Japanese translation. With the Western savants like le Bon who claimed to make a scientific study of humankind we come to what I think of as the kernel of Chou Tso-jen's thought, and consideration of it will bring us back to the masses only after a long detour.

Chou was in my experience very unusual among literary figures in reading and taking seriously substantial Western works about the human animal — as opposed to extracting and misusing attractive and exciting theories. Like everyone else he had read Yen Fu's translation of Huxley's *Evolution and Ethics*, but it all really began when in Shanghai, on his way to Japan, in 1906, he bought Sir Edward Burnett Tylor's *Anthropology* (1881), translated into Chinese as "Evolution."[33] In Japan foreign books were easy to obtain, and Chou began to build up a truly impressive collection on anthropology, mythology, fairy stories, sexology, local customs (mainly Japanese), and biology. We have already mentioned the names of authors who stand out in the catalogue: Andrew Lang, J. G. Frazer, Gustave le Bon, Havelock Ellis, Jane Harrison, and Henri Fabre. Mindful of the adage that you cannot measure the sea with a bushel, I shall not attempt to encompass the mind which had absorbed this body of knowledge, but only pick out some attitudes which seem to derive from it.

As an overture to the discussion I might quote Chou's remark from the postscript to *T'an hu chi* that "probably only the men of the eighteenth century [the "age of enlightenment" in Europe] were something of the same kind as me, only I am not so optimistic as they were, for after Darwin and Frazer, philosophers' thought came down from the air to the ground and they became ordinary mortals."[34] This I take to mean that anthropology had a sobering effect; it had in fact clipped the wings of the thought-spinners, who before its advent had been free to conceive of worlds peopled by rational beings like themselves, by driving home the concept of the human animal still for the most part governed by primitive instincts. For Chou anthropology and allied human sciences opened up two avenues of thought, the first leading to a life-style which was natural and good, the other overgrown by brambles of superstition, in which he saw so many innocents entangled. Both avenues led from the distant past and extended toward the future, but for a thousand years in China the traffic had been diverted into the second, and the first had been trod by only a few lone travelers. In Chou's own day the distribution did not seem to him to have changed very much, and indeed the tone of public life in Peking set by the warlord government could only lend objective support to his view.[35]

Policies of governments aside, it was Chou's basic thesis that the Chinese people as a whole still lived in a prescientific, one might even say prerational world, and so were prone to most of the perversities and excesses catalogued by psychologists and cultural anthropologists. To the instructed, these were as apparent as the habits, inappropriate to its domestic state, that the dog had inherited from the wolf.[36] The examples Chou gave included beliefs derived from the close association in the primitive mind between human procreation and the fertility of the soil and the belief that irregular sexual activity leads to social disasters: so a student was executed in Szechwan for adultery, and the governor of Hunan quit his wife's bed in order to precipitate rain.[37] Other unhealthy attitudes toward sex were attributed to the same kinds of superstitious repressions. For example, Chou regarded the prohibition against girls over ten using public baths in the Shanghai area[38] as inverted paidophilia and the prurient fascination with nudity as an example of Chinese "satyriasis";[39] he also criticized avoidance between the sexes, citing the instance of the splitting up of a coeducational school in Shaohsing.[40] The theoretical backing for most of these observations was Frazer's *The Psyche's Task.*

Other characteristics of primitive society which Chou saw in China included gerontocracy and what he called the rule of the tribal chief: the war between North and South was not in his eyes a war between northerners and southerners but an ideological war between tribalist and democratic thought.[41] Add to these his other evidences of barbarism, such as a universal and perennial lust for kill-ing[42] and cultural aberrations like the self-immurment and self-immolation of women, and we are left with a rather depressing picture. Understandably, Chou was at times seen to wring his hands in sheer frustration. At the end of an essay written in 1936 on the praising of female chastity and the simultaneous placing of concu-bines on pedestals, he bursts out: "Now, when the situation of our country is so grave, we could well lay off this stuff about relations between the sexes, but can such a debased specimen of humanity be equal to the task of saving the nation? I cannot but have my doubts."[43] Even more emotional and revealing was his response to the influx of refugees from warlord conflict into Peking in 1926. Instead of turning his anger agains the militarists, he is distressed by the connection he cannot help making between the plight of the refugees and the bound feet among the women; of course such people were going to be sheep led to the slaughter. "I know I am of the same race as them," he writes, "but I can't help thinking, your affliction is deserved, sad to say, you barbaric people!"[44]

Chou was not so silly as to think the Chinese were alone in their barbarism. He knew from the works of Andrew Lang and others of the survival of superstitious practices in Europe and of the obscur-antism in the West which had almost smothered the works of sexolo-gists, and he willingly accepted the generalization of Frazer that all civilized countries are barbaric under the skin.[45] Western countries had one vital advantage over China, however, and that was that the place of science had been firmly established in them. The few enlightened individuals in the Chinese past had struggled through to a sensible and rational view of things against the prevailing intel-lectual climate. Their much more numerous counterparts in the West had been swimming with the tide. Medicine provided a prime example of the difference between the two cultures. True, supersti-tion in medicine still survived in the West, despite the solid founda-tions laid by Hippocrates in the fifth century B.C., but in China it was rife among the educated class as well as the common people. In the West medicine had gone through all the evolutionary stages from instinctive, via magical and metaphysical, to scientific. In China progress was held up by the battle line thrown up by the force of reaction which extended right across the board. Chou thought the best chance of a breakthrough was still on the medical front, though, for as pure science it was relatively protected against the repression which had already more or less overtaken modernists in the fields of politics, economics, and morality, where the stigma of "redness" could be used. However, in view of the sponsorship of schools of native medicine by high officials, Chou was not very optimistic.[46]

It should be clear enough that Chou's criticisms were not a collection of random sideswipes at whatever touched him on a sore spot, but were guided by firm and consistent principles and backed by what he thought of as the most reliable analysis of human society available. His positive contribution was within the same framework — establishing rational norms by which aberrations could be seen as aberrations, explaining what was natural and permissible in sexual behavior, exposing the relativity of moral codes and the consequent wisdom of a liberating philosophy of live and let live, and showing how myths were made in order to "eliminate the terror from religion."[47]

A consequence of this estimation of the scientific attitude, logical but unfortunate for his political image, was his orientation toward the educated classes and neglect of the masses. Believing as he did that it was practically impossible to impart the principles of democratic politics to the Chinese villager, whose mind had only absorbed from Buddhism the ideas of reincarnation and retribution and from Confucianism a magical faith in the emperor-savior, it was only natural that he should invest his remaining hopes in the upper stratum, which was at least free from this immobilizing fatalism and fear of authority. In 1926 he noted Frazer's observation (in *The Psyche's Task*) that the gap between the leaders of the nation and the unthinking masses is like that between two different ages, and also Renan's remark that he trembled before the thought that civilization was sustained by such a small number of people. Thank god, Frazer concluded, for the leadership of the intellectual aristocracy. Amen, echoes Chou, "perhaps this is our only consolation and hope."[48]

Negative as Chou's impression of the rural masses was, it was borne out by most realistic fiction of the period. However, it is not Chou's powers of observation that we are interested in, but rather how his attitudes were formed and externalized. How far his own class background prepared him to accept this elitist view I do not know, but by his own confession these Western "dons" (I use the word because it sums up their remote and Olympian type of scholarship) made a strong impression on him, possibly a decisive one. That he was to some extent predisposed to believe their pessimistic evaluation is demonstrated by the credence he gave to le Bon's "researches," despite the fact that le Bon forcibly expressed certain views which Chou did not share, the most noticeable being that women are inferior beings. It was le Bon, we may recall, who taught Chou to "distrust the masses." In *Psychologie des foules*, le Bon applied the following epithets to the masses: impulsive, suggestible, credulous, simplistic, intolerant, authoritarian, servile, conservative; they are not amenable to reason and are hostile to change and progress.

Strong as its negative influence might have been, this work paled in significance in comparison with le Bon's other book which Chou mentioned, namely, *Lois psychologiques de l'evolution des peuples*. That work begins with these words:

The civilization of a people reposes on a small number of fundamental ideas. From these ideas derive its institutions, its literature, its arts. Very slow to form, they are also very slow to disappear. Long after they have become manifest errors to educated minds, they remain for the multitude incontestable truths and carry on their work in the lower depths of nations. If it is difficult to impose a new idea, it is not less difficult to destroy an old one. Humanity always clings desperately to dead ideas and dead gods.

Slowness to change is the keynote of the whole book. The character or mental constitution of a people is also something permanent, "as fixed as its anatomical characteristics."[49] The acceptance of a new religion, a new language, new institutions may seem to have effected vast changes, but when one studies these apparent changes, one soon perceives that "only the names of things vary, whilst the realities which hide behind the words continue to live and only transform themselves with extreme slowness."[50] All progress — scientific, literary, industrial—is due to a small intellectual elite; but this elite is unimportant from the point of view of the race: the power of a people depends on the quality of its character.[51] "It is an illusion to believe that governments and constitutions count for anything in the destiny of a people."[52] For a final flourish, "In order for a people to transform its institutions, its beliefs and its arts, it must first transform its soul."[53]

I have represented le Bon's message at some length because as a key it fits the lock of Chou's mind. I do not recall Chou heaping any special plaudits on le Bon, but the unspoken assumption behind his attacks on the weaknesses and evils that beset his country tallies with le Bon's analysis, namely that the seat of the trouble is the national character, and the political superstructure is a thing of transience and relatively little importance. This point may be illustrated by Chou's argument with regard to female emancipation that though institutional reforms such as creating job opportunities and getting equality of rights are all to the good, the real answer to the problem lies in self-awareness in women themselves. In le Bon's terms, in order to give substance and reality to institutional rights and freedoms won from men, women would need to "transform their soul."

The will to effect a change of heart and mind and to inaugurate a new age of reason was, I suppose, the chief inspiration of the May Fourth movement. To the extent to which it had been superseded on the left by considerations of social engineering, Chou had been left behind. The turning point in Lu Hsun's intellectual awareness was precisely in his acquainting himself with social science, as a complement to the vestiges of his earlier evolutionary view and an alternative to the Nietzschean vision of the Apocalypse. Chou Tso-jen never took this step. The events of the Northern Expedition, rather than forcing a revision of his ideas, confirmed his gloomiest doubts. The reversion to primitive bloodletting and the all-too-familiar struggle for the position of "top dog" shredded the standard of democracy that he had once seen as flying over the Kuomintang forces and would seem to have provided final proof of le Bon's contention that the words may change but the realities behind them persist. It was in November 1928 that he declared for positively the last time his intention to retreat behind closed doors and let the rest of the world go by,[54] in the spirit of the old saying, "You get on with

your banditry and I'll look after my city gate; it's bugger all to do
with me."[55]

There were two main strands in the essay, "Reading behind closed
doors," which Chou himself regarded as marking a watershed in his
life between involvement and withdrawal. One was the depression
and cynicism that the study of Chinese history engenders. The
burden of Chou's argument, namely, that history proves that succeeding ages do not throw up new people, only later models of the
same ones, we have met before. It is worth noting now, though, that
however much modern scholars may dispute the validity of the
cyclical theory of Chinese history, China's unique position of having
preserved roughly the same geographical identity and roughly the
same system of government for two thousand years did inevitably
lead to similar situations recurring and similar patterns being
repeated time after time. With this in mind, it would in a sense have
required an act of faith for Chou *not* to think of his own age as
another interregnum, another period of intellectual ferment and
political chaos like that at the end of the Ming, which would be
brought to an end by the emergence of a new strong man who would
reimpose a new strict orthodoxy and quell dissent. That at any rate
was the picture Chou had, and fading out politically was his way of
anticipating the latter eventuality. Chou liked to call this strategy
"saving one's skin in times of turmoil." This policy tied in with the
second strand of the "Closed doors" essay, the consequences of
materialism: if only the material world exists, there is no soul, so
there is only this life to live. Chou recognized that religious dedication could be channeled into social movements, and that some
would have the courage to prefer a good death to a bad life, but the
majority of ordinary people like himself would be incapable of such
resolve. To throw away one's life by accident through indiscreet
criticism would, given such premises, be the height of folly.
Caution, then, was to be the byword in public.

In compensation for the loss of the public sphere, Chou felt that
one's private life should be as rich and enjoyable as one could make
it — not, however, an endless pursuit of pleasures that would blot out
disagreeable reality, nor even a turning in on a mental world of
gentle melancholy, as practiced by some of the poets who eventually

became known as the "Contemporaries" (*Hsien-tai p'ai*), but investing significance in the routine activites of everyday life, making a space on the ledger, so to speak, for those necessary things which are normally devalued because they are habitual. Already in 1925 he had drawn up a rough prospectus:

Some people divide life up into sections and only want to select a few from among them and discard the bits that don't suit them. We can put this approach down as "drawing a blade to cut water" or "wielding a sword to carve clouds." Broadly speaking, life consists of eating and drinking, love, procreation, work, aging, and death, but they are all bound up together and you can't pick out one or two to please yourself . . . I don't pretend that people can sleep all day or subsist on tea or wine, but I feel sleeping or drinking tea or wine are not to be despised, because they do have their place in life. A hundred years ago, in Japan, there was an artist who was an expert in tea ceremony. Once he went on a trip and at every inn where he lodged he would bring out his utensils and serenely make his tea to drink by himself. Someone remonstrated with him, saying, "What is the need for this when one is traveling?" His answer was a good one: "Are you suggesting that when traveling one is not living?" Only someone who thinks this way can value and enjoy his life. Walter Pater once said, "The aim of our life is not the fruit of experience but experience itself."[56]

Chou's interest in popular customs now falls better into place, for it would seem not only to be based on the importance he consciously placed on the way the routine business of life was conducted; it also seemed to have a positive feedback into his own life, in that learning of other people's ways stimulates awareness of one's own. Even the most paltry thing can gain in status when strung in a net of cross references, as every academic knows.

Chou's philosophy of "saving one's skin," which led to the contraction in upon his personal life, was hardly a noble one. It was not one he accepted willingly, however temperamentally inclined toward it he may have been. Ironically, when the Japanese *Shun-t'ien shih-pao* recommended it to the Chinese on the occasion of the execution of Li Ta-chao, Chou was up in arms, stung by the implication that the Chinese could not measure up to the Japanese, whose own modern reformers had obviously been willing to lay down their lives for the cause they believed in.[57] Yet accept it he did, for himself. One does not know how much weight should be given to the fact that within his family he was at birth assigned the role of monkhood; it was a thing he joked about in his "Fiftieth Birthday Poem," but he may nevertheless have been tempted to fulfill the prediction. We do know from his own confession, however, that he was a timid person, afraid of physical danger. In 1928 he recalled five violent incidents which he clearly had not enjoyed and had become involved in either fortuitously or as an unlooked-for consequence of his own activities,[58] and later he described how alarmed he was when approached by a military policeman while waiting for a train back to Peking from Paoting in 1934.[59]

For himself again, Chou felt that the time for getting mixed up in movements and demonstrations was past. Now that he had entered middle age, he said in 1930, with the true Chinese scholar's sense of the type of behavior appropriate to the different ages of life, he should be sitting back and watching the passing cavalcade.[60] He was quite willing that the doers should do. He several times urged disgruntled young men to go off and work for revolution instead of sitting at home and fuming,[61] and he offered some pertinent advice on doing propaganda work among the military, where he thought it would count most.[62] The type of people he could not abide were the pseudorevolutionaries and the literary men who acted as if they were military men.[63] The honesty that made him so vulnerable through confessing his own weaknesses would not let him pass over the pretensions of those who from positions of sanctuary urged others to do or die,[64] or — and the categories overlap — of those who had never done an honest day's work but still claimed to write proletarian literature. As support for the latter was a touchstone of progressiveness, we had best expand a little on the subject.

Chou took a plain person's view of the proletarian literature movement. As he saw it, the propertied and propertyless classes of China were much alike; evidently relying on his knowledge of the rural poor he stuck fast to the view that the propertyless class of men too only desired riches, prestige, and women. More awkward still, he denied that one could talk about classes with regard to literature. On this last point Chou's argument is a little difficult to follow, but it seems to be on the premise that individuals cannot and do not in themselves embody class consciousness, and since individuals are the makers of literature, the theory of class literature must therefore be invalid. He conceded that ideas and attitudes expressed in literature can be legitimately ascribed to a certain class or age, but to do so is to extract them from their literary matrix. The language of sociology cannot be used to describe the totality of a work of literature, which is the mirror of its author's mind. Authors being human beings, their motivations are complex and not reducible to ideal patterns derived from economic models.[65] In sum, Chou could see no good coming out of the proletarian literature movement for three reasons: it would be if anything retrogressive in matters of mores; the term "literature" could not be anything but a misnomer; and the whole enterprise was intellectually dishonest.

In this context we do indeed see Chou in the role of the "aloof and incorruptible scholar." While more strongly motivated individuals might accept without qualms, and sometimes without reflection, the idea that to assist the work of angels, or history, it was necessary to live a lie, he balked at it. His case nicely illustrates the point Lu Hsun made with reference to *Yü ssu*:

Though *Yü ssu* may be said to have often displayed the spirit of resistance, yet too it was frequently tinged with weariness, probably because it saw the underlying reality of China too clearly, so inevitably tended to lose hope. This shows that too discerning a view of things leads to failure of nerve in action. Chuang-tzu's saying that "the lot of the man who can make out the fish in the deep is not a happy one" one would think not only means that other people fight shy of him but also that his own prospects will be seriously impaired.[66]

As we saw from the "Feminine Question" essay, Chou prided himself on not seeing the world through rose-colored spectacles but daring to face the darkness. Lu Hsun naturally also thought of himself as one who could "make out the fish in the deep," but the contrast between the two men is again instructive. Lu Hsun was wise enough to listen eventually to that small voice which told him, "When many people pass one way, a road is made" where none existed before.[67] From regretting, in his 1922 preface to *Na-han* (Battle cries), that he had introduced to order the odd note of optimism in his stories against his better judgment, he managed to curb his instinctive pessimism sufficiently to support a platform in which he seemed not to have fully believed. This strength of will was lacking in Chou Tso-jen.

Lu Hsun also showed better historical judgment than his brother in diverting his attack from the Chinese people as a whole to the class enemy. Chou, with his ideas about national character, stuck to the original target, thus earning some compliments but probably little loyalty or affection. He thus put himself, in the eyes of the left, in unsavory company. Already in 1923 Teng Chung-hsia, a member of the Central Committee of the Chinese Communist Party, spoke out against detraction of the people's customs and morals among fawning Westernizers and demanded works which would express the great spirit of the Chinese people.[68]

As to the negative side of the people's customs, Chou was far from dissociating himself from it; in fact he actively advocated the study of to him obnoxious aspects of China's cultural tradition like old plays and *pa-ku wen* (eight-legged essays) because they represented sides of the perennial Chinese character. He felt that the nation's past, bad as well as good, should be known and acknowledged, as it lived on in the present. But being aware of the inheritance did not imply that it could be either freely repudiated or deliberately per-petuated. The course of events was not to be determined by the human will. It is clear from his view on certain cultural questions[69] that he regarded history as a continuum which remains unbroken however much we care to think of the present age as a new depar-ture. In this perspective individuals are placed at a given point in the impersonal process of evolution, and through this consideration their private burdens are lightened.

Chou's habits of thought in the post-May Fourth period seem to be basically, though limitedly evolutionary in that progress in sci-entific scholarship, on which he put so much value, does increasing-ly tend to put things on a more rational footing and conversely undermine the irrational. He was still inclined to analyze the history of branches of human knowledge and art into evolutionary stages of development; to the example of medicine might be added his account of the growth of individual out of collective literature and his corresponding assertion that the familiar essay was "the ultimate in the development of literature."[70] To see the past in such terms but to think the process had universally come to a halt would not be sensible. Advances like these could continue in the face of mass inertia, as they belonged to the sphere of the enlightened few.

The frame of mind which Chou was fighting through to when buoyed up by such optimistic thoughts envisaged the individual in a more positive role. It was put into words by Havelock Ellis which earned his high praise: he accorded Ellis' attitude the accolade of "natural," "scientific," "calm and unflinching"—all qualities that Chou aspired to himself. This attitude took account of the fact that we live permanently in a transitional age, at the conjunction of past and future, and of the further fact that the world cannot be without traditions nor life without activity. In Ellis' metaphor, he and his fellows were the present bearers of the torch of light; soon they would be overtaken and in turn fade into the darkness, but in the meantime they had to ensure that the means were there for the torch to be passed on.[71] Chou could not know that another procession altogether would sweep by and extinguish the liberal flame. For him it was enough that there were still areas of Chinese life after the May Fourth movement which it could yet illuminate.

At the same time the belief in at least the possibility of progress was encroached on and overlaid by the doctrine of recurrence—"the cycle of existence repeating itself" (shih-shih lun-hui), as he called it in 1931.[72] It was this alternative doctrine which was applied to Chinese history, as we have seen. It also lay behind Chou's formulation in 1932 of the thesis of the pendulum swing rather than linear development in the story of Chinese literature.[73] But theories are only the elevated highways of the mind. The landscape out of which this one rose was littered with the signs of the bad old China reasserting itself and the collapse under the pressure of grim reality of the dreams of the future. Chou's attitude is better reflected in a personal response to the famous passage in Ecclesiastes about there being "nothing new under the sun." He grants that the world is peopled by "ghosts," in the sense that one sees reenacted about one the same follies that fill the chronicles of former ages, and is aware that the tradition at times works through oneself, as an instrument, pure and simple. But if this be the "vanity of vanities," then it should not be allowed to cause "vexation of spirit"; the only way to cope with the fact is to pursue vanities, to find them out and know them, even if this is bathing one's sores. To do so is to demonstrate the truth of Pascal's proposition that "man is a thinking reed," fragile and helpless it is true, but superior to the world that destroys him in that he is conscious of what is happening to him.[74]

The bearer of the torch or the thinking reed? Undoubtedly it was the latter metaphor which was more constantly before Chou Tso-jen in middle age. It offered no refuge in the past, present, or future, but was a way of accepting the most unpalatable truths about himself and his historical identity, and thus of remaining alive intellectually. The attitude seemed to appeal to depths of Confucian stoicism and skepticism uncovered as the Western liberal-progressive front crumbled. If faith in human potential is what ultimately separates radicals from conservatives, this alone put Chou on the right of the universal political spectrum, but the peculiar form his conservatism took was not that of allegiance to feudalism but of acceptance of his style of Chinese personality, both as a burden and a consolation.

CONTRIBUTORS
NOTES
GLOSSARY
INDEX

Contributors

Guy Alitto received his Ph.D. from Harvard University with a dissertation on Liang Shu-ming which he is currently revising into a book. He is a Fellow of the Center for Chinese Studies at the University of California, Berkeley.

Martin Bernal is an Associate Professor at Cornell University. He was a Fellow and Tutor of King's College, Cambridge, from 1965 to 1972, and he has recently completed a book on Chinese socialism up to 1907.

Hao Chang is Associate Professor of History, The Ohio State University, and the author of *Liang Ch'i-ch'ao and Intellectual Transition in China 1890-1907* (Harvard University Press, 1971).

Arif Dirlik is Assistant Professor of History at Duke University, and the author of a number of articles on Marxist historiography and historical materialism in Republican China.

Lloyd E. Eastman is Professor of History at the University of Illinois, and a specialist in the history and politics of Kuomintang China. His latest book, *The Abortive Revolution: China Under Nationalist Rule 1927-1937,* appeared in 1974 (Harvard University Press).

Charlotte Furth received her Ph.D. from Stanford, and is Associate Professor of History at California State University at Long Beach. She is the author of *Ting Wen-chiang: Science and China's New Culture* (Harvard University Press, 1970).

Lin Yü-sheng received his B.A. from National Taiwan University and his Ph.D. from the University of Chicago. A specialist in classical and modern Chinese intellectual history, he teaches as Associate Professor of History and East Asian Languages and Literature at the University of Wisconsin.

David E. Pollard is Lecturer in Modern Chinese at the School of Oriental and African Studies, University of London. He is the author of *A Chinese Look at Literature: The Literary Values of Chou Tso-jen in Relation to the Tradition* (Berkeley, University of California Press, 1973).

Laurence A. Schneider is the author of *Ku Chieh-kang and China's New History* (Berkeley, University of California Press, 1971), and a member of the Department of History at the State University of New York at Buffalo.

BENJAMIN I. SCHWARTZ, Professor of History and Government at Harvard, is known for his work on the history and theory of communism in China, and on the broad range of Chinese intellectual history. His books include *Chinese Communism and the Rise of Mao* (Harvard University Press, 1951), and *In Search of Wealth and Power: Yen Fu and the West* (Harvard University Press, 1964). In 1974-75 he was Eastman Professor at Oxford University.

TU WEI-MING is Assistant Professor of History at the University of California, Berkeley, and a specialist in the history of Chinese philosophy and religion. He is currently writing a book on Wang Yang-ming.

ERNEST P. YOUNG teaches history at the University of Michigan, and is an authority on the politics of the early Chinese Republic. He is the author of *The Presidency of Yuan Shih-k'ai: Liberalism and Dictatorship in Early Republican China*.

Notes

1   **Notes on Conservatism in General and in China in Particular**
Benjamin I. Schwartz

     1. *Reflections on the Revolution in France* (New York: The Liberal Arts Press, 1955), p. 99.
     2. Michael Oakeshott, *Rationalism in Politics* (London: Methuen, 1974).

2   **Culture and Politics in Modern Chinese Conservatism**
Charlotte Furth

     1. For secondary works reflecting new culturalist interpretations of the relationship of their movement to tradition, see Kuo Chan-po, *Chin wu-shih nien Chung-kuo ssu-hsiang shih* (The history of Chinese thought in the past fifty years; 1st ed., Peiping, 1935), and Chow Tse-tung, *The May Fourth Movement* (Cambridge, Mass.: Harvard University Press, 1960).
     2. Joseph R. Levenson, *Confucian China and Its Modern Fate,* 3 vols. (Berkeley: University of California Press, 1958-1965).
     3. For the distinction between conservatism and the traditional "vegetative patterns of life," see Karl Mannheim's classic analysis, "On Conservative Thought," reprinted in *Essays on Sociology and Social Psychology* (London: Routledge & Paul, 1969), pp. 74-164.
     4. K'ang first presented the idea in a memorial to the throne in 1898. See "Chronological Autobiography of K'ang Yu-wei," translated in Jung-pang Lo, *K'ang Yu-wei: A Biography and a Symposium* (Tucson, Ariz.: University of Arizona Press, 1967), p. 99. See K'ang's "Chung-hua chiu-kuo lun" (On China's salvation), in *Pu-jan tsa-chih* (Compassion magazine) 1:21-22 (March 1913), for a succinct statement of his view: "European countries . . . separate religion and government. Thus religion maintains its awesome power and morality is honored, even while dissension rages. This is to 'drive a cart on two wheels.' "
     5. The idea of a "restoration strategy" is developed by J. G. A. Pocock, who opposes such creative restructuring of history to the more truly conservative theories of historical transmission that stress the presumption of continuity between past and present. See "Time, Institutions and Action: An Essay on Traditions and Their Understanding," in *Politics and Experience: Essays Presented to Professor*

Michael Oakeshott on the Occasion of his Retirement (Cambridge, Eng.: Cambridge University Press, 1968).

6. Hsu Shou-sheng, *Chang Ping-lin* (Chengtu, 1945), has an exaggerated but nonetheless suggestive evaluation of the classical scholar's tutelary relationship to Sun. See pp. 1-19. Chang Ping-lin refers to his discussions with Sun on various ancient institutions in *Ch'iu-shu* (Shanghai, 1904), nos. 42 and 53. National Essence scholars wrote most of the historical pieces for Sun's revolutionary journal, *Min pao* (People's journal).

7. Both Chang and Liang were leaders of a variety of wartime "third force" political groups, such as the Association for National Construction in 1939 and the Democratic League in 1941-1945.

8. This view of political conservatism makes it necessary to struggle with the concept of "modernization" and with the tendency of that thorny term to imply an impersonal yet benign historical process leading toward some preestablished future historical culmination. To a certain extent, it is possible to de-mythologize modernization, for although to some people nationhood and mass participation in politics may appear to be desirable, they do not have to be looked at as morally valuable ends. It may also be possible to use the concept of modernization intelligibly without suggesting that the historical pattern at work creating nationhood and mass societies down to today necessarily constrains the future, which is after all fluid. Nonetheless there is at work here an inescapable tendency to define historical issues and periods in terms of the contemporary third world, and to suggest that if modernization is not an impersonal process at work with an inherent dynamic casting its shadow on the future, it is at least the product of the energies of people desiring change, so that their hopes cast such a shadow.

9. Other terms common during the early Republic were *kuo hun* (national soul) and *kuo hsing* (national character). The frankly spiritualistic "national soul" was preferred by K'ang Yu-wei who liked its religious connotations. See his "Chung-kuo huan hun lun (Recalling the soul of China), *Pu-jen tsa-chih* 8 (Nov. 1913). In discussing "national character" Liang Ch'i-ch'ao made just the distinction between living custom and formal canon that is at issue here. He said that the essence of Chinese morality was expressed in the national character traits of "reciprocity," "respect for station," and "concern for posterity." Liang reserved *kuo ts'ui* for categorizing the essential teachings of Confucius, to his mind those on personal self-cultivation. See Liang's "Chung-kuo tao-te chih ta yuan" (Fundamentals of Chinese morality), *Yung yen* (Justice), 1,2 and 1,4 (Dec. 16, 1912, Jan. 16, 1913); and his "Kung-tzu chiao-i shih-chi pi-i yü chin-jih kuo-min che ho tsai yü chang-ming chih ch'i tao ho yu" (How is it that Confucianism is of practical benefit to Chinese today and how do we wish to promulgate it?), in *Ta Chung-kuo* (Great China), 1, 2 (Feb. 1916).

10. For an analysis of the similar evolution of the idea of culture in nineteenth-century British thought, see Raymond Williams, *Culture and Society 1780-1950* (New York: 1958).

11. For an interesting analysis of these terms see Fung Yu-lan, *Hsin shih-lun* (New culture and society; Changsha, 1941), pp. 154-173. Pagination is from the reprint in Wang Yun-wu, ed., *Jen jen wen k'u* (Humanistic treasury; Taipei, 1967), vol. 371-372.

12. Ch'ien Mu, *Kuo shih ta-kang* (Outline of Chinese history), 2 vols. (Changsha, 1940; reprinted Shanghai, 1947). For a brief statement of Ch'ien Mu's theory of Chinese culture, see his "Chung-kuo wen-hua chih ch'eng-ch'ang yü fa-chan" (On the historical perfection and future development of Chinese culture), in *Tung hsi wen-hua* (Eastern and Western Cultures) 10: 1-12 (April 1968).

13. In Ch'ien Mu's analysis "legitimate institutions" were contrasted with "political strategies." The distinction was not between formal government structures and spheres of personal decision-making, but between government actions in the service of legitimate public interests, and those carried out for personal ends of power holders. See his *Chung-kuo li-tai cheng-chih te-shih* (Historical strengths and weaknesses of Chinese politics; Hong Kong, 1959), pp. 116ff.

14. For a Turkish example see Serif Mardin, "Center-Periphery Relations: A Key to Turkish Politics?" in *Daedalus* (Winter 1973), pp. 169-190. In its centralization ideal and relationship to the peasantry, the KMT seems closer to the Kemalists in Turkey than to the provincial groups which supported neotraditional Islam.

15. For the relationship between late Ch'ing scholarship and the revisionist "antiquity doubters" of the 1920s see Ch'ien Mu, *Kuo hsueh kai lun* (General introduction to national learning; Taipei, 1956), pp. 136-161; and Laurence Schneider, *Ku Chieh-kang and China's New History* (Berkeley: University of California Press, 1971).

16. This debate has been summarized in Wing-tsit Chan, *Religious Trends in Modern China* (New York: Columbia University Press, 1953). For an interesting argument for Confucianism as a religion see Chang Tung-sun, "Yü chih Kung-chiao kuan" (My view of Confucianism), *Yung Yen* (Justice) 15 (July 1913). Chang Ping-lin's views may be found, inter alia, in "Po chien-li Kung-chiao i" (Against the establishment of a Confucian religion), *Ya Yen* 1.1 (1919).

17. Definitions of religion are notoriously elusive. The problem is made more complicated here because so many educated Chinese — in reaction against the anthropomorphism and sacramentalism of both Christianity and Chinese popular worship — often tried to reserve the neologism *tsung-chiao* for belief systems with these presumably cruder characteristics. However, in saying that religion is a lower form of philosophy, they assumed that philosophy dealt with what outsiders would call questions of religious doctrine. If we shift the definition of religion away from doctrine and think instead of the feelings of awe and mystical aspiration inspired by a set of beliefs or their symbols, the religiousness of modern Confucianism is also clearly seen. See Chan, *Religious Trends*.

18. Quoted in Chan, *Religious Trends*, p. 226.

19. Technically the term "new Confucianist" (*hsin ju-chia*) is reserved for the more subjectivist modern Confucian metaphysicians like Hsiung Shih-li or Mou Tsung-san, as contrasted with the objectivist metaphysician Fung Yu-lan. Since the philosophical differences among these thinkers were comparatively complex without, it seems to me, rendering it impossible to talk about them as a group, I use "new Confucianism" as a generic term for the movement.

20. For a general survey of the new Confucianism, see in addition to Chan, *Religious Trends*, Ho Lin, *Tang-tai Chung-kuo che-hsueh* (Contemporary Chinese philosophies; Nanking, 1947). For a critical overview, see Yin Hai-kuang, *Chung-kuo wen-hua ti chan-wang* (The Future of Chinese culture; Taipei, 1966), chap. 8.

21. The term is Chan's; see his *Religious Trends*, p. 217.

22. For a similar analysis of the relation of science and value in modern Islam, see Clifford Geertz, *Islam Observed: Religious Development in Morocco and Indonesia* (New Haven: Yale University Press, 1968).

23. Ho Lin, pp. 63-64.

24. Ibid., pp. 16-18.

25. Ch'en Li-fu, *Philosophy of Life,* trans. Jen Tai (New York, 1958). This work is a translation of *Sheng chih yuan-li,* first published in 1944, which in turn was an expanded version of lectures Ch'en gave in 1934 and published shortly thereafter under the title *Wei-sheng lun* (Vitalism).

26. Fung Yu-lan, *Hsin yuan tao* (New treatise on the way; Shanghai, 1946; reprinted Hong Kong, 1961), pp. 205-206. For an English translation see E. R. Hughes, *The Spirit of Chinese Philosophy* (London: 1947).

27. Ibid.

28. For example, on this point Fung Yu-lan argued that historically the unconditional moral obligation was the personalized one of filiality, whereas today people owed unconditional allegiance to the nation as the most comprehensive social community existing in the present stage of evolution. Therefore, acts formerly characterized as righteous (*i*) — that is, acts which could not be considered obligatory because no reciprocal return could be expected — must now be seen in a new light. *Hsin shih lun,* pp. 77-86.

29. Ho Lin, pp. 19-21.

30. Ibid., p. 19.

31. See for example Ch'en Li-fu, *Philosophy of Life*, pp. 83-87; and Chiang Kai-shek, "Ta-hsueh chih tao" (The way of the "Great Learning"), in *Chiang Tsung-t'ung yen-lun hui-pien* (Collected speeches of President Chiang; Taipei, 1956), 12:1-24. Speeches of Sept. 11 and Sept. 15, 1934.

32. Chiang Kai-shek, "Hsin sheng huo yun-tung chih chung-hsin chun-tse" (Central guide to the New Life movement), *Collected speeches,* 11:120-124. Speech of March 5, 1934.

33. Fung Yu-lan, *Hsin shih lun.*

34. Ibid., p. 71.

35. Fung, *Hsin yuan tao*, pp. 189-190. Fung explained that the term "empty" (*k'ung*) was not meant to be taken in the negativist Taoist or Chan Buddhist sense.

36. *Wen-hua chien-she yueh-k'an* (Cultural construction monthly), Oct. 1934-July 1937. The first issue has a lead article by Ch'en Li-fu, "Chung-kuo ti wen-hua chien-she lun" (On Chinese cultural construction). For the manifesto itself see "Chung-kuo pen-wei ti wen-hua chien-she i-yen" (Manifesto on cultural construction on a Chinese base) 1.4:1-5. Later issues include articles by many of the "ten professors," and outside comments on the manifesto by twenty-two scholars and publishers based on a public symposium held in Shanghai in late January 1935. Besides T'ao Hsi-sheng, signers of the manifesto included Ho Ping-sung (European historian and editor of the Shanghai Commercial Press and of *Chiao-yü tsa-chih* [Educational magazine]); Sun Hsi-lin (professor of law at Ling-nan University and chief editor of Li-ming Book Company); Huang Wen-shan (social scientist and professor at Ling-nan); Chang I (head of the education department at Fu-tan

University); Fan Chung-yun (professor of literature and international relations at Fu-tan and Ling-nan); Wang Hsin-ming (author and chief editor of *Ch'en pao* newspaper); Chen Kao-yung (scientist); Wu Hsu-kan; and Sa Meng-wu.

37. For sociological thinking among the "ten professors," see Wang Hsin-ming, "Chung-kuo tsung-chiao ti fu-chan chi ch'i i-shih" (The development of Chinese religion and its ceremonies), *Wen-hua chien-she yueh-k'an* 1.1:83-92; Ho Ping-sung, "Chung-kuo ti feng-su" (Chinese customs), ibid. 1.1:93-100; Ch'en Kao-yung, "Chung-kuo ti lun-li ssu-hsiang" (Chinese ethical thought), ibid. 1.1:35-42; and his "Tsen-yang pien Chung-kuo k'o-hsueh hua" (How to make China a scientific society), ibid. 1.2:21-26. In response to communist-anticommunist battlelines, polemic was brisk throughout the 1930s concerning what constitutes philosophical materialism. Neither Fung Yu-lan nor Ch'en Li-fu passed as pure materialists, of course, since Fung said that the supraphenomenal realm of metaphysics did objectively exist, while Ch'en gave culture some autonomous role in the historical process. In the present context, however, their purely theoretical positions are less germane than their actual social thought.

38. Hu Shih bitterly satirized the manifesto as a "fashionable manifestation of today's reactionary atmosphere," but his accompanying argument that the "scientific method" could become a subjective slogan used by anybody applied equally well to himself. See *Wen-hua chien-she yueh-k'an*, 1.7:103-105.

39. The place of the *I ching* in Wang Fu-chih's historical thought is sensitively analyzed in James H. Zimmerman, "Wang Fu-chih as Historian: An Image of Sung History," paper presented to the Yale Seminar on Chinese Historiography, 1969. Wang used the word *"ch'üan"* (balance) to describe the proper style of action at each successive stage of changing circumstance. See *Wang Chüan-shan p'u* (Treatise on Wang Fu-chih) by Chang Hsi-t'ang (Shanghai, 1936), pp. 113-114.

3   National Essence and the New Intelligentsia
Laurence A. Schneider

1. For general polemics about the nature of the "national essence" and what was required of scholars and poets, see for example editorial prefaces to the *Kuo-ts'ui hsueh-pao* (National essence journal; hereafter *KTHP*), 1:1 (1905); Teng Shih, "Kuo-hsueh chen lun" (A true critique of national studies), ibid., III:2 (1907); and editorial introduction to the first anthology of Southern Society literature, *Nan-she,* 1st collection (Shanghai, 1909), reprinted in Hu Huan-shen, "Shang-hai hsueh-shu kai-yao" (Sketch of Shanghai scholarship), in *Shang-hai-shih t'ung-chih-kuan ch'i-k'an* (Journal of the gazetteer bureau of Shanghai), vol. II (June 1934-March 1935), p. 848.

2. Compare the observations of contributors in Benjamin Schwartz, ed., *Reflections on the May Fourth Movement* (Cambridge, Mass.: Harvard University Press, 1972), particularly those of Leo Lee (p. 74) and Jerome Grieder (p. 98).

3. For summary of membership data see Liu Ya-tzu, *Nan-she chi-lueh* (Recollections of the Southern Society; Shanghai, 1940; hereafter *NSCL*), p. 43 and passim.

4. See Feng Tzu-yu, *Ko-ming i-shih* (Fragments of revolutionary history;

Taipei reprint, 1969), II, 227-229; and *NSCL*, pp. 4-5.

5. For Huang Chieh see Howard L. Boorman, ed., *Biographical Diction-ary of Republican China* (New York: Columbia University Press, 1967-1970; here-after *BDRC*), II, 187; and Wu Mi, "Shih hsueh tsung shih Huang Chieh hsueh-shu" (The art of our venerated teacher Huang Chieh), in Huang Chieh, *Shih hsueh* (Poetics), Hong Kong edition, 1964.

6. For Ch'en Ch'u-p'ing see *NSCL,* p. 6; and *Chin-tai shih-hsuan* (An-thology of contemporary poetry; Peking, 1963; hereafter *CTSH*), p. 425; and also Feng Tzu-yu, *Ko-ming i-shih,* I, 196.

7. See "Correspondence to Liu Ya-tzu," in *CTSH,* p. 429; and "Epitaph for Liu Tao-i," ibid., p. 442.

8. *Chung-kuo chin-tai wen-hsueh shih-kao* (Draft history of contempor-ary Chinese literature; Shanghai, 1960; hereafter *CKCTWH*), p. 327; *NSCL,* p. 6; and also see Ch'en Ch'u-p'ing's entry in the "Publication notices" section of *KTHP* III:6 (1908).

9. *NSCL,* p. 43 and "Membership" appendix; *CTSH,* p. 452; and see membership photographs prefacing Nan-she (publisher), *Wen-lu* (Prose), 20th collection (Shanghai, 1917).

10. Mary Rankin, *Early Chinese Revolutionaries* (Cambridge, Mass.: Har-vard University Press, 1971), p. 109; *CKCTWH,* p. 341; *CTSH,* p. 484; and Hu P'u-an, ed., *Nan-she ts'ung hsuan* (Southern Society Anthology; Taipei reprint, Wen-hai, 1969 [?]; hereafter *NSTH*), I, 598-600, and II, 534.

11. Quoted in Ai Ying, *Wan-Ch'ing wen-i pao-kan shu-lueh* (Literature of the late Ch'ing; Shanghai, 1958), p. 42.

12. *NSTH,* I, 470.

13. *CTSH,* pp. 445-446.

14. Ch'en Ch'u-p'ing, "notice" of the Shen chiao society literary anthology in *KTHP* III:6 (1908).

15. *CTSH,* pp. 445-446, 462; *NSCL,* p. 47. Among the periodicals in question: *Min-li pao* (People's stand), 1909-1913; *Min Sheng* (People's voice), edited by Ning T'ai-i; and the *T'ai-p'ing-yang pao* (Pacific Ocean), 1911-1912, edited by Yeh Ch'u-ts'ang.

16. *NSCL,* p. 110.

17. Cited in William Ayers, *Chang Chih-tung and Educational Reform in China* (Cambridge, Mass.: Harvard University Press, 1971), p. 249.

18. See Lu Shao-ming, "Chiu hsueh hun" (Former study of soul), *KTHP* I:5 (1905); Teng Shih, preface to "Ming mo ssu hsien-sheng hsueh-shuo" (Research theories of four teachers of the late Ming), *KTHP* II:1 (1906), and preface to *KTHP* IV:3 (1908).

19. See Chang's *Ch'üan hsueh p'ien,* chaps. 5 and 8; and Ayers, *Chang Chih-tung,* pp. 50-51, 171-173, et passim.

20. See Wu Mi, "Shih hsueh tsung shih Huang Chieh," p. 24.

21. *NSTH* I, 137.

22. For example see Teng Shih, ed., *Feng-yu lou ts'ung-shu* (Collections of the wind and rain tower; Shanghai, 1910), 27 vols.

23. See also the *Kuo-ts'ui ts'ung-k'an* (National essence collection; Shang-hai, 1907-1911), which had Liu Shih-p'ei as general editor of the 27 titles; *Shen-*

chou kuo-kuang chi (China national revival collection; Shanghai, 1909-1912), for which Teng Shih served as general editor; and *Mei-shu ts'ung-shu* (Art collection; Shanghai, 1920-1928), also produced under the general editorship of Teng Shih.

24. For example "Ni she kuo-ts'ui hsueh-t'ang ch'i" (An explanation of the National Essence Academy), *KTHP* III:1 (Jan. 1907).

25. Hsu Fu-ch'eng, "Lun kuo-ts'ui wu tsu yü Ou-hua" (National essence is not hampered by Westernization), *KTHP* I:7 (July 1905).

26. Huang Chieh's "history" began with issue I:1 in 1905.

27. For a detailed discussion of these formulations and adaptations see the essays by Martin Bernal and Charlotte Furth in this volume.

28. These materials were published collectively under the general title of *Feng-yu lou ts'ung-shu* (Shanghai, 1910).

29. *CTSH*, p. 488 (dated 1902). And see Liang Ch'i-ch'ao's 1903 "Shih hua" (Poetics) in Liang's *Yin-ping wu wen-chi* (Taiwan: Chung-hua edition, 1960). vol. 16. Here Liang cites many examples, some from his own writings, of such patriotic poetry and sample national anthems.

30. *CTSH*, p. 488 (dated 1903). The "Violent Men" and the "Song of the Typhoon" are references to Liu Pang and his stalwarts who rescued China from the depredations of the Ch'in and established the Han dynasty in the third century B.C.

31. From Liu's "Fang-ko" (Song of liberation), *CKCTWH*, p. 343.

32. "Tzu-yu" (Freedom), *CTSH*, pp. 476-477.

33. *NSTH*, II, 657-658.

34. *CTSH*, p. 439.

35. For example, see Kao Hsu's formulation in *NSTH*, I, 534-538.

36. See essays by Lu Shao-ming and Teng Shih cited in note 18 above; and also see Teng Shih, "Kuo-hsueh fu-hsing lun" (The revival of national studies), *KTHP* I:9 (Sept. 1905).

37. *NSTH*, I, 1; *NSCL*, p. 43.

38. *NSTH*, I, 34, and II, 817; *CTSH*, p. 464; *Nan-she,* 13th collection (Shanghai, 1915); *NSTH*, III, 1369, and *CTSH*, pp. 450-451, for elegies.

39. See *CTSH*, pp. 450-451; *NSCL*, pp. 122-123; *NSTH* I, 217-219.

40. *NSCL*, pp. 110-111, 120-128, 133-134, 219-220.

41. Chow Tse-tsung, *The May Fourth Movement* (Cambridge, Mass.: Harvard University Press, 1960), pp. 62-63.

42. See Huang K'an's editorial preface to *Kuo ku* I:1 (1919).

43. See the debate between *Renaissance* and *National Heritage* in Mao Tzu-shui, "Kuo ku ho k'o-hsueh te ching-shen" (National heritage and the spirit of science), *Hsin ch'ao* (Renaissance) I:5 (April 1919); Chang Hsuan's response in *Kuo ku* (National heritage) I:3 (1919); and Mao Tzu-shui's rebuttal in *Hsin ch'ao* II:1 (August 1919).

44. See Yü Shih-chen's editorial on "Ku chin hsueh-shu . . . " (Old and new scholarship . . .) in *Kuo ku* I:1; and Huang K'an's editorial cited in note 42.

45. Huang K'an editorial.

46. This can be seen throughout Chow, *May Fourth Movement.*

47. Wu Mi, "Shih hsueh tsung shih Huang Chieh . . . ," p. 27b.

48. *NSCL,* membership appendix; and *Nan-she,* 13th collection for samples of their contributions.

49. *CTSH,* p. 425; *NSTH* I, 575; and see Ch'en Ch'u-p'ing, *Kao Ke tang shih shao* (Poetry of Kao Ke; n.p. 1924). This last title is a Festschrift volume in honor of Ch'en's fiftieth birthday. In addition to Ch'en's poetry, there are many congratulatory pieces from Southeastern University faculty, including prominent members of the *CR.*

50. Important *CR* formulations on these topics can be seen in Wu Fang-chi, "San lun yu-jen yen chung chih hsin-chiu wen-hsueh kuan" (Third discussion regarding the viewpoints on old and new literature), *Hsueh heng* (Critical review; hereafter *CR*), no. 31 (1924); Liu P'u, "Pi wen-hsueh fen kuei-tsu p'ing-min chih-wei" (Criticism of the division of literature into aristocratic and popular), ibid., no. 32 (August 1924); Ts'ao Mu-kuan, "Lun wen-hsueh wu hsin-chiu chih i" (Literature does not have old and new), ibid.

51. Liu Ya-tzu, preface to Ch'en Ch'u-p'ing, *Sung-ling wen-chi,* reprinted in *NSTH* II, 658.

52. For examples: *CTSH,* pp. 445-446, 457; *NSTH,* I, 577.

53. *NSTH,* I, 506.

54. Rankin, *Early Chinese Revolutionaries,* pp. 15, 173.

55. Ibid., pp. 15, 124.

56. Ibid., p. 124.

57. See Frederic Wakeman, Jr., "The Price of Autonomy: Intellectuals in Ming and Ch'ing Politics," *Daedalus* (Spring 1972), p. 63.

58. Ibid., p. 41.

59. Ibid., p. 37.

60. Ibid., p. 63.

63. Rankin, *Early Chinese Revolutionaries,* p. 15.

62. Wakeman, p. 47.

63. See Shirleen Sao-wan Wong, "Kung Tzu-chen: The Poet," Ph.D. dissertation, University of Washington, 1970. And also see David Nivison, "Protest Against Conventions and Conventions of Protest," in A. F. Wright, ed., *Confucianism and Chinese Civilization* (New York: Atheneum, 1964), pp. 248-249.

64. See Liu Ya-tzu's "Epigraph to Ma Chien-wu's Poetry," in *Nan-she,* 2d collection, 1908, cited in *CTSH,* p. 444. Also see Wu, "Shih hsueh tsung shih Huang Chieh . . . ," p. 24, for the influence of Kung Tzu-chen on Huang Chieh. The most thorough documentation of Kung's influence on the Southern Society circle is in Kurata Sadayoshi, *Chūgoku kindai shi no kenkyū* (Study of modern Chinese poetry; Tokyo, 1969).

65. *NSTH,* I, 11 (dated 1923).

66. The Japanese *shishi* may well have had some influence here too. Wakeman's essay speaks of the influence of this image on late nineteenth-century intellectual self-images in China; and Liang Ch'i-ch'ao and Ku Hung-ming's reverence for the samurai spirit is well known.

67. I have purposely borrowed from Frederick Mote's short study of the poet Kao Ch'i. It is sometimes extremely suggestive of the poets of the Southern Society. Some of Mote's well-crafted words: "Poetry in its own right could be a guarantor of immortality [for Kao Ch'i's circle]. At best, the creation of poetry could in itself assume the proportions of a heroic deed." ("A Fourteenth-Century Poet: Kao Ch'i," in Arthur Wright and Dennis Twitchett, *Confucian Personalities,*

Stanford: Stanford University Press, 1962, p. 251.)

68. For the popularity of Arnold see Bonnie S. McDougall, *The Introduction of Western Literary Theories into Modern China, 1919-1925* (Tokyo, 1971), p. 221. Reference to Arnold is constant throughout the *CR*. For an analysis of Arnold pertinent to our "culture/society" approach see Raymond Williams, *Culture and Society, 1780-1950* (New York: Doubleday, 1960), especially p. 272.

69. Wu Mi, "Lun An-ju-te chih shih" (On Arnold's Poetry), reprinted from *CR* in Wu Mi, *Wu Mi shih chi* (A collection of Wu Mi's poetry; Shanghai, 1935), pp. 65-71.

70. Wu Mi, "Shih hsueh tsung shih Huang Chieh . . . ," pp. 25a-26b.

71. Quoted ibid., p. 25a.

72. Mei Kuang-ti, "P'ing chin jen t'i-ch'ang hsueh-shu chih fang-fa" (Critique of the methods for scholarship promoted by contemporaries), original in *CR*, no. 2 (1922), reprinted in *Mei Kuang-ti wen lu* (Mei Kuang-ti anthology; Taipei, 1968), p. 9.

73. Mei Kuang-ti, "Lun chin-jih yu kuo-hsueh-shu-chieh chih hsiu-yao" (The needs of present-day national studies), *CR*, no. 4 (1922), and *Mei Kuang-ti wen-lu*, pp. 10-14.

74. Wu Mi, "Shih hsueh tsung shih Huang Chieh . . . ," p. 25b, formulates the poet-as-priest ideal, based on Arnold's arguments.

75. Liu I-cheng, "Lun ta-hsueh-sheng chih tse-wen" (The responsibility of university students), *CR*, no. 6 (1922). The phrase "reform their minds" could probably be rendered in Americanese as "have a change of heart."

76. Mei Kuang-ti, "Humanism in Modern China" (in English), reprinted in *Mei Kuang-ti wen-lu*, pp. 12-13. Original in *The Bookman*, n.p., 1931; and Mei's "P'ing t'i-ch'ang hsin wen-hua che" (A critique of those who advocate the new culture), *CR*, no. 1 (1922).

77. "P'ing chin jen t'i-ch'ang hsueh-shu chih fang-fa," p. 7; and "Is the West Awakening?" (in English), reprinted in *Mei Kuang-ti wen-lu*, pp. 1-9, from *The Nation*, April 21, 1926.

78. Mei Kuang-ti, "Lun chin-jih yu kuo-hsueh-shu-chieh chih hsiu-yao"; and also the example formulated by Hu Hsien-su, "P'ing ch'ang-shih chi" (A collection of criticisms against [recent] experiments), *CR*, no. 2 (1922).

79. Mei Kuang ti, "Lun chin-jih yu kuo-hsueh-shu-chieh chih hsiu-yao" and Mei, "P'ing-t'i-ch'ang hsin wen-hua che."

80. For example see Wu Mi, "Lun An-ju-te chih shih."

81. For examples, see Wu Mi, *Wu Mi shih chi,* last section, pp. 73-75, 108ff.

82. Ibid.

83. On Huang Tsun-hsien see Julia C. Lin, *Modern Chinese Poetry: An Introduction* (Seattle: University of Washington Press, 1972), chap. 2.

84. *Shih-hua,* pp. 41, 51.

85. *CTSH,* p. 24; *CKCTWH,* p. 340.

86. *CKCTWH,* p. 329.

87. *NSTH,* I, 185-186; and also see Liu Wu-chi, *Su Man-shu* (New York, 1972).

88. *Shih-hua,* p. 41, and also p. 87 for further examples.

89. *NSCL,* pp. 202-203.

90. Erich Heller, "Autobiography and Literature," in Thomas Mann, *Death in Venice* (New York: Modern Library Random House, 1970), p. 117.

91. Wu Mi, "Lun chin-jih wen-hsueh chuang-tsao chih cheng-fa" (The capital punishment of present-day literary creativity), in *Wu Mi shih chi,* last section, pp. 73-75.

92. For example, Cheng Chen-to, "Hsin yu chiu" (New and old), reprinted from *Wen-hsueh chou-pao* (Literary weekly), no. 136 (1924), in Cheng Chen-to, ed., *Chung-kuo hsin wen-hsueh ta-hsi* (An outline of China's new literature; Shanghai, 1935), part one, pp. 132-135.

93. Translated in McDougall, *The Introduction of Western Literary Theories,* p. 128. Kuo Mo-jo's statement dated 1919.

94. Huang K'an, editorial introduction to *Kuo ku* I:1 (1919).

95. For an example of the use of this metaphor see Liu Ya-tzu, *NSTH,* III, 1369. The poet-critic Wang Shih-chen may be the source of this image of the Yangtze as a moat. Wang (1634-1711) had spent much time as an official in the South, and in one of his poems lamented that the river no more acted as a protective boundary to the precious culture of the South: "The strategic position of the natural moat makes my sadness grow." (See Richard John Lynn, "Tradition and Synthesis: Wang Shih-chen as Poet and Critic," Ph.D. dissertation, Stanford University, 1971, pp. 175-176.)

96. McDougall sees the *CR* literary critics as the "only" counters to historicized literary history at the time. See *The Introduction of Western Literary Theories,* p. 230.

97. Karl Mannheim, *Essays on Sociology and Social Psychology* (New York: Oxford University Press, 1953), p. 140.

98. Ibid.

99. Quoted in Michael Curtis, *Three Against the Third Republic: Sorel, Barres, and Maurras* (Princeton: Princeton University Press, 1959), p. 113.

4   Liu Shih-p'ei and National Essence
Martin Bernal

1. This distinction is Weber's. See Karl Mannheim, *Essays on Sociology and Social Psychology* (New York: Oxford University Press, 1953), p. 95.

2. See "Chia-chen-nien tzu-shu-shih" (Poetic autobiography in the year 1904), printed in five installments in *Ching-chung jih-pao* (The Alarm Bell; hereafter CCJP) 9/7, 8, 10, 11, and 12 (1904). See also Ch'ien Hsuan-t'ung, "Hsu" (Introduction) to *Liu Shen-shu hsien-sheng i-shu* (Collected works of Mr. Liu Shen-shu [Shih-p'ei]; hereafter cited as LIS), ed. Nan P'ei-lan and Cheng Yü-fu, 74 sections (1934-1938) reprinted in 4 vols. (Taipei, 1965); pagination according to reprint, I, 34-38.

3. See Liang Ch'i-ch'ao, *Intellectual Trends in the Ch'ing Period,* trans. Immanuel Hsü (Cambridge, Mass.: Harvard University Press, 1959), p. 38; and T'an Ssu-t'ung, *Jen-hsueh* (Study of benevolence; Shanghai ed., 1958), p. 50.

4. Arthur Hummel, *Eminent Chinese of the Ch'ing Period* (Washington, D.C., 1943-1944; hereafter cited as ECCP); and Ozawa Bunshirō, *I-cheng Liu-*

Meng-shan nien-p'u (Chronological biography of Liu Meng-shan), in *Liu Nien-p'u* (Peking, 1939; reprinted Taipei, 1968), p. 218. There seems to have been a wider wave of antibarbarian and anti-Manchu feeling in Yangchow in the 1840s, perhaps because of the disgust at Manchu abuses among the high officials who were attempting to reform the salt administration there.

5. For details on this see my *Liu Shih-p'ei* (Ithaca, N.Y.: Cornell Monograph, 1974).

6. LIS, p. 34.

7. It is reprinted in LIS, I, 675-714. Liu though younger is named as the senior author. For a description of this see Onagawa Hidemi, "Ryū Shi-bai to Museifushugi" in *Tōhō Gakuhō* 36:695-720 (1964), published in English as "Liu Shih-p'ei and Anarchism," *Acta Asiatica* 77:70-99 (1967).

8. For a summary of Huang's views in English see Theodore de Bary, *Sources of Chinese Tradition,* text ed., 2 vols. (New York: 1964), I, 530-542.

9. LIS, I, 677.

10. LIS, I, 678. This is close to the Marxist view of memories of primitive communism inspiring democratic ideas in slave societies. See Hou Wai-lu, *Chung-kuo ssu-hsiang t'ung-shih* (General history of Chinese thought), 5 vols. (vol. IV in 2 pts.; Peking, 1957-1958), I, 261-263; and Joseph Needham, *Science and Civilisation in China* (Cambridge, Eng.: Cambridge University Press, 1954), II, 194-195.

11. LIS, I, 686. See Hsun tzu's section "Li lun" translated in *Hsun Tze: Works from the Chinese,* by H. H. Dubbs (London: 1928), pp. 213-214. The *Lü shih ch'un-ch'iu* was compiled under the patronage of the statesman Lü Pu-wei, the putative father of Ch'in Shih Huang-ti.

12. LIS, I, 680.

13. *Mencius* Book III, 1, Ch. IV, 1-6.

14. Yen Fu's translation of *The Wealth of Nations* appeared in 1900. Liu and Lin used his title, *Yuan fu.*

15. *Lun-yü,* Book XIV, 17-18.

16. *Kung-yang chuan* (Shanghai, 1930), Ssu-pu pei-yao ed., 10, 8a.

17. The Sung writer Sun Fu (*tzu* Ming-fu) wrote a book entitled *Ch'un-ch'iu tsun-wang fa-wei* (The secret message of *tsun-wang* in the *Ch'un-ch'iu*). See Liang Ch'i-ch'ao, "*Ch'un-ch'iu Chung-kuo i-ti pien* hsu" (Introduction to "Discrimination between Chinese and barbarians in the *Ch'un-ch'iu*"), *Shih-wu pao* 36:4-4b (Aug. 8, 1897). The most explicit early Ch'ing references to this were by Lü Liu-liang. See Ch'ien Mu, *Chung-kuo chin san-pai nien hsueh-shu shih* (History of Chinese learning in the last three hundred years; 2 vols. Taipei reprint, 1968) I, 83-84; and Mi Chu Wien's "Anti-Manchu Thought During the Early Ch'ing," *Harvard Papers on China* 22a:9 (1969).

18. It was ironic that a phrase so closely associated with hegemony should have been used against the Japanese hegemon or shogun, whose full title was *seii tai shogun* (commander of forces against the barbarians).

19. See T'an Ssu-t'ung's attempt to explain Confucius' approval of Kuan Chung in other terms: *T'an Liu-yang ch'üan-chi* (Collected writings of T'an Liu-Yang [Ssu-t'ung]; Taipei reprint, 1962), pp. 382-384.

20. *Jang shu* is reprinted in LIS, I, 762, and Onogawa, "Liu Shih-p'ei," p. 77.

21. There are striking resemblances between the ideas expressed in *Ch'iu shu* and *Jang shu*. See for instance the arguments on the totems of tribal peoples, *Ch'iu shu* 38 and *Jang shu*, LIS, II, 754. *Ch'iu shu* was first written between 1899 and 1902, before the appearance of *Jang shu*. However, it was substantially reworked and republished in 1904 (the edition reprinted in Taipei) after the publication of Liu's book, which Chang would have been able to read in prison. It is probable that Liu was influenced by the earlier edition and that given the relative similarity of educational background and political passion, the two men were more or less independently attracted to the same Western and Japanese theories on China.

22. LIS, II, 755. Spencer never to my knowledge said this explicitly, but it is implicit throughout his work.

23. Liu alleged that the Po in Szechwan had fur and the Fan had tails. LIS, II, 755.

24. Benjamin Kidd's *Social Evolution,* which stressed these aspects of progress, was translated into Chinese under the title *Ta-t'ung hsueh* (Study of *ta-t'ung*) in 1899.

25. LIS, II, 755.

26. Mi Chu Wiens, 8.

27. LIS, II, 760.

28. See Wang's *Ssu-wen lu* "Wai pien" (Peking ed., 1956), pp. 72-73.

29. LIS, II, 761-762.

30. Spencer had a major influence on all "progressive" Chinese intellectuals of the period. The section of *Ch'iu shu* entitled "Hsu chung hsing" (Introducing races and clans) was largely based on Terrien de Lacouperie.

31. "Memorial Notice of Prof. Terrien de Lacouperie," *Babylonian and Oriental Record* (hereafter BOR) 7:262-264 (1894).

32. BOR 3:64 (1889).

33. BOR 3:64-65 (1889) and 5:26 (1891). He talked of "about a dozen Bak tribes." *The Languages of China Before the Chinese* (London, 1887), p. 9.

34. BOR 5:257-264 (1891). He maintained that *pai, pak* in archaic Chinese came from "Bak."

35. LIS, II, 721. Ario Tainokuni, *Shina bummei shi* (History of Chinese culture). It is almost certain that there were other Japanese transmissions of Terrien de Lacouperie's theories. From September 1903 to January 1905 Chiang Kuang-yun (*ming* Chih-yu) published a large section of Terrien de Lacouperie's *Western Origin of Chinese Civilisation* in the *Hsin-min ts'ung-pao* (The renovation of the people).

36. See Liu's "Chung-kuo min-tsu-chih" (History of the Chinese nation), written in 1905, in which he disagreed with Lacouperie that Chinese and European culture had a common place of origin in central Asia. LIS, II, 721. Chang Ping-lin rejected the notion that Huang-ti was an immigrant. See "P'ai Man p'ing-i" (Critical essay on driving out the Manchus), *Min-pao* 21:4-6 (June 10, 1907).

Despite these retractions, interest in Lacouperie's ideas has not died out. In the 1940s Ku Chieh-kang was still writing about the Chou conquest of Shang and Duke Mu of Chao in terms very reminiscent of Terrien de Lacouperie. See Lawrence Schneider, *Ku Chieh-kang and China's New History* (Berkeley: University of

California Press, 1971), p. 296. In 1970 the Ch'eng Wen publishing company in Taipei considered it worthwhile to reissue *The Languages of China Before the Chinese.*

37. LIS, II, 755. This scheme completely contradicts that set out in *The Theme of Social Contract in China,* in which classes were supposed to have arisen from a homogeneous society.

38. For a discussion of this see Joseph Levenson, *Confucian China and Its Modern Fate: The Problem of Intellectual Continuity* (London: Routledge and Kegan Paul, 1958), pp. 76-78. He points out that reactionaries also used the argument that there were ancient Chinese precedents for every aspect of European civilization. See also C. de Harlez, "The Antiquity of the Ancient Chinese Sacred Books," BOR 5:45-48.

39. See for instance Coke's "invention" of Magna Carta and the seventeenth-century myth of the "Norman yoke" and the desire to return to Saxon England.

40. Because of their doubts on early texts the reformers were unable to speculate about China's past or about the possible origin of equivalences between East and West.

41. Chang, *Ch'iu shu,* p. 42.

42. Fung Yu-lan, *A History of Chinese Philosophy,* 2 vols., trans. Derk Bodde (Princeton: Princeton University Press, 1952), I, 160 and 167-168; and Needham, II, 232-236.

43. For a list of Chinese references to him see Terrien de Lacouperie, BOR 4:258-259 (1890). See also Fung Yu-lan, I, 160; Needham, II, 238; and Hou Wai-lu, I, 649-651.

44. In Chinese cosmology yellow is the color of earth, the center and hence of the "central states," or China.

45. *Kuo-min jih-jih pao hui pien* (Collection from the China national gazette; reprinted, Taipei, 1968; 2 vols.), pagination of reprint, I, 276.

46. "Lun chi-lieh ti hao-ch'u" (On the advantages of extremism), reprinted in Chang Nan and Wang Jen-chih, *Hsin-hai ko-ming ch'ien shih-nien shih-lun hsuan-chi* (Selection of contemporary articles from the decade before the 1911 revolution; Peking, 1962; 2 vols., two sections each), I, 1:888-889.

47. See James Y. Liu, *The Chinese Knight Errant* (London: Routledge and Kegan Paul, 1967).

48. "Lun chi-lieh ti hao-ch'u," p. 890. In the autumn of 1904, Liu actively promoted the unsuccessful assassination attempt on the corrupt Ch'ing official Wang Chih-ch'un.

49. Yang T'ien-shih," Lun hsin-hai ko-ming ch'ien ti Chung-kuo kuo-ts'ui chu-i ssu-ch'ao" (On the current of Chinese national essence before 1911; Hsin Chien-she, 1965), II, 75.

50. Quoted in Mannheim, *Essays on Sociology and Social Psychology,* pp. 148-149.

51. Quoted in Nobutaka Ike, *The Beginnings of Political Democracy in Japan* (Baltimore: Johns Hopkins University Press, 1950), p. 183.

52. "*Nihonjin* ga kaihō suru tokoro no shigi o koku hakasu" (Explanation of the principles held by *The Japanese*), in *Shiga Shigetaka Zenshū* (Complete

works of Shiga Shigetaka; Tokyo, 1927-1929; 8 vols.), I, 1.

53. Kenneth B. Pyle, *The New Generation in Meiji Japan: Problems of Cultural Identity 1885-1895* (Stanford: Stanford University Press, 1969), pp. 60-61, 68-69.

54. Pyle, p. 69.

55. Barbara Teters, "The Genro In and the National Essence Movement," *Pacific Historical Review* 31.4:359-371 (1962), and George M. Wilson, *Radical Nationalist in Japan, Kita Ikki 1883-1937* (Cambridge, Mass.: Harvard University Press, 1969), p. 13.

56. Quoted in *Hsin-min ts'ung-pao* 20:49-50 (Oct. 1, 1902), Yang T'ien-shih, p. 68, and Ting Wen-chiang, *Liang Jen-kung hsien-sheng nien-p'u ch'u-kao* (First draft of a chronological biography of Mr. Liang Jen-kung [Ch'i-ch'ao]; Taipei, 1962; 2 vols.), I, 161.

57. *Hsin-min ts'ung pao* 20:50; Ting Wen-chiang, I, 164.

58. See the references to it in an advertisement of *Jang-shu*, CCJP (April 14, 1904). It is interesting that the term does not appear in the pamphlet itself nor in *Ch'iu shu* or Tsou Jung's *Ko-ming chün*. This suggests that some new source of information on the Japanese movement became available early in 1904.

59. Yang T'ien-shih, p. 69, and *Kuo-ts'ui hsueh-pao* (hereafter KTHP) 1:19 (Feb. 23, 1905).

60. KTHP 1:14 and 37.

61. Huang Chieh, in KTHP 1:16.

62. Hsu Shou-wei, "Lun kuo-ts'ui wu tsu yü Ou-hua" (On national essence not being a block to Europeanization), KTHP 7:772-773 (Aug. 20, 1905). The idea of a "Chinese Renaissance" was later taken up by Hu Shih and others.

63. KTHP and LIS. It was Liu's studies of this period that laid the basis of much of the work of his pupil Fung Yu-lan.

64. Advertisement for *Jang shu*, CCJP April 14, 1904.

65. Chang Chih-tung, *Chang Wen-hsiang kung ch'üan-chi* (Complete works of Mr. Chang Wen-hsiang [Chih-tung]), ed. Wang Shu-nan (Peking, 1928), 68:27.

66. Chang Chih-tung, 190:3.

67. Chang Chih-tung, 190:3-4.

68. Chang Chih-tung, 68:26-32b.

69. Chang Chih-tung, 199:10-10b.

70. William Ayers, *Chang Chih-tung and Educational Reform in China* (Cambridge, Mass.: Harvard University Press, 1971), p. 248.

71. Chang Chih-tung, 68:26-26b; and Ayers, p. 240.

72. Ayers, p. 251.

73. See for instance ECCP, I, 31.

74. Chang Chih-tung, 68:29b.

75. Chang Chih-tung, 97:7b.

76. Ting Wen-chiang, ed., *Liang Jen-kung hsien-sheng nien-p'u chang-pien ch'u-kao* (Taipei, 1962; 2 vols), I, 222.

77. Yang T'ien-shih, p. 68. Hao Chang considers 1907 to be the turning point in Liang's development.

78. Yang T'ien-shih, p. 68. Benjamin Schwartz in his *In Search of Wealth and Power: Yen Fu and the West* (Cambridge, Mass.: Harvard University Press,

1964), says that the break between Yen's westernizing and conservative phases came in 1908, but states that this is an approximation; pp. 212-213.

79. Ku Chieh-kang, *The Autobiography of a Chinese Historian,* trans. A. W. Hummel (Leyden: Brill Ltd., 1931), p. 20.

5   The Sage as Rebel: The Inner World of Chang Ping-lin
Charlotte Furth

1. *Ch'iu shu* (Bood of raillery; Shanghai, 1904), reprinted in Lo Chia-lun, ed., *Chung-hua min-kuo kuo shih ts'ung liao* (Collection on the history of the Chinese republic; Taipei, 1967). For the circumstances of its composition see *Chang T'ai-yen tzu-ting nien-p'u* (Chronological autobiography of Chang T'ai-yen; Hong Kong, 1965), p. 9. The book was further revised by Chang during the heat of the *Su pao* case in 1903 and printed by friends in 1904. An obscure pun, the title is typical of the book's style, cloaking polemic in erudite irony.

2. In addition to Chang's own chronological autobiography, there are two short books on his life: Hsu Shou-sheng, *Chang Ping-lin* (Chengtu, 1945); and Shen Yen-kuo, *Chi Chang T'ai-yen hsien-sheng* (Memoir of Chang T'ai-yen; Shanghai, 1946). For surveys of his thought, see Hou Wai-lu, *Chin-tai Chung-kuo ssu-hsiang hsueh shuo shih* (Interpretive history of recent Chinese thought; Shanghai, 1947), pp. 784-859; and Hsiao Kung-ch'üan, *Chung-kuo cheng-chih ssu-hsiang shih* (History of Chinese political thought; Taipei, 1964, 5th ed., 1968), 6:843-879. As Hou emphasizes the rationalist and reformer, while Hsiao sees the racialist and individualist, the two studies complement each other; alone, each should be used with caution.

3. Material on K'ang Yu-wei is drawn from Hsiao Kung-ch'üan, *History,* 5:681-711; Hou Wai-lu, *Interpretive History,* pp. 594-772; and K'ang Yu-wei, *Ta-t'ung shu* (Book of the great commonwealth; Shanghai, 1935).

4. *Ch'iu shu,* "Ch'ing ju" (Ch'ing Confucian scholars), pp. 20-25. This view was widely shared. See for example Liang Ch'i-ch'ao, *Intellectual Trends in the Ch'ing Period,* trans. Immanuel C. Y. Hsü (Cambridge, Mass.: Harvard University Press, 1959), pp. 51-75.

5. For an account that covers modern movements, see Chou Yü-t'ung, *Ching ku chin wen hsueh* (Old and new texts of the classics; Shanghai, 1926).

6. *Liu Tzu-cheng Tso shih shuo* (On Liu Hsin and Master Tso). This and a companion piece, *Ch'un-ch'iu Tso shih ch'uan hsu-lu* (Notes on Master Tso's *Spring and Autumn Annals*) were published serially in *Kuo-ts'ui hsueh-pao* (National Essence Journal), nos. 26-33 and 40-44 in 1907 and 1908. For the date of writing, see Chang's *Nien p'u,* p. 5.

7. *Nien p'u,* p. 5.

8. Kuo Chan-po, *Chin wu-shih nien Chung-kuo ssu-hsiang shih* (History of Chinese thought in the past fifty years; 2d ed., Peiping, 1935-1936), pp. 63-69.

9. Chang's views on history are summed up most succinctly in "Cheng hsin lun" (On verification) and "Hsin shih" (Truth in history), *Chang T'ai-yen wen-lu ch'u pien* (Writings of Chang T'ai-yen: first series; Chekiang, 1919; photolithographed reprint, Taipei, 1970) 1:45-51 and 51-61. See also *Ch'iu shu,* "Ch'ing ju," pp. 23-26.

10. *Ch'iu shu,* no. 59, "Ai Ch'ing shih" (Lament for Ch'ing history), pp.

193-202, discusses this plan. A proposed table of contents for the history is on p. 202.

11. *Ch'iu shu,* p. 26.

12. *Wen lu,* 1:51. *P'ing-i,* a New Text term, connotes determining the truth on the basis of a correct reading of a text.

13. Hou Wai-lu, *Interpretive History,* p. 823.

14. *Ch'iu shu,* pp. 25-26.

15. David Nivison, *The Life and Thought of Chang Hsueh-ch'eng* (Stanford: Stanford University Press, 1966). See esp. pp. 60-61.

16. *Ch'iu shu,* pp. 2-4. Nivison notes that this was a step that Chang Hsueh-ch'eng never took though it was claimed for him by enthusiastic moderns like Hu Shih. Rather, for Chang the classics "lose none of their holiness, and other 'actual things' begin to share it," p. 296.

17. In the *Ch'iu shu,* see particularly nos. 58 and 59, "Ai fen shu" (Lament for the bookburning), and "Ai Ch'ing shih" (Lament for Ch'ing history).

18. See for example Ch'ien Mu, *Chung-kuo li-tai cheng-chih te-shih* (Historical strengths and weaknesses of Chinese politics; Hong Kong, 1959), pp. 116-146.

19. A good example is in *Min pao* 6, "Yen-shuo lu" (Account of an address), a reprint of a speech Chang gave upon accepting the editorship of the journal in July 1906. See pp. 10-11.

20. *Min pao* 21:22.

21. Quoted in Hou Wai-lu, *Interpretive History,* p. 787.

22. See *Min pao* 6, "Yen-shuo lu."

23. Chang Ping-lin, *Kuo ku lun heng* (Critical essays on antiquity; Taipei, photolithographed reprint, 1971), "Yü-yen yuan-chi shuo" (On the origins of language), pp. 39-45.

24. This account of Chang's view of the relationship of historical and modern linguistic forms is taken from "Po Chung-kuo yung wan-kuo hsin-yü shuo" (Against the Chinese adoption of Esperanto), *Min pao* 21:1-24. This essay was written as a reply to the language reform proposals of Wu Chih-hui's Paris group, and was also reprinted in *Kuo-ts'ui hsueh-pao.* Chang's criticism of Esperanto was needless to say withering.

25. "Against Esperanto," p. 7.

26. In addition to *Kuo ku lun heng,* which provides a general introduction to Chang's theories on language, see "Hsin fang-yen" (Modern dialects), *Kuo-ts'ui hsueh-pao,* nos. 34 to 43; and *Wen shih* (The origins of language; 1914, Taipei, photolithographic reprint, 1970).

27. Material on Wang Fu-chih is drawn largely from Hsiao Kung-chüan, *History,* pp. 629-654; and from a superficial reading of Wang's *Huang shu* (Yellow book; reprint, Peking 1965). See also Chang Hsi-t'ang, *Wang Chuan-shan p'u* (Treatise on Wang Fu-chih; Shanghai, 1936).

28. See Benjamin Schwartz, *In Search of Wealth and Power: Yen Fu and the West* (Cambridge, Mass.: Harvard University Press, 1964).

29. Herbert Spencer, "Progress, Its Law and Cause," *Westminster Review* (April 1857). Reprinted in *Spencer's Essays: Scientific, Political and Speculative,* I (New York, 1904), 8-62. The translation, "Ssu-pin-so-erh wen chi," appeared

serially in *Chang yen pao* (Plain speech), nos. 1, 2, 3, 4, and 5. It was a collaboration between Chang and Tseng Kuang-ch'üan, the diplomat and grand-nephew of Tseng Kuo-fan, who had served as an attaché at the London legation when his adopted father, "Marquis" Tseng Chi-tse, was minister. The Chinese essay is more of an interpretation than a true translation, omitting most of Spencer's technical language and interpolating freely.

30. "Progress, Its Law and Cause," was in fact written before Darwin had published his theory of natural selection, and of course long before the surfacing of Mendelian genetics. Darwin himself came to recognize the important role which environment does play in evolution in the form of selection pressures.

31. I must thank my friend Linda Shin for making available to me her unpublished seminar paper, "Min-tsu: An Introduction," upon which the above is based. The German "nation" is best translated into English as "people."

32. See for example *Ch'iu shu*, p. 40: "Those who emphasize 'nation' (*kuo min*) glorify government; those who stress 'people' (*tsu min*) glorify family and race." Later in the *Min pao* Chang said that the concept nation (*kuo chia*) is a mechanical abstraction based upon political boundaries and forms of organization; while only *min-tsu*, based on land and people, can give the abstraction any concrete reality. See "Wu wu lun" (The five negatives), *Min pao* 16:10.

33. *Ch'iu shu*, nos. 16-20, "Yuan jen" (Human origins); "Hsu chung hsing" (Succession of races and names); "Yuan pien" (Origins of change); and "Tsu chih" (Clan governance). See pp. 32-67.

34. Ibid., p. 37.

35. Ibid., p. 39. T'ai Po is an alternate name for Fu Hsi. Ch'un-wei is a name given the presumed Hsia dynasty ancestors of the *Hsiung-nu* barbarians. The descendants of Hsi Ho and of Yü were presumed to have been barbarian peoples.

36. *Ch'iu shu*, pp. 40-41. See also Albert Etienne Jean Baptiste Terrien de Lacouperie, *Western Origins of the Early Chinese Civilization from 2300 B.C. to 200 A.D.* (1st ed., 1894; reprint, Osnabruck, 1966), esp. pp. 23ff. For the dissemination of Terrien de Lacouperie's theories in China see Martin Bernal's essay in this volume. Chang later abandoned the idea of such Western origins for early Chinese civilization as farfetched. See *Min pao* 21:2-8.

37. *Ch'iu shu*, pp. 39 and 61-62.

38. A source Chang relied on heavily in constructing his genealogies was the *Shih pen* (Generations from earliest times), a work purporting to chronicle events from the Yellow Emperor's time to the Ch'in. It was quoted by Ssu-ma Ch'ien, but has been lost except for fragments since the Sung. Chang accepted the tradition that the *Shih pen* was compiled by the author of the *Tso chuan*. This idea, as well as the authenticity of surviving portions, is disputed. See *Ch'iu shu*, no. 56, "Tsun shih" (In honor of the historian). Chang's theory of early surnames is disputed by Creel, who gives quite different hypotheses for the earliest meanings of *shih* and *hsing*. See Herrlee G. Creel, *The Origins of Statecraft in China* (Chicago: University of Chicago Press, 1970), I, 333-334.

39. *Ch'iu shu*, p. 39.

40. Ibid., p. 58.

41. Ibid., pp. 39-40.

42. Ibid., pp. 58-59. On eugenics, see pp. 61-65.

43. Ibid., p. 34. *Shou, min,* and *jen* are all psychological classifications. The difference between *min* and *jen* seems to be only that the former term refers to organic self-conscious social groups, while *jen* is individuating.

44. Chang speculated that certain groups of modern primates might in fact be descendants of tribes of primitive people, by a process of reverse evolution. See pp. 60-61.

45. Ibid., p. 34.

46. Ibid., p. 60. The name "Ma-liu" derives from the name of the Han dynasty military commander, Ma Yuan, who led the colony.

47. Ibid., p. 60.

48. Ibid., p. 64.

49. *Chang yen pao* 5:1. Spencer's original reads, "The universe at large like every organism was once homogeneous; as a whole and in every detail it has increasingly advanced toward greater heterogeneity . . . Progress is not an accident, not a thing within human control, but a beneficent necessity." See "Progress, Its Law and Cause," p. 60.

50. "Chü-fen chin-hua lun" (On progress as differentiation), *Min pao* 7:1-13. Here as elsewhere in *Min pao,* Chang based his analysis upon the theories of "consciousness only" (*wei-shih*) Buddhism.

51. See specially *Min pao* 16:4-7; 20:1-3; 22:11-14.

52. The debate between advocates of *feng-chien* and *chün-hsien* was almost as old as the Han dynasty itself, and even by the late Ming had acquired a complexity which defies the simple polarization suggested above. In the reform generation the question was more than ever one of the proper mix of autonomy *and* central control, and the appropriate density of the administrative infrastructure — all in a context of general rejection of hereditary officeholding as an appropriate form of localism. The differences between Chang and K'ang were ones of emphasis along this spectrum.

53. Quoted in Hou Wai-lu, *Interpretive History,* p. 786.

54. See Hsiao Kung-ch'üan, *History,* p. 634, quoting Wang's *Tu T'ung ch'ien lun* (On reading "The comprehensive mirror").

55. Ibid., pp. 595-606. For Huang see also William Theodore de Bary, "Chinese Despotism and the Confucian Ideal: A Seventeenth Century View," in *Chinese Thought and Institutions* (Chicago, 1957), pp. 163-203.

56. "Fei Huang" (Against Huang), *T'ai-yen wen-lu* 1:123-129.

57. Ibid., pp. 125-126.

58. For Chang's views on criminal justice see "Hsing kuan" (Criminal justices), *Ch'iu shu,* no. 37; and "Ting lü" (Firming the laws), ibid., no. 38. For his views on Legalism in general see no. 5, "Ju fa" (Confucianist and Legalist); and no. 35, "Shang Yang."

59. See "Ming ch'ieh" (The profound separation), ibid., no. 30.

60. *Ch'iu shu,* no. 35, "Shang Yang," p. 130.

61. Ibid., pp. 130-133. The Han statutes which established the tradition of imperial law, associated with legal statesmen like Hsieh Ho under Han Kao-tsu and Chang T'ang under Han Wu-ti, Chang dismissed as corruptions of Legalism. Laws made by "spying out the ruler's mind and making distinctions of high and low based on this" served the imperial person, and no more.

62. "Chieh hsin tang lun" (Admonitions to new parties), *Min pao* 10.

63. Chang's word was *chuan chih.* He did not like the term "enlightened despotism," which he regarded as connoting a Western style of personal rule and as a code term for constitutionalist ideas.

64. Han Fei-tzu, *Basic Writings,* trans. Burton Watson (New York: Columbia University Press, 1964). See especially section 9, "Wielding Power," pp. 35-42.

65. "Ko-ming chih tao-te" (Revolutionary morality), *Min pao* 8. See esp. pp. 3-5.

66. "Ssu huo lun" (The four doubts), *Min pao* 22:1-22, especially the discussion of *kung li.* There is a good analysis of Chang and the term *kung li* in Fung Yu-lan, "Chang T'ai-yen Min pao shih-ch'i ti che-hsueh ssu-hsiang" (Chang T'ai-yen's philosophical thought at the time of the *People's Journal*), *Wen hui pao* (The literary fount), July 14, 1961.

67. The late Ch'ing revival of Buddhism is often said to have been pioneered by New Text intellectuals, but Chang, especially after his prison experience, also became a serious student of the subject. For Chang's exposition of the *wei-shih* doctrine, see "Progress as differentiation" and also "Chien-li tsung-chiao lun" (On established religion), *Min pao* 9.

68. "The four doubts," pp. 9-10. The expression quoted from Chuang-tzu is *"wu wu pu jan; wu wu pu k'o."* Hegel aside, there are theoretical conflicts between Chuang-tzu's philosophy and *wei-shih* Buddhism: for example, Chuang-tzu described reality as an undifferentiated continuum of phenomena, while *wei-shih* taught that phenomena are not ontologically real. In *Min pao,* Chang's interpretation varied, but in 1912 he published a short philosophical work, *Ch'i wu lun shih* (Elucidation of "On seeing things as equal"), which attempted a synthesis of the two systems.

69. "Wu wu lun" (On the five negatives), *Min pao* 16. See also "P'ai Man p'ing lun" (Critical essay on driving out the Manchus), *Min pao* 21. The feud between Wu and Chang dated back to the *Su pao* case when Wu, who also had been placed under arrest, left Shanghai and did not stand trial.

70. "On the five negatives."

71. Chang, *Kuo ku lun heng,* pp. 159-163.

72. Chang Chih-tung, "Ch'üan hsuch p'icn" (Exhortation to learn). See chaps. 5 and 8.

6   **The Suicide of Liang Chi: An Ambiguous Case of Moral Conservatism**
Lin Yü-sheng

1. Liang Chi, *Kuei-lin Liang hsien-sheng (Chi) i-shu* (The posthumous works of Mr. Liang [Chi] of Kuei-lin; hereafter referred to as *I-shu*), ed. Liang Huan-nai and Liang Huan-ting [Liang Sou-ming] (Taipei: Wen-hai ch'u-pan she, reprint, n.d.), "I-pi hui-ts'un" (Collection of bequeathed letters), 1a.

2. ·Ch'en Tu-hsiu, "Tui-yü Liang Chü-ch'uan hsien-sheng tzu-sha chih kan-hsiang" (Reflections on the suicide of Mr. Liang Chü-ch'uan [Chi]), *Hsin ch'ing-nien* (New youth; hereafter referred to as *HCN*) 6.1:19, Kyūko Shoin reprint

(hereafter referred to as KS reprint) 25 (Jan. 15, 1919).

3. T'ao Lü-kung (T'ao Meng-ho), "Lun tzu-sha" (On suicide), *HCN* 6.1:12-18, KS reprint 17-23 (Jan. 15, 1919).

4. Hsü Chih-mo, "Tu Kuei-lin Liang Chü-ch'uan hsien-sheng i-shu" (On reading the posthumous works of Mr. Liang Chü-ch'uan of Kuei-lin), in Chiang Fu-ts'ung and Liang Shih-ch'iu, eds., *Hsü Chih-mo ch'üan-chi* (The complete works of Hsü Chih-mo; Taipei: Chuan-chi wen hsueh ch'u-pan-she, 1969), III, 146.

5. Liang Sou-ming, "Letter to Ch'en Tu-hsiu," *HCN* 6.4:427-431, KS reprint 477-481 (April 15, 1919).

6. The following summary of Liang Chi's life is based on the chronological biography of Liang Chi written by Liang Huan-nai and Liang Sou-ming in *I-shu*, "Nien-p'u," la-29a; Liang Sou-ming, *Wo-ti tzu-hsueh hsiao-shih* (A short account of my self-education; Shanghai: Hua-hua shu-tien, 1947); and Liang Sou-ming, *Tzu-shu* (Autobiographical account; Tsou-p'ing, Shantung: Shantung hsiang-ts'un chien-she yen-chiu yüan, 1935).

7. "Nien-p'u," 9a.

8. Ibid., 16b.

9. Liang Sou-ming, *Wo-ti tzu-hsueh hsiao-shih*, p. 10.

10. "Nien-p'u," 16b-17a.

11. As I have said in my "Radical Iconoclasm in the May Fourth Period and the Future of Chinese Liberalism," in Benjamin I. Schwartz, ed., *Reflections on the May Fourth Movement* (Cambridge, Mass.: Harvard University Press, 1972), pp. 23-58, the stress on the intellectual-moral function of the mind was a continuing mode of thinking assumed by both traditional Confucian literati and members of the emerging intelligentsia. For a more detailed analysis, see my forthcoming *The Crisis of Chinese Consciousness: Radical Antitraditionalism in the May Fourth Era* (Madison: University of Wisconsin Press, 1976), chaps. II and III.

12. "Nien-p'u," 24a.

13. Liang Chi, *I-shu*, "I-pi hui-ts'un," 13a; "Fu-luan lu," 26b.

14. Liang Chi, *I-shu*, "I-pi hui-ts'un," 10b-11a.

15. Ibid., 14b-15a.

16. "Nien-p'u," 23a.

17. Liang Chi, *I-shu*, "Fu-luan lu," 1b. Liang Sou-ming also said on a number of occasions that his father was scornful of bookish learning and literary composition, regarding traditional Chinese scholars and men of letters as "useless creatures." Liang Sou-ming, *Tzu-shu*, p. 7, and *Wo-ti tzu-hsueh hsiao-shih*, p. 29.

18. See Liang Chi, *I-shu*, "Shih-chi jih-chi" (Dairy of attending [my mother's] illness), 2a-4a. Also, although his father died when Liang was only seven years old, he was influenced by his father in many ways. He recalled that he was deeply moved by his father's moral concerns and rectitude as revealed in the latter's correspondence, which Liang read after he had grown up. *I-shu*, "Hsin-jen lei kao" (Various drafts of 1911-1912), 17a.

19. Wm. Theodore de Bary has elucidated this theme with clarity in his "Individualism and Humanitarianism in Late Ming Thought," Wm. Theodore de Bary and others, *Self and Society in Ming Thought* (New York: Columbia University Press, 1970), pp. 145-247, especially p. 169.

20. *Mencius,* IVB.6.

21. Liang Chi, *I-shu,* "Hsin-jen lei kao," 16a. The Ministry of Police was changed shortly afterwards to be the Ministry of Civil Affairs.

22. Liang Chi, *I-shu,* "Hsin-jen lei kao," 17a-b.

23. Such as asking Sun Yü-wen, a friend of his father, to recommend him to a teaching position in an academy during his first visit to Sun — Sun could not do it, however, because Sun was already out of office — and requesting Sun Chia-nai, another friend of his father, to write a couplet to honor his mother's birthday. Liang Chi, *I-shu,* "Hsin-jen lei-kao," 18a-b.

24. Liang made this statement earlier in *I-shu,* "Hsin-jen lei-kao," 17a.

25. Ibid., 19a.

26. Liang Chi, *I-shu,* "Kan-ch'ü shan-fang jih-chi chieh-ch'ao" (Selections from the diary from the study of appreciating [my mother's] toil), 2a.

27. Liang Chi, *I-shu,* "Shih-chi jih-chi," 2a-3a.

28. Ibid., 24a. Liang Chi, for fear of failing the metropolitan examination, actually made an initial arrangement a few days before the official announcement of the list of successful candidates for a loan to purchase a title in order to please his formal mother and natural mother. But he later decided to decline the loan even though he failed the examination. Ibid., 23a.

29. Liang Chi, *I-shu,* "Pieh-chu tz'u-hua chi" (On saying farewell to bamboos and flowers), 8b.

30. Ibid., 6b.

31. For a discussion of the Confucian concept of moral autonomy from the point of view of its historical background as well as its philosophic coherence (and ambiguity), see my "Evolution of the Pre-Confucian Meaning of *'Jen'* and the Confucian Concept of Moral Autonomy," to be published in *Monumenta Serica* 31 (1975).

32. Benjamin Schwartz, "Some Polarities in Confucian Thought," in D. S. Nivison and A. F. Wright, eds., *Confucianism in Action* (Stanford: Stanford University Press, 1959), pp. 50-58.

33. Liang Chi, *I-shu,* "I-pi hui-ts'un," 8b, 38b; "Hsin-jen lei kao," 23a.; "Fu-luan lu," 5b.

34. Liang Chi, *I-shu,* "I-pi hui-ts'un," 51b.

35. Ibid., 11a; "Fu-luan lu," 16a-b, 24a-26a.

36. Liang Chi, *I-shu,* "I-pi hui-ts'un," 10b.

37. Ibid., 10b-11a, 13a-14b, 57b-59a; "Pieh-chu tz'u-hua chi," 1a-11b.

38. Liang Chi, *I-shu,* "I-pi hui-ts'un," 62a.

39. Liang Ch'i-ch'ao, "Kuo-hsing p'ien" (On [Chinese] national character), *Yung-yen* ("The Justice") 1.1:1-6 (Dec. 1, 1912).

40. Wu Ting-ch'ang, "Wei-lai chih Chung-kuo" (The future of China), *Yung-yen* 1.19:1-5 (Sept. 1, 1913).

41. Liang Chi, *I-shu,* "I-pi hui-ts'un," 59b.

42. Ibid., 60b.

43. Liang Chi formally used *cheng-t'ung ssu-hsiang* to refer to what he wanted to preserve after he read Kuang Sheng, "Chung-kuo kuo-min-hsing chi ch'i jo-tien" (The Chinese national character and its weakness), *HCN* 2.6:4, KS reprint 574 (Feb. 1, 1917). See Liang Chi, *I-shu,* "Fu-luan lu," 26b. *Cheng-t'ung ssu-*

hsiang in the context of Liang Chi's thought should not be translated as "orthodox thought." Liang was not consciously interested in partisan advocacy of any particular Confucian school, although his life-style was more in line with the Lu-Wang school than the Ch'eng-Chu school. What he meant by *cheng-t'ung ssu-hsiang* was the essential elements of the Confucian tradition.

44. To be sure, tensions existed within the complex Confucian moral system, and many of these tensions remained unresolved. For instance, the relative importance of loyalty to the universal king and filial piety to parents had been problematic. It can be justifiably said, however, that Confucian moral values at least on the concrete level were derived from particularistic concerns of family ethics, with filial piety as the most important virtue.

45. See my article and book cited in note 11.

46. I should like to acknowledge the summer grant in 1972 from the Research Committee of the University of Wisconsin, Madison, which facilitated the research for this paper.

7   The Hung-hsien Emperor as a Modernizing Conservative
Ernest P. Young

Abbreviations Used in the Notes

CFKP: *Cheng-fu kung-pao* (Government gazette; Peking, 1912-1926).
FO: Great Britain, Foreign Office, Archives, Public Record Office, London.
Goodnow Collection: Frank J. Goodnow, private papers, Goodnow Collection (14,600 items), Lanier Room, Johns Hopkins University, Baltimore, Maryland.
MP: George Ernest Morrison Papers, uncatalogued manuscript, Mitchell Library, Sydney, Australia.

1. Karl Mannheim, "Conservative Thought," in *Essays on Sociology and Psychology* (New York: Oxford University Press, 1953), pp. 94-95, 99.

2. Joseph R. Levenson, *Confucian China and Its Modern Fate* (Berkeley and Los Angeles: University of California Press, 1964), II, 137.

3. This essay is largely drawn from the author's book, forthcoming from the University of Michigan Press, *The Presidency of Yuan Shih-k'ai: Liberalism and Dictatorship in Early Republican China.*

4. Huang Yen-p'ei put Yuan's wives at fifteen or sixteen: introduction to Pai Chiao, *Yuan Shih-k'ai yü Chung-hua min-kuo* (Yuan Shih-k'ai and the Republic of China; Shanghai, 1936, Taipei reprint, 1962), p. 4. G. E. Morrison believed they had become twenty-four in the fall of 1914: Cyril Pearl, *Morrison of Peking* (Sydney: Angus and Robertson, 1967), p. 305. For Yuan's pronouncement on the evil consequences of sexual equality: *CFKP* 807 (August 4, 1914), reprinted edition, 28.1:55-56.

5. *CFKP* 860 (Sept. 25, 1914), reprinted edition, 29.1:291-292. An earlier presidential order said: "Naturally it would be inappropriate to establish a national religion, since this would do violence to the sentiments of the masses." *CFKP* 631:8 (Feb. 8, 1914). The sentiments referred to were the divergent beliefs of

the five nationalities. See also *CFKP* 563:1 (Nov. 27, 1913) and *CFKP* 631:7 (Feb. 8, 1914).

Chow Tse-tung's statement that Yuan "became an enthusiastic patron of the Confucian movement" seems to me misleading, since Yuan rejected the main demand of the Confucian Society. Chow Tse-tung, "Anti-Confucianism in Early Republican China," in Arthur F. Wright, ed., *The Confucian Persuasion* (Stanford: Stanford University Press, 1960), p. 291.

6. *Republican Advocate* (Shanghai) 1.29:1152 (Oct. 19, 1912). Cheshire, Consul-general in Canton, to Calhoun, Secretary of State (Oct. 31, 1912), 893.00/1507, National Archives, Washington, D.C. *Ta-kung-ho jih-pao* (Republican Times; Shanghai, Oct. 10, 1912), p. 4.

7. *Republican Advocate* 1.43:1700 (Jan. 25, 1913).

8. *CKFP* 1022 (March 14, 1915), reprinted edition, 35.1:554. Kirke, Consul in Nanking, to Jordan, Minister in Peking (Oct. 13, 1914), FO 228/1909.

9. *Peking Daily News* (Jan. 16, 1914).

10. *Peking Daily News* (Jan. 24 and Jan. 30, 1914). *CFKP* 631:4-5 (Feb. 8, 1914).

11. For a description of the ceremony, see Jerome Ch'en, *Yuan Shih-k'ai*, 2d ed. (Stanford: Stanford University Press, 1972), pp. 162-163. For Yuan's order generalizing the ceremony, a point absent from Ch'en's description: *CFKP* 945 (Dec. 21, 1914), reprinted edition, 32.1:208. See also: *CFKP* 631:4-5 (Feb. 8, 1914).

12. *Peking Daily News* (Oct. 11, June 19, June 25, and Sept. 22, 1914). *CFKP* 543:1 (Nov. 7, 1913). Ibid. 867 (Oct. 31, 1914), reprinted edition, 30.1:48. Huang Yuan-yung, *Yuan-sheng i-chu* (Posthumous collection of writings of Huang Yuan-yung; Taipei reprint, 1962), 2:247-248.

13. *Peking Daily News* (Dec. 28, 1914). Ts'ao Ju-lin, *I-cheng chih hui-i* (A lifetime's recollections; Hong Kong, 1966), p. 154. *CFKP* 1295 (Dec. 15, 1915), reprinted edition, 44.2:535-536. Ibid. (Jan. 16, 1916), reprinted edition, 45.2:571-572.

14. Edgar Snow, "A Conversation with Mao Tse-tung," *Life* 70.16:46 (April 30, 1971).

15. Jordan to Grey, Foreign Secretary (Nov. 14, 1911), FO 405/205. G. E. Morrison Diary (Nov. 20, 1911), MP item 91.

16. G. E. Morrison diary (Dec. 9, 1911), MP item 91.

17. Fei Hsing-chien (pseud. Wo-chiu chung-tsu), *Tuan Ch'i-jui* (Shanghai, 1921), p. 35. Chang I-lin, *Hsin-t'ai-p'ing-shih chi* (Collection of Chang I-lin's works; 1947), p. 41.

18. *K'ai-kuo kuei-mo* (Patterns in the inauguration of the republic), ed. Committee of the Compilation of Documents on the Fiftieth Anniversary of the Founding of the Republic of China (Taipei, 1962), pp. 640-641.

19. For example, *T'ien-to pao* (The Bell; Shanghai, May 13, 1912), and in many other issues of this newspaper in May and June, 1912.

20. Jordan to Langley, Peking, June 1, 1914, Jordan Papers, FO 350/12.

21. *Chung-kuo T'ung-meng hui tsa-chih* (Magazine of the Chinese Alliance Society; Canton, Sept. 11, 1912), *chu-shu* section, p. 11.

22. "Notes on the Political Situation," Frank W. Hadley, Shanghai (March 4, 1913), 893.99/1611, National Archives, Washington, D.C.

23. *Nihon gaikō bunsho* (Documents on Japan's diplomacy), 1914, II, 743-745.

24. G. E. Morrison diary (Sept. 25, 1915), MP item 104. The aide was Ts'ai T'ing-kan.

25. Report of a conversation with Ts'ai T'ing-kan, G. E. Morrison diary (May 26, 1915), MP item 104.

26. G. E. Morrison diary (Aug. 17, 1915), MP item 104.

27. Jordan to Grey (Dec. 22, 1911), FO 405/205.

28. Ts'ao Ju-lin, p. 132.

29. *CFKP* 554 (Dec. 30, 1914), reprinted edition, 32.1:319.

30. Pai Chiao, pp. 191-221. For a useful but inaccurate translation: B. L. Putnam Weale (pseudonym of B. Lennox Simpson), *The Fight for the Republic in China* (New York: Dodd, Mead and Co., 1917), pp. 150-171.

31. "Inaugural Address of President to the Council of Government" (Dec. 15, 1913), FO 228/1852. For an edited version of the remarks, see *CFKP* 585:2 (Dec. 19, 1913).

32. *Papers Relating to the Foreign Relations of the United States 1915* (Washington, D.C., 1924), pp. 66-67.

33. *Peking Daily News* (March 14, 1916).

34. Ch'en Tu-hsiu, "Chiu ssu-hsiang yü kuo-t'i" (Old thought and [the problem of] the national polity), *Hsin ch'ing-nien* (The new youth; May 1, 1917), Daian edition, III, 207-208.

35. *CFKP* 1294 (Dec. 14, 1915), reprinted edition, 44.1:497.

36. Pai Chiao, p. 297. Reginald F. Johnston, *Twilight in the Forbidden City* (London: Victor Gollancz, 1934), p. 114.

37. *CFKP* 1295 (Dec. 15, 1915), reprinted edition, 44.1:535-536. Ibid. 1299 (Dec. 19, 1915), reprinted edition, 44.2:713. Ibid. 1303 (Dec. 23, 1915), reprinted edition, 44.2:906.

38. Pai Chiao, pp. 194, 196, 199.

39. Gabriel A. Almond, "Introduction: A Functional Approach to Comparative Politics," in Almond and James S. Coleman, eds., *The Politics of the Developing Areas* (Princeton: Princeton University Press, 1960), pp. 13-15.

40. Morrison to Captain Tsao, Peking, Oct. 29, 1913, MP item 178. "Published in the Peking Gazette, 31 Oct. 1913 — by Frank Johnson Goodnow," MP item 133. "The Draft Constitution. Professor Goodnow's Criticism" (printed), "Criticisms of the Draft Constitution" (MS.), "The Constitution and the President" (printed in the *Peking Daily News*, Nov. 18, 1913), Goodnow Collection.

41. G. E. Morrison diary (Nov. 23, 1913), MP item 99; Goodnow to Nicholas Murray Butler, Peking, Jan. 2, 1914, and March 30, 1914 ("Miscellaneous Correspondence"), Goodnow Collection.

42. Goodnow to Butler, Peking, May 18, 1914 ("Miscellaneous Correspondence"), Goodnow Collection.

43. F. J. Goodnow, "The Parliament of the Republic of China," *American Political Science Review* 8.4:560 (Nov. 1914). My comments in this paragraph are also based on: ibid., pp. 541-562; G. E. Morrison diary (Nov. 23, 1913), MP item

99; Goodnow to Butler, Peking, Jan. 2, 1914, and Feb. 16, 1914 ("Miscellaneous Correspondence"), Goodnow Collection.

44. F. J. Goodnow, "Reform in China," *American Political Science Review* 9.2:209-224 (May 1915).

45. Goodnow wrote of seeing Yuan K'o-ting twice a week on a regular basis at the beginning of 1914, and there are evidences of a continuing closeness. Goodnow to Butler, Peking, Jan. 2, 1914, and Feb. 26, 1914 ("Miscellaneous Correspondence"), Goodnow Collection. G. E. Morrison diary (Feb. 16, 1914), MP item 100.

46. Goodnow's private views are recorded in G. E. Morrison diary (July 16, July 28, and Aug. 11, 1915), MP item 104.

47. Dr. Frank J. Goodnow, "Republic or Monarchy?" in MP item 139.

48. G. E. Morrison diary (July 28, Aug. 11, Aug. 17, and Aug. 31, 1915), MP item 104. *Washington Post* (Aug. 17, 1915), 893.00/2299, National Archives, Washington, D.C., *Papers Relating to the Foreign Relations of the United States.*

49. Pai Chiao, pp. 205-207.

50. Mannheim, p. 115.

51. *CFKP* 726:2 (May 15, 1914).

8   The Kuomintang in the 1930s
Lloyd E. Eastman

1. The research for this essay, part of which is adapted from the author's study *The Abortive Revolution: China Under Nationalist Rule, 1927-1937* (Cambridge, Mass.: Harvard University Press, 1974), has been aided by grants from the Committee on Exchanges with Asian Institutions and the Joint Committee on Contemporary China, both of the Social Science Research Council; the Center for Asian Studies, the Center for International Comparative Studies, and the University Research Board, all of the University of Illinois; and the East Asian Research Center, Harvard University.

2. Roberto Michels, "Conservatism," *Encyclopaedia of the Social Sciences* (New York: Macmillan, 1931), IV, 230. Michels' definition delineates what may be called "true" political conservatism. This can be differentiated from what I have called, for want of a better term, "subjective" political conservatism—that is, actions and attitudes that did not tend to maintain the status quo, but that were thought in the context of the time to be somehow less "radical" than the actions and attitudes of another person or movement. In my view, Chiang Kai-shek, Yuan Shih-k'ai, and Liu Shao-ch'i—each of whom has been labeled a conservative—were conservative only in the sense of subjective conservatism. For a more extensive discussion of the differences between true and subjective conservatism, see Lloyd E. Eastman, "Political Conservatism in a Revolutionary Society: China," *American Behavioral Scientist* 17.2:293-308 (Nov.-Dec. 1973).

The definition of true conservatism employed here has been propounded by other scholars. Samuel P. Huntington, for example, has rejected claims that conservatism implies some specific ideational content, remarking, "What is the political vision of conservatism? Is it possible to describe a conservative society? On the contrary, the essence of conservatism is that it is literally, in Mühlenfeld's phrase, *'Politik ohne Wunschbilder.'* " "Conservatism as an Ideology," *American Political Science Review* 51.2:457 (June 1957). See also Peter Witonski, "Introduction," *The Wisdom of Conservatism*, ed. Peter Witonski (New Rochelle, N.Y.: Arlington House, 1971), I, 15-39; and Mark N. Hagopian, *The Phenomenon of Revolution* (New York: Dodd, Mead and Co., 1974), pp. 353-354, 384-385.

3. Mary C. Wright, "From Revolution to Restoration: The Transformation of Kuomintang Ideology," *The Far Eastern Quarterly* 14.4:515-532 (Aug. 1955). This was reprinted in revised form in Mary Clabaugh Wright, *The Last Stand of Chinese Conservatism: The T'ung-Chih Restoration, 1862-1874* (Stanford: Stanford University Press, 1957), chap. 12.

4. The discussion of the Blue Shirts is based largely on Eastman, *The Abortive Revolution*, chap. 2.

5. Kao Ching-chai, "Chung-kuo ko-ming yü wo-men te lu-hsien" (The Chinese revolution and our line), *Ch'ien-t'u* (Future) 2.1:1 (Jan. 1, 1934).

6. Kan Kuo-hsun, "Chui-ssu Liu Chien-ch'ün ping shih lan-i-she" (Recollections of Liu Chien-ch'ün and revelations regarding the Blue Shirts), *Chuan-chi wen-hsueh* (Biographical literature) 21.3:18 (Sept. 1, 1972).

7. Jerry Bernard Seps, "German Military Advisers and Chiang Kai-shek, 1927-1938," Ph.D. dissertation, University of California, Berkeley, 1972, pp. 35, 82, 160, et passim; and Karl Mehner, "Die Rolle deutscher Militärberater als Interessenvertreter des deutschen Imperialismus und Militarismus in China (1928-1936)," Inaugural dissertation, Karl-Marx-Universität, Leipzig, 1961, pp. 69-71, 99-100, 118-121, et passim.

8. Interview with Liu Chien-ch'ün, Hsin-tien, Taiwan, May 9, 1969.

9. Editorial, *She-hui hsin-wen* (The society mercury) 3:354 (June 9, 1933).

10. Chang Yun-fu, "Wen-hua t'ung-chih te i-i chi fang-fa" (The meaning and method of cultural control), *Ch'ien-t'u* 2.8:1 (Aug. 1, 1934).

11. Yü Wen-wei, "Chung-hua min-tsu hsien-tsai hsu-yao ho-chung chiao-yü" (What kind of education does the Chinese nation need?), *Ch'ien-t'u* 1.7:3 (July 1, 1933). Emphasis added.

12. Ibid.

13. Ibid., pp. 2-6.

14. Ch'en Shao-hsiao [pseudonym of Ch'en Fan], *Hei-wang lu* (Record of the black net) (Hong Kong, 1966), p. 287.

15. Ch'en Li-fu, "Chung-kuo wen-hua chien-she lun" (On China's cultural construction), *Wen-hua chien-she* (Cultural construction) 1.1:14 (Oct. 10, 1934); and "K'ung-tzu yü Sun Chung-shan hsien-sheng" (Confucius and Sun Yat-sen), speech delivered in Aug. 1934, in *Ch'en Li-fu hsien-sheng yen-lun chi* (A collection of Ch'en Li-fu speeches), ed. Lu Yuan-chün (Taipei 1967), p. 11. An extensive English summary of Ch'en Li-fu's major writings is in A. T. Roy, "Confucian Thought in China in the Nineteen Thirties: Ch'en Li-fu," *The Chung Chi Journal* 7.1:72-89 (Nov. 1967), and 8.1:63-82 (Nov. 1968).

16. The declaration may be found in *Wen-hua chien-she* 1.4:1-5 (Jan. 10, 1935). Ch'en Li-fu's part in the drafting of the declaration is remarked in Ou-yang Tsung, *Chung-kuo nei-mu* (The inside story in China) (Shanghai, 1941), p. 2; and Meng Kung-jen, "Ch'ung-ch'ing chih cheng-tang p'ai-pieh yü wai-chiao lu-hsien"

(Political factions and the diplomatic line in Chungking), *Chung-kuo kung-lun* (Chinese opinion) 6.3:15 (Dec. 1, 1941).

17. S. N. Eisenstadt, "Tradition, Change, and Modernity: Reflections on the Chinese Experience," *China in Crisis,* ed. Ping-ti Ho and Tang Tsou (Chicago: University of Chicago Press, 1968), vol. 1, book 2, p. 754. See also Alfred Diamant, "The Nature of Political Development," *Political Development and Social Change,* ed. Jason L. Finkle and Richard W. Gable (New York: John Wiley, 1968), pp. 93-94.

18. Remarks by Mao made in 1956, quoted by Stuart Schram in *The New York Times,* Feb. 22, 1972, p. 15:4; and "On New Democracy," *Selected Works of Mao Tse-tung* (Peking, 1965), II, 380-381.

19. "Lun tu-ching" (On reading the classics), *Kuo-wen chou-pao* (National news weekly), 12.4:1 (Jan. 21, 1935).

20. Theodore de Bary and others, eds., *Sources of Chinese Tradition* (New York: Columbia University Press, 1960), p. 856. See also Lü Chin-lu, "Ju-chia ssu-hsiang yü hsien-tai-hua Chung-kuo" (Confucian thought and China during the process of modernization), *Tung-fang tsa-chih* (Eastern miscellany), 32.19:163-175 (Oct. 1, 1935).

21. "K'ung-tzu yü Sun Chung-shan hsien-sheng," p. 13.

22. "Chung-kuo wen-hua chien-she lun," p. 14.

23. Ibid.

24. Fang Chih, "Min-tsu wen-hua yü min-tsu ssu-hsiang" (National culture and national thought), *Wen-hua chien-she* 1.2:20 (Nov. 10, 1934).

25. Chang Chi-t'ung, "Kuan-yü Chung-kuo pen-wei te wen-hua chien-she" (Regarding cultural construction on a Chinese basis), *Kuo-wen chou-pao* 12.10:articles p. 1 (Mar. 18, 1935).

26. "Hsin-sheng-huo yun-tung chih yao-i" (Essentials of the New Life movement), *Chiang-tsung-t'ung ssu-hsiang yen-lun chi* (A collection of President Chiang's thoughts and speeches), XII, 103.

27. Ibid., pp. 105-106.

28. Ibid., p. 106.

29. *Hsin-sheng-huo yun-tung hsu-chih* (Essential information for the New Life movement) (Nanking, 1935), pp. 216-220.

30. "Hsin-sheng-huo yun-tung chih yao-i," pp. 109-110.

31. Ibid., p. 110.

32. Quoted in [Iwai Eiichi], *Ranisha ni kansuru chōsa* (An investigation of the Blue Shirts; issued by the Research Division of the Japanese Foreign Ministry, marked "secret," 1937), pp. 37-38.

33. "Hsin-sheng-huo yun-tung chih yao-i," p. 111.

34. The leading role of the Blue Shirts in the New Life movement is indicated in a textbook used by the Blue Shirts. See *Wo-men te hsun-lien* (Our training; n.p., 1936), pp. 14, 169-170. See also Kan Kuo-hsun, pp. 19-20. There were, of course, other than Blue Shirt influences in the movement. The Christian missionary role is discussed in James C. Thomson, Jr., *While China Faced West: American Reformers in Nationalist China, 1927-1937* (Cambridge, Mass.: Harvard University Press, 1969), pp. 151-195.

35. Unsigned, "Chiang Kai-shek Developing a Fascism à la Chine," *China*

Weekly Review 68.10:387 (May 5, 1934).

36. Thomson, p. 183.

37. John Israel, *Student Nationalism in China, 1927-1937* (Stanford: Stanford University Press, 1966), p. 100.

38. "Hsin-sheng-huo yun-tung chih chung-hsin chun-tse" (The central precept of the New Life movement), *Chiang tsung-t'ung ssu-hsiang yen-lun chi,* XII, 116-117.

39. Chen Li-fu, *Philosophy of Life* (New York: Philosophical Library, 1948), pp. 74-82 et passim.

40. Gauss to Johnson, Sept. 16, 1934, State Dept. Archives 893.000/12842, p. 1.

41. Jürgen Domes, *Vertagte Revolution* (Berlin: Walter de Gruyter & Co., 1969), pp. 605-607; *China Year Book, 1936,* p. 32.

42. H. R. Ekins and Theon Wright, *China Fights for Her Life* (New York and London: Whittlesey House, 1938), p. 27. Much the same view was expressed, if less cuttingly, by an editorial in *I-shih pao* (Social welfare), reprinted in *Kuo-wen chou-pao* 9.23: editorials p. 8 (June 13, 1932).

43. See, for example, Chiang Kai-shek, "The Cause and Cure of Rural Decadence," in Wang Ching-wei and Chiang Kai-shek, *China's Leaders and Their Policies* (Shanghai, 1935), pp. 31-32.

44. Tsiang T'ing-fu, "Tui kung-ch'an-tang pi-hsü te cheng-chih ts'e-lueh" (Political measures needed to oppose the Communist party), *Tu-li p'ing-lun* (Independent review), 11:6-8 (Aug. 31, 1932); George E. Taylor, "The Reconstruction Movement in China," *Problems of the Pacific, 1936,* ed. W. L. Holland and Kate L. Mitchell (Chicago: University of Chicago Press, n.d.), p. 391; T. H. Shen, *Agricultural Resources of China* (Ithaca, N.Y.: Cornell University Press, 1951), p. 100.

45. Chiang's speech to the fourth plenary session of the Central Executive Committee, June 1934, quoted in *Report of the Technical Agent on His Mission in China from the Date of His Appointment until April 1st, 1934* (Geneva: League of Nations, 1934), pp. 28-30.

46. Y. C. Wang, *Chinese Intellectuals and the West, 1872-1949* (Chapel Hill: University of North Carolina Press, 1966), p. 463.

47. Franklin L. Ho, "The Reminiscences of Ho Lien (Franklin L. Ho)" as told to Crystal Lorch (unpub. manuscript in Special Collections Library, Butler Library, Columbia University, postscript dated July 1966), p. 144.

48. "Influential Elements in the Kuomintang (and National Government)" dated Jan. 24, 1943, in *The Amerasia Papers: A Clue to the Catastrophe of China* (Washington, D.C.: U.S. Government Printing Office, 1970), I, 236.

49. Rajchman letter to Dragoni, Aug. 4, 1934, League of Nations archives, R. 5687.

50. Frank Tamagna, *Banking and Finance in China* (New York: Institute of Pacific Relations, 1942), p. 195; *Agrarian China: Selected Source Materials from Chinese Authors,* comp. and trans. the Research staff of the Secretariat, Institute of Pacific Relations (Chicago, 1938), pp. 213 and 216; *Problems of the Pacific, 1936,* p. 390.

51. *Problems of the Pacific, 1936,* p. 166. Italics added.

52. Gideon Chen, *Chinese Government Economic Planning and Recon-*

struction since 1927 (China Institute of Pacific Relations, 1933), p. 24 et passim.

53. Ibid., pp. 25-26.

54. "Hsiu-ming nei-cheng yü cheng-ch'ih li-chih" (Reform internal administration and rectify rule by officials), *Chiang tsung-t'ung ssu-hsiang yen-lun chi* XI, 130.

55. "Chiao-fei yao shih-kan" (To exterminate the communists, we must work effectively), *Chiang tsung-t'ung ssu-hsiang yen-lun chi* XI, 137.

56. I have discussed several possible explanations in *The Abortive Revolution* (see note 1).

57. Clinton Rossiter, "Conservatism," *International Encyclopedia of the Social Sciences* (New York: Macmillan, 1968), III, 292.

9   The Conservative as Sage: Liang Shu-ming
Guy Alitto

Abbreviations Used in the Notes

TH: Liang Shu-ming. *Tung-Hsi wen-hua chi ch'i che-hsueh* (Eastern and Western cultures and their philosophies). Shanghai, 1922.

SC: _____ *Shu-ming sa-ch'ien wen-lu* (Liang Shu-ming's writings before the age of thirty). Shanghai, 1924.

KLL: _____ and Liang Nai-ting, eds. *Kuei-lin Liang hsien-sheng i-shu* (The Collected Writings of Mr. Liang of Kweilin). 4 vols. Peking, 1927.

SH: _____ *Shu-ming sa-hou wen-lu* (Liang Shu-ming's writings after the age of thirty). Shanghai, 1930.

CW: _____ *Chung-kuo min-tsu tzu-chiu yun-tung chih tsui-hou chueh-wu* (The final awakening of the self-salvation movement of the Chinese people). Peiping, 1932.

WC: _____ *Hsiang-ts'un chien-she lun-wen chi* (Collection of writings on rural reconstruction). Tsou-p'ing, 1934.

CY: _____ *Liang Shu-ming hsien-sheng chiao-yü wen-lu* (Liang Shu-ming's writings on education). Tsou-p'ing, 1935.

LL: _____ *Hsiang-ts'un chien-she li-lun* (The theory of rural reconstruction). Tsou-p'ing, 1937.

SY: _____ *Hsiang-ts'un chien-she shih-yen* (Experiments in rural reconstruction). Vol. 1, Shanghai, 1936; vols. 2-3, Shanghai, 1938.

CH: _____ *Chao-hua* (Morning talks). Changsha, 1940.

HS: _____ *Wo-ti tzu-hsueh hsiao shih* (A short account of my self-education). Shanghai, 1947.

YI: _____ *Chung-kuo wen-hua yao-i* (The essence of Chinese culture). Shanghai, 1949.

1. This paper is based on primary sources far too numerous to include in the notes, which are meant to be suggestive rather than exhaustive. Also contributing to my overall understanding of Liang Shu-ming and his rural reconstruction work are several hundred hours of personal interviews conducted in Taiwan and Hong Kong. I have limited my discussion of Liang's thought to his major ideas on

culture, education, and rural reconstruction, which he reiterated in scores of books and articles. Perhaps the most systematic expression of them may be found in *TH, LL,* and *YI.* Interviewees included students and colleagues from Liang's rural reconstruction work as well as scholarly associates like T'ang Chün-i, Mou Tsung-san, and Ch'ien Mu. I also interviewed prominent Republican period political or intellectual figures like Li Tsung-huang, Wang Yun-wu, and Ch'en Li-fu, all of whom had contact with Liang in various ways and to varying degrees.

2. Benjamin Schwartz has made this observation in many of his articles on modern Chinese intellectual history. See his "Intellectual History of China: Pre-liminary Reflections," in John K. Fairbank, ed., *Chinese Thought and Institutions* (Chicago: University of Chicago Press, 1957), pp. 15-30; and "The Limits of 'Tra-dition Versus Modernity' as Categories of Explanation: The Case of the Chinese Intellectuals," *Daedalus* (Winter 1972), pp. 71-88.

3. See for example Hu Shih, "Tu Liang Shu-ming hsien-sheng ti *Tung-Hsi wen-hua chi ch'i che-hsueh*" (After reading Mr. Liang Shu-ming's Eastern and Western cultures and their philosophies), in *Hu Shih wen-ts'un* (Collected works of Hu Shih), 4 vols. (Taipei, 1953), II, 59-89; and Wu Chih-hui, "I-ko hsin-yang ti yu-chou-kuan chi jen-sheng-kuan" (The cosmology of a new faith and philosophy of life), in *K'o-hsueh yü jen-sheng-kuan* (Science and philosophy of life), 2 vols. (Shanghai, 1923), II, 120-130.

4. From interviews with former colleagues of Liang Shu-ming.

5. See for example Yang Ming-chai, *P'ing Chung-Hsi wen-hua-kuan* (A critique of views on Chinese and Western cultures; Peking, 1924), pp. 1-106; Ch'en Hsu-ching, "Tung-Hsi wen-hua kuan" (Views concerning Eastern and Western cultures), *Ling-nan hsueh-pao* (The Lingnan journal) 5.1:90-98; and Ts'ai Shang-ssu, "Liang Shu-ming ssu-hsiang ti p'ing-chieh" (A critical introduction to Liang Shu-ming's thought), *Shih yü wen* (The times and writing) 3.1:6-8, 3.2:23-24, 3.3:39-40, 3.4:55-57, and 3.5:71-75 (Shanghai, April-May, 1948).

6. See for example *Liang Shu-ming ssu-hsiang p'i-p'an* (Criticism of Liang Shu-ming's thought; Peking, 1955); and Ai Ssu-ch'i, *P'i-p'an Liang Shu-ming ti che-hsueh ssu hsiang* (Criticism of Liang Shu-ming's philosophical thought; Peking, 1956).

7. Ts'ui Te-li and Liang Tou-hsing, *Chung-kuo wen-hua kai-lun* (A gen-eral discussion of Chinese culture: Taipei, 1968). Various Kuomintang connected people with whom I talked in Taiwan referred to Liang as a "fellow traveler."

8. The articles which appeared in the conventionalized thought-reform campaign directed against Liang Shu-ming in 1955-1956 are an exception, but in such formal campaigns, casting aspersions on the "personalized target's" character is *de rigueur.*

9. *TH,* "Preface," p. 4; ibid., p. 137.

10. Liang Shu-ming, "Hsiang-kang t'o-hsien chi K'uan Shu liang erh" (A letter to my two sons [P'ei]-k'uan and [P'ei]-shu on my escape from Hong Kong). This was a letter Liang wrote to his sons after he had fled the Japanese occupation of Hong Kong and had reached Wu-chou, Kwangsi. The letter was published in a Kweilin newspaper in February 1942. I have seen a handwritten copy preserved by one of Liang's students now in Taiwan, but it bears no date or newspaper name. Parts of the letter are quoted in: Chou Shao-hsien, "T'an Liang Shu-ming hsien-

sheng chih ssu-hsiang" (A discussion of Mr. Liang Shu-ming's thought), *Hsin hsia* (New Cathay) 5:73-76 (Nov. 7, 1969), nos. 5-10 (Nov. 7, 1969-March 15, 1970); Mou Tsung-san, "Wo yü Hsiung Shih-li hsien-sheng" (Mr. Hsiung Shih-li and I), *Chung-kuo hsueh-jen* (Chinese scholar), no. 1 (Hong Kong, 1970); and Hu (Ying)-han, "Chi Liang Shu-ming hsien-sheng" (Remembering Mr. Liang Shu-ming), *Chin-jih shih-chieh* (Today's world; Hong Kong, May 15, 1952).

11. See for instance Tseng Ch'i's letter to Liang in *Tseng Mu-han hsien-sheng i-chu* (Mr. Tseng Mu-han's collected writings; Taipei, 1954), p. 209, in which he refers to Liang's urging him to write in *pai-hua*.

12. *TH*, pp. 202, 204-206, 210-211.

13. *SC*, pp. 197-198; *TH*, pp. 207-209.

14. *CW*, pp. 21, 22, 333. *LL*, pp. 279-280. The term "nodding acquaintance" was used by Ch'en Li-fu himself during an interview in Taipei, May 19, 1971.

15. Karl Mannheim, "Conservative Thought," in *Essays on Sociology and Social Psychology* (New York: Oxford University Press, 1953), pp. 74-164.

16. Raymond Williams, *Culture and Society 1780-1950* (New York: Harper and Row, 1958), p. xvi.

17. The internal spiritual element sometimes appears as "civilization" (as with W. von Humbolt, A. Schaeffle, P. Barth) and sometime as "culture" (as in A. Weber's famous formula and in some others like F. Oppenheimer). These contrasted concepts, as well as the general prominence of *Kultur*, appear as a natural development of earlier German romantic thought, especially that of Herder and Schiller.

18. There is a short biography of Liang Chi (T. Chü-ch'uan) in the *Ch'ing shih-kao* (A draft history of the Ch'ing dynasty; Mukden, 1937), chüan 496, pp. 20b-21a. Liang Shu-ming's mother, Chang Ying (T. Ch'un-i), was a highly educated woman from an old established scholar-official family. In 1904 she participated in the establishment of Peking's first modern girls' school and taught Chinese literature there. Mme. Liang also vigorously supported her husband's reform endeavors. She died in 1912. *KLL*, "Nien-p'u," 7b, 19b, 24b; *HS*, pp. 3-4, 20.

19. Liang Chi's nonofficial activities such as his efforts at popular journalism or theatrical innovations all aimed at raising national consciousness. See *KLL*, pp. 19b, 20, 28, 29b; *HS*, pp. 18, 31-33; and *SC*, pp. 100-102; and *WC*, p. 4.

20. *HS*, p. 12; and *KLL*, "Nien-p'u," p. 26b; *WC*, pp. 2-4.

21. *WC*, pp. 17, 19; *CW*, pp. 4-8, 101-107; *HS*, pp. 14-15, 27-33, 36-37; *SH*, pp. 99, 191, 198; *CY*, pp. 88-91, 232-233.

22. *KLL*, "Hsin-jen lei kao" (Notes from 1911 and 1912), chüan 4, p. 4b.

23. See "Ni-ch'eng min-cheng-pu-chang kuan ch'ing tai ti shu-kao" (Draft memorial to the minister of the interior), in *KLL*, chüan 4.

24. *CY*, p. 233.

25. *KLL*, "Nien-p'u," pp. 23b-24; *SH*, pp. 100-101; *HS*, pp. 37-39; *WC*, pp. 1-31; *CY*, p. 232; *CW*, p. 4; and Liang Shu-ming, "Erh-shih-wu nien kuo-ch'ing chi-nien" (Commemorating the twenty-fifth national day), *Hsiang-ts'un chien-she* (Rural reconstruction) 6.5 (Oct. 16, 1936).

26. *KLL*, "Nien-p'u," p. 24.

27. Liang Shu-ming, "Erh-shih-wu nien kuo-ch'ing chi-nien," p. 3; *KLL*,

"Nien-p'u," pp. 23b, 24a; *HS*, pp. 38-39; *CW*, p. 4; *WC*, pp. 16, 19, 20; *CH*, p. 55.

28. *KLL*, "Nien-p'u," p. 24.

29. Ibid.; also *KLL*, "I-shu," chüan 1, p. 10b and chüan 6, p. 1b.

30. Liang Shu-ming, "Ju shu" (Confucianism), *Chia-yin tsa-chih* (The tiger magazine) 1.8 (August 1915) and "Fo li" (The essence of Buddhism), ibid. 1.10 (October 1915).

31. *KLL*, "Nien-p'u," p. 26b; *SA*, p. 47; *WC*, pp. 1-31; and Liang Shu-ming, "Chi-nien Ts'ai hsien-sheng" (Commemorating Mr. Ts'ai), *Wen-hua tsa-chih* (Culture magazine; Kweilin) 2.1 (March 1942).

32. *CH*, pp. 1-4; *HS*, pp. 30, 39; *YI*, pp. 1-3; *SC*, pp. 15-16, 151; *CY*, pp. 83-85; *CW*, pp. 3-4, 101-102; and *WC*, pp. 1-31.

33. In "Chiu yuan chueh i lun" (On studying the origin and solving doubts), *Tung-fang tsa-chih* (Eastern miscellany) 13.6:9 (June 10, 1916) and 13.7:8 (July 10, 1916), for instance, while still committed to Buddhism, he finds certain aspects of the Buddhist and earlier Confucian (Sung-Ming) philosophy of life similar. In the summer of that year he undertook his first serious study of the Confucian classics. That fall, in "Chung-hua hsueh-yu hsuan-yen" (Statement of the China Alumni Associaton) in *SH*, pp. 59-60, he first used the term "culture" (*wen-hua*) to refer to a transcendent entity independent of the forms it assumed in history and transmitted from earliest times. Upon accepting a professorship of Indian philosophy at Peking University in late 1917, he purposely proclaimed to Ts'ai Yuan-p'ei and Ch'en Tu-hsiu that he had come to elucidate the teachings of Buddha *and* Confucius. *TH*, p. 15. A few months later he had started a study of Confucius and Mencius and had founded a Confucian Philosophy Research Society. Ibid., p. 16; and Ts'ai Yuan-p'ei, *Ts'ai Yuan-p'ei tzu-shu* (Ts'ai Yuan-p'ei's self-account; Taipei, 1967), p. 23.

34. Scholars have generally put forth the tempting but somewhat facile interpretation that Liang converted to Confucianism and Chinese culture primarily as a consequence of his father's suicide. See for example Kuo Chan-p'o, *Chin wu-shih nien Chung-kuo ssu-hsiang shih* (Chinese intellectual history of the past fifty years; Peiping, 1935), p. 176; Wei Cheng-t'ung, *Ch'uan-t'ung ti t'ou-shih* (A penetrating look at tradition; Taipei, 1965), p. 118; Chester C. Tan, *Chinese Political Thought in the Twentieth Century* (New York: Doubleday and Co., 1971), p. 278. Certainly the impact of Liang Chi's suicide cannot be lightly dismissed. Liang Shu-ming himself said that his personal decision to lead a Confucian life took place "in March and April [of 1921]" which was two and a half years after his father's death. ("Preface," *TH*, p. 2; *WC*, p. 16.) Yet analysis of Liang's life and writings suggests that his conversion was the culmination of a long, gradual process beginning with his breakdown in 1912, and throughout which he felt guilty for disobeying and disregarding his father. Moreover, even before his father's suicide his thought contained all the seeds that would grow into his later cultural theories. (See note 33.)

35. Erik Erikson, *Young Man Luther* (New York: Norton and Co., 1962), pp. 161-162.

36. Liang Shu-ming, "Chiu yuan chueh i lun."

37. See n. 10. The above section of the letter is also quoted in Jen Chi-yü,

"Hsiang Liang Shu-ming ti fan tung ssu-hsiang chan-k'ai tou-cheng" (Opening the struggle against Liang Shu-ming's reactionary thought), in *Liang Shu-ming ssu-hsiang p'i-p'an* (Criticism of Liang Shu-ming's thought; Peking, 1956), II, 19-29.

38. *SC*, pp. 15-17. See also Huang Yuan-sheng, "Hsiang ying lu" (Some reflections), *Tung-fang tsa-chih* 13:2 (Feb. 10, 1916), which Liang referred to as the immediate stimulus for writing his own article.

39. Wang Hung-i, influential Shantung political figure and educator, first met Liang Shu-ming at Tsinan in 1921 when Liang was delivering his series of lectures on Eastern and Western cultures. They remained in close contact until Wang's death in 1930. In 1924 Wang and others of his clique of traditionalist North China gentry formulated a program of agrarianist cultural reconstruction. Liang found their ideas agreeable but unrealistic. Wang started the Peking *Ts'un chih yueh-k'an* (Village government monthly) in 1929 and finally prevailed upon Liang, by then an active advocate of rural reconstruction, to associate himself with the group. This association led Liang to warlord Han Fu-ch'ü's patronage and eventually to the founding of his famous rural reconstruction projects in Shantung in 1931. *CW*, pp. 11-14, 18, 19, 325-331; *SY*, I, 31-38; *LL*, 346. See also note 54.

40. *TH*, pp. 48-55, 80-87; *SC*, pp. 107-126.

41. *TH*, p. 199.

42. *TH*, pp. 118-138, 146-150; *SC*, pp. 137-138.

43. The modern Chinese term *li-hsing* is a borrowed Japanese neologism meaning "reason" or "rationality." Liang himself had often used the word in this sense in the past. (*TH*, pp. 33, 45, 75-76, 155-157, 173-175; *SH*, p. 133.) He first imbued the term with its new meaning in 1930 (*CW*, pp. 136-137, 170-176), at the same time adumbrating the theory of Chinese and Western cultures and societies which he continued to develop for the next twenty years. His last book, *Chung-kuo wen-hua yao-i* (The essence of Chinese culture), published in 1949, set forth the theory in final form.

44. *YI*, pp. 138, 132, 133. Also see ibid., pp. 129, 185, 247, 260, 289, 321.

45. *YI*, p. 125; *CY*, pp. 82-84.

46. *YI*, p. 128.

47. Liang Shu-ming, "Chi-ko wen-ti ti t'ao-lun" (A discussion of a few questions), *Hsiang-ts'un chien-she* 6.1 (Aug. 16, 1936).

48. What he does say is that in Western culture intellect is strong and well developed while *li-hsing* is "shallow" and "weak." In Chinese culture the opposite is true. *YI*, pp. 129, 289-293; *LL*, 39-43; *CW*, pp. 170-175; *CY*, p. 79; *CH*, p. 61.

49. *KLL*, chüan 1. See especially "Liu shih erh-nu shu" (Parting instructions to my children), pp. 57b-62. Liang Chi also linked the *t'ien-li* with *min-i* (the people's natural disposition, that is, their inherent goodness).

50. *TH*, p. 163.

51. *TH*, p. 165.

52. In the early 1920s, Liang pointed to certain Western trends like instinct psychology and socialism, or to individual thinkers, like Nietzsche, William James, Henri Bergson, Rudolph Eucken, Bertrand Russell, and even Einstein (*TH*, pp. 77-79, 118-119, 166-186; *SC*, pp. 177-182) as proof of the Western change in cultural direction. After this, while still continuing to quote Russell's praise of China and criticism of the West (for example, *CW*, pp. 59-61; 65, 143, 175; *WC*,

p. 31; *YI*, p. 8, 128, 292, 322) and occasionally quoting other Western self-criticism (*LL*, p. 2), he never again attempted to prove that the West would change, but simply assumed that it must. In his last statement on the subject he ominously ruminated that "in the future, if [modern Western culture] does not create unlimited happiness for all people then it will certainly destroy all people." Liang Shu-ming, "Mien-jen wen-hsueh-yuan ch'uang-pan yuan chi ch'i chih-ch'ü (The founding and purpose of the Mien-jen Academy) in *Mien-jen wen-hsueh-yuan yuan-k'an* (The Mien-jen Academy journal), no. 1 (Pei-p'ei, Szechwan, May 1949).

53. See for example *CW*, pp. 140-179, 207, 289; *WC*, pp. 173-177; *CY*, pp. 257-258, 162, 171; *YI*, pp. 143, 146, 163, 168; *SH*, p. 276; and *LL*, pp. 138, 383.

54. In 1925 Liang sent three students south to participate in the Northern Expedition. When in 1926 they returned full of enthusiasm for the Communist party, one having already joined and another on the verge of following, Liang experienced a sudden awakening to the unsuitability of Western political and economic institutions and committed himself to rural reform as a solution to China's crisis. *CW*, pp. 9-11, 15-16; and *WC*, pp. 26-28. Already in 1922 Liang had identified China's cities as infected by Western selfish individualism (*SC*, pp. 194-195) and had already heard about Chang Shih-chao's rural revival plan. He also generally agreed with Wang Hung-i's own adoption of Chang's program but it was not until the communists' success in the south that he "dared believe in it." *CW*, pp. 5-26.

55. In 1927 he personally witnessed the communists' success in organizing a militant Kwangtung peasantry. *CY*, pp. 176-177; *LL*, pp. 273-274.

56. *KLL*, chüan 4, "Hsin-jen lei kao."

57. Wang Shao-sheng, "Hsu Ming-hung" (Biography of Hsu Ming-hung) in "Feng-shun hsien chih kao" (Draft gazette for Feng-shun hsien); *CH*, pp. 1-3.

58. *SH*, pp. 17, 55-69, 71-85, 118; *CH*, p. 1; *CY*, pp. 3, 100; and "Chi-nien Ts'ai hsien-sheng."

59. *CW*, pp. 19-21.

60. Both friends and critics of Liang have interpreted his rural reconstruction program in this way. See Mao I-heng, "Liang Shu-ming yü pei Sung Lü hsueh" (Liang Shu-ming and the doctrines of the Lü family of the northern Sung) in *Tzu-yu wen-hsuan* (Selections from liberty magazine; Taipei, 1956); Kao Tsan-fei, "Ts'ung li-lun ho shih-chien shang lai k'an Liang Shu-ming ti 'hsiang-ts'un chien-she' ti fan-tung hsing" (Looking at the reactionary nature of Liang shu-ming's 'rural reconstruction' in theory and practice) in *Hsin hua yueh-k'an* (New China monthly; Peking) no. 5 (1955); Yuan Fang, "P'i-p'an Liang Shu-ming ti hsiang-ts'un chien-she yun-tung" (A criticism of Liang Shu-ming's rural reconstruction movement), pp. 64-65, and Tsou Lu-feng and others, "P'i-p'an Liang Shu-ming ti fan-tung chiao-yü ssu-hsiang" (A criticism of Liang Shu-ming's reactionary educational thought), pp. 166-173 in *Liang Shu-ming ssu-hsiang p'i-p'an*, vol. I (Peking, 1956).

61. See the biography of Lü Ta-fang in the *Sung shih* (History of the Sung dynasty) chüan 340; Chu Hsi, "Tseng-sun Lü-shih hsiang-yueh" (An emendation of the village compact of Mr. Lü) in Shen Chieh-fu, ed., *Yu shun lu*; Wang Yang-ming, "Nan-Kan hsiang-yueh" (The village compact for southern Kanchow) in

Wang Yang-ming ch'üan-chi (The collected works of Wang Yang-ming; Taipei, 1971), "tsou i" chüan 9, pp. 58-62. Lü, Chu and Wang's versions all differ to an extent, but the fundamental concept is the same.

62. *CY*, pp. 202-203; see also *LL*, pp. 187-215; Liang Shu-ming, *Hsiang-ts'un chien-she ta-i* (The gist of rural reconstruction; Tsou-p'ing, 1936), pp. 127-129; *CW*, pp. 53-63.

63. Liang first met Mao in 1918 in Peking at the home of Mao's father-in-law, Yang Ch'ang-chi, who was Liang's friend and colleague in the philosophy department of Peking University. Liang met Mao on a few occasions after this, including a week of all-night discussions in Mao's Yenan cave during January 1938. See Liang Shu-ming, "Fang-wen Yen-an" (Visit to Yenan), *Kuang-ming pao* (Light journal; Hong Kong, October 5, 1941).

64. *SY*, III, 62; Liang Shu-ming, "Hsiang-ts'un kung-tso chung i ko tai yen-chiu t̠ai shih-yen wen-t'i—ju-ho shih Chung-kuo jen yu t'uan-t'i tsu-chih" (A problem awaiting research and experimentation in rural work—how to make Chinese have group organizations), *Ta kung pao* (L'Impartial), Hsiang-ts'un chien-she supplement no. 66 (Jan. 1, 1936); Liang Shu-ming, "Liang nien lai wo yu le na-hsieh chüan-pien" (What changes I have had in the past two years), *Kuang-ming jih-pao* (Light daily; Peking, Oct. 5, 1951); Liang Shu-ming, "Wo-men liang ta nan-ch'u" (Our two great difficulties), appended to *LL*.

65. This Mencian attitude is especially clear when Liang attempts to define his program to political power holders. See for example, "Ju-ho k'ang-ti" (How to resist the enemy), *Szu-ch'uan chiao-yü* (Szechwan education) 1.7-8:61-66 (Aug. 1937).

66. See for example *SY*, III, 301-302; *CW*, pp. 312-351, 177, 299; *LL*, pp. 314-320; *SH*, pp. 252, 269-273; and Liang Shu-ming, "Wo-men liang ta nan-ch'u."

67. *LL*, p. 197.

68. *LL*, p. 17; Liang Shu-ming, *Hsiang-ts'un chien-she ta-i*, p. 56.

69. While not a nationalist in the usual sense, Liang was nevertheless a fervid anti-imperialist and even once publicly accused Hu Shih of being soft on imperialism. *CW*, pp. 333-342. But his anti-imperialism was a kind of Luddite vexation at the very existence of the modern West and the consequent need for China to modernize in self-defense.

70. Agrarianism in this sense, of course, is a modern phenomenon. Liang's rural reconstruction has the same relationship to the traditional Chinese emphasis on agriculture as the European Romantics' agrarianism had to the premodern agrarian tradition of Hesiod, Cato, and St. Augustine.

71. Liang Shu-ming, "Tung yu kuan-kan chi-lueh" (Impressions from a trip to Japan), *Hsiang-ts'un chien-she* 6:1 (Aug. 16, 1936).

72. P. L. Ford, ed., *Works of Thomas Jefferson* (New York: G. P. Putnam's sons, 1904), XI, 503-505. In a letter of 1816 to Benjamin Austin, Jefferson admits that the war of 1812 caused him to retreat from the stand he had taken against cities and manufacturing in his 1784 *Notes on Virginia*.

73. Liang did hedge a bit too. He allowed that cities could function as political and economic centers (*chūng-hsīn*) but that rural society must be the center of gravity (*chùng-hsīn*). *SY*, II, 14-16; *LL*, p. 376.

74. Liang Shu-ming, "Tui-yü tung-sheng shih-chien chih kan-yen" (Heartfelt words on the Manchurian incident), *Ta kung pao* (Tientsin, Oct. 7, 1931).

75. Liang Shu-ming, "Wo-men tsen-yang ying-fu tang-ch'ien ta-chan?" (How shall we deal with the great war facing us?), *Ta kung pao* (Shanghai, Aug. 12 and 13, 1937); and "Ju-ho k'ang-ti."

76. *CY,* pp. 87-90.

77. *The Analects of Confucius,* trans. Arthur Waley (London: George Allen & Unwin Ltd., 1938), 14.41:190.

10   Hsiung Shih-li's Quest for Authentic Existence
Tu Wei-ming

1. Joseph R. Levenson, *Confucian China and Its Modern Fate: A Trilogy* (Berkeley: University of California Press, 1968), pp. ix-x. It should be noted that the passage originally appeared in Levenson's *Liang Ch'i-ch'ao and the Mind of Modern China* (Cambridge, Mass.: Harvard University Press, 1953).

2. Ibid., p. xi.

3. Ibid., p. xvi.

4. Ibid.

5. Ibid., p. ix.

6. Wing-tsit Chan, *A Source Book in Chinese Philosophy* (Princeton: Princeton University Press, 1963), p. 743.

7. Levenson, *Confucian China,* p. xvi.

8. For example, see Sha Ming, *K'ung-chia tien chi ch'i yu-ling* (Confucius and sons and their ghosts; Hong Kong: Wen-chiao Press, 1970), pp. 53-68.

9. For an excellent study on this, see Herbert Fingarette, *Confucius: The Secular as Sacred* (New York: Harper Torchbooks, 1972), pp. 1-17.

10. It should be added that the struggle continued in a most vigorous way in the People's Republic. Levenson's notion of "museumified" Confucius can hardly account for intellectual attack against the so-called Confucian elements during the Cultural Revolution. See Levenson, *Confucian China,* III, 76-82. Cf. Sha Ming, pp. 54-55.

11. Benjamin I. Schwartz, "Some Notes on Conservatism in General and in China in Particular," p. 20.

12. Ibid.

13. Ibid. This refers to a point particularly emphasized by Levenson.

14. Levenson, *Confucian China,* p. x.

15. An indication of this uncommonly significant response was Hsiung's memorial service held by the Department of Philosophy at New Asia College and the Oriental Society of Humanism in Hong Kong on July 14, 1968. See a brief report on the occasion in *Young-sun,* no. 388 (Aug. 1968), pp. 2-3.

16. This information was given to me by some of Hsiung's closest associates, such as Professor T'ang Chün-i of New Asia College in Hong Kong. For an example of the kind of intellectual discourse T'ang had with Hsiung, see Hsiung Shih-li, *Shih-li yü-yao* (Essential Sayings [Dialogues] of Shih-li; Taipei: Kuang-wen Book Company, 1962; reprint), 2:11b-20. Hereafter referred to as *Yü-yao.*

17. One could argue that this was probably due to Hsiung's lack of socio-political influence. There is also reason to believe that his preferential treatment was actually sanctioned by the highest authority in Peking because of his reputation abroad.

18. Shen Yu-ting, Ho Ch'ang-ch'ün, and Jen Chi-yü were greeted either as his junior friends or as his students. For reference, see *Yü-yao*, 3:12b-13, 3:17a-b (Shen); 2:65-69b (Ho); and 2:70b-71b (Jen). Chang Tung-sun was one of his closest friends; for example, see *Yü-yao*, 1:47b-55 and 2:2-6. Ma I-fu later invited him to join Ma's Fu-hsing Academy as a professor, but their friendship failed shortly afterwards.

19. For a monographic account of Hu Shih, see Jerome B. Grieder, *Hu Shih and the Chinese Renaissance: Liberalism in the Chinese Revolution, 1917-1937* (Cambridge, Mass.: Harvard University Press, 1970).

20. I have in mind particularly Professors Mou Tsung-san and T'ang Chün-i at New Asia College, Professor Liu Shu-hsien at the University of Southern Illinois, and Professor Fu Wei-hsun at Temple University.

21. For an account of this kind of personal animosity, see Mou Tsung-san, "Wo yü Hsiung Shih-li hsien-sheng" (Master Hsiung Shih-li and I), in his *Sheng-ming te hsueh-wen* (The learning of life; Taipei: San-min Book Company, 1970), pp. 143-144. It should be noted that the account given is based on Professor Mou's personal reminiscences.

22. Hsiung fully acknowledged the strength of Ch'ing scholarship. What he really criticized was the mentality of scholasticism. See Hsiung Shih-li, *Tu-ching shih-yao* (Essential ways of reading the Classics; Taipei: Kuang-wen Book Company, 1960; reprint), 1:8-11. Hereafter referred to as *Tu-ching*.

23. *Yü-yao*, 1:46-47b.

24. Ibid., 1:46b.

25. Ibid., 1:47.

26. It should be noted that although the entire book was published more than two decades after the May Fourth movement, letters and discussions in the book actually represent his intellectual position since the 1920s. The term "Dialoque" here refers to his *Yü-yao*, for the sayings included are mainly in the format of questions and answers.

27. *Yü-yao*, 3:63.

28. Ibid., 3:63b.

29. In fact, since the Sung neo-Confucian revival, Confucian learning has frequently been referred to as *shen-hsin chih hsueh* (the learning of the body and mind) and *sheng-jen chih hsueh* (the learning of the sages). The designation *hsin-hsing chih hsueh* (the learning of mind and human nature) has also been widely used.

30. *Yü-yao*, 3:64.

31. In this connection, I have to take issue with Donald J. Munro. See his "Humanism in Modern China: Fung Yu-lan and Hsiung Shih-li," in *Nothing Concealed; Essays in Honor of Liu Yü-yun*, ed. Fred Wakeman, Jr. (Taipei: Chinese Materials and Research Aids Service Center, 1970), pp. 179-192.

32. *Yü-yao*, 3:64.

33. For a discussion on this issue, see Wei-ming Tu, "Subjectivity and

Ontological Reality—An Interpretation of Wang Yang-ming's Mode of Thinking," in *Philosophy East and West,* 23.1-2:187-205 (Jan., April 1973).

34. See *Chung-yung* (Doctrine of the mean), chap. 20 in Wing-tsit Chan, *A Source Book in Chinese Philosophy,* pp. 107-108. The quotation is a condensed version of the original statement.

35. This refers particularly to Mencius' distinction between those who labor with their minds and those who labor with their strength. The idea was originally intended to advocate a form of division of labor. See *Mencius,* 3A:4. For an English version of this passage, see *Mencius,* trans. D.C. Lau (Penguin Classics, 1970), pp. 100-104.

36. Hsiung maintained that "the greatest cultural issue today is to make analytical distinctions between China and the West." The ultimate purpose is to arrive at a mutual appreciation of cultural values. Hsiung seems to argue that without sophisticated understanding of the difference, the possibility for a new synthesis at a higher level is quite slim. See *Yü-yao,* 3:73.

37. See Hsu Fu-kan's introduction in Hsiung Shih-li, *Fo-chia ming-hsiang t'ung-shih* (Buddhist Concepts Explained; Taipei: Kuang-wen Book Company, 1961), Preface, p. 4.

38. The late Professor Yin Hai-kuang of Taiwan University told me that although he was basically in conflict with Hsiung on philosophical grounds, he was overpowered by Hsiung's personality and style of writing. Yin, as a disciple of Chin Yueh-lin, the famed scholar of British empiricism, was noted for his discipline in logic and clarity of expresson.

39. See *Tu-ching,* 2:31-32.

40. For example, see *Yü-yao,* 2:102 and 3:72b-73.

41. Peter Boodberg, "The Semasiology of Some Primary Confucian Concepts," *Philosophy East and West,* 2:327-330 (1953).

42. See Wing-tsit Chan, *A Source Book of Chinese Philosophy,* p. 791. For an ontological account on this issue, see Mou Tsung-san, *Tsai-hsing yü hsuan-li* (Native endowments and metaphysical principles; Hong Kong: Young-sun Press, 1963), pp. 128-139.

43. Levenson, *Confucian China,* I, 132-133.

44. Ibid., p. 110.

45. Ibid.

46. For a brief account of the Fa-hsiang (or Wei-shih) school, see Kenneth K. S. Chen, *Buddhism in China* (Princeton: Princeton University Press, 1964), pp. 320-325. Also see Wing-tsit Chan, *Religious Trends in Modern China* (New York: Columbia University Press, 1953), pp. 105-106. A succinct account of Hsiung's association with the tradition is found in *Religious Trends,* pp. 126-135.

47. See Kenneth Chen, pp. 321-322.

48. See Wing-tsit Chan, *Religious Trends,* p. 107. It is also cited in Kenneth Chen, p. 323.

49. O. Briere, *Fifty Years of Chinese Philosophy,* trans. Laurence G. Thompson (New York: Frederick A. Praeger, Inc., 1965), p. 42.

50. The text had been lost in China for centuries; it was presented to Yang Wen-hui by the renowned Japanese Buddhist scholar Bunyu Nanjio in 1880. Its subsequent publication in China marked the beginning of Buddhist revival in modern China. See Wing-tsit Chan, *Religious Trends,* pp. 109-110.

51. Ch'en Po-sha (Hsien-chang, 1428-1500), a leading neo-Confucian thinker in the Ming, has been widely acclaimed as the precursor of Wang Yang-ming's dynamic idealism.

52. *Ta-i* in this connection refers to the idea of "great transformation" in the *Book of Changes.*

53. Hsiung Shih-li, *Hsin wei-shih lun* (New exposition on the conscious-ness-only doctrine; Taipei: Kuang-wen Book Company, 1962; reprint), I, 82b-83. Cf. Wing-tsit Chan, *Religious Trends,* pp. 126-127.

54. Hsiung Shih-li, *Hsin-lun,* Preface, p. 1.

55. Ibid.

56. Frederick W. Mote, *Intellectual Foundations of China* (New York: Alfred A. Knopf, 1971), p. 15. For a general interpretation of the *Book of Changes,* see Richard Wilhelm, trans., *The I Ching,* rendered into English by Cary F. Baynes (Princeton: Princeton University Press, 1967), pp. xlvii-lxii.

57. See Jung's foreword to *The I Ching,* in Wilhelm, pp. xxi-xxxix. Also See C. G. Jung, *Psychology and Religion: West and East (Collected Works,* vol. XI), trans. R. F. C. Hull (New York: Pantheon Books, Bollingen Series, 1958), pp. 82 and 96.

58. See *Hsin-lun,* I, 28b-29b. Quotation from Wing-tsit Chan, *Religious Trends,* p. 34.

59. For a brief account of Chang Tsai's philosophy, see T'ang Chün-i, "Chang Tsai's Theory of Mind and Its Metaphysical Basis," *Philosophy East and West,* 7.2:113-136 (July 1956). See also Wing-tsit Chan, *A Source Book of Chinese Philosophy,* pp. 495-517.

60. Wing-tsit Chan, *Source Book,* p. 503.

61. Wang Fu-chih's influence on Hsiung is omitted in the present study. But in a more comprehensive analysis of the intellectual formation of Hsiung's thought, it is imperative that Wang's philosophical reflections on reality be noted as a background. For a controversial study on Wang's approach to *t'i-yung,* see Chu Po-k'un, "Wang Fu-chih *lun pen-t'i ho hsien-hsiang*" (Want Fu-chih on ori-ginal substance and phenomenal appearance) in *Chung-kuo che-hsueh shih lun-wen chi* (Collected essays on the history of Chinese philosophy; Peking: Chung-hua Book Company, 1965), pp. 66-99.

62. See *Hsin-lun,* I, 57b-66. For the quotation, see Clarence Burton Day, *The Philosophers of China* (New York: The Citadel Press, 1962), p. 328.

63. Day, *Philosophers of China,* p. 328.

64. See *Yü-yao,* 2:85.

65. For a serious critique of Hsiung's new approach from a Buddhist point of view, see Yin-shun, *P'ing Hsiung Shih-li ti hsin wei-shih lun* (A review of Hsiung Shih-li's new exposition of the consciousness-only doctrine; Hong Kong: Cheng-wen Press, 1950).

66. It should be noted that Hsiung defines the original mind as an abso-lutely nondependent wholeness. First, it is called *heart* because it is the real sub-stance of myriad things but is not itself a thing. Second, it is called (genuine) *inten-tion* for it develops according to the unceasing creativity of its own nature. Third, it is called (pure) *consciousness* for it comprehends as it creates. And it is in the unity of heart, intention, and consciousness where the true meaning of the original mind lies. See *Hsin-lun,* IIIA, 100b-101b.

67. *Mencius,* 3A:4.

68. Ibid.

69. *Hsin-lun,* IIIA, 79b-80.

70. Day, *Philosophers of China,* pp. 329-330.

71. O. Briere, *Fifty Years of Chinese Philosophy,* p. 42.

72. Professor Hamilton's piece is otherwise a pertinent summary of Hsiung's philosophical orientation.

73. *Hsin-lun,* IIIB, 66a-b. See Liu Shu-hsien, "Hsiung Shih-li's Theory of Causation," *Philosophy East and West,* 19.4:407, n. 18 (Oct. 1969).

74. *Hsin-lun,* IIIB, 65-66. Reference is also made to John Dewey and Bertrand Russell. Similarly, his critique of Social Darwinism is made from an ontological perspective, see *Hsin-lun,* IIB, 10.

75. It should be noted here that although Hsiung had high respect for T'an Ssu-t'ung, he repeatedly criticized K'ang Yu-wei for his uncritical adaptation of Western ideas as a way of making Confucianism relevant to the modern times.

76. Joseph R. Levenson, "The Genesis of *Confucian China and Its Modern Fate,*" in Perry L. Curtis, Jr., ed., *The Historian's Workshop* (New York: Basic Books, 1972), p. 285.

77. Ibid.

78. Ibid.

79. Cited by Levenson, ibid.

11   The New Confucianism and the Intellectual Crisis of Contemporary China
Hao Chang

1. I am indebted to Professor Shu-hsien Liu who read the last version of this essay and gave me helpful advice and corrections. Mou Tsung-san and others, "Wei Chung-kuo wen hua ching-kao shih-chieh jen-shih hsuan-yen" (A manifesto to the world on Chinese culture), to be abbreviated as "Hsuan-yen" hereafter, in *Min-chu p'ing-lun* (Democratic Tribune) 9:1 (1958).

2. Mou Tsung-san, *Sheng-ming ti hsueh-wen* (An existential learning; Taipei, 1970), pp. 132-156; T'ang Chün-i, *Chung-kuo wen-hua chih ching-shen chia-chih* (The spiritual value of Chinese civilization; Taipei, 1965), to be abbreviated as *Chia-chih* hereafter, pp. 2-3; see also Hsu Fu-kuan, "Editor's preface," in Hsiung Shih-li, *Fu-chia ming-hsiang t'ung-shih* (A general annotation of Buddhist concepts; Taichung, 1961), pp. 3-4.

3. Ho Lin, *Tang-tai Chung-kuo che-hsueh* (Contemporary Chinese philosophies; Nanking, 1947), pp. 9-16.

4. Wing-tsit Chan, *Religious Trends in Modern China* (New York: Columbia University Press, 1953), pp. 5-8.

5. James R. Pusey, "K'ang Yu-wei and Pao-chiao: Confucian Reform and Reformation," in *Papers on China* 20:144-176 (1966).

6. Joseph R. Levenson, *Confucian China and Its Modern Fate* (Berkeley: University of California Press, 1958), pp. xiii-xix.

7. Ibid. For some cultural historians, this emotional complex seems to

represent the core of the Chinese crisis of cultural identity. But, important as this complex is, the Chinese need for cultural identity also involves some significant nonemotional components such as the intellectual-evaluative need to define the meaning of one's cultural tradition and to appraise it with reference to other cultures in the world. To see the Chinese quest for cultural identity as no more than an emotional complex smacks of a psychological reductionism which distorts a major phase of China's intellectual crisis.

8. "Hsuan-yen," pp. 5-6, 9-11, 11-14, 16-20; also see *Chia-chih,* pp. 1-16, 345-409.

9. To be sure, the word "crisis" is not used here to connote impending catastrophe. Rather it is used to designate a turning point, a crucial period, when development moves in new directions involving changes of unprecedented scope and depth at a greatly accelerated tempo. For reasons why the intellectual crisis began with the closing years of the 1890s, see Hao Chang, *Liang Ch'i-ch'ao and Intellectual Transition in China, 1890-1907* (Cambridge, Mass.: Harvard University Press, 1971).

10. Ibid.

11. Chow Tse-tsung, *The May Fourth Movement: Intellectual Revolution in Modern China* (Cambridge, Mass.: Harvard University Press, 1960), p. 59.

12. Paul Tillich, *The Courage To Be* (New Haven: Yale University Press, 1965), pp. 32-57.

13. Ho Lin, pp. 9, 13.

14. For understanding the concept of scientism, see Charlotte Furth, *Ting Wen-chiang: Science and China's New Culture* (Cambridge, Mass.: Harvard University Press, 1970), pp. 14-15; see also D. W. Y. Kwok, *Scientism in Chinese Thought, 1900-1950* (New Haven: Yale University Press, 1965), pp. 3-30.

15. D. W. Y. Kwok, pp. 135-160.

16. Liang Shu-ming, *Tung-Hsi wen-hua chi ch'i che-hsueh* (Eastern and Western civilizations and their philosophies; Shanghai, 1922), pp. 25-34, 114-160. Chang Chün-mai, "Wo chih che-hsueh ssu-hsiang" (My philosophical thinking), in *Min-chu she-hui* (Democratic society) 6.1:1-4 (Feb. 1970).

17. Liang Shu-ming, pp. 121-130, 149-150.

18. Chang Chün-mai, "Wo chih che-hsueh ssu-hsiang," pp. 2-3.

19. Wei-ming Tu, "Hsiung Shih-li's Quest for Authentic Existence," in the present volume.

20. Wing-tsit Chan, *Religious Trends,* pp. 33-43; see also Hsiung Shih-li, *Shih-li yü-yao* (The essential sayings of Shih-li; Taipei, 1962), I, 48b-55, II, 11b-24.

21. Hu Shih, "Ch'ing-tai hsueh-che ti chih-hsueh fang-fa," (The methodology of the Ch'ing scholars); and "Lun kuo-ku hsueh" (On the study of national heritage), in *Hu Shih wen-ts'un* (A collection of essays by Hu Shih; Taipei, 1953), chi 1, chüan 2, pp. 383-412, 440-442; "Kuo hsueh chi-k'an fa-k'an hsuan-yen" (A preface to the opening issue of the journal of the study of Chinese heritage), in *Hu Shih wen-ts'un,* chi 2, chüan 1, pp. 1-18.

22. Ch'ien Mu, *Chung-kuo chin san-pai-nien hsueh-shu shih* (An intellectual history of China during the past three hundred years; Shanghai, 1937), pp.

306-379, 453-522, 596-632. I use the concept "subjective" primarily in the Kierke-
gaardian sense.

23. Laurence A. Schneider, *Ku Chieh-kang and China's New History*
(Berkeley: University of California Press, 1971), pp. 53-84; see also D. W. Y. Kwok,
pp. 83-131.

24. Hsiung Shih-li, *Shih-li yü-yao* II, 2b-6, 11b-20.

25. Liang Shu-ming, pp. 68-80; Chang Chün-mai, pp. 1-4.

26. "Hsuan-yen," pp. 4-5. The four signers of the manifesto among themselves do not necessarily understand the work *chih-chueh* (intuition) in the same
way, although they all place great emphasis on the concept. In fact Carson Chang,
being heavily influenced by Bergsonian intuitionism, tended to use the term with a
cognitive thrust. Meanwhile the other three, especially Mou Tsung-san and T'ang
Chün-i, are inclined to use intuitionism primarily in a moral-existential sense. This
is also the sense in which the concept is used in the manifesto.

27. Ibid., pp. 6-7.

28. Ibid., p. 6.

29. Ibid., pp. 6-7.

30. Ibid., pp. 8-9; see also Mou Tsung-san, *Chung-kuo che-hsueh ti t'e-
chih* (The distinguishing characteristics of Chinese philosophy; Hong Kong, 1963;
hereafter abbreviated as *T'e-chih*), pp. 5-7, 79-88; *Hsin-t'i yü hsing-t'i* (The substance of mind and the substance of nature; Taipei, 1968), pp. 4-6. I borrow the
term "numinous" from Rudolph Otto's writings but I want to avoid some of the
connotations in his usage of the term, which stem from his Christian theological
background. In my usage the "numinous" simply refers to the ineffable, ultimate
power in the beyond.

31. "Hsuan-yen," p. 8.

32. Ibid., pp. 8-9; see also Mou Tsung-san, *Hsin-t'i yü hsing-t'i*, p. 40; *T'e-
chih*, p. 60.

33. *T'e-chih*, p. 70.

34. Ibid., pp. 52-78.

35. "Hsuan-yen," p. 7; see also *T'e-chih*, pp. 17-39.

36. T'ang Chün-i, *Chia-chih*, pp. 326-344; *T'e-chih*, pp. 89-101.

37. *T'e-chih*, pp. 68-78.

38. *T'e-chih*, pp. 89-101; *Chia-chih*, pp. 326-344.

39. Mou Tsung-san, *Hsin-t'i yü hsing-t'i*, p. 6.

40. Ibid.

41. *T'e chih*, pp. 25-31, 93-95.

42. Ibid., pp. 96-98.

43. Ibid., pp. 68-78, 96-97.

44. *Chia-chih*, pp. 405-406; Mou Tsung-san, *Hsin-t'i yü hsing-t'i*, pp. 4-6.

45. *Chia-chih*, pp. 130-178, 281-309; see also Mou Tsung-san, *Tao-te ti
li-hsiang chu-i* (Moral idealism; Taipei, 1959), pp. 39-67; *T'e-chih*, pp. 68-78.

46. *Chia-chih*, pp. 68-78.

47. Hsu Fu-kuan, *Chung-kuo jen-hsing lun-shih* (A history of Chinese
thought on human nature; Taichung, 1963), pp. 96-97.

48. Mou Tsung-san, *Cheng-tao yü chih-tao* (The political way and the
administrative way; Taipei, 1960), pp. 1-25; see also his *Li-shih che-hseuh* (Philos-

ophy of history; Hong Kong, 1962), pp. 183-184.

49. Mou Tsung-san, *Li-shih che hsueh,* pp. 164-193.

50. Ibid.

51. "Hsuan-yen," pp. 11-13; Mou Tsung-san, *Li-shih che-hsueh,* pp. 168-172.

52. Mou Tsung-san, *Li-shih che hsueh,* pp. 172-174, 181-189; *Cheng-tao yü chih-tao,* pp. 1-43; "Hsuan-yen," pp. 13-14.

53. *Li-shih che-hsueh,* appendix II, pp. 24-25.

54. "Hsuan-yen," pp. 13-14.

55. Ibid.; *Cheng-tao yü chih-tao,* pp. 163-224.

56. "Hsuan-yen," pp. 11-13; *Li-shih che-hsueh,* pp. 164-181.

57. "Hsuan-yen," pp. 11-13; *Li-shih che-hsueh,* pp. 181-230; *Cheng-tao yü chih-tao,* pp. 163-224.

58. *Tao-te ti li-hsiang chu-i,* pp. 56-58.

59. Ibid., pp. 56-57; *Li-shih che-hsueh,* pp. 30-34, pp. 149-230; *Cheng-tao yü chih-tao,* pp. 225-269; *T'e chih,* p. 11.

60. "Hsuan-yen," pp. 17-18.

61. T'ang Chün-i, *Jen-sheng chih t'i-yen hsu-pien* (A sequel to philosophy of life; Hong Kong, 1961), pp. 41-43.

62. Ibid., pp. 41-63.

63. Hsu Fu-kuan, pp. 20-24; see also Mou Tsung-san, *Chung-kuo che-hsueh ti t'e-chih,* pp. 11-17.

64. T'ang Chün-i, *Jen-sheng chih t'i-yen hsu-pien,* pp. 87-102.

65. "Hsuan-yen," pp. 7-8.

66. Ibid., p. 9; *T'e-chih,* pp. 5-6, 9-13, 40-51.

67. *T'e-chih,* pp. 9-13, 93-101.

68. "Hsuan-yen," pp. 4-6.

69. Mou Tsung-san, *Sheng-ming ti hsueh-wen,* pp. 21-39; *Hsin-t'i yü hsing-t'i,* pp. 4-11.

12   T'ao Hsi-sheng: The Social Limits of Change
Arif Dirlik

1. For T'ao's involvement in the writing of *China's Destiny,* see Philip Jaffe, "The Secret of China's Destiny," in Chiang Kai-shek, *China's Destiny and Chinese Economic Theory* (New York: Roy, 1947), p. 21. Jaffe seems to agree with those who contended that the book was compiled mainly by T'ao himself and checked by Chiang. Jaffe, however, is quite wrong on a number of facts concerning T'ao. T'ao was never educated in Japan, as Jaffe claims, and it is quite misleading to describe him as a man "hostile to Western political and economic concepts." (Ibid.) The concepts that T'ao employed in his political and economic analyses were wholly of Western origin. Furthermore, T'ao's explanations of China's decline and his ideas on traditional Chinese political and economic thought were very different from those in Chiang's books, which were more reminiscent of the ideas of Kuomintang thinkers such as Hu Han-min. Neither is it possible to argue that T'ao gave up his own ideas after 1937. His last major work on Chinese history, *Chung-kuo she hui shih* (History of Chinese society; Chungking, 1944), was still very much

in keeping with his Marxist analyses. Under such circumstances, I see little reason to challenge T'ao's own account of his editorial function in the composition of the book. He claims that the task was at first to be undertaken by Ch'en Pu-lei. When Ch'en became ill, the task devolved on T'ao, who was at the time Ch'en's secretary. See T'ao Hsi-sheng, *Ch'ao-liu yü tien-ti* (The tide and the drop; hereafter CLTT; Taipei, 1964), p. 204.

2. Interview, Taipei, 1969.

3. For a detailed discussion of the social history controversy, see Arif Dirlik, "Mirror to Revolution: Early Marxist Images of Chinese History," *Journal of Asian Studies,* 33.2:193-223 (Feb. 1974).

4. The left-Kuomintang position was that the revolution was primarily political in nature. It was to eliminate warlords and bureaucrats and achieve independence. The communists saw class struggle as a prerequisite to the achievement of these aims. The Stalinists in the CCP, arguing that China was a feudal society, included landlords among their targets. The Trotskyites, on the other hand, argued that China was already a capitalist society and advocated a struggle of the proletariat and the peasantry against the bourgeoisie, the landlords, and the imperialists.

5. Before 1927, T'ao was first a teacher and then an editor at the Commercial Press. His only involvement with politics before 1927 was a brief association with Ho Kung-kan's Tu-li ch'ing-nien tang (Independent Youth party). For a while, he was editor of one of the journals of that party, *Tu-li p'ing-lun* (The independent review; to be distinguished from the journal published by Hu Shih later).

6. CLTT, pp. 87-103. The Special Committee was established in Nanking in September 1927 upon the initiative of warlords who had joined the party during the Northern Expedition (Li Tsung-jen and Pai Ch'ung-hsi were leading spirits) and members of the Western Hills group within the KMT. Its intention was to supplant the second Central Executive Committee dominated by radicals.

7. Ibid., pp. 110-112.

8. *Hsin sheng-ming* (The New Life monthly) was the most prominent of a number of journals published by KMT partisans at this time. Its political orientation, as indicated by its editors, was somewhat more ambivalent than other journals that were more unequivocally for Wang Ching-wei and opposed to the post-1927 leadership. At first, Ch'en Pu-lei, Tai Chi-t'ao, Ch'en Kuo-fu, and Chou Fu-hai all cooperated in the undertaking. See Ch'en Pu-lei, *Ch'en Pu-lei hui-i lu* (Memoirs of Ch'en Pu-lei; Taipei, 1957), p. 74.

9. CLTT, p. 55.

10. E. Adamson Hoebel in *International Encyclopedia of the Social Sciences* (New York: Macmillan and Free Press, 1968), article on Henry Maine, IX, 530-533.

11. H. S. Maine, *Ancient Law* (Boston: Beacon Press, 1963), p. 23.

12. Ibid., p. 22.

13. There is little doubt that T'ao accepted this scheme. See T'ao Hui-tseng (T'ao Hsi-sheng), *Ch'in-shu fa ta-kang* (An outline of family law; Shanghai, 1927), especially the introduction of Part II, "Basis of Law." This was repeated unequivocally in a work published nearly ten years later, *Min-fa ch'in-shu* (Kinship in civil law; Shanghai, 1936).

14. *Ch'in-shu fa ta-kang,* p. 142.

15. R. Gettell, *History of Political Thought* (New York: The Century Co., 1924), p. 352.

16. Maine had undertaken his study of ancient law to demonstrate "its connection with the early history of society and its relation to modern ideas." T'ao wanted to do the same for China. His concern with the present, if anything, was more urgent because it was a period of reform, and the reformers had a need to understand what they were trying to reform. *Ch'in-shu fa ta-kang,* p. 7. T'ao applied the idea of the social determination of law even to the revolutionary situation in China and suggested that at a time when social contradictions abound, legislation must reflect such contradictions. See "Li-fa cheng-ts'e yü li-fa chi-shu" (Legislative policy and legislative technique), in *Hsin sheng-ming* (hereafter HSM) 1.10:1-2 (Oct. 1928).

17. *Ch'in-shu fa ta-kang,* preface to Part III.

18. CLTT, p. 111.

19. In his memoirs, T'ao says that he first analyzed Chinese society in terms of the two classes, *shih-tai-fu* and peasantry, in an article published in the *Tu-li p'ing-lun* in 1926. I have not been able to locate this article. See CLTT, p. 82, for his brief description.

20. F. Oppenheimer, *The State: Its History and Development Viewed Sociologically* (Indianapolis, 1914), p. 25.

21. T'ao Hsi-sheng, ed., *Chung-kuo she-hui chih hui-ku yü chan-wang* (Chinese society: retrospect and prospect; hereafter CKSHCHKYCW; Shanghai, 1930), pp. 1-2.

22. Wang I-ch'ang, "Chung-kuo she-hui shih lun shih" (History of the discussion of Chinese social history), *Tu-shu tsa-chih* (Research magazine) 2.2-3:22-23 (Feb.-March 1932). T'ao Hsi-sheng's ideas on commercial capital can be traced to chapter 20 of *Capital,* vol. 3, "Historical Facts about Merchant's Capital." Commercial capital, Marx suggested, was not peculiar to any type of society but could exist in all types. Its power, when it existed independently of production, was primarily disintegrative; that is, it could lead to the disintegration of the existing mode of production without necessarily creating a new one. T'ao translated this chapter in HSM, 3.4 (April 1939), introducing it as the theory of one of the "major economists" of the nineteenth century.

23. T'ao, "Chung-kuo she-hui tao-ti shih-shen-mo she-hui?" (What kind of society is Chinese society?") in *Chung-kuo she-hui chih shih ti fen-hsi* (Analysis of Chinese social history) (hereafter CKSHCSTFH; Shanghai, 1929), p. 32.

24. Yu Chih (Ku Meng-yü), "Nung-min yü t'u-ti wen-t'i" (Peasantry and the land question), in T'ao, CKSHCHKYCW, pp. 261-262.

25. T'ao, CKSHCSTFH, p. 26. T'ao's original statement was: "The feudal system has disappeared, feudal forces remain."

26. See *Chung-kuo she-hui yü Chung-kuo ko-ming* (Chinese society and the Chinese revolution; hereafter CKSHYCKKM; Shanghai, 1929), pp. 1-2 and 191. For further descriptions of these characteristics of commerce see Fang Yueh (T'ao Hsi-sheng), "Chung-kuo feng-chien chih-tu chih hsiao-mieh" (The demise of the Chinese feudal system), HSM, 2.3, 4, 5 (March-May 1929), Part II, and T'ao, "T'ung-i yü sheng-ch'an" (Unity and production), HSM, 3.4 (April 1930).

27. T'ao, "Kuan-liao chi chün-tui chih feng-chien ti hsing-t'ai" (The feudal nature of the bureaucracy and the military), in CKSHCSTFH, p. 131.

28. T'ao, "Kuan-liao ti fa-sheng fa-chan chi ch'i tsai cheng-chih shang ti ti-wei" (The origins and development of the bureaucracy and its political role), CKSHCSTFH, p.93.

29. "Chung-kuo she-hui tao-ti shih shen-mo she-hui?" CKSHCSTFH, p. 38.

30. T'ao, "Chung-kuo she-hui shih ti i-ko k'ao-ch'a" (An examination of Chinese social history), CKSHCSTFH, p. 260.

31. "Kuan-liao chi chün-tui chih feng-chien ti hsing-t'ai," CKSHCSTFH, p. 136.

32. T'ao was criticized severely for this view by his communist opponents. See Li Chi, "Tui-yü Chung-kuo she-hui shih lun-chan ti kung-hsien yü p'i-p'ing" (Contributions and critique on the controversy on Chinese social history), Part III, Tu-shu tsa-chih, 3.3-4:1-86 (April 1933), 33.

33. T'ao, "Chung-kuo shang-jen tzu-pen chi ti-chu yu nung-min," HSM, 3.2 (February 1930), 7.

34. Ibid., p. 12.

35. "Kuan-liao ti fa-sheng, fa-chen chi ch'i tsai cheng-shih shang ti ti-wei," in CKSHCSTFH, p. 99.

36. "Chung-kuo she-hui tao-ti shih shen-mo she-hui?" in CKSHCSTFH, p. 42.

37. "Kuan-liao chi chün-tui chih feng-chien ti hsing-t'ai," CKSHCSTFH, p. 143.

38. See the series of articles published in HSM on this issue: T'ao, "T'ung-i yü sheng-ch'an" (Unity and production), 3.4 (April 1930); T'ao, "Ch'ang ch'i ho-p'ing chih cheng-tuan" (Prognosis of a long period of peace), 3.11 (Nov. 1930); Sa Meng-wu, "Kuo-min ko-ming yü she-hui ko-ming" (National revolution and social revolution), 1.8 (Aug. 1928); Sa, "Ti-i t'ung ti-erh sheng-ch'an" (First unity then production), 3.5 (May 1930); Sa, "Ko-ming yü t'ung-i" (Revolution and unity), 3.6 (June 1930); Chung Wen, "Yu Chung-kuo hsien chieh-tuan shuo-ming min-sheng chu-i ti ching-chi cheng-ts'e" (An exposition of the economic policy of people's livelihood from the present stage of Chinese society), 2.7 (July 1929).

39. In theory, T'ao regarded unity and production as subject to a mutual cause-effect relationship. See "T'ung-i yü sheng-ch'an," p. 13. But there is no doubt that in the practice of revolution unity had to precede the growth of productive forces. See "Kuo-min-tang ti ko-ming fang-lüeh" (The revolutionary strategy of the Kuomintang), HSM, 1.8:5-11 (Aug. 1928).

40. Ibid.

41. T'ao, "T'ung-i yü sheng-ch'an," p. 13. For the importance of making cities dominant over rural areas, see "Ch'ang ch'i ho-p'ing chih cheng-tuan."

42. "Kuo-min-tang ti ko-ming fang-lüeh."

43. "Chung-kuo chih shang-jen tzu-pen chi ti-chu yü nung-min," p. 16.

44. Fang Yüeh (T'ao Hsi-sheng), "San-min chu-i chih she-hui shih ti i-i" (The sociohistorical significance of the three principles of the people), HSM, 2.6:10-12 (June 1929). T'ao says here that he first realized this problem of rural China when he was a cadre in Wuhan. The same idea is repeated in his memoirs.

See CLTT, p. 94. The idea of "consumer socialism," which he used to describe the peasant rebellions of the past as well as the communists of the present, was probably derived from K. Kautsky's *Foundations of Christianity,* trans. H. F. Mins (New York: S. A. Russell Publ., 1953). He says in his memoirs that this book was more important for his thinking than the works of Marx and Lenin, a statement which I am inclined to doubt in spite of the importance of this distinction between socialism and "consumer socialism."

45. Chou Fu-hai, *San-min chu-i chih li-lun ti t'i-hsi* (The Theoretical System of the Three Peoples Principles) (Shanghai, 1928), pp. 233-234.

46. Ibid., pp. 231-232. The quote from p. 232.

47. CLTT, p. 122.

48. T'ao, "Chung-kuo ku-yu ti she-hui ssu-hsiang" (Native social thought in China), *Wen-hua chien-she yueh-k'an* (Cultural reconstruction monthly) 1.1:33 (Dec. 1934).

49. Kuo Chan-po, *Chin wu-shih nien Chung-kuo ssu-hsiang shih* (History of Chinese thought of the past fifty years; Hong Kong, 1965), p. 338.

50. Ibid., pp. 339-343.

51. Ibid., pp. 343-344.

52. T'ao, "Wei-shen-mo fou-jen hsien-tai ti Chung-kuo" (Why reject present day China?" in *Wen-hua chien-she yueh-k'an,* 1.7:101-103 (April 1935).

53. T'ao, Editorial, *Shih huo pan-yueh-k'an* (Food and commodities semimonthly), 1.1:29-30 (Dec. 1, 1934).

54. T'ao, "She-hui k'o-hsueh chiang-tso (Colloquium on social science), HSM, 2.5:1 (May 1929).

55. T'ao, "Ssu-hsiang chieh ti i-ko jo-tien" (A weakness of the intellectual world), *Tu-li p'ing-lun* (Independent critic) no. 154 (June 9, 1935), pp. 10-14. Here T'ao argued against Hu Shih's demands for political freedom on the grounds that political freedom would interfere with economic development.

56. Kuo Chan-po, p. 345.

57. From Fung Yu-lan's lecture at the National Normal University in Peking in 1935. Quoted in Kuo Chan-po, pp. 221-224. The "explainers of antiquity" included participants in the social history controversy who were dissatisfied with Ku Chieh-kang's "destructive" work in Chinese history. See T'ao, "I-ku yü shih-ku," *Shih huo pan-yueh-k'an,* 3.1:1 (Dec. 1, 1935), where he complains about the excesses of both approaches. He repeated this in our personal interview.

58. The participants in the social history controversy regarded the controversy on the philosophy of life as the most important debate to precede their own and saw it as having put an end to "metaphysics" in Chinese thought. But it is also noteworthy that they thought of the "victors" in that controversy as already having had their day. Since then, formal logic, the "insufficient" weapon of the victors, had yielded to dialectical materialism. See Wang Li-hsi, "Chung-kuo she-hui shih lun-chan hsu-mu" (Introduction to the controversy on Chinese social history), *Tu-shu tsa-chih* 1.4-5 (Aug. 1931).

59. The working definition of historicism adopted here is the broad one suggested by M. Mandelbaum: "Historicism is the belief that an adequate understanding of the nature of any phenomenon and an adequate assessment of its value are to be gained through considering it in terms of the place which it occupied and

the role which is played within a process of development." See *History, Man and Reason* (Baltimore: Johns Hopkins University Press, 1971), p. 42.

60. Wang Li-hsi, pp. 9-10.

61. For a discussion of this ambiguity, see Karl Mannheim, *Essays on Sociology and Social Psychology* (New York: Oxford University Press, 1953), p. 93, and Mandelbaum, pp. 70-76.

13   Chou Tso-jen: A Scholar Who Withdrew
David E. Pollard

1. Ernst Wolff ably presents the facts of Chou's life and works in his book, *Chou Tso-jen* (New York: Twayne Publishers, Inc., 1971).

2. Some facts are clearly relevant to Chou's collaboration, such as his wife being Japanese, but what else went into his decision one has no means of knowing.

3. Wang Yao, *Chung-kuo hsin wen-hsueh shih kao* (A draft history of new Chinese literature; Shanghai, 1953), pp. 130-131.

4. It first appeared in *Wen-hsueh* (Literature), III, 1, and was reprinted in Mao Tun, ed., *Tso-chia lun* (On authors; Shanghai, 1936).

5. "Wu-shih tzu-shou shih" (Fiftieth birthday poem), *Jen-chien shih* (This human world), no. 1 (April 5, 1934).

6. *Chih-t'ang hui-hsiang lu* (Memoirs of Chih-t'ang; Hong Kong, 1970), p. 571.

7. Ibid., p. 461.

8. "I sui huo-sheng chih yü" (Addendum to "Street cries throughout the year"), *Yeh tu ch'ao* (Notes from night reading; Shanghai, 1934).

9. Quoted in Ts'ao Chü-jen, *Lu Hsun p'ing-chuan* (Critical biography of Lu Hsun; Hong Kong, 1961), p. 69.

10. Preface to *Tse-hsieh chi* (Water plantains; Shanghai, 1927).

11. "Liang-ke kuei" (Two demons), *Yü ssu* (Tattler), 91 (Aug. 9, 1926).

12. "Liang-ke kuei ti wen-chang" (Essays of two demons; 1944), in *Kuo-ch'ü ti kung-tso* (Past work), pp. 76-77.

13. Printed in *Yung-jih chi* (Endless days; Shanghai, 1929).

14. "Wu-p'eng ch'uan" (Black awninged boats), *Tse-hsieh chi*, p. 64.

15. "He ch'a" (Drinking tea), *Yü-t'ien ti shu* (Rainy day book; Shanghai, 1927), p. 73.

16. "Pei-p'ing ti ch'a-shih" (Teacakes of Peking), *Chou Tso-jen san-wen ch'ao* (Anthology of Chou Tso-jen's prose works; Shanghai, 1932).

17. "Pei-p'ing ti hao-huai" (The good and bad sides of Peking), *Kua tou chi* (Melons and beans; Shanghai, 1934), pp. 113-114.

18. *Chou Tso-jen tai-piao tso* (Representative works of Chou Tso-jen; Shanghai, 1937), p. 142.

19. "Tsai lun ch'ih ch'a" (Tea drinking again), *Yeh tu ch'ao* p. 250.

20. His program was set out in most detail in his essay "Jen ti wen-hsueh" (A literature of human beings) in 1918; see my article "Chou Tso-jen and Cultivating One's Garden," in *Asia Major* 11.2 (1965), esp. pp. 186-189. In this essay he dismissed "bandit" literature like *Shui-hu chuan* and "superstitious" literature like *Hsi-yu chi,* but later on more than one occasion confessed his liking for these two novels.

21. "Pei-p'ing ti hao-huai," *Kua tou chi,* pp. 111-112.

22. John Service, "Edgar Snow: Some Personal Reminiscences," *China Quarterly* 50:211-212 (April-June 1972).

23. "Tai k'uai-yu" (In place of an express letter), *T'an hu chi* (Talking of tigers; Shanghai, 1928), p. 175.

24. "Tzu-pen-chu-i ti chin ch'ang" (Suppression of prostitution under capitalism), *T'an hu chi.*

25. "Ou-chou cheng-tun feng-hua" (Moral reform in Europe), *Yung-jih chi.*

26. "Ch'uan ch'ün yü pu ch'uan ch'ün" (Wearing skirts and not wearing skirts), *Yü ssu* 142 (July 30, 1927).

27. "Wai-hang ti an-yü (Comments of an outsider), *T'an hu chi,* p. 263.

28. Ibid., p. 265.

29. Chou visited "new villages" in 1919. They were established by Mushakoji Saneatsu and were chiefly inspired by Tolstoy's example. Chou wrote about them in three articles in *I-shu yü sheng-huo* (Art and life; Shanghai, 1926), pp. 401-468. For his later reflections on the semireligious humanism of the movement see *Chih-t'ang hui-hsiang lu,* pp. 390-393.

30. "Nü-tzu Hsueh-yüan ti huo" (Fire at the Women's College), *Yü ssu* 108 (Dec. 4, 1926).

31. "Shih-tzu chieh-t'ou ti t'a" (The tower at the crossroads; 1925), *Yü-t'ien ti shu,* p. 103.

32. "Fu-nü wen-t'i yü tung-fang wen-ming teng," *Yung-jih chi,* p. 222.

33. *Chih-t'ang hui-hsiang lu,* p. 686.

34. P. 623.

35. See Jerome Ch'en, "Defining Warlords and Their Factions," *Bulletin of the School of Oriental and African Studies,* 31.3:570 (1968).

36. "Kou chua ti-t'an" (Dogs scratching carpets), *Yü ssu* 3 (Nov. 1, 1924).

37. "Sa-man ti li-chiao ssu-hsiang" (Shamanistic religious thought; 1925), *T'an hu chi.*

38. "Feng-chi chih jou-ts'ui" (The fragility of moral standards; 1925), *T'an hu chi.*

39. "Pan-ch'un" (Semivernal; 1927), *T'an hu chi.*

40. "Ye-man min-tsu ti li-chiao" (The religion of barbarous peoples), *T'an hu chi;* this was written originally in 1920, but repeated in 1927.

41. "K'u-yü-chai ch'ih-tu 8" (Letters from bitter rain studio, no. 8), *Yü ssu* 104 (Nov. 6, 1926).

42. "Tsen-mo shuo ts'ai hao?" (What to say?), *Yü ssu* 151 (Oct. 1, 1927).

43. "Kuan-yü chen-nü" (On chaste women), *Kua tou chi,* p. 283.

44. "Wo-men ti hsien-hua 14" (Our causeries, no. 14), *Yü ssu* 83 (June 14, 1926).

45. "Ying-chi-li yao-su hsü" (Preface to English Folklore; 1931), *K'an yun chi* (Cloud-gazing; Shanghai, 1932), p. 163.

46. See "I-hsueh chou k'an chi hsu" (Preface to "Selections from the Medical Weekly"; 1927), and "Hsin-chiu i-hsueh tou-cheng yü fu-ku" (The struggle between new and old medicine and revivalism; 1928), in *Yung-jih chi.*

47. The words are Jane Harrison's; see *Chih-t'ang hui-hsiang lu,* pp. 682-683.

48. "Hsiang-ts'un yü tao-chiao ssu-hsiang" (Villages and Taoist thought), *Yü ssu* 100 (Oct. 9, 1926), and *T'an hu chi,* p. 353.

49. Gustave le Bon, *Lois psychologiques de l'evolution des peuples,* 9th ed. (Paris: Bibliothèque de Philosophie Contemporaine, 1909), p. 5.

50. Ibid., p. 66.

51. Ibid., p. 26.

52. Ibid., p. 104.

53. Ibid., p. 5.

54. In "Pi-hu tu-shu lun" (on reading behind closed doors), *Yung-jih chi.*

55. These words are used in "Han-i *Ku-shih chi* shen-hua chuan hsu" (Preface to the Chinese translation of the mythological section of *Kojiki*), *Yü ssu* 65 (Feb. 8, 1926).

56. "Shang hsia shen" (Above and below the belt; 1925), *Yü-t'ien ti shu,* pp. 107-108.

57. "Jih-pen-jen ti hao-i" (The kind intentions of the Japanese), *Yü-ssu* 131 (May 14, 1927).

58. "Tsai Nü-tzu Hsueh-yuan pei ch'iu chi" (Imprisoned in the Women's College; 1928), *Yung-jih chi.*

59. *Chih-t'ang hui-hsiang lu,* p. 548.

60. "Chung-nien" (Middle age; 1930), *K'an yun chi.*

61. "Ta hei lang ti ku-shih hsu" (Preface to "Stories of big black wolves"; 1928), *Yung-jih chi.*

62. "Pieh-chen yü t'ien-kang" (Pins and high winds), *Yü ssu* 45 (Sept. 21, 1925).

63. "Chu-yao man-ch'ao" (Decoctions: random notes), *K'u chu tsa-chi* (Bitter bamboo miscellany; Shanghai, 1936), p. 44.

64. As n. 60.

65. See "Kuei-tsu-ti yü p'ing-min-ti" (Aristocratic and plebian), in *Tzu-chi ti yuan-ti* (One's own garden; Shanghai, 1932); "Ta Yun-shen hsien-sheng" (In reply to Mr. Yun-shen), and "Wen-hsueh t'an" (On literature), in *T'an lung chi* (Talking of dragons; Shanghai, 1929).

66. Quoted Ts'ao, *Lu Hsun p'ing-chuan,* p. 176.

67. "Ku-hsiang" (Hometown), *Lu Hsun ch'üan chi* (Complete works of Lu Hsun; Peking, 1961), I, 71.

68. "Kung-hsien yü hsin shih-jen chih ch'ien" (For the attention of our new poets), quoted Li Ho-lin, *Chung-kuo hsin wen-hsueh shih yen-shiu* (Researches into new Chinese literature; Peking, 1951), p. 47.

69. For example, Chou refused to deny a place to classical Chinese in the modern age on the ground of the continuity of the Chinese language, in "Kuo-yü wen-hsueh t'an" (On literature in the national language; 1925), in *I-shu yü sheng-huo;* and his opinion that innovations in literature only expand on what has gone before, stated in "Wen-i shang ti k'uan-jung" (Tolerance in literature; 1922), in *Tzu-chi ti yuan-ti.*

70. Introduction to vol. 6 of *Chung-kuo hsin wen-hsueh ta-hsi* (Compendium of new Chinese literature; Hong Kong reprint, 1962), p. 6.

71. "Hsing ti hsin-li" (The psychology of sex; 1933), *Yeh tu ch'ao,* pp. 48-49.

72. "Tsao yü Ch'iao ti hsu" (Preface to "Dates" and "Bridge"), *K'an yun chi,* p. 197.

73. In Chou Tso-jen, *Chung-kuo hsin wen-hsueh ti yuan-liu* (Sources of the new Chinese literature; Peiping, 1934).

74. "Wei-ta ti pu-feng" (Great vexation of spirit; 1929), *K'an yun chi.*

Glossary

an-hsin li-ming 安心立命
Ariga Nagao 有賀長雄

Chang Chih-tung 張之洞
Chang Chün-mai 張君勱
Chang Hsueh-ch'eng 章學誠
Chang Hsun 張勳
Chang I 章益
Chang I-lin 張一麟
Chang Ping-lin (t. T'ai-yen) 章炳麟
　　（太炎）
Chang Tsai 張載
Chang Tung-sun 張東蓀
Chang Yun-fu 張雲伏
Ch'ang-chou 常州
Ch'ang yen pao 昌言報
chen 眞
Chen Kao-yung 陣高傭
Ch'en Ch'u-ping 陳去病
Ch'en Huan-chang 陳煥章
Ch'en Kung-po 陳公博
Ch'en Kuo-fu 陳果夫
Ch'en Li-fu 陳立夫
Ch'en Po-sha 陳白沙
Ch'en Pu-lei 陳布雷
Ch'en T'ien-hua 陳天華
Ch'en Tu-hsiu 陳獨秀
Cheng Ch'eng-kung 鄭成功
cheng-hui 證會
cheng-li kuo-ku 整理國故
cheng-tao 政道
cheng-t'ung ssu-hsiang 正統思想
ch'eng 誠
Ch'eng-Chu 程朱
ch'eng-te chih chiao 成德之教
Ch'eng wei-shih lun shu-chi 成唯識論述記
Chi-shui T'an 積水潭

chi-wu 己物
ch'i 氣
ch'i chün-tzu 七君子
ch'i-shih 奇士
ch'i wu 齊物
Ch'i wu lun 齊物論
chia fa 家法
chiang-hsueh 講學
chiang-hu 江湖
Chiang Kai-shek 蔣介石
chiao 教
chiao-chu 教主
Ch'ien Hsuan-t'ung 錢玄同
Ch'ien-k'un yen 乾坤衍
Ch'ien Mu 錢穆
chih-chien 知見
chih-chueh 直覺
chih-hui 智慧
chih-shih chieh-chi 智識階級
chih-tao 治道
chih tu 制度
chih yung 致用
ch'ih 恥
Ch'ih Yu 蚩尤
Chin Sheng-t'an 金聖歎
chin-shih 進士
Chin Yueh-lin 金岳霖
Ch'in Shih-huang 秦始皇
Ch'in-shu fa ta-kang 親屬法大綱
ching 敬
Ching-hua jih-pao 京話日報
ching-shen 精神
ching shih 經世
ch'ing-kao ming-shih 清高名士
chiu ke-lu, hsin ts'ai-liao 舊格律新材料
chiu-kuo 救國
Ch'iu Chin 秋瑾

Ch'iu shu 訄書
Chou En-lai 周恩來
Chou Fu-hai 周彿海
Chou Ping-lin 周炳琳
Chou Tso-jen 周作人
Chou Tzu-ch'i 周自齊
Chu Ch'i-ch'ing 朱齊青
Chu Hsi 朱熹
Chu-ko Liang 諸葛亮
chu tzu 諸子
ch'u-ch'i tzu-pen chu-i 初期資本主義
Ch'un-wei 淳維
chü-jen 舉人
Ch'ü Yuan 屈原
chuan chih 專制
Ch'uan-hsi lu 傳習錄
Ch'üan hsueh p'ien 勸學篇
Chuang-tzu 莊子
chueh-wu 覺悟
chün-hsien 郡縣
chün-tzu 君子
chung 忠
Chung-hua min-kuo 中華民國
Chung-hua ti-kuo 中華帝國
Chung-kuo chiao-yü hui 中國教育會
chung-lei 種類
Chung yung 中庸

Erh ya 爾雅

Fa-hsiang 法相
Fan Chung-yen 范仲淹
Fan Chung-yun 樊仲雲
fan-shen k'e-chi chih kung 反身克己之功
Fang Chih 方治
feng-chien 封建
feng-chien ssu-hsiang suo chih-p'ei ti
    ch'u-ch'i tzu-pen chu-i 封建思想所
    支配的初期資本主義
feng-ke 風格
Feng yü t'an 風雨談
Fo-chia ming-hsiang t'ung-shih 佛家名相通釋
fu chiang 富強
Fu Hsi 伏羲
Fu-hsing (Academy) 復性
fu hsing (restoration of glory) 復興
Fu hsing she 復興社

fu-ku 復古
Fu she 復社
Fu Wei-hsun 傅偉勳
Fung Yu-lan 馮友蘭

gagaku 雅樂

Han Fei 韓非
Han Fei-tzu 韓非子
Han Fu-chü 韓復榘
Han hsueh 漢學
Han Wu 漢武
hao sheng chih hsin 好勝之心
Ho Ch'ang-ch'ün 賀昌群
Ho Chen 何震
Ho Ping-sung 何炳松
Ho-tse 菏澤
Hou-pu yuan-wai-lang 候補員外郎
hsi 翕
hsi-hsin 習心
Hsia 夏
Hsia Tou-yin 夏斗寅
Hsiang chien p'ai 鄉建派
Hsiang Yü 項羽
hsiang yueh 鄉約
hsiao hsueh 小學
hsiao-t'i 小體
hsien-tai hua 現代化
hsien-tai p'ai 現代派
hsin (faithfulness) 信
hsin (mind; mind-heart) 心
Hsin ch'ao 新潮
Hsin ch'ing-nien 新青年
hsin-hsing chih hsueh 心性之學
Hsin ju-chia 新儒家
hsin-ku p'ai 信古派
Hsin sheng-ming yueh k'an 新生命月刊
Hsin Wei-shih lun 新唯識論
hsing (family names) 姓
hsing (nature) 性
hsing-chih 形式
Hsing shih shu 姓氏書
hsiu-shen 修身
Hsiung Shih-li 熊十力
Hsu Chieh 許傑
Hsu Chih-mo 徐志摩
Hsu Fu-kuan 徐復觀

Hsu Hsing 許行
hsuan-hsueh ti chen-li 玄學的眞理
Hsueh heng 學衡
hsueh-hui 學會
Hsun-tzu 荀子
Hu Hsien-su 胡先驌
Hu Shih 胡適
Hua kuo 華國
Huan 桓
Huang Chieh 黃節
Huang-fu Mi 皇甫謐
Huang Hsing 黃興
Huang shih 黃史
Huang shu 黃書
Huang-ti 黃帝
Huang-ti hun 黃帝魂
Huang Tsun-hsien 黃遵憲
Huang Tsung-hsi 黃宗羲
Huang Wen-shan 黃文山
hun 魂
Hung-hsien 洪憲

i 義
I ching (Book of changes) 易經
i-ching (embody new states of meaning)
    意境
i-hsia 義俠
i-ku p'ai 疑古派
I-li (Ceremonies and rituals) 儀禮
i-li (moral-metaphysical) 義理

jang-i 攘夷
Jang-shu 攘書
jen (benevolence; humanity) 仁
jen (people; human being) 人
Jen Chi-yü 任繼愈
Juan Yuan 阮元
Jung 戎
Jung-lu 榮祿

K'an yun chi 看雲集
kang-ch'ang ming-chiao 綱常名教
K'ang Yu-wei 康有爲
Kao Ch'i 高啓
Kao Hsu 高旭
kao ming 高明
k'ao-chü 考據

Kato Hiroyuki 加藤弘之
ko wu 格物
kokusui, *see* kuo ts'ui
kokusui hozon 國粹保存
kokusui kansho 國粹勸獎
Ku Chieh-kang 顧頡剛
Ku Hung-ming 辜鴻銘
Ku-liang 穀梁
Ku Meng-yü 顧孟餘
Ku Yen-wu 顧炎武
K'u ch'a sui-pi 苦茶隨筆
K'u chu tsa chi 苦竹雜記
Kua tou chi 瓜豆集
K'uai Kuang-tien 蒯光典
Kuan Chung 管仲
Kuan-tzu 管子
kuang-fu 光復
Kuang-fu hui 光復會
K'uei-chi 窺基
kung 公
kung li 公理
kung-t'ung sheng-huo 共同生活
Kung Tzu-chen 龔自珍
Kung yang 公羊
k'ung 空
K'ung Wen-hsien 孔文軒
kuo 國
Kuo Chan-po 郭湛波
kuo chia 國家
kuo hsing 國性
Kuo hsing p'ien 國性篇
kuo hsueh 國學
Kuo hsueh chen-ch'i she 國學振起社
Kuo hsueh pao 國學報
Kuo hsueh pao-ts'un hui 國學保存會
kuo hun 國魂
kuo ku 國故
Kuo ku 國古
kuo min 國民
Kuo Mo-jo 郭沫若
kuo ts'ui (kokusui) 國粹
kuo-ts'ui hsueh-p'ai 國粹學派
Kuo-ts'ui hsueh-pao 國粹學報
Kuo-ts'ui ts'ung-k'an 國粹叢刊
kuo-wen 國文

lao-hsin che 勞心者

lao-li che 勞力者
Lao-tzu, *Lao-tzu* 老子
li 禮
li-chih 吏治
li-hsiang 理想
li-hsing 理性
li-min 黎民
Li Po 李白
li-shih fa-hsueh p'ai 歷史法學派
Li Ta-chao 李大釗
Liang Chi 梁濟
Liang Ch'i-ch'ao 梁啓超
Liang Shih-i 梁士詒
Liang Shu-ming (or Liang Sou-ming) 梁漱溟
Liang Tun-yen 梁敦彥
Liang Yuan-tung 梁園東
lien 廉
Lin Hsieh 林懈
Lin Shu 林紓
Liu Hsin (t. Tzu-chün) 劉歆 (子駿)
Liu I-cheng 柳詒徵
Liu K'an-yuan 劉侃元
liu-mang 流氓
Liu Shao-ch'i 劉少奇
Liu Shih-p'ei (t. Shen-shu) 劉師培 (申叔)
Liu Shu-hsien 劉述先
Liu Wen-ch'i 劉文淇
Liu Ya-tzu 柳亞子
Lu Hsun 魯迅
Lu-Wang 陸王
Lü Ho-shu 呂和叔
Lü Liu-liang 呂留良
lü-shih 律詩
Lü-shih ch'un-ch'iu 呂氏春秋

Ma Chün-wu 馬君武
Ma I-fou 馬一浮
Ma-liu 馬流
Ma Yuan 馬援
Mao Tse-tung 毛澤東
Mei Kuang-ti 梅光迪
Miao 苗
min 民
Min-chu p'ing-lun 民主評論
Min-chu she-hui tang 民主社會黨
min-ch'üan 民權
min-i 民彝

Min pao 民報
min sheng 民生
min-tsu (minzoku) 民族
min-tsu chu-i 民族主義
min-tsu hsing 民族性
min-tsu kuang-fu 民族光復
ming-liu hsueh-che 名流學者
Ming-ti 明帝
minzoku, *see* min-tsu
Miyake Setsurei 三宅雪嶺
Mou Tsung-san 牟宗三
mu fu 幕府

Na-han 吶喊
Nan she 南社
Nei-ko chung-shu 內閣中書
nei-sheng wai-wang 內聖外王
Nihonjin 日本人
Ning T'ai-i 寗太一
nung-min yun-tung chiang-hsi suo 農民
    運動講習所

Ou-yang Ching-wu 歐陽竟無

pa-ku wen 八股文
pai-hsing 百姓
pai-hua 白話
pao-chiao 保教
Pao huang hui 保皇會
pen-hsin 本心
pen-t'i 本體
pen-t'i lun 本體論
Peng I-chung 彭翼仲
pi-chi 筆記
Pi-hu tu-shu lun 閉戶讀書論
p'i 闢
pien 變
pien-hua 變化
p'ing-i 平議
p'o hsueh 樸學

Sa Meng-wu 薩孟武
san-min chu-i 三民主義
Shang shu 尚書
Shang Yang 商鞅
she-hui fa-hsueh p'ai 社會法學派
She Ts'un-tung 施存統

Shen Chou 神州
shen-hsin chih hsueh 身心之學
Shen Nung 神農
shen-shih 紳士
Shen Ts'ung-wen 沈從文
Shen Yu-ting 沈又鼎
sheng-jen chih hsueh 聖人之學
Shiga Shigetaka 志賀重昂
shih 氏
Shih chi 史記
Shih hua 詩話
shih-kan 實幹
shih-ku 釋古
shih-ku p'ai 釋古派
shih kuan 史館
Shih pen 世本
shih-shih lun-hui 世事輪廻
shih-tai-fu 士大夫
shou 獸
shu (reciprocity) 恕
shu (techniques) 術
Shui-hu-chuan 水滸傳
Shun 舜
Shun-t'ien shih-pao 順天時報
Shuo wen 說文
sonnō jōi 尊王攘夷
ssu 私
Ssu-ma Ch'ien 司馬遷
Su Man-shu 蘇曼殊
Su pao 蘇報
Su Tung-po 蘇東坡
Sun Fo 孫科
Sun Hsi-lin 孫錫麟
Sun Yat-sen 孫逸仙
Sun Yü-wen 孫毓汶
Sung Chiang 宋江
Sung Chiao-jen 宋教仁

Ta Ch'ing-kuo 大淸國
ta-hua 大化
ta-i 大易
ta-t'i 大體
ta-t'ung 大同
Ta-t'ung shu 大同書
Tai Chen 戴震
Tai Chi-t'ao 戴季陶
t'ai-p'ing 太平

T'ai-po 泰伯
T'an hu chi 談虎集
T'an Ssu-t'ung 譚嗣同
T'ang Chün-i 唐君毅
tao 道
tao-te ti tsung-chiao 道德的宗教
tao t'ung 道統
T'ao Hsi-sheng 陶希聖
T'ao Meng-ho 陶孟和
te 德
Teng Ch'u-min 鄧初民
Teng Chung-hsia 鄧中夏
Teng Shih 鄧實
Teng Yen-ta 鄧演達
ti 悌
Ti-ch'iu yun-yen 地球韻言
t'i 體
t'i-jen 體認
t'i-yung 體用
t'ien 天
T'ien-an-men 天安門
t'ien-hsia 天下
t'ien-hsia wei kung 天下爲公
t'ien-jen ho-i 天人合一
t'ien-li 天理
t'ien-tao 天道
Ts'ai O 蔡鍔
Ts'ai Yuan-p'ei 蔡元培
Tseng Kuo-fan 曾國藩
Tso chuan 左傳
tso-yu ming 座右銘
tso-yung 作用
ts'o hsin yü wu 措心於無
Tsou Jung 鄒容
tsu 族
tsu min 族民
tsun-wang 尊王
Ts'un-ku hsueh-t'ang 存古學堂
tsung-chiao 宗敎
tsung-fa 宗法
Tu Fu 杜甫
Tu-li ch'ing-nien tang 獨立靑年黨
Tu-shu tsa-chih 讀書雜誌
Tuan Chih-kuei 段芝貴
Tuan-fang 端方
Tung-Hsi wen-hua chi ch'i che-hsueh 東西
　　　文化及其哲學

Tung-lin 東林
Tung-nan ta-hsueh 東南大學
t'ung-ch'ing yü ching-i 同情與敬意
T'ung meng hui 同盟會
t'ung shih 通史
tz'u k'o 刺客

Wang Chih-ch'eng 王志澄
Wang Ching-wei 汪精衛
Wang Ching-wen 王景文
Wang Fu-chih 王夫之
Wang Hsin-ming 王新命
Wang Kuo-wei 王國維
Wang Li-hsi 王禮錫
Wang Mang 王莽
Wang Nien-sun 王念孫
Wang Pi 王弼
Wang Shih-chen 王士珍
Wang Yang-ming 王陽明
Wang Yin-chih 王引之
Wang Yun-wu 王雲五
Wei-lai chih Chung-kuo 未來之中國
Wei-shih 唯識
wei yen ta-i 微言大義
Wei Yuan 魏源
wu (non-being) 無
Wu (people) 吳
Wu-ch'ang 武昌
wu cheng-fu chu-i 無政府主義
Wu Chih-hui 吳稚暉
Wu Hsu-kan 武壻幹
Wu Mi 吳宓
Wu Ting-ch'ang 吳鼎昌
wu wei 無爲
wu wu pu jan; wu wu pu k'o 無物不然,
   無物不可
Wu Yueh 吳樾

Yang Ch'ang-chi 楊昌濟
Yang Ch'üan 楊詮
Yang Ting-tung 楊廷棟
Yang Tu 楊度
Yang Wen-hui 楊文會
Yao 堯
yeh 業
Yeh tu ch'ao 夜讀抄
Yen Chih-t'ui 顏之推
Yen Fu 嚴復
Yen-tzu 晏子
Yen Yuan 顏元
Yin Hai-kuang 殷海光
Yin-ming ta-su shan-chu 因明大疏刪注
yin-yang 陰陽
Ying 嬴
ying-shih 英士
yu 憂
yu-hsia 游俠
yü 禹
yü-lu 語錄
Yü ssu 語絲
yü t'ien-ti wan-wu wei i-t'i 與天地萬物
   爲一體
Yü Wen-wei 余文偉
Yü Yueh 余樾
Yuan-ju 原儒
Yuan K'o-ting 袁克定
Yuan Shih-k'ai 袁世凱
Yuan ts'ai 原才
Yueh 越
Yueh Fei 岳飛
Yun Tai-ying 惲代英
yung 用
Yung jih chi 永日集
Yung-yen pao 庸言報

Index

Addams, Jane, 240
Addison, Joseph, 336
Alarm Bell, 104
Alitto, Guy, 14, 41, 44
Almond, Gabriel A., 184
Ariga Nagao, 184-185
Arnold, Matthew, 74, 75, 79, 81, 228
Ataturk, Kemal, 207

Babbitt, Irving, 73-74, 75, 81
Bakunin, Mikhail, 343
Barres, Auguste Maurice, 89
Bergson, Henri, 227, 252, 260, 272, 287
Bernal, Martin, 31, 60
Blue Shirts, 193-196, 203, 204, 205, 210
Bluntschli, J. K., 131
Boodberg, Peter, 261
Book of Changes, see *I ching*
Bradley, F. H., 273, 274
Briere, Father, 266, 272
Buber, Martin, 246
Burke, Edmund, 16-17, 200; and con-
    servatism, 5, 7-8, 9, 11, 12, 13
Byron, George Gordon, Lord, 78, 79,
    81, 83

Calhoun, John Caldwell, 240
Carsun Chang, *see* Chang Chün-mai
CC Clique, 203, 204, 205, 210; and
    Chinese modernization, 196-200
Central Daily, 309
Central Independent Division, 309
Chang Chih-tung, 25, 74, 87; academy
    proposed by, 31, 63-64; his "Exhorta-
    tion to learn," 63, 64-65; and
    national essence, 107-108, 216; on
    excessive change, 110; and Chang

Ping-lin and K'ang Yu-wei, 148; and
    t'i-yung, 200, 215, 261
Chang Chün-mai (Carsun Chang), 27,
    37, 226, 295; and New Confucian-
    ism, 276-277; and scientism, 283-
    284, 285; Western impact on, 287
Chang Hsueh-ch'eng, 75, 122-123
Chang Hsun, 162
Chang I-lin, 178
Chang Piao, 255
Chang Ping-lin (Chang T'ai-yen) 16,
    26, 34, 51, 66; cultural conservatism
    of, 17-18, 30; and National Essence
    movement, 31, 73; and moderniza-
    tion of Confucianism, 36; and Chou
    Tso-jen, 53; and Ch'en Ch'u-p'ing,
    61; and *National Essence Journal*,
    64; and Shanghai academy and
    library, 65; political conservatism of,
    92; and *kuang-fu*, 95; influence of
    Lacouperie on, 96; and Liu Shih-
    p'ei, 97, 98, 99, 109, 111; release
    from prison of, 110; "The Sage as
    Rebel: The Inner World of Chang
    Ping-lin," 113-150; *Ch'iu shu*, 113,
    128, 131-132, 141-142
Chang T'ai-yen, 215, 217, 233
Chang Tsai, 269
Chang Tung-sun, 37, 245, 249, 272,
    273
Chang Yün-fu, 195
Ch'en, Kenneth, 265
Ch'en Ch'u-p'ing, 72; and *National
    Essence Journal*, 61; and Southern
    Society, 62, 63; *Sung-ling Literary
    Anthology*, 68; and Southeastern
    University, 74
Ch'en Huang-chang, 174

Ch'en Kung-po, 308, 309, 310, 315
Ch'en Kuo-fu, 196
Ch'en Li-fu, 47, 48, 49, 51, 149, 150;
  and scientific spirit of Confucianism,
  40; and CC Clique, 196-197; on
  Chinese modernization, 198-199; and
  t'i-yung, 200; philosophic outlook of,
  203-204; neotraditionalism of, 216,
  217
Ch'en T'ien-hua, 144
Ch'en Tu-hsiu, 72, 111, 151, 182
Cheng Ch'eng-kung, 76
Chiang Kai-shek, 23, 29, 42, 150, 189;
  New Life movement of, 19, 200-205;
  commitment of, to nationhood, 28;
  and Kuan-tzu, 44; Mary Wright on,
  191-192; and the Blue Shirts, 193,
  194, 195; and CC Clique, 196; and
  conservative face of Kuomintang,
  205-206, 210; on bureaucracy, 209;
  and Yuan Shih-k'ai, 217; and T'ao
  Hsi-sheng, 305
Ch'ien Hsuan-t'ung, 122
Ch'ien Mu, 34, 35, 39, 46, 150
Chin Sheng-t'an, 67
Ch'in Shih-huang, 150, 236
China's Destiny, 305
Chinese Educational Association
  (Chung-kuo chiao-yü hui), 61
Chinese Renaissance, 36
Ch'iu Chin, 61, 63, 69
Chou En-lai, 217
Chou Fu-hai, 309, 310, 323
Chou Ping-lin, 309
Chou Tso-jen, 32, 52-53; conservatism
  of, 19-20; and national studies, 109;
  "Chou Tso-jen: A Scholar Who
  Withdrew," 332-356; collections of
  essays by, 335
Chou Tzu-ch'i, 182
Chu Ch'i-ch'ing, 310
Chu Hsi, 64-65, 234, 251
Chu-ko Liang, 236
Ch'ü Yuan, 78
Chuang-tzu, 4, 145, 146, 147
Coleridge, Samuel Taylor, 228
Condorcet, Marquis de, 6

Confucianism: doctrine (chiao), 25, 26;
  as a religion, 25-26, 36-37; movement to modernize, 30, 36-37; New
  Text and Old Text, 36, 37; scientism
  and, 37; social mission of, 40; and
  moral heroism, 43; rationalisms in,
  44; and Yuan Shih-k'ai, 174-175; in
  modern China, 242-249. See also
  New Confucianism
Confucius, 94, 98, 99, 227
Conservatism: unreflective forms of, 3-
  4; and liberalism, 4, 10-12, 15, 16;
  and radicalism, 4-5, 9, 10, 15, 16,
  20; and determinism, 5; and political
  realm, 6-7; and historicism, 7-8, 9;
  and sociologism, 8; and nationalism,
  8-9, 10, 11, 16; and modernization,
  12, 14, 18-19, 20; in America, 13;
  and skepticism, 15, 20; and social
  interests, 15-16; in China, 16-21; and
  national essence, 16; cultural, 16-18,
  19, 20; traditionalistic, 18; of despair, 19-20; Liang Shu-ming and
  Chinese cultural, 215-217
Critical Review (CR; Hsueh heng), 66,
  73-75, 79-80, 87-89; founding of, 58;
  and national essence, 60, 215; and
  the intelligentsia, 80-81; and Old
  School and New School of poetry, 82,
  84, 85
Cultural Construction, 48-49

Darwin, Charles, 131, 252, 344
Darwinism, 51-52; and National
  Essence movement, 31, 33
Day, C. B., 272
de Gaulle, Charles, 176
"Declaration of Cultural Construction
  on a Chinese Basis," 197
Democratic Socialist (formerly National
  Socialist) party, 276
Dewey, John, 11, 233, 251, 252, 253
Dirlik, Arif, 46
Disraeli, Benjamin, 199
Doctrine of the Mean (Chung yung),
  38, 40
Durkheim, Émile, 230

Eastman, Lloyd, 28, 29
Eisenstadt, S. N., 197
Ellis, Havelock, 335, 344, 355
Epstein, Klaus, 5
Erikson, Erik, 213, 224
Eucken, Rudolph, 287
Examination system, abolition of, 110

Fabre, Henri, 335, 344
Falkland, Lord, 306
Fan Chung-yen, 255
Fang Chih, 199
Feuerbach, Ludwig Andreas, 6
Frazer, J. G., 335, 344, 345, 346, 347
Fu Hsi, 125, 132
Fu she (Revival Society), 63, 69, 76, 79
Fung Yu-lan, 37, 38, 51, 112, 245, 249;
    and sage within and king without,
    40, 41; on culture and industrial and
    social change, 47-48; and *Cultural
    Construction* group, 49; utopianism
    of, 52; and Hsiung Shih-li, 258; on
    "explainers of antiquity," 328

Gandhi, Mohandas Karamchand, 228,
    241
Gauss, Clarence, 204
Glazer, Nathan, 14
Gobineau, Joseph de, 97
Goldwater, Barry, 12, 13
Goodnow, Frank J., 183-187
Great Commonwealth (*ta-t'ung*), 48,
    49-50
Great Learning, 44

Hamilton, Clarence H., 272
Han Fei, 139, 140, 141, 143, 144, 146-
    147
Han Wu, 236
Hao Chang, 37
Harrison, Jane, 335, 344
Hegel, Georg Wilhelm Friedrich, 8, 9
Heller, Erich, 84
Hippocrates, 346
Hitler, Adolf, 194, 207
Ho, Franklin, 206
Ho Ch'ang-ch'ün, 249

Ho Chen, 92
Ho Shen, 254-255
Hobbes, Thomas, 93
Hsia Tou-yin, 309
Hsiang Yü, 144
Hsieh Yu-wei, 272-273
Hsin ch'ing nien, see *New Youth*
Hsin sheng-ming (New life monthly),
    310
Hsiu Shih-lin, 61
Hsiung Shih-li, 18, 41; cultural con-
    servatism of, 30; and Confucianism,
    37; his "experiential recognition,"
    38; "Hsiung Shih-li's Quest for
    Authentic Existence," 242-275;
    Dialogues, 254, 260; *Yuan-ju*, 256;
    Ch'ien-k'un yen, 256; *Buddhist Con-
    cepts Explained*, 266; *Commentary
    on the Great Treatise on Buddhist
    Logic*, 266; influence of, 276-277;
    existential problems of, 281-282;
    intellectual outlook of, 284-285;
    effect of Western thought on, 287
Hsu Chieh, 333-334, 337-338, 341
Hsu Chih-mo, 32, 152
Hsu Fu-kuan, 259, 276, 294, 299
Hsu Hsing, 94
Hsuan-t'ung, 109
Hsun-tzu, 93, 140, 142
Hu Hsien-su, 74
Hu Shih, 88, 112, 197-198, 226, 233,
    285; and liberalism, 11, 12; and
    Chang Ping-lin, 122, 126; and Liang
    Shu-ming, 214; and Hsiung Shih-li,
    250-251; and pragmatic philosophy,
    253; and Ten Professors Manifesto,
    325-326, 327-328; empirical scien-
    tism of, 329
Huan of Ch'i, Duke, 94
Huang Chieh, 65, 81, 215; and
    National Essence Journal, 61; his
    "Yellow History," 66, 86-87; and *CR*
    circle, 73, 80; and Wu Mi, 74; and
    Liu Shih-p'ei, 104, 105
Huang-fu Mi, 98-99
Huang Hsing, 179
Huang-ti, 98-99, 132

Huang Tsun-hsien, 82, 103-104
Huang Tsung-hsi, 67, 91, 92, 93, 140-141
Hung-hsien Emperor, *see under* Yuan Shih-k'ai
Huxley, Thomas H., 252, 344

I ching (Book of Changes), 40, 51, 227, 267-268
Intelligentsia (*chih-shih chieh-chi*), 80-81

Japanese, The (*Nihonjin*), 101, 102
Jaspers, Karl, 281
Jefferson, Thomas, 6, 240
Jen (benevolence), 33, 42, 227, 229, 271-275, 291-293, 294
Jen Chi-yü, 249
Juan Yuan, 91
Justice, The (*Yung-yen pao*), 163

K'ang Yu-wei, 25-26, 27, 30, 50, 73, 98; and movement to modernize Confucianism, 36-37, 174, 216, 277-278; and human evolution, 46, 49, 51; his *Ta-t'ung shu*, 48; utopianism of, 52, 93-94; and *jang-i*, 95; and Liu Shih-p'ei, 105-106; and Chang Ping-lin, 113, 115-117, 147-148; domination of New Text studies by, 119; institutional innovations of, 119-120; on documentary records, 123; on *jen*, 138-139, 273; and administrative issues, 140, 142; and Huang Tsung-hsi, 141; and Liang Chi, 153
Kant, Immanuel, 260
Kao Hsu, 62, 67, 72, 89; his poetry, 82, 83; on national spirit, 100
Kato Hiroyuki, 131
Kollontai, Alexandra, 343
Koo, Wellington, 182
Kropotkin, Pëtr Alekseevich, 341
Ku Chieh-kang, 111, 112, 122, 127, 285
Ku Meng-yü, 308, 309, 314-315, 315-316
Ku Yen-wu, 67, 96, 118, 133, 255
K'uai Kuang-tien, 107
Kuan Chung, 94

Kuan-tzu, 44, 140
K'uei-chi, 266
kung (public-mindedness), 27, 34, 42
Kung, H. H., 206
Kung Tzu-chen, 78, 119
K'ung Wen-hsien, 309
Kuo Chan-po, 328
kuo hsing (national character), 34, 229
Kuo Mo-jo, 32, 85, 112, 127, 309
Kuomintang: "The Kuomintang in the 1930s," 191-210; and T'ao Hsi-sheng, 305, 307, 309-310

Lacouperie, Terrian de, 66, 96-98, 99, 132
Lang, Andrew, 335, 344, 346
Langer, Susanne, 280
Language: classical versus vernacular, 33; Chang Ping-lin on scholarship and, 118-128
Lao-tzu, 4, 98, 146, 261
le Bon, Gustave, 344, 348-349
Levenson, Joseph, 22-23, 172, 219, 263, 327; on "traditionalist" and "traditionalistic" thinking, 18; on Yuan Shih-k'ai's monarchical movement, 189; on Confucianism, 243-245; and syncretism, 256; on intellectual history, 273-274
li-hsing, 228, 229, 230, 231, 239
Li Po, 83
Li Ta-chao, 10, 51, 217, 351
Liang Chi, 221-224, 232; "The Suicide of Liang Chi: An Ambiguous Case of Moral Conservatism," 151-168
Liang Ch'i-ch'ao, 98, 110, 131, 236, 244, 328; on liberalism, 11; his call for a "new people," 31, 138; "Poetics," 82; on poetic and political forms, 83-84; and Liu Shih-p'ei, 91; and national essence, 103, 104; and national studies, 109; and Kuan-tzu, 140; and Liang Chi, 153, 163-164, 222; and Yuan Shih-k'ai, 172; and Liang Shu-ming, 222; *Reflections on a European Journey*, 226
Liang Shih-i, 182
Liang Shu-ming (Liang Sou-ming), 14,

18, 39, 44, 245, 249; support for democratic oppositionist groups by, 27; on need for religion, 37; his "intuitive knowledge of the good," 38; and sage within and king without, 41; cultural conservatism of, 42, 248; and Liang Chi, 151, 152-153, 154; "The Conservative as Sage: Liang Shu-ming," 213-241; *Eastern and Western Cultures,* 225, 226, 241, 283; and Hsiung Shih-li, 258, 276-277; existential problems of, 281-282; and scientism, 283-284, 285; Western impact on, 287

Liang Tun-yen, 179

Liang Yuan-tung, 315

Lin Hsieh, 92-94

Lin Shu, 84

Liu Hsin, 119

Liu I-cheng, 73, 75, 80, 87

Liu K'an-yuan, 309

Liu Shih-p'ei, 26, 31, 66, 73; and *National Essence Journal,* 60-61; and National Learning Protection Society, 65; support of, for restoration, 71; and Peking University, 72; and *National Heritage,* 72, 85; death of, 73; "Liu Shih-p'ei and National Essence," 90-112; *The Theme of Social Contract in China,* 92-94; *Book of Expulsion,* 94-99; *The Soul of the Yellow Emperor,* 99; and Chang Ping-lin, 114, 115; and *kuo-ts'ui,* 215

Liu Wen-ch'i, 91

Liu Ya-tzu, 62, 63, 68, 69, 71; on Fu she, 76; and Southern Society, 78, 81; and "classical acrobatics," 84

Lu Hsun, 109, 221, 336-337, 349; and Chang Ping-lin, 127; and Chou Tso-jen, 332, 333, 353-354

Lu Liu-liang, 67

Lü Ho-shu, 234

Ma Chün-wu, 68, 82-83, 84

Ma I-fou, 40, 245, 249

Maine, Henry, 324, 331; *Ancient Law,* 310-313

Maistre, Joseph Marie de, 100-101

Mannheim, Karl, 88, 171, 187, 188; and conservatism, 4, 7, 8, 9, 12, 15, 301; on rationalism, 218; and Vitalism, 227

Mao Tse-tung, 18, 23, 29, 51, 188, 207; and westernization, 112, 197; and Ch'in Shih-huang, 150; on emperor worship, 177-178; and Liang Shu-ming, 217, 234-236, 237

Marx, Karl, 5, 229, 232, 313, 314, 324; on materialist doctrine, 6; and idea of growth, 9-10

Materialism, 307-308, 330-331

May Fourth movement, 22, 30, 45, 252

Mei Kuang-ti, 74, 75, 81, 215

Mencius, 158, 174, 271, 290

Michels, Roberto, 191

Mill, J. S., 11, 252

Min-chu p'ing-lun (Democratic tribune), 276

Min pao, 113, 137

Min-tsu hsing (national character), 34

Ming Tung-lin Academy, 69, 76, 79

Miyake Setsurei, 101, 102, 105

Montesquieu, 5

Möser, Justus, 5, 7

Mou Tsung-san, 30, 38, 276, 295; on Confucianism, 289-293, 299; and nationalism, 297

Müller, Adam, 7

Munro, Donald J., 256

Mussolini, Benito, 194

National Customs, 109

National Essence Journal (Kuo-ts'ui hsueh-pao), 58, 59, 64, 69-70, 85; and Liu Shih-p'ei, 60-61, 104, 106, 111; and Huang Chieh, 61; and Ch'en Ch'u-p'ing, 61; and Southern Society, 63; promotion of syncretism by, 65-66; writings in, 66-67; disintegration of, 70-71; and *National Heritage,* 72; and *CR* circle, 74; and Chang Ping-lin, 115

National Essence (*kuo ts'ui*) movement, 26, 27, 30-36, 38-39, 75-76; fragmentation of, 70-71; emphasis on locale and site of, 86; summarized, 85-89; and Liang Shu-ming, 215-217. *See also National Essence Journal*

National Essence Protection Association, 26

National Heritage (Kuo ku), 72-73, 85

National Salvation Movement, 207

National Studies (Kuo hsueh pao), 103

National Studies school (Kuo hsueh), 64

Nativism, 35, 40

Neuman, Cardinal, 228

New Confucianism (*hsin ju-chia*), 37-51 *passim*, 301-302; and 1958 cultural manifesto, 276-278, 287-289; and concept of cultural identity, 278-280; and crisis of meaning, 280-283, 301-302; as reaction against scientism, 283-287, 301; and emphasis on tradition, 287-288; and doctrine of mind and nature, 289-291; and *jen*, 291-293, 294; and ideal of "sage within and king without," 293-294; and failure to develop science and democracy, 294-297; and nationalism, 297; and "spirit of modernization," 297-298; and problem of death, 299-300; and moral awakening, 300

New Culture movement, 22, 47, 49, 59, 111, 112

New Life movement, 19, 35; Chiang Kai-shek and, 200-205

New Youth (Hsin ch'ing nien), 46, 71, 111, 151, 165, 332

Nietzsche, Friedrich, 252

Ning T'ai-i, 62, 71

Oakeshott, Michael, 4, 13, 14

Oppenheimer, F., 313

Ou-yang Ching-wu, 255, 264, 266

Park, Robert, 240

Pascal, Blaise, 356

Peking University, 71-72, 73, 249, 252

Pekingese Daily (Ching-hua jih-pao), 154

Peng I-chung, 154

People's Friend, The, 102

People's Journal, 109

Plain Speech (Chang yen pao), 128

Pocock, J. G. A., 3

Politics and morality, Chang Ping-lin on, 139-147

Pollard, David, 19, 52

Pragmatism, 49, 51, 253

Protect the Emperor Society (*Pao huang hu*), 26

Pu-yi, Henry, 162

Race and evolution, Chang Ping-lin on, 128-139

Radhkrishnan, S., 246

Rajchman, Ludwig, 208

Rankin, Mary, 76, 77

Regenerationist Society (Fu-hsing she), 194. *See also* Blue Shirts

Renaissance (Hsin ch'ao), 72

Renovation of the People, 109

Revolutionary Alliance (T'ung meng hui), 60-61, 62, 63, 65, 76; Tokyo, 113; and Yuan Shih-k'ai, 114

Rossiter, Clinton, 29, 209-210

Rousseau, Jean Jacques, 8, 10, 93

Rural Reconstruction Group (Hsiang chien p'ai), 239

Russell, Bertrand, 252, 260

"Sage within and king without" (*nei-sheng wai-wang*), 40-41, 293-294

Schneider, Laurence, 31, 33

School for the Preservation of Antiquity (Ts'un-ku hsueh-t'ang), 107

Schopenhauer, Arthur, 252

Schwartz, Benjamin, 24, 247

Science and metaphysics debate ("philosophy of life" debate; 1923), 37, 225, 283, 285-286

Scientism, 37, 51; New Confucianism as reaction to, 283-287, 301

Service, John, 340

Shakespeare, William, 83

Shang Yang, 142

She Ts'un-t'ung, 309

Shelley, Percy Bysshe, 83, 229

Shen Nung, 132
Shen Ts'ung-wen, 197-198
Shen Yu-ting, 249
Shiga Shigetaka, 101-102, 105
Smith, Adam, 94, 232
Snow, C. P., 228
Snow, Edgar, 340
Social history controversy, 308, 314-322, 330
Society for the Promotion of National Studies (Kuo-hsueh chen-ch'i she), 109
Society for the Protection of National Studies (Kuo hsueh pao-ts'un hui), 58, 61, 62, 65; founding of, 60, 104
Soong, T. V., 206, 207, 208
Southeastern University (Tung-nan ta-hsueh), 58, 73, 74
Southern Society (Nan she), 26, 58, 59, 75, 83, 85; founding of, 61-62; activities of, 62-63; writings in, 67, 68-69, 74; and Ma Chün-wu, 68; disintegration of, 71; political milieu of, 76, 77-79; and CR circle, 81, 82; emphasis on locale and site of, 86; conservatism of, 88
Spencer, Herbert, 11, 95, 96, 99, 101; and Chang Ping-lin, 128, 136-137; his laws of nature and history, 130-131; translation of works of, 252
Spirit, of Chinese culture, 34-35
Stalin, Joseph, 207
Su Man-shu, 78, 83
Su pao, 113
Su Tung-po, 20
Sun Fo, 207
Sun Yat-sen, 175, 197, 308, 322; refusal of, to be politically anti-Western, 27; and Chang Ping-lin, 114; his "Principle of the People," 131; and Yuan Shih-k'ai, 179; his view of revolution, 323, 327
Sun Yü-wen, 156
Sung Chiao-jen, 65, 179
Suzuki Daisetz, 246

Tagore, Rabindranath, 251

Tai Chen, 118
Tai Chi-t'ao, 34, 46, 149, 216
T'an Ssu-t'ung, 91
T'ang Chün-i, 167, 276, 294, 297, 298-299
T'ao Hsi-sheng, 16, 46-47, 48, 51, 149; conservatism of, 18, 19; and Chou Tso-jen, 52-53; "T'ao Hsi-sheng: The Social Limits of Change," 305-331; An Outline of Family Law, 312-313
T'ao Meng-ho (L. K. Tao), 151-152
Ten Professors Manifesto, 48-49, 325-328
Teng Ch'u-min, 309
Teng Chung-hsia, 354
Teng Shih, 65, 67, 104, 105
Teng Yen-ta, 207
Tennyson, Alfred, Lord, 83
Thoreau, Henry David, 240
T'i-yung formula for change, 25, 33, 200, 215, 228, 245, 260-261
Tillich, Paul, 246
Tocqueville, Alexis de, 8
Ts'ai O, 172
Ts'ai Yuan-p'ei, 40, 61, 62, 88; and Peking University, 71-72; and Yuan Shih-k'ai, 178; and Chou Tso-jen, 341
Tseng Kuo-fan, 91, 161, 328
Tsou Jung, 61, 115
Tu Fu, 80, 83
Tu-shu tsa-chih (Research magazine), 330
Tu Wei-ming, 37, 38, 50, 284
Tuan Chih-kuei, 178
Turgot, Anne Robert Jacques, 6
Tylor, Sir Edward Burnett, 344

United Front, 308
"Unity of knowledge and action," 43
Utopianism, Chinese moral, 50

Vernacular Literature movement, 73, 74, 82, 83, 85
Vitalism, 227

Wakeman, Frederick, 76-77

Wang, Y. C., 206
Wang Chih-ch'eng, 315
Wang Ching-wei, 308
Wang Ching-wen, 338
Wang Fu-chih, 52, 93, 95, 130, 135; and Liu Shih-p'ei, 91, 96; *Yellow Book*, 92, 99, 128-129, 132; and *National Essence Journal*, 104; and Chang Ping-lin, 128, 131, 143; traditional culturalism of, 136; and institutional reform, 140, 141; and Hsiung Shih-li, 255, 262; philosophy of, 269
Wang Kuo-wei, 64, 281
Wang Li-hsi, 329-330
Wang Mang, 119
Wang Nien-sun, 118
Wang Pi, 261
Wang Yang-ming, 234, 271, 283; school of, 42-43; his *Ch'uan-hsi lu*, 67; and Hsiung Shih-li, 257, 269-270
Wang Yin-chih, 118
Weber, Max, 4, 218, 298
Wei-shih (consciousness only) Buddhism, 227, 255-256, 264-269, 272
Wei Yuan, 119, 140
Whitehead, Alfred North, 273
Williams, Raymond, 219
Wing-tsit Chan, 267, 268
Wright, Mary C., 191-192, 205
Wu Chih-hui, 109, 114, 145, 214, 328, 329
Wu Mi, 40, 89, 215; and *CR* circle, 73-74, 79-80, 82; and Western influence, 75; and poetic form, 84-85
Wu Ting-ch'ang, 163, 164
Wu Yueh, 144

Yang Ch'üan, 207
Yang Shih-fu, 69
Yang Ting-tung, 93
Yang Tu, 186-187
Yen, James Y. C., 237
Yen Chih-t'ui, 335
Yen Fu, 73, 110, 344; and liberalism, 11, 138; and modernization, 19; and human evolution, 46; conservatism of, 109; and Herbert Spencer, 130
Yen Yuan, 335
Young, Ernest, 26, 28, 29, 30
Yü ssu (Tatler) magazine, 333, 337, 353
Yü Wen-wei, 195
Yü Yueh, 118, 120
Yuan K'o-ting, 178, 185
Yuan Shih-k'ai, 19, 30, 86, 217; attempt of, to establish dynasty, 26, 92, 171-190; as a conservative modernizer, 28, 29; and National Essence movement, 70-71; and Southern Society, 80; and Chang Ping-lin, 114; and Liang Chi, 162; "The Hung-hsien Emperor as a Modernizing Conservative," 171-190; significance to Confucianism of collapse of regime of, 243
Yueh Fei, 69, 76
Yun Tai-ying, 309

HARVARD EAST ASIAN SERIES

1. *China's Early Industrialization: Sheng Hsuan-huai (1884-1916) and Mandarin Enterprise.* By Albert Feuerwerker.
2. *Intellectual Trends in the Ch'ing Period.* By Liang Ch'i-ch'ao. Translated by Immanuel C. Y. Hsü.
3. *Reform in Sung China: Wang An-shih (1021-1086) and His New Policies.* By James T. C. Liu.
4. *Studies on the Population of China, 1368-1953.* By Ping-ti Ho.
5. *China's Entrance into the Family of Nations: The Diplomatic Phase, 1858-1880.* By Immanuel C. Y. Hsü.
6. *The May Fourth Movement: Intellectual Revolution in Modern China.* By Chow Tse-tsung.
7. *Ch'ing Administrative Terms: A Translation of the Terminology of the Six Boards with Explanatory Notes.* Translated and edited by E-tu Zen Sun.
8. *Anglo-American Steamship Rivalry in China, 1862-1874.* By Kwang-Ching Liu.
9. *Local Government in China under the Ch'ing.* By T'ung-tsu Ch'ü.
10. *Communist China, 1955-1959: Policy Documents with Analysis.* With a foreword by Robert R. Bowie and John K. Fairbank. (Prepared at Harvard University under the joint auspices of the Center for International Affairs and the East Asian Research Center.)
11. *China and Christianity: The Missionary Movement and the Growth of Chinese Antiforeignism, 1860-1870.* By Paul A. Cohen.
12. *China and the Helping Hand, 1937-1945.* By Arthur N. Young.
13. *Research Guide to the May Fourth Movement: Intellectual Revolution in Modern China, 1915-1924.* By Chow Tse-tsung.
14. *The United States and the Far Eastern Crisis of 1933-1938: From the Manchurian Incident through the Initial Stage of the Undeclared Sino-Japanese War.* By Dorothy Borg.
15. *China and the West, 1858-1861: The Origins of the Tsungli Yamen.* By Masataka Banno.
16. *In Search of Wealth and Power: Yen Fu and the West.* By Benjamin Schwartz.
17. *The Origins of Entrepreneurship in Meiji Japan.* By Johannes Hirschmeier, S.V.D.
18. *Commissioner Lin and the Opium War.* By Hsin-pao Chang.
19. *Money and Monetary Policy in China, 1845-1895.* By Frank H. H. King.
20. *China's Wartime Finance and Inflation, 1937-1945.* By Arthur N. Young.
21. *Foreign Investment and Economic Development in China, 1840-1937.* By Chi-ming Hou.
22. *After Imperialism: The Search for a New Order in the Far East, 1921-1931.* By Akira Iriye.
23. *Foundations of Constitutional Government in Modern Japan, 1868-1900.* By George Akita.
24. *Political Thought in Early Meiji Japan, 1868-1889.* By Joseph Pittau, S.J.
25. *China's Struggle for Naval Development, 1839-1895.* By John L. Rawlinson.

26. *The Practice of Buddhism in China, 1900-1950.* By Holmes Welch.

27. *Li Ta-chao and the Origins of Chinese Marxism.* By Maurice Meisner.

28. *Pa Chin and His Writings: Chinese Youth Between the Two Revolutions.* By Olga Lang.

29. *Literary Dissent in Communist China.* By Merle Goldman.

30. *Politics in the Tokugawa Bakufu, 1600-1843.* By Conrad Totman.

31. *Hara Kei in the Politics of Compromise, 1905-1915.* By Tetsuo Najita.

32. *The Chinese World Order: Traditional China's Foreign Relations.* Edited by John K. Fairbank.

33. *The Buddhist Revival in China.* By Holmes Welch.

34. *Traditional Medicine in Modern China: Science, Nationalism, and the Tensions of Cultural Change.* By Ralph C. Croizier.

35. *Party Rivalry and Political Change in Taishō Japan.* By Peter Duus.

36. *The Rhetoric of Empire: American China Policy, 1895-1901.* By Marilyn B. Young.

37. *Radical Nationalist in Japan: Kita Ikki, 1883-1937.* By George M. Wilson.

38. *While China Faced West: American Reformers in Nationalist China, 1928-1937.* By James C. Thomson, Jr.

39. *The Failure of Freedom: A Portrait of Modern Japanese Intellectuals.* By Tatsuo Arima.

40. *Asian Ideas of East and West: Tagore and His Critics in Japan, China, and India.* By Stephen N. Hay.

41. *Canton under Communism: Programs and Politics in a Provincial Capital, 1949-1968.* By Ezra F. Vogel.

42. *Ting Wen-chiang: Science and China's New Culture.* By Charlotte Furth.

43. *The Manchurian Frontier in Ch'ing History.* By Robert H. G. Lee.

44. *Motoori Norinaga, 1730-1801.* By Shigeru Matsumoto.

45. *The Comprador in Nineteenth Century China: Bridge between East and West.* By Yen-p'ing Hao.

46. *Hu Shih and the Chinese Renaissance: Liberalism in the Chinese Revolution, 1917-1937.* By Jerome B. Grieder.

47. *The Chinese Peasant Economy: Agricultural Development in Hopei and Shantung, 1890-1949.* By Ramon H. Myers.

48. *Japanese Tradition and Western Law: Emperor, State, and Law in the Thought of Hozumi Yatsuka.* By Richard H. Minear.

49. *Rebellion and Its Enemies in Late Imperial China: Militarization and Social Structure, 1796-1864.* By Philip A. Kuhn.

50. *Early Chinese Revolutionaries: Radical Intellectuals in Shanghai and Chekiang, 1902-1911.* By Mary Backus Rankin.

51. *Communications and Imperial Control in China: Evolution of the Palace Memorial System, 1693-1735.* By Silas H. L. Wu.

52. *Vietnam and the Chinese Model: A Comparative Study of Nguyễn and Ch'ing Civil Government in the First Half of the Nineteenth Century.* By Alexander Barton Woodside.

53. *The Modernization of the Chinese Salt Administration, 1900-1920.* By S. A. M. Adshead.

54. *Chang Chih-tung and Educational Reform in China.* By William Ayers.

55. *Kuo Mo-jo: The Early Years.* By David Tod Roy.

56. *Social Reformers in Urban China: The Chinese Y.M.C.A., 1895-1926.* By Shirley S. Garrett.

57. *Biographic Dictionary of Chinese Communism, 1921-1965.* By Donald W. Klein and Anne B. Clark.

58. *Imperialism and Chinese Nationalism: Germany in Shantung.* By John E. Shrecker.

59. *Monarchy in the Emperor's Eyes: Image and Reality in the Ch'ien-lung Reign.* By Harold L. Kahn.

60. *Yamagata Aritomo in the Rise of Modern Japan, 1838-1922.* By Roger F. Hackett.

61. *Russia and China: Their Diplomatic Relations to 1728.* By Mark Mancall.

62. *The Yenan Way in Revolutionary China.* By Mark Selden.

63. *The Mississippi Chinese: Between Black and White.* By James W. Loewen.

64. *Lang Ch'i-ch'ao and Intellectual Transition in China, 1890-1907.* By Hao Chang.

65. *A Korean Village: Between Farm and Sea.* By Vincent S. R. Brandt.

66. *Agricultural Change and the Peasant Economy of South China.* By Evelyn S. Rawski.

67. *The Peace Conspiracy: Wang Ching-wei and the China War, 1937-1941.* By Gerald Bunker.

68. *Mori Arinori.* By Ivan Hall.

69. *Buddhism under Mao.* By Holmes Welch.

70. *Student Radicals in Prewar Japan.* By Henry Smith.

71. *The Romantic Generation of Modern Chinese Writers.* By Leo Ou-fan Lee.

72. *Deus Destroyed: The Image of Christianity in Early Modern Japan.* By George Elison.

73. *Land Taxation in Imperial China, 1750-1911.* By Yeh-chien Wang.

74. *Chinese Ways in Warfare.* Edited by Frank A. Kierman Jr. and John K. Fairbank.

75. *Pepper, Guns, and Parleys: The Dutch East India Company and China, 1662-1681.* By John E. Wills Jr.

76. *A Study of Samurai Income and Entrepreneurship: Quantitative Analyses of Economic and Social Aspects of the Samurai in Tokugawa and Meiji Japan.* By Kozo Yamamura.

77. *Between Tradition and Modernity: Wang T'ao and Reform in Late Ch'ing China.* By Paul A. Cohen.

78. *The Abortive Revolution: China under Nationalist Rule, 1927-1937.* By Lloyd E. Eastman.

79. *Russia and the Roots of the Chinese Revolution, 1896-1911.* By Don C. Price.

80. *Toward Industrial Democracy: Management and Workers in Modern Japan.* By Kunio Odaka.

81. *China's Republican Revolution: The Case of Kwangtung, 1895-1913.* By Edward J. M. Rhoads.

82. *Politics and Policy in Traditional Korea.* By James B. Palais.

83. *Folk Buddhist Religion: Dissenting Sects in Late Traditional China.* By Daniel L. Overmyer.

84. *The Limits of Change: Essays on Conservative Alternatives in Republican China.* Edited by Charlotte Furth.